MW00764403

"It's Not Your Nationality," Song Cover. From right to left: Turkish houri, French mademoiselle (with pentagonal star on her beret), Spanish señorita, Scottish lassie, Dutch girl and Stars and Stripes gal (with Jewish Star of David on her crown).

Although many previous publications have alluded to Jewish influences on American popular music, the references usually are anecdotal. Few books support such assertions with musical examples. This is the first book ever to present an exhaustive account of the evidence with the support of an ancillary CD. The book shows how a minority culture can infuse a majority culture, enrich it and still retain its own identity.

Now in the new millennium, it has become possible to gain a perspective on a sweeping panorama of songs from the first half of the twentieth century (1914-1964).

From Tin Pan Alley, song examples by:

Maury Abrams (b. Maurice Abrahams), Lew Brown (Louis Brownstein), Sammy Cahn (Samuel Cohen), Ziggy Elman (Harry Finkelman), Gus Kahn & Grace Leibowitz (husband and wife, Gustav K. Gerson & Grace LeBoy), Nora Bayes (Dora Goldberg), Harry Von Tilzer (Aaron Gumbinsky), Saul Chaplin (Saul Kaplan), Billy Rose (William Rosenberg), Fred Fisher (Albert Von Breitenbach), et al.

From Broadway, song examples by:

Harold Arlen (b. Hyman Arluck), Irving Berlin (Isadore Baline), Leonard (Lewis) Bernstein, George & Ira Gershwin (Jacob & Isadore Gershovitz), Edgar "Yip" Harburg (Isadore Hochberg), Burton Lane (Burton Levy), Jerry Ross (Jerold Rosenberg), Jule Styne (Julius Kerwin Stein) and Cole Porter (although not Jewish, he wrote in a Jewish idiom), et al.

From Hollywood, song and background score examples by:

Sammy Fain (b. Samuel Feinberg), Doris Fisher, Mack Gordon (Morris Gitler), Max (Maximilian Raoul) Steiner, Dimitri Tiomkin, Franz Waxman (Wachsman), as well as Victor Young and Harry Warren (Salvatore Guarangna)—both not Jewish, but Warren once wrote under the pseudonym of Harry Herschele— et al.

From Yiddish Theater, song examples by:

Abraham Ellstein, Abraham Goldfaden (b. Avrom Goldinfodim), Adolph King (Kaiser), Jacob Koppel Sandler, David Meyerowitz, Alexander Olshanetsky (a.k.a. Alex Olshey), Sholom (Samuel) Secunda, Isaac Reingold, Joseph Rumshinsky, Herman Wohl, Herman Yablokoff, et al.—and how their songs filtered through mainstream music.

From Jewish musicologists and cantors:

Abraham Zvi Idelsohn, Eric Werner, Baruch Cohon, Adolph Katchko, Israel Alter, et al.

Russian songs and dances as well as Yiddish folk songs by:

Yehuda Leib Cahan, Mordecai Gebirtig, Itzik Manger, Mark Warshavsky, Abraham Reisen, et al.

Funny, It Doesn't Sound Jewish

Funny,

It Doesn't Sound Jewish

How Yiddish Songs
and Synagogue Melodies
Influenced Tin Pan Alley,
Broadway, and Hollywood

JACK GOTTLIEB

STATE UNIVERSITY OF NEW YORK

in association with

THE LIBRARY OF CONGRESS

This book was funded in part by grants from:
  The Leonard Bernstein Family Foundation, Inc.
  The Aaron Copland Fund for Music, Inc.
  The Leonore and Ira Gershwin Trust for the Benefit
  of the Library of Congress

For the Library of Congress
W. Ralph Eubanks, Publisher
Iris Newsom, Editor
Stephen Kraft, Designer

For SUNY Press
Michael Haggett, production
Fran Keneston, marketing
James Peltz, editor

Library of Congress Cataloging-in-Publication Data
Gottlieb, Jack.
  Funny, it doesn't sound Jewish : how Yiddish songs and synagogue melodies influenced
Tin Pan Alley, Broadway, and Hollywood / Jack Gottlieb
      p. cm.
  Includes bibliographical references and indexes.
  ISBN 0-8444-1130-2
   1. Jews--United States--Music--History and criticism. 2. Popular music--United
States--History and criticism. 3. Folk songs, Yiddish--History and criticism. I. Title.

ML3776.G65 2004
781.64'089'924073--dc22   2003044257

In loving memory of my father (1890-1957)

Born Moshe ben Pesakh—"Moses, son of Pascal"—in Pinsk, Russia. Moses, meaning "drawn from the water," was a harbinger of his future occupation as a small hand-laundry owner. He became Morris after his arrival at Ellis Island in 1909 via Rotterdam, Holland. Morris, meaning "moorish" or "swarthy," was an unlikely symbolic change since he labored indoors from pre-dawn to after sundown. His greatest joy was to write Yiddish lyrics and sing them to his own mandolin playing.

In my father's youth, the following statement appeared in print:
"If the statistics are right, the Jews constitute but one per cent of the human race. It suggests a nebulous dim puff of star dust lost in the blaze of the Milky Way. Properly, the Jew ought hardly to be heard of; but he is heard of, has always been heard of . . . His contribution to the world's list of great names in literature, science, art and music, finance, medicine and obtuse learning are very out of proportion to the weakness of his numbers."

—MARK TWAIN, "Concerning the Jews," *Harpers Magazine,* September, 1899

Contents

Illustrations

(Unless otherwise indicated on the illustration page, all materials are from the collections of the author or the Library of Congress.)

Efforts made to trace the designers of song covers used on the dust jacket have not yielded results. Should rightful owners be ascertained, the author would appreciate notification for inclusion in future editions.

Foreword

Two extra-terrestrials land in Jerusalem.
"Hi! Who are you?" asks one. "3369. And you?" "1836." "Funny, you don't look Jewish."
ADAPTED FROM LEO ROSTEN, *The Joys of Yinglish*

While I was feeding the computer the final music example that I was to input for this book (see Ex. 11 9a), it suddenly dawned on me why I had subconsciously saved this one for last. Called "Dovid un Ester," it comes from the title song of the very first Yiddish musical my father took me to see. The printed sheet music reveals it was a Julius Nathanson production that played in 1938 at the National Theater on Second Avenue at Houston (pronounced 'House-ton') Street, New York City. The place and time of action of this self-styled "Romance" was Russia at the Polish border, also 1938, the year when Yiddish Theater was having its last hurrah and Europe was trembling on the brink of the abyss. But I knew nothing of this or of the fact that musician-refugees fleeing Europe were being regarded as threats to the livelihoods of native-born Americans. An impassioned exchange of pro and con letters to the *New York Times*, including commentaries by concert-hall composers Howard Hanson and Roger Sessions, fail to report that most of these foreigners were Jews. Synagogue composer Lazare Saminsky, on the other hand, does make mention of a cantor forced to become a dishwasher.[1]

Although *Dovid un Ester* was boilerplate melodrama—lovers pledging eternal devotion even if they have to subsist on bread and water—only the song made a lasting impression on me because my brother is a David and my mother was an Esther. I was delighted there was a song written with their names, and no doubt I drove my folks crazy by singing the opening phrase at them for days thereafter. This was one year or so after the Andrews Sisters' recording of "Bay mir bist du sheyn" had become all the rage. My chauvinistic basking in its success, however, was deflated when Italian kids on my block challenged me to come up with any other Jewish title that could compare to the imperishable favorites of "Chiribiribin"—especially the Harry James recording—"Come Back to Sorrento," "Funiculi Funicula," "O Sole Mio," or "Santa Lucia." Alas, I could not; but with the onset of World War II, I was proud to stand up in front of an audience at a Hebrew school *purimshpil* (Purim play) and warble to the tune of "Bay mir bistu sheyn":

"Herr Hitler, you'd look good/In a box made of pine wood;
Herr Hitler, you'd look good/If you were dead."[2]

Now here I was, decades later, having a moment of epiphany, wondering if this book had been preordained by those early years.

As a former professor of Jewish music theory, as a composer for both the theater and the synagogue, and as a first generation American Jew, I am as qualified as anyone could be to do a book about the Jewish influence on American popular music. These musical arenas are not as mutually exclusive as they may initially seem. In fact, my synagogue compositions have now and then been criticized for being pop-flavored while some of my show songs (not necessarily on Jewish themes) have been regarded as too serious-minded for the stage—translation, "not commercial enough." It is only in recent years that I have come to comfortable terms with my inner voice. Trying to conform to other people's standards of aesthetic propriety was not going to solve my so-called problem, however my output may have been characterized.

I straddle the two worlds of popular musical idioms and elitist music, a not uncommon American—to say nothing of Jewish-American—dilemma. The same dualism exists in this book. It is designed to be read by lovers of popular music, but leavened with a modest dose of technical terminology. Ethno-musicologists may sneer at the informal tone of my writing style, while other readers may occasionally find themselves at sea. The latter is due to a built-in problem. I use copious musical examples, and music, alas, is a language not read by everyone. The CD recording appended to this book will help to alleviate some of that predicament. However, there were difficulties. The BMG/RCA recording company refused permission, while other labels ignored numerous requests to use a few of their holdings, presumably because it was not worth their time. If approval had been forthcoming, recordings now sitting forgotten in dark vaults would have been resuscitated; and even though a CD-ROM could open up a whole new world of attractive possibilities, the experience with such recalcitrant companies makes this desideratum unlikely. Until this situation changes, there is no better way to illuminate my subject in book form than by printed examples.

This book has been a long time aborning. Ideas for the project started to perk in the early 1970s when I was Music Director of a large Reform temple in St. Louis. I was asked to oversee a production of *Fiddler on the Roof* at my congregation, but demurred on the grounds that it had been overdone and better done at other local amateur venues. But it started me thinking about what to do instead: *Milk and Honey*, an Israeli setting? *Funny Girl*, about Fanny Brice, the Jewish comedienne? A revue of Gershwin songs, but only because he was born Jewish? Perhaps there was something Jewish about *Porgy and Bess*? (And how!) What about other Jewish writers? The numbers of them were stunning. Perhaps there was a show in that.

This led to a lecture-entertainment called *From Shtetl to Stage Door (A Melting Potpourri)* either with me alone at the piano or with another singer. The program took off when it was registered with a lecture bureau that arranged for me to present it around the country for several years to Jewish groups. Continually being reworked, its title was eventually changed to *Funny, It Doesn't Sound Jewish*. One of these performances was seen by a university press editor who felt a book was lurking therein. The revised lecture was conceived in order to get me going on the book, but it took on a surprising life of its own. In the 1980s I presented it almost forty times in appearances as diverse as the topic itself: the Library of Congress, the Smithsonian Institution, the Museum of the Diaspora in Tel Aviv, the Rebecca Crown Auditorium in Jerusalem, the Technion Society in Winnipeg, Jewish centers and synagogues, museums, the Village Gate in New York City, and the Universities of Illinois and Indiana.

Everywhere I went, I was asked to make the talk more widely available. It was evident I had sparked a nostalgic nerve in people because they responded in a most personal way. Now at long last, the written word takes center stage. In addition to musical examples, illustrations of song covers, photographs, and reproductions of illustrated song slides will serve to convert more cogently for the eye material originally written for the ear. Whereas the original lecture included nonmusical personages, this book only pertains to music. Jewish comics, playwrights, and producers, among others, are whole subpopulations in American theater that demand and have produced their own studies.[3]

Some explanations for the skewed numbers of Jewish writers in the American musical theater are to be found in Jewish history itself and the role theologians played in stifling the evolution of sacred music (Chapter 1). This repression indirectly led to an explosion of activity in America between 1914, the year of Irving Berlin's first full stage score *Watch Your Step*, and 1964, the premiere of *Fiddler on the Roof*, a half-century suffused by a musical legacy from Jewish music sources (the bulk of this book). Although the main thrust of my study is focused on this fifty-year period, there are side trips before and after. For the most part, I deal far less with Jewish influences in post-1960s music since such motivating forces are less clear, if and when present. This means, I regret to say, that Stephen Sondheim, the consummate theater composer of our time, plays little part in my study. His song "Poor Baby" (from *Company*, 1970) could be included mainly because it is a gloss on Gershwin, who in turn was Jewishly oriented. The Alan Menken-Howard Ashman song "Mushnik and Son" (from *Little Shop of Horrors*, 1982) would be another example since it too recalls other novelties written in the same vein from an earlier era.

Nor is this book a survey or an overview of popular music. There is little discussion of jazz and none whatsoever of country or other genres such as soul, new wave, rock 'n' roll, or rap. It is, instead, a documentation of analogues between the music of Tin Pan Alley, Broadway, and Hollywood and the music of Eastern European Yiddish folk songs, Yiddish theater songs, and traditional synagogue modes and melodies. Although this requires me to be a tune detective, I am not remotely interested in determining guilt or innocence. Unlike the late Sigmund Spaeth, who had a popular radio show about tune detection and who was often called upon to testify in plagiarism cases, I have found, more often than not, that attempts to establish who is the borrower and who is the lender of musical phrases (as opposed to whole songs) is a futile exercise. More satisfying to me has been the discovery of how certain melodic fragments tend to cluster into family groupings and how these groupings have ethnic or allegiant connotations.

Problems of Permissions

Although there are numerous books on popular music, few use musical examples and for good reason. Some publishers of sheet music—thankfully, not all—either do not grant permissions, feeling that even limited quotations would compromise their own music sales, or they deny consent for reasons known only to themselves. It took me more than a year to obtain the clearances needed for the almost two hundred copyrighted titles from which I quote excerpts; and, in fact, this may well be the first book ever to contain that many copyrighted examples of both melody lines and lyrics from popular songs. Remarkably, only one publisher refused me: the Walt Disney Company. Terms could not be negotiated with two other publishers due to a requirement known as the "most favored nations" clause. Basically, this stinger states that after a fee is set between two parties, if a third party demands a larger sum and receives it, all boats rise with the tide and the author must cough up the difference between the two amounts.

Most examples that do get used in books are either diluted by abridgement or by piano reduction only or by words and vocal line alone or melody by itself. Alec Wilder's classic book *American Popular Song* cites song phrases in piano reduction; no lyric is quoted. Moreover, Wilder, along with many others, found out to his despair that Irving Berlin would not give permission to reproduce any samples of his work. Berlin was particularly mean-spirited concerning Wilder's writing, dismissing it in 1971 as "pretentious, stupid analysis crap."[4] More politely perhaps, some elitist academics would have sided with Berlin back then and still would today, invalidating popular music as not being strong enough to support analysis—a position I regard as insupportable.

For the most part, I have skirted the issue of Fair Use, a practice that would allow copyrighted material to be reproduced without owner consent. Fair usage and cases of plagiarism share one factor in common, and that is the number of notes deemed sufficient to determine the validity of either claim. How many notes can one quote from someone else's work without requiring permission? How few notes constitute a parallel identity between two different melodies? Often difficult to determine. "Because music unfolds in time and not in space—because it's serial not parallel—a little sonic quotation goes a long way."[5]

* * *

I was once asked by a jingle firm to evaluate a musical pattern since they had recorded it for a commercial:

They feared they would get into legal hot water because the riff was also a main source for Elmer Bernstein's background score to the 1956 film *The Man with the Golden Arm* and in "I'm a Woman," the Peggy Lee 1961 hit by Lieber and Stoller. I found it hard to understand their concern if other pieces had already set a precedent. Furthermore, I pointed out, the riff could be heard in "Trouble," another number written by Lieber and Stoller for Elvis Presley in the 1958 movie *King Creole*, as well as in a song recorded by Brook Benton, "Make Me Feel Good, Kiddy-O." But if they wanted real assurance insurance, no less than the Austrian master-composer Gustav Mahler had used this motivic idea in the opening of his *Symphony No. 9*, where its assertive punch was transformed into a nervous twitch:

The same accompaniment figure can be used melodically, as in Ruggiero Leoncavallo's classic Italian song "Mattinata," subsequently converted into the 1948 popular American hit "You're Breaking My Heart":

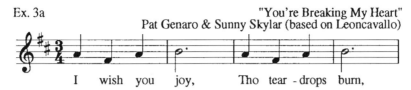

If the case had gone to trial and I were to decide the issue, these obviously unintentional connections would be more than enough to justify dismissal of plagiarism charges. Furthermore, I would have maintained that infringement of material, at the least, has to take place in the foreground as part of a main melodic line, not as a background motive or as an accompanying frill or filler. But if all else failed, and if heavenly protection were needed, the riff also appears in the traditional blessing chanted before the reading of the weekly Torah portion:

Perhaps an argument could be made that Berlin himself was inadvertently "guilty" of lifting a tune. Compare the big tune in Vincent d'Indy's *Symphony on a Mountain Air* (1887) to Berlin's "This Is the Army, Mr. Jones" of 1943. What is one to make of the similarity between the opening of Sondheim's "No One Is Alone" (from *Into the Woods*, 1987) and an earlier Sammy Davis, Jr., hit "The Candy Man" (1961)? An eleven-note resemblance was more than enough to brand Jerry Herman's 1964 "Hello, Dolly/Well Hello, Dolly/It's so . . ." as an infringement of Mack David's 1948 "She's a Sunflower/She's my Sunflower/And (I) . . .". In fact, Herman had to make restitution with the sum of a half-million dollars.

Beatle George Harrison, one of the writers of the 1980 "My Sweet Lord," was sued for appropriating the 1962 Ronald Mack song "He's So Fine" (popularized in a hit record by the girl group known as The Chiffons) in a suit brought by Bright Tunes Music Corp., publisher of "He's So Fine." During a protracted and labyrinthic court battle, Judge Richard Owen, himself a composer, concluded that Harrison indeed was guilty of plagiarizing and was to be penalized more than one and a half million dollars. It is not clear what the actual final damages were as a result of the litigation; but to add insult to injury, in 1975 The Chiffons recorded Harrison's song to which he rejoined, one year later, by writing "This Song," with lyrics such as "This song . . . don't infringe on anyone's copyright" and "This tune has nothing Bright [i.e., the suing publisher] about it."

In other instances, the number of notes shared in common was not the culpable factor. The Milanese publishing house of G. Ricordi was awarded $25,000 in damages on a claim that the minor key of the aria "E lucevan le stelle" (from Giacomo

Puccini's opera *Tosca,* 1900) was pilfered by conversion into a major tonality of the pop song "Avalon" (by Vincent Rose and Al Jolson, 1920). There is a grim irony in this since Puccini had vigorously campaigned to get the rights to write the score and had ruthlessly snatched the libretto away from a fellow composer, Alberto Franchetti.

In another court case, Morris Albert, a Brazilian composer-performer, tried to palm off the song "Feelings" (1975) as his own, but was contested by Louis Gasté, a Frenchman, who maintained "Feelings" was a rip-off of his cabaret song "Pour Toi," written twenty years earlier. Rather than have the case drag on for years, a settlement was reached, and today "Feelings" is credited to both Mauricio Kaiserman (Albert's real name) and Gasté.[6] Big band leader Stan Kenton could have also joined the fray against Morris Albert since the tune resembles Kenton's theme song "Artistry in Rhythm." French composer Maurice Ravel might also have laid claim with an important theme from his ballet score *Daphnis et Chloé,* while Giuseppe Verdi could have argued that a secondary melodic motive from his aria "Addio del passato" from *La Traviata,* 1853, is exactly the same as a secondary motive from Gasté's "Pour Toi." Verdi, in turn, may have been influenced by a Ladino tune (see Chapter 1). So who began the begat?[7]

Other Books

There are few existing books known to me that demonstrate Jewish influences on American popular music with actual musical examples; and these examples are only treated incidentally. Mark Slobin, in his basically splendid book *Tenement Songs,* equates Yiddish folk and synagogue music solely with the so-called *frigish*[8] mode (see my Chapter 7), but this is only one of various traditional synagogue modes. He also describes (p. 95) the "Kibitzer's Theme" in the movie *The Jazz Singer* not only as being in the *frigish* mode, but as a "mock-Hasidic tune" perfected by the likes of Yiddish theater composers Abraham Goldfaden and Sigmund Mogulesco. However, the tune is actually based on earlier Yiddish folk songs, a lullaby "Az ikh volt gehat dem kaysers oytsers" (Were I to Have the Emperor's Treasures), and the first eight bars of "In der shtot Yerusholayim" (In the City of Jerusalem).[9] There is nothing mock, or theater-derived, or probably Hasidic, or even *frigish* about either of them.

Slobin also criticizes *Fiddler on the Roof* for not being faithful to the original Sholem Aleichem stories.[10] This line of reasoning could lead to condemnation of a host of other Broadway shows based on literary sources—for example, *Man of La Mancha* or *South Pacific,* which do not adhere, respectively, to their original stories by Cervantes and Michener. In another book he edited, *Old Jewish Folk Music,* Slobin refers to *Fiddler* as a "stereotype" (p. xi), as if it were *Fiddler's* responsibility to teach the American public the proper facts of Jewish history. If nothing else, *Fiddler* may have actually reawakened interest in the Yiddish language.

Stephen J. Whitfield makes mention of the semblance between the Hebrew camp-fire song "Heiveinu shalom aleichem" (We've Brought Greetings) and Gershwin's "It Takes a Long Pull to Get There" from *Porgy and Bess.* Otherwise, he feels that possible analogues of Broadway and synagogue melodies "could [only] be traced in a vague way."[11] Entertainer Michael Feinstein states that such notions are only explainable as the product of "cultural osmosis," with no actual references. Indeed, Henry Spoznik goes so far as to say that "there are no long-lived harmonic, thematic, or stylistic influences of Jewish music discernible in American popular music."[12]

Several books on Gershwin incorporate musical examples. In *Fascinating Rhythm*, Deena Rosenberg talks about the impact of Jewish inflections on Gershwin, but her illustrations fail to back up her claims.[13] Other books by Joseph P. Swain, Steven E. Gilbert and Allen Forte—the latter two brilliant Schenker analysts—dive into much deeper Gershwin waters, but none of their writing pertains to Jewish subject matter.[14]

However, Charles Schwartz[15] does make some feeble attempts through musical examples to prove the Jewishness of certain Gershwin pieces. Much of it, he avers, is based on the interval of the minor 3rd which leads to at least one ridiculous conclusion. Because Gershwin's song "'S Wonderful" and Goldfaden's Yiddish song "Noakhs teyve" (Noah's Ark) both open with the dotted figure of a descending minor 3rd, they are deemed analogous.[16] This is a bit like comparing an acorn to the entire oak tree. The Goldfaden song, if anything, is closer to Mozart's "Non più andrai" from *The Marriage of Figaro*.

Orthography and Abbreviations

A uniform transliteration of Yiddish is not easily accomplished. Despite variances, I have in general followed guidelines set forth by YIVO (acronym for *Yidisher visnshaftlekher institut*), the Institute for Jewish Research. Exceptions are those Yiddish words which have penetrated English and now are in common usage: "chutzpah," not "khutspe"; "Eli," not "Eyli," except when published otherwise as in "That Eili, Eili Melody." "Bei mir bist du schoen," the Germanic spelling, is how the sheet music was titled in its heyday. Some other variant spellings include "shain" and "shoen." Current standards transliterate this as "Bay mir bistu sheyn." Following YIVO style, romanization of titles uses initial capitals only for the first word.

For the standardization of musical/typographical wordings, the *Chicago Manual of Style* is emulated: (a) show and other titles are italicized; (b) song titles in any language are in roman and contained in quotes; (c) quotations in foreign languages and foreign song texts in body copy and in musical examples are italicized, usually followed by English translations in parentheses.

If a title or other phrase is used frequently within a chapter, it is replaced by its acronym after a second mention: e.g., "Bay mir bistu sheyn" (in its alternate spellings) becomes "BMBDS;" *Adonai malakh* mode becomes *AM* or the *AM* mode, etc. Broadway teams usually are listed by composer first, lyricist second, as in Rodgers and Hammerstein, but this is not always the case: Lerner and Loewe are the other way around. If it is not clear who wrote what, the musical partner is labeled (M) and the wordsmith (W).

A sensitive issue is how to characterize authors not of Jewish birth. "Gentile" is too restrictive (but I use it); WASP is offensive; nomenclature such as nJ for "non-

Jewish" has the effect of creating unintended segregation; and *goy*, which may have been a neutral term when spoken by Yiddish speakers, becomes loaded (like the word *shvartse*, Yiddish for "black") once it comes into English usage. Although it is not the best solution, the asterisk* is employed to distinguish such writers. When I am not certain, I use a superscripted (?). I have no qualms using the word "Jew" regularly, but historically it has been an appellation fraught with baggage. Isaac Meyer Wise, the founder of American Reform Judaism, found it unbecoming. It is rarely used in any English popular song. "Jewish" has been used in lyrics a bit more, sometimes replaced by "Hebrew," "Yiddish," or "Israelite." A position paper, "for the guidance of editors," states:

> The application of the word *Jew* or *Jewish* to any individual is to be avoided . . . unless the facts have some relation to his being . . . Thus, if a Jew is convicted of a crime, he should not be called a *Jewish criminal*; . . . if a Jew makes a great scientific discovery, he should not be called an eminent *Jewish scientist*. The word *Jew* is a noun, and should never be used as an adjective or verb.[17]

Since standard concert and pop song repertoires are more readily accessible than printed Yiddish songs or cantorial recitatives, I have provided sources only for the Jewish music examples that come from collections. If no source is given, it usually means the example was printed individually as sheet music. Some of the out-of-print collections may be located in libraries, but songs are often duplicated in compilations that are available. Abbreviations for these anthologies follow:

GSOTYT = Great Songs of the Yiddish Theatre
HOM = Hebräisch-Orientalischer Melodienschatz (Treasury of Hebrew Oriental
    Melodies)
KJTS = Kammen Jewish Theatre Songs, vols. 1 & 2
Katchko1 = Services for Sabbath Eve and Morning by Cantor Adolph Katchko
Katchko2 = Rosh Hashono Service by Cantor Adolph Katchko
Katchko3 = Services for Sabbath Eve and Morning and *Three Festivals*
      by Cantor Adolph Katchko
MTAG = Mir trogn a gezang (We Carry a Song)
NPOYS = New Pearls of Yiddish Song
POYS = Pearls of Yiddish Song
SOMP = Songs of My People
TOJFS = *A Treasury of Jewish Folk Song*
TSWS = The Songs We Sing
YFS (SC) = Yiddish Folk Songs, Schack-Cohen

NOTES

1. Olin Downes, "Music of the Times," Sunday column, section IX, *New York Times,* 19 January-23 February 1941 inclusive.

2. At Purim time in the mid-1940s, Jews in Displaced Persons camps lampooned Nazis. The 1942 movie *Reunion in France* had a nightclub scene with a black male vocalist parodying Sam Theard's 1931 song, "I'll Be Glad When You're Dead, You Rascal You," "and Adolf too."

3. See Lawrence J. Epstein, *That Haunted Smile: The Story of Jewish Comedians in America.* In a 2002 exhibition at the Jewish Museum, NYC, even still photography was scrutinized as a Jewish artistic medium. At the Museum in 2003, an important book was released in tandem with an exhibition on Jewish entertainment: J. Hoberman, Jeffrey Shandler, et al., *Entertaining America: Jews, Movies, and Broadcasting.*

4. Laurence Bergreen, "Irving Berlin's Last Hurrah," *Esquire*, January 1990. When the New York City Ballet approached Berlin to use his songs as the basis for a dance work, his letter of refusal said: "I don't want my music to be danced by ballet dancers." Matthew Gurewitsch, *New York Times*, Arts and Leisure, 16 January, 2004.

5. Professor Kevin J. H. Dettmar, *New York Times*, 3 October 1998.

6. John Nathan, of Overseas Music Inc., representative for Fermata Intl. Melodies Inc. and Loving Guitar Music, joint publishers of "Feelings," phone conversation with author, 6 November 1989. Kaiserman is probably Jewish. See also *Variety*, "Rules 'Feelings' Was Plagiarized from French Songwriter," 5 August 1987.

7. In the early 1980s, performer Seymour Rockoff parodied "Feelings" as "Tefilin" (i.e., phylacteries, the Jewish prayer boxes). It works well due to the affinity between the tearjerker and the synagogue mode known as *Magein avot*. Recorded on *The Almost Complete Collection of Rechnizer Rejects*.

8. Or *freygish*, a Yiddishism for "Phrygian."

9. See Abraham Idelsohn, *HOM*, IX, nos. 90 and 219.

10. Mark Slobin, *Tenement Songs*, p. 11. In his contributory essay to *From Hester Street to Hollywood* (Sarah B. Cohen, ed.), Slobin also states that the *Fiddler* songs have only occasional references to ethnic content. I disagree; at least seven of the songs are quite specific.

11. Stephen J. Whitfield, *In Search of American Jewish Culture*, p. 63.

12. Michael Feinstein, *Nice Work If You Can Get It*, p. 63. Henry Sapoznik in *Klezmer!*, p. 140.

13. Instead, Rosenberg deftly demonstrates how Gershwin quotes from himself. I do not always concur with her conclusions: e.g., that a passing tone in a phrase from "But Not for Me"—a passage reminiscent of the opening to Strauss's *Till Eulenspiegel*—has the same meaning as the flatted 6th step at the end of "Embraceable You" (see Deena Rosenberg, *Fascinating Rhythm*, p. 178).

14. Joseph P. Swain, *The Broadway Musical*; Steven E. Gilbert, *The Music of Gershwin*; Allen Forte, *The American Popular Ballad of the Golden Era*. Another book by Forte, *Listening to Classic American Popular Songs*, is aimed at the lay reader.

15. Charles Schwartz, *Gershwin, His Life and Music*.

16. Ibid., p. 28.

17. H. L. Mencken, *The American Language*, p. 298.

Introduction

Jews are not that bad, homosexuals do not bother me, communists are okay, as long as
they are not in large numbers. But Jewish, homosexual, communist composers, that's
where I draw the line!

ATTRIBUTED TO HOWARD HANSON

Making Lists

Investigations of American popular music often begin with the historical
approach of "up the river from New Orleans,"[1] and while the influence of jazz
and its offshoots on popular song is indisputable, my book contends that within the chronicle of popular songs there was a concurrent passage "from the East
River across town to Tin Pan Alley and Broadway." Were it not for composers and
lyricists of Jewish origin, the touchstone classics of the American musical theater
would be nonexistent. The turning-point works—those that advanced the
Broadway musical into the realm of higher art—have not been matched by the output of non-Jewish writers. As historian Edward Pessen states:

The big five, if lyricist and melodist are treated as one, were Berlin, Porter, Rodgers and
Hart, Ira and George Gershwin, and Kern and his various collaborators, and they wrote
about two-fifths of the fine songs.

That makes four out of five who were Jewish. Pessen continues:

Seventy-five percent of the lyricists appear to have been Jewish, as do fifty percent of the
composers of the melodies of the good songs. The sixty percent of the good songwriters
who were Jewish wrote about seventy percent of the songs, since almost all the most pro-
lific among them were Jewish. [Even though Jews] were thus inordinately represented
among all songwriters, [they were] three times as heavily represented among the elite of
talent and creativity.[2]

American Jews—probably Jews everywhere—tend to be list-happy. One of the
likely reasons for this propensity is that public education in the early twentieth century rarely taught the significant role of Jews in national and world history. Other
motivations may be debatable notions of the Jewish self-image as outsider with the
concomitant need to belong. As a result, there are books, articles, etc. on Jews in
sports, the arts, the sciences, and the like. Originally, I had intended to jump onto
this bandwagon, and spent countless hours compiling tabulations of major and
journeymen Jewish songwriters, lyricists, performers, publishers and their shows of
social significance, Jewish themes, African-American themes, etc. But then I found
myself asking if any of this truly mattered, and concluded that it did not if all the
busy work were merely going to be a matter of statistics, however impressive the
numbers might be. My inventory has been replaced with only one birth-death list-
ing of almost all the names (Jewish or otherwise) mentioned in this book, a task
that proved to be equally daunting. And watch out:

To talk about Jews in the arts—or, for that matter, in the media, finance, psychiatry and

1

many other fields—is to risk echoing anti-Semitic ravings about Zionist conspiracies. Every salute to Jewish achievement carries with it the danger of buttressing the paranoia of nut cases, as well as the discreet bigotry of polite society.[3]

Indeed, such lists evoke intimations of the Spanish Inquisition Index, Senator Joseph McCarthy's blacklist of the Hollywood Ten (i.e., screen writers), and Joseph Goebbels's Nazi propaganda. Under the aegis of Nazi officialdom, the *Lexikon der Juden in der Musik* by Herbert Gerigk and Theophil (Gottlieb in Greek!) Stengel was published as an *Erforschung der Judenfrage* (Investigation of the Jewish Question), citing historical as well as then current names. American composers George Antheil and Louis Moreau Gottschalk are marked with an iron cross as among "those whose Jewish descent can be confirmed, but which cannot be completely proven." Boris Blacher, my Tanglewood teacher, is listed *unter den lebenden Vierteljuden* (under living one-quarter Jews[4]) and Georges Bizet as *er hat einer Jüdin verheiratet war* (he was married to a Jewess). Perversely, death dates are marked with crucifix signs. Due allegiance is paid to *Reichsleites* [Dr. Alfred] Rosenberg, the so–called Jewish specialist.

When I asked to make copies of some pages from this notorious publication, I was refused permission by the New York Public Library since the document held the notice in English: "Copyright 1943 Berhard Hahnefeld Verlag, Berlin." If the notice had been in German, there would have been no problem. My protest that "we were at war with them" cut no ice against strict library policy. Most chilling for me was to see, on one page, six Gottlieb names listed, stamped with the Nazi insignia of eagle atop a swastika, the only sheet, other than the title page, to receive this dubious distinction.

A century ago, Mark Twain made it clear that animosity towards Jews had more connection to envy than to religion. He wrote:

I feel convinced that the Crucifixion has not much to do with the world's attitude toward the Jews; that the reasons for it are older than that event . . . I am persuaded that . . . nine-tenths of the hostility to the Jews comes from the average Christian's inability to compete successfully with the average Jew in business. . . .[5]

Still, the need for Jews to make inventories has grown out of a basic insecurity to prove one's Jewish self to the non-Jewish world. Although problems of American-Jewish self-identity are not based on the cohesive community that some mass media and anti-Semites would have us believe, a commonality among Jews of all persuasions is an ongoing awareness of some kind of Jewishness in their backgrounds. No matter how far removed from their forebears' traditions or how much it has blended into American society, it is there. Some would say that whatever a Jew may think of himself, the Gentile will always remind him who he is. Defined by centuries of outward hostility and inward religious sensibilities, Jews are ambivalent, caught—in the words of S. Anski's subtitle for his play *The Dybbuk*— "Between Two Worlds." In 1942, writer Ben Hecht challenged Hollywood producer David Selznick to ask three non-Jews if they considered Selznick an American or a Jew. If any of them had replied "American," Hecht would not persist in asking Selznick to lend his name to a Jewish cause. After all three had replied "Jew," Selznick lent his name.[6] Late in their careers, Broadway composers who had previously shown little or no need to express their Judaism turned to Jewish themes: Burton Lane, working on a treatment of *Chelm*, Richard Rodgers in *Two By Two*, Jule Styne in *Bar Mitzvah Boy*, and Cy Coleman in *The Great Ostrovsky*, among others.

What's in a Name?

There were objections to the title of this book even before I started writing it, reactions such as: "too coy, too sophomoric, too demeaning of the subject." Curiously, the naysayers were all Jews. Was their negative reception due to unease about their Jewishness? Perhaps I was rationalizing. My critical pundits evidently regard punny language as *pun*ishment. Nevertheless, I hereby unabashedly declare I love puns, double entendres, word twists, fractured idioms—the groanier the better, but I have been persuaded to tone them down in this volume. My title pinpoints what the book is about—melodic puns or, to be more accurate, musical homophones. Like words that sound the same but have different meanings in different contexts, musical phrases, too, can have multiple resonances depending upon the cultural experiences of both the creator and the listener. A person learning English as a second language might learn the word "run" as a verbal signal for rapid movement. But he could then confuse it with politicians who—or noses that—run.

The title with its allusion to the catchphrase "Funny, you don't look Jewish" was the more likely turnoff for my critics. With that reference, however, the title raises a paradoxical question: why are we so fascinated with the real names of celebrities, which in turn leads to the knowledge that someone is Jewish? Can you identify the following well-known comics?

(a) Easy ones first: M. Berlinger, L. Hacker, D. Kaminsky, P. Silversmith

(b) Less easy: N. Birnbaum, B. Kubelsky, I. Lahrheim, J. Levitch, J. Molinsky

(c) Difficult: A. Chwatt, J. Gottlieb, I. Iskowitz, A. Konigsberg, Albert Einstein

(c) Red Buttons, Joey Bishop, Eddie Cantor, Woody Allen, Albert Brooks
(b) George Burns, Jack Benny, Bert Lahr, Jerry Lewis, Joan Rivers
(a) Milton Berle, Buddy Hackett, Danny Kaye, Phil Silvers

Tell the truth—did you react: "I didn't know that!" And if you did not, are you still piqued by such trivia of de-Judaization? Indeed, both Jews and non-Jews often have the same reaction. Is it envy (or worse) on the part of non-Jews?, "there they go, showing off again!" Pride on the part of Jews?, "one of us made it big!" Or is this attitude only from the psyche of someone from an older generation? Does anyone ever remark on the "Catholic look"—or whatever—of a prominent personality? Well, yes, it is true the acronym WASP has been heard in the land.[7]

Such considerations, nevertheless, lie at the heart of my subject. Iskowitz, for example, may be too Jewish sounding for show-biz, but funny how Jewish Eddie's name change to "Cantor" sounds. Chwatt might have been too much to chew on, but when Red Buttons sings "Strange Things Are Happening," funny how "Buttons" keeps us in stitches. And if Joey Gottlieb had become a Jewish cleric, the name Rabbi Bishop would have been even funnier.

Pianist-comedian Victor Borge once quipped, "My father called me Borge; he couldn't remember any of our names."[8] The joke here is that Borge indeed is his first name; the last name is Rosenbaum. Playwright Arthur Laurents was born

Arthur Levine; Myron S. Rubin became musical comedy book writer Michael Stewart; Broadway and Hollywood producer Mike Todd changed his name from Avrom (Yiddish for Abe) Hirsch Goldbogen, but more, one suspects, for reasons of Americanizing rather than to mask his Jewishness.[9] After perusing a New York City telephone book for ideas, Catherine Conn became actress Kitty Carlisle; actor Tony Randall was born Leonard Rosenberg; Gyorgy Stern was transformed into Gyorgy Solti, then conductor Georg Solti. The list is a long one.

In the midnineteenth century, it was customary for English-speaking opera performers to adopt Italian names to help them get ahead. A century later, conductor Julius Rudel, in his early days with small opera companies, Italianized his moniker to Rudolfo di Guilio. Edward Johnson, who later became manager of the Metropolitan Opera, in his early days was known as Edoardo di Giovanni. Even Joan Sutherland was urged to Italianize her name. Ironically, however, in the world of popular songs, American-born male singers of Italian ancestry felt compelled to go in the opposite direction in order to enhance their professional status. Broadway matinee idol Alfred Drake was born Alfredo Capuro, movie star Mario Lanza was originally Alfredo Arnold Cocozza, and pop singers Antonio Dominic Benedetto, Ruggiero Eugenio di Rodolfo Columbo, Dino Paul Crocetti, Vito Farinola, Francis Avallone, John Pompeo, Walter [Walden?] Robert Cassotto, Aldo Sigismondi, and Nick Perido became, respectively: Tony Bennett, Russ Colombo, Dean Martin, Vic Damone, Frankie Avalon, Johnny Raye, Bobby Darin (he coined his professional name after the word "mandarin"), Alan Dale, and Perry Como (a.k.a. Pierino Roland Como).

Certainly the name-changing practice of actors and performers, Jewish and non-Jewish,[10] has continued in more recent times. On the musical stage, Debbie Shapiro was in for a while, but disappeared when she became Debbie Gravitte. Winona (a town in Minnesota) Horowitz changed into actress Winona Ryder; Peter Slutzker renamed himself Peter Marx (he had played Chico in a revival of the Marx Brothers classic *Coconuts,* a case of changing from one Jewish name to another). But for the most part, in the latter half of the twentieth century, there were many who no longer felt the need to follow this well-trodden route. Although it is true that the team of Simon and Garfunkel was originally known as "Tom and Jerry," that is not how they established their fame. Imagine Gregg Edelman, Michael Feinstein, Madeline Kahn, Lainie Kazan, Bette Midler or Mandy (Mandel) Patinkin using their real names if they had starred in the days of Asa Yoelson (i.e. Al Jolson). In fact, Terri Sue Feldshuh reverted to her Hebrew name of Tovah.

Whereas before stage names were à la mode, now they are often meaningless. The same custom was experienced by at least one songwriter. When a college musical *Pippin, Pippin* opened in 1967, the score was by one Lawrence Stephens who by the time the show—now called simply *Pippin*—opened in 1972, had returned to his given name of Stephen Schwartz. His *Godspell* was one of the earliest musical theater works to embrace rock 'n' roll (1971, the same year as Gary William Friedman's *The Me Nobody Knows*). The unfettered formats of rock musicals have not in general lent themselves very well to the disciplines required of the stage nor have they created lasting works of art—with the moot exceptions of *Godspell, Hair* (MacDermot, Ragni & Rado), and *Jesus Christ Superstar* (Lloyd Webber). Look at some of the other titles with their authors, mostly grade-B shows and only one

Jewish-sounding name among them: *Aida* (John), *Bring in 'da Noise, Bring in 'da Funk* (Wolf & Glover), *Dude* (Ragni & MacDermot), *Grease* (Jacobs² & Casey), *Mamma Mia!* (ABBA), *Promenade* (Fornés & Carmines), *Rock-a-Bye Hamlet* (Cliff Jones), *Tommy* (Townshend & The Who), *Two Gentlemen of Verona* (Guare & MacDermot), *Via Galactica* (Gore & MacDermot), *The Wiz* (Brown & Smalls), and *Your Own Thing* (Hester & Apolinar). *Hedwig and the Angry Inch* (Trask² & Mitchell) packs a terrific wallop, but has not added any further measure to American musical history. Scores for two successful rock shows: *The Full Monty* (Yazbek) and *Rent* (Larson) are by Jewish (or half-Jewish) songwriters; but two "rocky" shows that failed were written by Jews: Paul Simon's *The Capeman* and Randy Newman's version of *Faust*.

Where once the Jewish songwriter prospered, now he flounders. Could it be that, when the struggle between alienation and assimilation was resolved and the comic spirit born of that conflict was diminished, the incentive to create musical comedy lost its punch? Is it just coincidence that the dearth of new works has come with the fading away of the first generation of American-Jewish show composers? How else to account for the endless revivals of the 1980s and 1990s? With few exceptions (e.g., *The Producers* and *Hairspray*), almost no musical has scored big on the Great White Way in recent years.[11]

Yiddish into English

In the early twentieth century, the struggle among Jews to establish the supremacy of Hebrew over Yiddish as the national language of Israel resulted in sharp divisiveness. In fact, government policy went so far as to discourage actors of the Yiddish Theater from performing in the newly created State.[12] However, the resurgence of Hebrew would not have been possible without the ongoing invention of new words and words borrowed from other tongues. A language, of course, stays alive only as long as it remains in a state of continual flux. Until the 1908 Yiddish Conference held in Czernowitz (then capital of the Austro-Hungarian province of Bukovina), Yiddish had been designated, even by some of its proponents, as "jargon."[13] But others objected to this notion since it implied that Yiddish was not a genuine language with its own grammar, syntax, and spelling.

Nevertheless, there is no question that Yiddish constructions have infiltrated English, expressions such as "you should live so long," "it shouldn't happen to a dog," "how come?" "so what?" and "for free." More subtle are the Yiddish permeations of statements phrased as questions, subjects moved to the end of sentences, and questions answered by questions. Pioneer studies by H. L. Mencken,[14] Eric Partridge, and Lillian Mermin Feinsilver have amply demonstrated this.[15]

Language not only shapes vocal music, but instrumental pieces as well. German music is heavy, French is light, Hungarian stresses frontal syllables, Hebrew stresses penultimate and final syllables. All these tongues are part of the eclectic Yiddish mix: German, Jewish-French, and Italian account for about 70 percent and Hebrew for 20 percent. The remaining 10 percent derives from Slavic tongues (Russian, Ukrainian, Polish), from Romanian, Hungarian, and from other borrowed words, including English.[16]

Possibly the most exhaustive scrutiny of Yiddish into English is Leo Rosten's *The Joys of Yinglish*, although a purist such as Maurice Samuel in his book *In Praise of Yiddish* denounced Rosten's list of dirty Yiddish words. But language does evolve from so-called corrupt usage to eventual acceptance. *The American Heritage Dictionary* (1992 edition), in addition to such stalwart words as *chutzpah, gonif, heimish, maven, mishegas, tchotchke, tsuris, kibitz, kvetch,* and *nebbish,* among others, lists a good number of Yiddishisms with the prefix "sch" that do indeed suggest *schmutstsik* (dirty) words, which have also crept into the vocabulary of American English. Among them—omitting the letter "c," a holdover from German—are such earthy expressions as *shmeer, shmooz, shnoz, shpritz, shtik, shlemiel, shlep, shlimazl, shlock, shiker, shlump, shmaltz, shmata, shmeck, shmigegi, shmendrik, shmo, shmuck, shnorrer* and *shnook.*

James Cagney, the Irish-Catholic film star actor who grew up in New York City's Yorkville district, uses "shnook" in speech and in a song by Allie Wrubel in the film *Never Steal Anything Small.*[17] In point of fact, the fronting of "sh" to English words has become very much an American-Jewish trait. Mitchell Parish, as one example, wrote a lyric to a tune by Sammy Fain that began "Wealthy, shmelthy, as long as you're healthy/Brother, you're a millionaire."

Rosten's methodical investigation of the impact of Yiddish interrogatory sentence structure and syntax upon American English, particularly in its sardonic inversions, is especially helpful. In the following list, the italicized phrases are Rosten's; the examples are mine, inspired by Rosten:

(1) *accentuating scorn or disdain by moving adjectives to the front of sentences*: "Patient? The Doctor isn't!"
(2) *accusing someone of idiocy by denying the obvious*: "The Pope is Catholic? You're kidding!"
(3) *adjectives converted into nouns for ridicule*: "In music, I'm bored by classical."
(4) *adjectives fronted for emphasis*: "Successful? It's a fluke."
(5) *advertising one's forbearance by repeating a question*: (question from a panhandler) "Have you got any change? (Reply) Have I got change? No, still unemployed, but thanks for asking."
(6) *agreement deployed to maximize contempt*: (in a theater) "Pardon me, but could you speak up a bit louder? Those actors on stage are getting in the way of your conversation."
(7) *anger converted to nominal exoneration*: "It's okay, dinner can get cold."
(8) *assent enthusiastically enlarged to denote mockery*: "Not to worry, she's only a little bit pregnant."
(9) *automatic and sarcastic repetition to maximize conviction*: "All right already, I'll eat it, I'll eat it."
(10) *automatic apposition*: "My kids the pests."

All this from only the "A" section of Rosten's book! Such Yiddish inflections could shift Hamlet's eloquence into something more querulous: "To be or not to be *that* [hand chop for emphasis] is the question." Or it can be turned into a Gertrude Stein kind of inquiry: "To be or not to be that [in disbelief] *is the question*?" About syntax, I quote from correspondence my father sent me from Miami Beach, early in 1956, the year before he died (punctuation added, spelling left intact):

Dear Son, Jake, Yankele,
Everything Jake here with me. Sorry did not write sooner. As the old saying goes, something like time is 90 percent answer to a letter. So here is the rest of 10 percent on the card. Your letter sure was very much *wilkomen*. If you can spare sometime, do it again, although you must not expect from me likewise. Plenty of time with me, though very little *geduld* [patience]. Just completed a *lainge megilah* [long story] to Mom at home, and if David will feel kind to a poor lonsome animal Jackie he'll mail it to you.

To my brother he had written:

So you fell more than skiied on your skiing venture. But don't mind. As we say in *Eddish, a gefalenen helft Got* [God helps the fallen ones]. With love and good wishes for big success in all your adventures,
      Pop, Moishe, Morris

The slang word "copacetic," meaning "everything's fine," may have entered English via Yiddish vaudeville. Although usually attributed to the black entertainer Bill "Bojangles" Robinson, one other fanciful origin that has been bandied about is from the Hebrew (say it fast) *ha-kol b'seder* (everything's in order). Other phrases enter English from Yiddish through popular entertainment: "out of this world" (the title of a 1945 Harold Arlen-Johnny Mercer song from a film of the same name) from *an oysham fun der velt*, "hole in the head"(*lokh in kop*) and the title of the 1959 Frank Sinatra movie which changed the original Jewish family name to an Italian one. In exasperation, Nathan Detroit, after plea bargaining with Adelaide, his girlfriend of long standing, exclaims in the song "Sue Me" (from *Guys and Dolls*): "All right, already/So sue me, sue me[18]/What can you do me/I love you." Pure New Yorkese Yiddishisms or, as one scholar terms it, "Jewspeech."[19]

The origin of "Ish Kabibble" is fuzzy. One possible derivation is from the Hebrew *ish k'bavel* (man from Babylon). Humorist Harry Hershfield claims it came from a Yiddishism used by Fanny Brice in a Ziegfeld Follies edition: *nisht gefidlt* (Don't fiddle or Don't fool around).[20] In their ditty "Ish Ga-bibble" (1913), songwriters Sam Lewis and George Meyer took it to mean "I should worry"—in Yiddish, *mayn bubbe's dayge* (my grandmother's worry). Novelty singer-trumpet player Mervyn Bogue, of the Kay Kayser Band, adopted it as his professional name.

Isolated Yiddish words also bespeckle the sweep of theater and pop songs. Louis Prima screams *gornisht* (nothing) in his recording of black composer Spencer Williams's 1916 song "I Ain't Got Nobody." "Without you I'm *bubkes*" (worth nothing) and "Like is for *pishers*" (in this context, nobodies) are lyrics from songs in the Cy Coleman-David Zippel musical, *City of Angels*. "Once I was a *shlepper* [clumsy performer]/Now I'm Miss Mazeppa" is a Stephen Sondheim couplet for a stripper in *Gypsy*.

"Bubba," which President Bill Clinton once described as a Southern American name for "mensh," has a Yiddish cognate in *bube*, meaning "grandmother." In southern Germany, *Bubi* means "little boy"; but it was via Yiddish that it seeped into American slang, as in Sondheim's show *Company*: "Bobby, baby, bubi . . ." or in Tony Bennett's recording of "Put on a Happy Face" where he tacks on "Come on and smile, bubi, it's your birthday." *Bubela* is the affectionate diminutive.[21] *Megillah*, not a diminutive word, is Hebrew-Yiddish for "scroll" or "overlong story," and has crept into American culture via a cartoon character, "Megillah

Gorilla." Frank Sinatra sings: "I'll give you the whole megillah in one word: reach!" in the title song for the movie *Come Blow Your Horn*.

Yiddish speech patterns tend to lift up at natural pauses within sentences and to dip down at the period. Ponder the parallel constructions of lyrics by E. Y. Harburg (from *Finian's Rainbow*), "When I'm not near the girl I love/I love the girl I'm near"[22] and a Yiddish proverb, which should be spoken aloud in order to be fully appreciated: *Az ale zukhn sheyne kales/Vu kumen ahin di miese meydn?* (With all the world looking for pretty brides/What becomes of the homely girls?). Harburg himself is said to have noted the Yiddish derived inflection in his lyric.[23] The inflection echoes the sing-song chanting typical of Talmudical dialectic, made with hand gestures: "On the one hand/But on the other . . ." Or, as in the Leonard Bernstein lyric from *Mass*: "Possibly yes, probably no."

In "Wintergreen for President," the opening choral number from *Of Thee I Sing*, Ira Gershwin characterizes the candidate as "the man the people choose/Loves the Irish and the Jews." Wintergreen admires girls who "are good at blintzes," but he prefers girls who can "make corn muffins." Less direct, the vox populi refers to the Supreme Court justices as "the A.K.s who give the O.K.s." A.K.s is the abbreviation for the Yiddish vulgarism *alte kockers* (old shitters),[24] meaning curmudgeonly old men. And when the French soldiers introduce their ambassador, they sing: "A vous toot dir veh, a vous?" mixing what sounds like French for Yiddish: "Are you [*vous*] hurting?" Or: "Where [*vu*] are you hurting?"[25]

Ira's lyric in "The Babbitt and the Bromide" (*Funny Face*, 1927): "Hello! How are you? Howza folks? What's new?," has a precursor in a song by James Kendis: "How Is Everyt'ing By You? By Me It's All Right Too" (1924), a Yiddish articulation. Brother George may have known the song since he cut a piano roll of another Kendis tune: "Nat'an! Nat'an! Tell Me For Vot Are You Vaitin', Nat'an?" (1916, Ex. 1a). Described as a "sure-fire hit in Jewish neighborhoods,"[26] it indirectly made ripples when a variant of the last phrase became the opening of a famous Gershwin song of 1924 (Ex. 1b), "Fascinating Rhythm." More significantly, the phrase has a parallel in the Torah blessing (Ex. 1c). By fiddling with the emPHAsis, one discovers how the "syn" in synagogue becomes the "syn" of syncopation:

Whereas Jews in the past metabolized foreign melodic elements into their sacred and secular music, and in the process transmuted these into something characteristically Jewish, the premise of this book is that they infused popular music of the United States with melodic elements from Yiddish folk and theater songs and from Ashkenazic[27] synagogue modes and tunes in the twentieth century, which came to be part of the American sound. For the first time since ancient history, when synagogue cantillation influenced church plain chant, Jews contributed significantly to the music of the mainstream: Tin Pan Alley, Broadway, and Hollywood.

NOTES

1. After the U.S. Navy successfully closed down the New Orleans red-light district known as Storyville, jazz musicians were forced to seek employment elsewhere.

2. Edward Pessen, "The Great Songwriters of Tin Pan Alley's Golden Age," *American Music* 3 (1985): 183-184.

3. Herbert Muschamp, "Architecture of Light and Remembrance," *New York Times*, 15 December 1996, section 2.

4. H. J. Moser dutifully refined this even further to a hierarchy of all half- and quarter-Jewish composers in yet another notorious index, *Musik Lexicon*, 1943.

5. Mark Twain, "Concerning the Jews," from *The Essays of Mark Twain*, pp. 242-243.

6. A. Scott Berg, *Goldwyn, A Biography*, p. 365.

7. The term WASP was coined by historian E. Digby Balzell in his book *The Protestant Establishment*.

8. *Victor Borge, Then and Now*, at Fox Theater, Detroit, PBS Television, 24 August 1992.

9. As a toddler, Avrom, the son of Rabbi Chaim Goldbogen, would say "toht" for coat, and the family nicknamed him "Tohti." He then named himself Michael after his first child. *The Jewish Week*, 14-20 August 1992, p. 29.

10. Because the spelling of his name was not considered to be a plus, in 1945 the African-American singer Billy Eckstein became Eckstine.

11. The "Great White Way" was coined in 1901 by O. J. Gude, an ad man, when Broadway converted to electric lighting.

12. As late as 1954, this was experienced by the family theatrical team of Pesach Burstyn, his wife Lillian Lux, and their twin children, Susan and Mike (who subsequently became a Broadway star).

13. See Emanuel Goldsmith, *Modern Yiddish Culture*. Repudiation of Yiddish as a legitimate language by Jews in West and Central Europe lasted at least until World War II.

14. In 1989 it was revealed that Mencken was a rabid anti-Semite, although apologists have rationalized this posture as symptomatic of Mencken's era. See *The Diary of H. L. Mencken*.

15. See Mencken, *The American Language*; for British English, see Partridge, *Slang Today and Yesterday*; Lillian Mermin Feinsilver in various journals: *American Speech, The Chicago Jewish Forum, Jewish Heritage*, and *The Jewish Digest*. For other sources, see Bratkowsky, *Yiddish Linguistics*.

16. Yiddish was used by gangsters, both Jewish and not, in nineteenth-century middle Europe as an in-group language, which prompted German police to learn the language. Jewish musicians also invented their own special lingo, a process comparable to coinages by jazz players. See Yale Strom, *The Book of Klezmer*, pp. 327-341.

17. As Jack Warner learned, when Yiddish was used as camouflage during negotiations, Cagney spoke it knowledgeably. He says his love of Yiddish, learned on the streets, was "because it's the one great language of vituperation." In three other films he speaks Yiddish: extensively in *Taxi* (1932) and fleetingly in both *Lady Killer* (1933) and *Something to Sing About* (1937). In *The Fighting 69th* (1940), his costar Pat O'Brien, as Father Duffy, delivers last rites in Hebrew to a Jewish soldier. See John McCabe, *Cagney*, pp. 24, 89, 91ff, 115, 158.

18. Perverted by Michael Jackson in 1995 to "Jew me, sue me." See note 7, Chapter 12.

19. David G. Roskies, Professor of Jewish Literature, Jewish Theological Seminary. See "Jazz and Jewspeech: The Anatomy of Yiddish in American Jewish Culture" in *Ideology and Jewish Identity in Israeli and*

American Literature, Emily Miller Budick, ed. (Albany: State University of New York Press, 2002), pp. 131-146.

20. Harry Hershfield, *Laugh Louder, Live Longer*, p. 14.

21. But the suffix "la" is not necessarily so: "rugela" is Yiddish Danish pastry, but arugula is something else altogether.

22. Compare this to the Crosby, Stills, and Nash lyric: "When you can't be with the one you love/You love the one you're with."

23. In discussion with Art D'Lugoff, founder of the Village Gate, New York City.

24. Deena Rosenberg misses the point by calling this Gershwin's "silliest lyric line." See *Fascinating Rhythm*, p. 235.

25. Sung by "French soldiers," but later in the scene they repeat the line with "veh" transliterated as "vay," Yiddish for "hurt."

26. Irving Howe, *World of Our Fathers*, p. 562.

27. Contrary to popular notion, Ashkenaz was not a name for "Germany," but for a biblical people, great-grandsons of Noah (*Genesis* 10:3 and *Jeremiah* 51:27). Jews in German-speaking countries borrowed the name for its similarity to As-Skandz (Saxony). Sepharad, the name for Spain, comes from another biblical source, *Obadiah* 1:20, and was chosen by Jews in Spanish-speaking lands as coming closest to the sound of Hesperia (Spain).

PART I
Secular Roots

CHAPTER 1

Slices of History

Adolphus Cusins, Salvation Army drummer: "It's a wedding chorus from one of Donizetti's operas, but we have converted it. We convert everything."

GEORGE BERNARD SHAW, *Major Barbara*, ACT II

A Search for Definitions

Ever since music of the Ashkenaz tradition was first published in the early six-teenth century there have been unresolved questions as to what constitutes Jewish musical practice. But just as the question, "Who is a Jew?" is prob-lematic, so answers to the question, "What is Jewish music?" are no less fragile. Does any work by a Jewish composer qualify it as a Jewish piece? Is music with a Hebrew text or an instrumental work with a biblical title ipso facto Jewish? What if a biblically inspired work is vocal and has Jewish idioms, but is written by a non Jew? Once, at a discussion about appropriate music for Jewish weddings, I asked colleagues of mine what they thought of an organ processional entitled—or so I informed them—"Rachel at the Well." They deemed it acceptable until I confessed that it was actually a Prelude by J. S. Bach.

There never can be a consensus on what constitutes Jewish music. What can be asserted is that, throughout history, the music of the Jewish people has been pre-eminently single-line vocal melody for solo voice or voices singing in unison. The reasons for this are mainly due, at least until the last two hundred years or so, to rabbinic pronouncements. One such injunction was that worship in song must be *b'kol echad* (in one voice), a doctrine of Jewish mysticism from the Kabbalah. Perhaps this guiding principle was derived from a sentence in the *Kedusha* prayer (Sanctification of the Creator) on which Christianity bases its *Sanctus* : "The holy beings that exalt the Almighty loudly proclaim with awe in *unison* [i.e., with one voice] the words of the living God." Singing in one voice, therefore, is a manifes-tation of monotheism, the central tenet of Judaism. Counterpoint was not likely to develop under such singular circumstances.

The prohibition against instrumental music in the synagogue is a legacy from rabbinical fiat of ancient days. Legend has it that this ban was a sign of mourning for the destruction of the Second Temple at the hands of Titus in the year 70 of the Common Era. It was after this calamity that the synagogue—the sanctuary for the ordinary citizen, which may have already existed—supplanted the Temple. A loose comparison can be made between Temple, the seat of authority, and syna-gogue as is made today between Vatican and church. The Temple, an institution of pomp and ceremony, had a trained choir and instrumental orchestra, but it was neither democratic nor participatory. Its function was twofold: first, to regulate sac-rifice, and second, to provide instruction. The synagogue (from the Greek *synago-goe*, a bringing together) replaced daily sacrifice ceremonies of the Temple with a verbal liturgy, and the high priestly arts of the Temple disappeared. The church went in the opposite direction. Whereas, at first, church officials also banned instrumental music, the organ eventually became an instrument of elevated art in cathedrals.

Temple musicians, from the tribe of Levi, were an ecclesiastical caste; and one of the customs of the Levites was to adapt older tunes to newer words, including Holy Writ, a practice known as contrafaction,[1] still very much with us today. In post-biblical days, the setting of new texts to already existing music came to be known as parody. Eventually done more often for comic effect than pragmatism, parody has come to signify humor. But in biblical times there was a more serious purpose. Certain psalms to be sung to then existing popular melodies—unknown to us—were so indicated in their opening line, contrafacts such as Psalm 22 to the tune of "The Hind of Morning," Psalm 45 to "Lilies," Psalm 56 to "The Silent Dove," Psalm 57 to "Destroy Not."

Although the destruction of the Temple was more than enough reason to dispense with its trappings, it is more likely that rabbis came to frown upon instruments—percussion, in particular—because such usage was considered to be an inducement to kinesthetic response, not appropriate for spiritual uplift. Women's voices similarly were forbidden, deemed as being too erotic for worship purposes (*kol be'ishah erva*: a woman's voice is [nakedness] indecent).[2] For like reasons, dancing between the sexes was prohibited centuries later. Although European dance houses (*tanzhausen*) could be the scene of forbidden games for randy youths and maidens, the held handkerchief, even today, separates dancing men and women of ultraorthodox persuasion.

A third interdiction by rabbis was against notated music (Hebrew is written right to left, the opposite direction of musical notation). Velvel Pasternak writes, "Once written down, they felt these melodies . . . might be used by secular institutions and other institutions not dedicated to the service of G-d."[3] It is paradoxical that "The People of the Book" sustained their musical heritage more through oral communication than by written form. Perhaps this anomaly is related to the biblical—and, thereafter, traditional—ban on the plastic arts in the synagogue. Jews do not erect statues; and although they depict pairs of hands on their stained-glass windows (symbol of the priestly blessing), full human representation is proscribed. Outside of worship contexts, Orthodox Jews refer to the Supreme Being by code substitutes. Torah scribes have clear restrictions on how to write down the Ineffable Name on parchment, a task that cannot be undertaken lightly.[4] Notated music also implies a threat of unspontaneous singing that could lead to mechanical worship. "To inspire," after all, means to breathe life into something, a concept at odds with the prescriptive permanence of written music. Singing improvised on the spur of religious fervor is, allegedly, "inspirational." The issue is cloudy and contradictory, like the student who wrote: "It is superstitious to believe in G-d," which, of course for skeptics, has its own built-in superstition.

Not only was there concern that transcribed melodies were deficient as an expression of the soul or in danger of being secularized, but that notation would contaminate the purity of the initial inspiration. Rabbis believed sacred music would become vulgarized if made widely available and set, for example, with Yiddish texts. An ancestor of Kurt Weill studied with Rabbi Jacob ha-Levi Molin (1365-1427), an authority who frowned upon the use of Yiddish, the lingua franca, as a substitute for Hebrew in religious music. But in the long run, it was a losing battle, and the authorities were not successful at excluding foreign intrusions into the music.

It took another century after Rabbi Molin for the first full-fledged synagogue music to be printed, notably by the Italian Salomone Rossi (ca.1570-ca.1630), a composer so highly regarded by the politicians that he was given immunity from having to wear the yellow badge of shame to which Jews were subjected since the days of Pope Innocent III's 1215 decree.[5] Rossi's choir settings were ahead of their time; the notion of choral singing in the synagogue had to wait another two hundred years before it became acceptable. A steady flow of written Hebraic musical works began in the late eighteenth century, but did not really proliferate until the nineteenth, with emphasis usually placed on one leading melody regardless of choral setting or keyboard accompaniment. This manner of synagogue composition has persisted into our own time, and as a result, large-scale synagogue works are rare. After all, the predominance of one melodic line obviously will not give rise to contrapuntal textures and polyphonic forms, and thereby generate a "Jewish Bach." Synagogue music, above all else, emphasizes melody. Rhythmic excitement, exotic harmony, intricate counterpoint, and busy accompaniments are, at least traditionally, regarded as pollutants that muddy the waters of vocalized prayer.

Jewish music of the past was disseminated by itinerant performers who learned their craft by apprenticeship. They consisted of merry-makers known as the *letz* (Hebrew: clown), the *marshalik* (German: marshal) or the master of ceremony called the *badchan* (Hebrew: versifier)—all jesters of one sort or another. Instrumental players were known as *klezmorim* (plural of *klezmer,* fusing two Hebrew words: *k'ley,* tools or vessels, and *zemer,* song). These entertainers not only played at weddings, bar mitzvahs, *purimshpils,* and other joyous events, but also at non-Jewish festivities: social dances, royal births and the like. Gentile musicians— particularly those of Rom (gypsy) background—also functioned at Jewish weddings, and so it was inevitable that cross-pollination would occur and that some of their melodies would be amalgamated into the Jewish repertoire.[6] Many times these manifestations of pleasurable pastimes were regarded by the rabbinic authorities as inimical to social control.

More respected than klezmers and badkhans were the *hazanim* (cantors) who took their role as *shlichei tsibur* (messengers of the congregation) quite literally, traveling with troupes of backup singers (*meshorerim*), who created an organlike foundation, wherever there were jobs. Their free-wheeling style of inserting passages into *piyyutim* (sacred poetry) got so out of hand during the medieval era that, again, rabbis felt obliged to intervene and put a stop to their show-off technique. This may have been the first time that the inevitable clash of clerical and musical egos came to a head. The rabbinic stance has been and continues to be, often to the dismay of cantors: "*le service c'est moi.*" This, after all, is how the clergy is trained.

All forms of preseventeenth-century Jewish vocal music depended on reiteration. Since there were few, if any, manuscripts, performers relied on *aides de mémoire.* Nonetheless, manuscripts would have had negligible meaning for the musically illiterate. In order to make it easier to remember the music, similarities of melodic patterns emerged to serve as mnemonic devices. Thus, even though there was no notation to follow, there evolved a repository of melodic fragments that recurred over and over. These melody-cells became sanctioned with time and ultimately sanction became sanctification.

This is as good a working definition of Jewish music as any other, particularly within the Ashkenaz tradition. (Recurrences of melody-cells are also integral to popular song traditions, whether or not they are consciously composed.) The singing of these memorable melodic patterns, particularly in the chanting of Torah passages, is called *cantillation.* Punctuating accents that follow phonetic signs over and below words of scripture dictate a continuous melodic flow according to syntactical rules. Other kinds of patterns also occur in the singing of prayers called *nusakh,* meaning variously: version, rite, text, copy, form, practice, and custom.

Much of synagogue music is assembled out of intertwined mosaics of motivic fragments, a procedure of compilation rather than organic development,[7] wherein music is tailored by stitching used pieces of material together into new musical cloth. Since the legacy of the past breeds familiarity, these referent bits and pieces take on cumulative meaning.

This also was the process adopted by Jewish musicians in selecting bits of tunes from their non-Jewish surroundings to create new assemblages or chains of melody. However, the interdependence of Jewish and Christian liturgy and music was a two-way street. Ever since the fourth century there has been traffic in both directions, particularly in text usage. The following are some of the texts that went from Jewish to Christian liturgy:

Synagogue	Church
Kaddish	*Pater noster* (The Lord's Prayer)
Kedusha	*Sanctus*
U'netane tokef	*Dies irae*
Eykha (Lamentations)	*Tenebrae* (Lessons)

The Tenebrae lessons even include the chanting of Hebrew letters in the otherwise Latin text, to preserve some semblance of the alphabetical acrostic form of the original.[8] As for music, the relics of parallelism that have come down to us from ancient times may not be the best examples that could have been found, but they are, nevertheless, among the very few that are extant.

For example, the cantillation of *Vayikra Moshe,* out of the Babylonian-Jewish tradition (Ex. 1-1a), wandered into a *Kyrie* of the *Processionale* in the Roman-Catholic rite (Ex. 1-1b)[9]:

From *Exodus* 12:21
Idelsohn, *Jewish Music*, p. 40

Ex. 1-1a

Va -yik - ra   Mo-she ____ l' - khol zik- nei Yis - ra- el   va - yo - mer a - lei - hem
(Then Moses called for all the elders of Israel, and said to them)

Ex. 1-1b

Gregorian Chant, Tone 3, 4th Century
Jewish Music, p. 42

Ky — ri - e e - lei - son,   Do - mi - ne ___ mi - se - re   re
(Lord have mercy, Lord have mercy)

The opening of this "Kyrie" is based on the melding of two Hebrew cantillation signs (also known as trope symbols), *munach*, meaning resting (a half-rectangular shape), and *r'vi-i*, meaning square (a diamond shape):

Subsequently, this became the opening for a fifteenth-century German folk-song (Ex.1-3a) which, a century later, was tossed back into the sacred music camp by Hans Leo Hassler (1564-1612) as a chorale tune (Ex. 1-3b):[10]

Johann Sebastian Bach (1685-1750) then harmonized the chorale tune in his immortal *Passion According to St. Matthew*:[11]

Thus history witnesses the ascendancy of lowly speech-song (i.e., the chanting of biblical text) to the elevated art music of the Baroque era.[12] But the journey does not end there. In the 1970s, Paul Simon personalized the Bach chorale melody as his "American Tune":

Then, in a peripheral mutation, singer Mandy Patinkin recorded a Yiddish version of the Simon tune on his 1998 album *Mamaloshen*, where the lyric became: *Toysnt*

yor hob ikh shoyn a sakh gehat (loosely, "I've been through a lot for a long time"). Is all of this serendipity or the evolution of a time-honored tune from ancient Jewish roots to a contemporary American-Jewish composer's take on what usually has been perceived to be a Lutheran hymn?

During medieval times, a raw mix of Jewish psalmody, minnesinger ballads, and Rhineland street songs gradually emerged into substantial fixed melodies that came to be recognized as the pinnacle of synagogue repertoire. Since they are regarded as delivered by Moses himself, they are known as *Mi-sinai* (from Mount Sinai) tunes, "in every way equal to the contemporary art-music of their Gentile environment."[13] Although they may have borrowed some materials from their so-called host societies, the Jews, to put it mildly, were not always welcome guests. One of the most compelling *Mi-sinai* melodies, for example, became a secret renunciation of enforced conversion, *Kol nidrei* (All Vows, the Yom Kippur dispensation of oaths). Musicologists have noted a resemblance between the opening of *Kol nidrei* and the first five bars of the sixth movement from Beethoven's String Quartet, C-sharp Minor, op. 131. One has stated:

It is unimaginable that Beethoven . . . heard the Kol Nidre theme since at the time. . . he was completely deaf. It is quite obvious that a similarity, if there is one . . . is nothing more than a coincidence.[14]

But another musicologist implies something else about this 1826 quartet:

In the previous year Beethoven was asked by the Israelitic community (in Vienna) to compose a cantata on the occasion of the dedication of the new temple . . . Beethoven considered complying . . . [he] might have occupied himself with synagogue tunes to become acquainted with the style. . . .[15]

Heretofore unmentioned in musicological literature is the startling similarity between another *Mi-sinai* tune and the opening theme of the slow movement of Beethoven's Symphony No. 3, the *Eroica* (written in 1803—years before Beethoven might have examined the *Mi-sinai* tunes):

Ex. 1-6

"Ochila lael" (from the Yom Kippur liturgy)
Werner, *A Voice Still Heard*, p. 39

O - chi_la la - el   a - ha - leh fa - nav esh - a - la_____ mi - me - nu ma - a - ne la - shon.
(I will hope in God, His presence I will entreat. I will ask Him the gift of speech.)

Symphony No. 3, Mvt II, Beethoven
(transposed from C-minor)

pp

A - sher bik'-hal am   a - shi - ra__u - zo__ A - bi - - a r' - no - not b'_ad mif - a - lav.
(That in the congregation of the people, I will sing of His power and render joyful melody for His deeds.)

In addition to *Kol nidrei*, significant Jewish melodies are the end result of melody-type concatenations. As documented by musicologists Abraham Z. Idelsohn and Eric Werner, these include *Hatikvah* (The Hope, the national anthem of Israel), *Maoz tsur* (Rock of Ages, the Chanukah hymn), *Eli tsiyon* (Lord of Zion, the Tisha B'Av lament), *Eyn keloheinu* (None Like Our God, the Sabbath hymn), and *Birkat hamazon* (grace after meals). All of them are migratory tunes based on materials borrowed from the surrounding environment and assembled like a patchwork quilt. *Maoz tsur*, for instance, consists of incongruous fragments from a Lutheran chorale, a German battle song and a love song.[16] In a midnineteenth-century study of migrating tunes, the German musicologist Wilhelm Tappert comments, *Manche Melodie gleicht die ewigen Juden dem die ruhenden, niemals sterben-den* (Many melodies are like the eternal Jew, restless, deathless).[17]

The investigations by Idelsohn and Werner place them in the front rank of twentieth-century Jewish musicology. Werner, who was Idelsohn's successor at Hebrew Union College (Cincinnati) was born 1901 in Ludenberg, near Vienna; Idelsohn in 1882, in Courland, Latvia. The east-west locations of these two birthplaces denote a caste system in European Jewry. Werner, who had limited patience and who commanded respect from all comers, reveals a blind spot in a telling passage from his magnum opus *The Sacred Bridge*:

A. Z. Idelsohn . . . cannot be fully absolved from fault or bias. Being himself of eastern Jewish extraction, he never freed himself completely from an affection for eastern Jewish tunes nor was he able to evaluate them with that detachment which behoves [sic] the critical scholar.[18]

In his defense, Werner does give some justifiable reasons for his rebuke of Idelsohn's stance in his later book, *A Voice Still Heard* (pp. 144-145). Even so, of all the 217 titles listed in a bibliography of Werner's writings, not one pertains to Yiddish folk (to say nothing of theater) music.[19] In contradistinction to this snobbery, there is Idelsohn's field work, particularly for our purposes, volumes VIII (Synagogue Songs of East-European Jewry), IX (The Folk Songs of East-European Jewry), and X (Songs of the Hasidim) of his exhaustive anthology (1914-1932).[20] The explanatory chapters to this ten-volume set are particularly helpful for their tables of comparative melodies. (see Illustration 1)

Over There—The Mediterranean Basin and Western Europe

Civilized societies begin life as settlements near bodies of water, since rivers and seas are as essential to the nourishment and growth of peoples as are amniotic fluids to a developing fetus. The mother that rocked the cradle of many diverse cultures was the Mediterranean Sea (note the French homonym of *mer* and *mère* for sea and mother). Not only did Jewish travelers on that expanse trade merchandise with their neighbors, but they must have exchanged musical wares as well. Hence, melodic semblances inevitably evolved among Hebraic, Semitic (including Arabic), Greek, Spanish, Neapolitan, and Moorish[21]—not necessarily black-skinned—societies. Traffic from the Mediterranean also went inland via the Aegean and Black Seas to the shores of Romania.

. . . in well-to-do and middle-class Jewish families there were often Ukrainian female servants . . . these girls brought Ukrainian melodies and song texts into Jewish circles, and perhaps vice versa: they may have transmitted Jewish melodies . . . to the Ukrainian milieu.[22]

Often these were improvisatory, elaborately ornamented nonmetrical modal tunes—called *doynas* in Romanian and *volekhl* or *volekhs* in Yiddish, named after the Romanian district of Walachia. Usually accompanied by a drone, the *doyna* had a plot:

A shepherd has lost a sheep . . . Weeping, he goes in search of it. He asks every passerby . . . but no one can tell him where it is. Finally he finds it and pours out his joy in a jolly dance tune.[23]

In America, klezmer musicians such as clarinetists David Tarras and Naftule Brandwein performed and recorded such southwest European folk recitatives. In fact, the opening clarinet solo of Gershwin's *Rhapsody in Blue* has been characterized as a "typical Yiddish-Romanian soliloquy in the style of a *doyna*."[24] If there is any validity to this claim, it might be attributed to the mixed modes of major and minor in the opening four bars (see Chapter 5, Ex. 5-27 for a representation of this composite).

* * *

In Act III of Verdi's opera *La Traviata* (1853), Violetta bids farewell to life and love in 6/8 time (Ex. 1-7a). The second half of an early nineteenth-century *romanza* in Ladino (the Spanish-Jewish tongue also known as Judesmo or Lo'ez) mourns lost love the same way, but in 4/4 time (Ex. 1-7b):[25]

The word Ladino literally means "translation"; and the song may have wended its way through various translations from Sarajevo in the Balkan States (home of a large settlement of Sephardic Jews) to Trieste, where it became part of Italian folklore.[26] There, however, Judeo-Italian (known as La'az) was more likely to be the vernacular for Jews.

These "borrowed" melodies are . . . quick to lose . . .specific national details that are not appropriate to the expressive means of the new user . . . for the sake of "exoticism" or for good-humored parody or not-so-friendly satire.[27]

However, "the distinction . . . lies not in the . . . common property of two or more peoples," but that

> no two peoples utilize the same complete body of motives . . . Certain motives are predominant, stamp[ing] the motive as typical . . .The difference lies in the way motives are used, how they are fused together, their succession and development. . . .[28]

Did Verdi adapt an Italian folk song? Was the folk song actually based on Ladino material?[29] Or did Sephardic Jews adapt the operatic aria? Whatever the answer, the crossbreeding of gentile melodies with Jewish forms of expression has clearly made for some strange offspring.

Other examples of operatic arias used incongruously in Hebrew prayer settings include Verdi's "Celeste Aida" (as "Eloheinu veiloheinu"), Mozart's "Si Vuol Ballare" ("L'cho dodi"[30]) and "Rachel! Quand du Seigneur" from Halévy's opera *La Juive*, despite its subject matter ("Mimikomo"), etc. Equally inappropriate were transferals from free-standing melodies such as Schubert's "Serenade" ("Ki lekakh tov") and "Kaddish" set to "La Marseillaise" and "The Girl I Left Behind Me," etc.

Then there is the phenomenon of Abraham Goldfaden, founder of the Yiddish Theater, who, in his 1883 musical drama *Bar Kochba* (the eponymous Jewish leader of Roman times), makes what seems to be the most bizarre borrowing of all. Surrounded by his followers, Bar Kochba—an assumed name, meaning "Son of the Star"—exacts an oath (*shvueh)* of fidelity from them in "Der Shverung" (Ex. 1-8), a contrafact of the "Hallelujah Chorus" from Handel's *Messiah*![31] Nonetheless, Goldfaden's choice turns out to be a canny one. A cursory examination of the life of Simeon Ben Kosebah—possibly his real name—reveals that as a rebel against the regime of Emperor Hadrian (early second century) he was hailed by the great Rabbi Akiba as the Messiah. Upon his defeat, however, the hero became known as Ben Koziba or "Son of the Lie"; and with his musical cross-reference, Goldfaden not only underscores Bar Kochba's Redeemer status, but also establishes its "falseness" by setting it in an anachronistic language unknown to the historical personages being portrayed on stage.[32]

(Pledge yourselves to me. We swear it. Swear it from your heart. We swear it!)

Biblical personalities have always been a source of inspiration for western composers of all faiths and stripes; but in the nineteenth century, Hebrew liturgy and sound materials—and, later, Yiddish folk songs—began to be explored by composers of renown. A sampling of non-Jewish composers—and Jewish converts to Christianity—may be of interest. Schubert did a setting of *Tov lehodot*, Psalm 92; Max Bruch made a concert setting of *Kol Nidre*; Elgar used a synagogue melody in *The Apostles*, an oratorio; Ravel made art songs out of the *Kaddish*, *Di alte kashe* (The Old Question), and *Meyerke mayn zun* (Little Meyer, My Son); Moussorgsky's "Samuel Goldenberg and Schmuyle" (with declamatory, then nattering rhythms) in *Pictures at an Exhibition* and the choral piece "Joshua" are based on Jewish motifs; Prokofiev wrote an *Overture on Hebrew Themes* (including the Yiddish song *Zayt gezunterheyt,* Stay Healthy); Stravinsky set *Abraham and Isaac* to a Hebrew text; works by Shostakovich use both explicit Yiddish melodies (e.g. *Oy, Abram*)[33] as well as more substantial hidden Jewish modalities.

Despite their conversions, Felix Mendelssohn, Anton Rubinstein,[34] and Gustav Mahler never completely escaped their origins. (Arnold Schoenberg, who wrote extensive Jewish-theme works and who had generations of cantors on his mother's side, converted to Christianity and then came back into the fold.) Although Mendelssohn (unknowingly) provided the music for a world famous Christmas carol: "Hark the Herald Angels Sing,"[35] he based a section of his oratorio *Elijah*: "Behold, God the Lord" on a German high holy day tune.[36] Rubinstein wrote an opera called *Christus*, but he also composed *Moses, Sulamith* and *The Macabees*—three dramatic works that utilized Hebrew melodies. The third movement of Mahler's Symphony No. 1 contains a parody of the *freylekh*, a Jewish wedding dance. Musicologist Hanoch Avenary[37] has even detected a Jewish speech pattern in the last movement of Mahler's *Das Lied von der Erde*. While he says this *Abschied* (Parting) is "a far cry from... practical solutions demanded . . . for synagogue song, which had to cope with tradition and habitude,"[38] Avenary's insight demonstrates the more intriguing process of how Mahler's Jewish heritage was internalized.

Author Howard Pollack has described a similar metamorphosis in Aaron Copland's trio, *Vitebsk*, how its depiction of harsh shtetl life "resurfaced in subsequent scores, including Copland's next two major works: *Symphonic Ode* and *Piano Variations*." Copland also refashioned parts of *Quiet City*, a "very urban and Jewish work," incorporating them into *Our Town* and *Appalachian Spring*, two very rural and non-Jewish works, which "throws an unexpected perspective on them."[39]

While none of this may have direct bearing on popular music in America, it does indicate that influences flow from Gentile to Jew and vice versa; and although it can be risky to deal with nuances open to interpretation, the fact cannot be ignored that Jewish idioms emerge almost in spite of themselves in non-Jewish contexts.

The route to American musical comedy came by way of theater composers, mainly through the precedent set by Jacques Offenbach, the father of modern European operetta. The enormous success of Offenbach could not have been lost on Goldfaden; and even more consequential for the history of the musical theater, it had direct bearing on the style of Gilbert and Sullivan throughout their entire oeuvre. Listen to "Never mind the why and wherefore" from *H. M.S. Pinafore*, and you can hear an Offenbach cancan kicking up its legs.

Offenbach's popularity also persuaded Johann Strauss, Jr., "The Waltz King," to change direction and write his first operetta, *Die Fledermaus*. Offenbach's Jewish ancestry is clear-cut (Chapter 9 addresses the slight Jewish content in his music); but the genealogy of the Strausses, both Sr. and Jr., is considerably more tangled. Junior's paternal grandparents, Wolf and Theresia Strauss, were Hungarian Jews. He was raised as a Catholic, and although the church did not recognize the divorce from his second wife (his first wife had died), it did not prevent him from marrying Adèle Deutsch, a Jewess who had a child from a previous marriage. In order to accomplish this, Strauss turned Protestant and left his native (Catholic) Vienna for the German (Protestant) city of Coburg, where he divorced Lilli (1882) and married Adèle. (According to Jewish law, if there had been any offspring from this third marriage, they would have been considered Jewish.) The female lead of *Die Fledermaus* (1874) is named Adèle, and the plot is a German adaptation of a French farce by two French Jews, Henri Meilhac and Lodovic Halévy, the same team that provided Georges Bizet the libretto for *Carmen*.[40] (Halévy was the son-in-law of Bizet and a cousin to Jacques Halévy, famous for the opera *La Juive*.) Whether or not there is any Jewish content in Strauss's stage works, "the bonhomie of 'Die Fledermaus' . . . was adored by . . . the Eastern European Jews pouring into the Leopoldstadt [the Jewish quarter in Vienna]."[41] It also was revered by Adolf Hitler.

Over Here–The USA, Mostly New York City

Ludwig Englander, a student of Offenbach, relocated to America, where he became best known for his operetta *The Casino Girl*. More illustrious émigré composers included Oscar Straus (*The Chocolate Soldier*), Emmerich Kálmán (*Countess Maritza*), Sigmund Romberg (*The Student Prince*), Rudolf Friml (*The Vagabond King*), and, more significantly, Kurt Weill. But, with the exception of the last, these West Europeans continued to write in a Offenbachian-cum-Straussian style even after they took up residence in the United States.

It was an American-born Jew of German-Bohemian parentage who broke the European bonds. Jerome Kern, virtually single-handedly, domesticated the imported sounds of the day. In his early musical comedies the remote figures of operetta royalty—countesses, princes and company—were usurped and replaced by "plain folk," even though Kern's earliest successes were produced, contrarily, at the Princess Theater on Broadway. Kern revealed his national origins in the song "Pick Yourself Up" (from the film *Swing Time*), a disguised Bohemian polka based on a famous tune from Jaromir Weinberger's opera *Schwanda, the Bagpiper*.[42] In *Show Boat* (1927), Kern wrote an historic score, alternating central European airs with quasiblack strains. The two streams come together in the River, which "just keeps rolling along." With one foot in Europe, the other on American soil, *Show Boat* was the touchstone work that turned an adjective into a noun. Thereafter, "musical comedies" became "musicals."

But Jewish input is minimal in Kern's output. The Kern-Harburg song "And Russia Is Her Name" from the movie *Song of Russia* (sung on the sound track by Cantor Moishe Oysher under the pseudonym of Walter Lawrence) was one of the few exceptions.[43] This is not surprising since Kern was not supportive of Zionist efforts to repatriate the remnants of Jewry who had escaped Hitler's annihilation. During Kern's era and earlier, the field of opera was the domain of Italians, while the symphonic field was controlled by German gentiles. In fact, the Philharmonic Society of New York, founded in 1842, was derided as "The German Philharmonic."

The fields of popular culture, on the other hand, were wide open. Newly found freedom and newly developing technology were an irresistible combination. What better way to become quickly Americanized than through recordings, vaudeville, radio, and movies? Along with socialism and nationalism, showbiz became the new secular religion. Between 1881 (when the Russian pogroms began in earnest) and 1924 (the year of the American National Origins Immigration Act), east European Jews rapidly became homesteaders as popular music managers, publishers, song pluggers, performers, and consummate songwriters.

Preceding them, Sephardic Jews had settled on American shores as early as the 1650s. By the 1820s, Jewish communities had become established in the South. Henry Russell (1812-1900), an English Jew, was a popular balladeer who toured the American provinces in the midnineteenth century. His best known number was "Woodman, Spare That Tree." There is no Jewish content in Russell's songs, despite one viewpoint that Russell's "Our Way Across the Mountain, Ho!" (1838), with words by Charles Mackay, Esq., is "a song of the religious variety based upon words from the psalms."[44] The earliest piece of printed American sheet music on a Jewish theme that I have traced comes out of Philadelphia, "Song of the Hebrew Captive" (1830), a florid paraphrase of Psalm 137. Another, out of Boston, is "The Sorrowing Jew" (1843). While its cover displays a poignant etching worthy of respect, its words reveal a different scenario: "Teach them their own pierced Messiah to view/And bring to His fold the poor sorrowing Jew."[45] (Illustration 2)

Pianist-composer Louis Gottschalk (1829-1869), the son of a marriage between a Jewish father and a Creole mother, was one of the first to incorporate Negro localisms into art music. Although the popular works of this darling of the mid-century salon had no Jewish content, the first edition of the Reform *Union Hymnal* (1892) adapted one of his melodies as "Happy Who Is Early Youth" (no. 96) without credit, but later attributed it to him in the 1914 and 1943 editions.

Beginning in the 1880s, Jewish immigrant types became provender for stage fare. Typically portrayed as unkempt with crooked noses, moustaches, scruffy beards and wearing derby hats, they were reckless in gesticulation as they spoke in a gibberish that was supposed to pass for Yiddish.

One of the first stage portrayals to be seen, if not the very first, was *Samuel of Posen*, an 1881 play by George Jessop (or Jessup?) about an Austrian Jewish peddler, popular enough to be made into a film in 1910. The refrain[46] of the eponymous title song by Isaac Scholem (W) and Roger Putnam (M) began:

"Machovis [?sic] he has plenty, and lots of stuff that's bad,
But if you speak against his goods/Oh, then don't he get mad!"

"Let Us Go to the Sheeney Wedding," by Harry Thompson, describes a free-for-all rather than a dignified affair. Frank Bush—not Jewish, but known as the "Jew comic"—portrayed "Solomon Moses," a clothing store owner: "I'm a Bully Sheeny Man." Among his other depictions as a ragman or a pawnshop dealer, Bush also performed a parody on Harrigan and Braham's "Babies on Our Block," as "Sheenies in the Sand," who "may be seen upon the beach/They come from Corbin's building . . .".[47] In 1879, Austin Corbin, president of the Long Island Railroad and a resort owner (and probably a German Jew) announced he would accept only so-called "white Jews" (i.e., those not from Eastern Europe) in his hotel on Manhattan Beach, Coney Island. Another composition based on this incident was "Corbin's Idea or No Jews Wanted," author and date unknown.[48] Besides Frank Bush, other "stage Jews" from this period included David Warfield (b. Wohlfelt), Andy Rice, Abe Reynolds, Julian Rose, Howe and Scott, Ben Welch, Lew Welch, and Joe Welch (relationship unknown). The opening line of Joe Welch's act "Mebbe you tink I'm a heppy man," became a catchphrase and the title—as "Maybe You Think I'm Happy?"—of a 1911 song by L. Wolfe Gilbert about "Cohn and his marriage to Kate O'Hare." It is not clear how many, if any, of these early entertainers were Jewish, but there is no question about the Jewishness of their successors who continued the boorish practices first as "Dutch" (i.e., *Deutsch*) actors and then, with the onset of World War I, as Jewish personae: Joe (b. Moishe Yossel) Weber and Lew Fields (b. Moishe Schoenfeld), Joe Smith (b. Sulzer) and Charles Dale (b. Marks), Lou Holtz and brothers Willie and Eugene Howard (b. Levkowitz). (see Illustration 3)

Among other early songs, there were "Moses Levi Cohen" (by W. H. Batchelor), "Solomon Levi," a college march tune, and "The Hebrew Picnic," a lengthy ditty of 1892, in which "after . . . rambling and scrambling and gambling/Some of the Jews got wrangling who settled the bill." It ends up in a free-for-all brawl. Ironically, "The Hebrew Picnic" was to be sung to an air called "The Tipperary Christening."[49] At "The Hebrew Fancy Ball" (words and music by Edwin R. Lang, 1892), another Moses Levy (how tiresome it gets!) affirms "A Hebrew staunch and true/But most everybody says I am a cranky Jew/I have been keeping pawnshop for nearly fifteen years/And when I lose my money, my eyes they fill with tears."[50]

Offsetting these tedious clichés, Alfred Bryan, a Catholic, wrote a refreshing item in 1908:

Verse: Sweet Lizzie Rosinsky and Izzy Kozinsky/Once worked in a buttonhole shop,
And both were delighted when they were invited/To come to the Tammany hop.
'Twas after Yom Kippur and both felt so chipper/They'd waltz til their shoes were worn out,
At twosteps or lanciers they beat all the dancers/For Lizzy to Izzy would shout:

Refrain: Dance With Me Till I'm Dizzy, Izzy/Left and right, hug me tight,
Hold on to your Lizzie, Izzy/Don't you mind the cost, you can be a sport,
Let your feet get busy, Izzy/One, two, three, can't you see
We won't have to stop for that buttonhole shop/Izzy, dance with me!

Verse: At five in the morning, without any warning/A big Irish loafer came in,
He saw Lizzy dancing so sweet and entrancing/And thought that a smile he could win.
Then brave little Izzy, he surely got busy/And made for that man a black eye,
I'm not a boxfighter, said he, but I'll right her/And then little Lizzy did cry:

[Refrain.][51]

Obviously, most of this material was prejudicial,[52] but while it was reflective of then current social mores, blatant offensiveness probably was not intended to be more than "anything for a laugh." The 1880s mark the beginning of the ethnic-stereotype age when Mexicans and Turks are viewed as crapshooters, Germans as agitating socialists, Italians as organ-grinders, Asians as opium-addicted "Heathen Chinee," Irish as lazy drunks and arm-twisting politicians. Negroes wield razors and dine on watermelon, and long-nosed Jews are grubby tailors and hard-nosed pawn shop proprietors. "Political correctness" was a yet-to-be-heard-from term. While so-called native Americans (which, of course, has since come to mean American Indians—equally subject to bigoted clichés) would laugh at these stage images, newcomers from the other side laughed along with them.

Among the probable non-Jewish German or Irish writers mentioned above, Isaac Scholem doubtless was Jewish. So was Fred Fischer, the author of another song about Jewish cowardice, making it a particularly hard pill to swallow:

Verse: Hark, hark the bugle is calling,/See the soldiers are marching away,
           Rosenbaum, ain't you going to fight for the U. S. A.?
           Give up your bus'ness for your duty,/Fight for your country, not for gold,
           Meet the en'my face to face,/Don't you run, it's a disgrace,
           Be a hero brave and bold.

Refrain: Rosenbaum, he was a soldier,/But a sword he never drew,
           He said to me: the deuce with fighting,/'Taint no bus'ness for a Jew.
           Butcher, Baker, Real Estator,/Those are men of great reknown;
           When the bugle call would sound/He was never to be found,
           Oi, what a fighter was Rosenbaum.

Verse: Right where the bullets were thickest/They found Rosenbaum, so they tell,
           Under the ammunition wagon/Far from the shot and shell,
           There was no fight./The captain shouted:
           Why did you run? Then Rosen cried:/I saw the enemy advance
           So I run and took no chance./Don't be angry, Rosen cried. [Refrain]

Although copyrighted 1909, a 1936 publication states "Rosenbaum" was written in 1903. The new edition also added the couplets:"Oh he won the Croix de Guerre,/ In a crap game over there," and "When it came to shot and shells,/He was with the Mad'moiselles"—implying that it was a World War I song. Equally ludicrous, the three-syllabled "gentleman" awkwardly replaces "Jew," as if that could ameliorate the despicable portrait.

The composer of "Rosenbaum," words and music, was a man of contradiction. Born in 1875 as Albert von Breitenbach in Cologne, Germany, in 1900 he emigrated to the United States, where he assumed the name of Fred Fischer—Friedrich for its Germanic strength and Fischer from a sign he read on a passing truck. With the onslaught of World War I, he decided Fischer was too Germanic and so he modified it to Fisher. Yiddish for him was a bastardized tongue, a point of view consistent with his background. Another one of his Jewish-based tunes, "Good-Bye Beckie Cohen" (1910), appears to be a gloss (or outright plagiarism) on an earlier number, "Good-Bye Dolly Gray" (1900) by Will Cobb and Paul Barnes.

Then this German-born composer made it into Ripley's "Believe It or Not" column for writing more Irish songs than anyone else—"Ireland Must Be Heaven for My Mother Came from There" (with Howard Johnson and Joe McCarthy, the authors of this book's frontispiece), and the classic "Peg o' My Heart," with Alfred

Bryan, among other titles. Other Fisher standards include "Come Josephine in My Flying Machine" (again with Bryan), and the evergreen "Chicago (That Toddling Town)," for which he wrote both words and music. He preferred composing comic songs, a decision he came to regret when he realized ballads had greater lasting power. He committed suicide in 1942, throwing himself out of a window, despondent over having colon cancer.[53]

In sharp contrast to the likes of "Rosenbaum," is the lyric for "The Cohens" by one Maurice Morris, who was inspired by a *New York Herald* article based on a War Records Bureau report (probably 1919) that the name Cohen was the most frequent to appear among enlistees:[54]

Verse: They have told in song and story of the Kalmuck and the Turk,
Sang the everlasting glory of the Kelly, Shea and Burke.
But apologies should flow in to the fiercest warrior clan,
Yes, the newest name is Cohen, he's the top hole fighting man.

Refrain: Here's to Ikey, Abe and Izzy/Here's to Ignace, Moe and Jake,
Sure the pace they set was dizzy/And they made the Heinies quake.
Some said gold was their delighting/And that business was their soul,
Well, they made their business fighting/And kicked the Kaiser for a goal.

Verse: You will find them in the Bowery and in Hester Street and Grand,
And their manner may seem flowery as they talk with either hand.
But you'll do well to remember that those hands can turn to fists,
And that three years, come November those same Cohens led the lists.

Refrain: Here's to Ike and Abie, shout them/Here's to Ignatz, Jake and Moe,
We have had our jests about them/Now what's underneath we know,
Boasted not the flag above them/Nor for country-valuted land,
But they showed best how to love them/And they've done the city proud![55]

* * *

Irish performers Harrigan and Hart dominated the American musical stage of the late nineteenth century. Edward Harrigan was the wordsmith and one-half of the performing team, but Tony Hart, the other half, was not the tunesmith. The scores were composed by a Jew born in London, David Braham— a name probably shortened from Abraham. Was David related to the renowned English synagogue and opera singer John Braham (1774-1856)? The son of Cantor Abraham Singer and a disciple of Cantor Meyer Leon,[56] John Braham was composer of the well-known hymn tune used by both synagogue and church "Praise to the living God" (Yigdal), and was named as co-composer (but not in actuality) with Isaac Nathan of the music to Lord Byron's "Hebrew Melodies."

Jewish musicians had been known to inhabit the sixteenth century palaces of Henry VIII. Although as Jews they could live freely in the ghetto, the art music of which they were masters was not encouraged there. On the other hand, in gentile society, they could be musicians, but not practicing Jews. [57]

Two hundred years later, John Braham had no such problems. He sired seven children.[58] The genealogy after David Braham is of interest since it established an American musical dynasty as had John Braham's before him in England. David had two brothers: Joseph and John Joseph, both orchestra leaders at music halls in New

York City—Tony Pastor's and the Casino Theater. To keep it all in the family, David became Edward Harrigan's son-in-law when he married one of Harrigan's ten children, sixteen-year-old daughter Annie, in 1876. David's and Annie's son Harry became Lillian Russell's first husband (she of Gay Nineties stage fame). Although the magic was gone, son Charles succeeded his father as Harrigan's composer, when David died. Harrigan died in 1911. The youngest Harrigan child, a girl named Nedda, married film actor Walter Connolly and, after his death, Joshua Logan, the theater director and writer. Nedda, President of the Actors' Fund, died in 1989 at age 89.

Harrigan and Braham captured New York City street life as vividly as Dickens did in London, influencing the naturalist course of the American musical theater. Indeed, George M. Cohan was in their direct line of descent. Among their more than two hundred songs about the likes of the Widow Nolan (who had a goat whose "whiskers were long like the Wandering Jew man"), Paddy Duffy, the Mulligan Guard, and many other Irish types, there was, from the 1882 show of the same name, *Mordecai Lyons*, a Christian-Jewish melodrama of mistaken identities:

Verse: My name it is Lyons, a merchant by trade,/Oh, I'm in the old clothing line,
           I'd sell you new trousers and second-hand boots,/I warrant them all superfine;
           Suspenders and socks, Hats, neckties and bows,/Oh, it's garters and shoelaces, too;
           Oh, take them at cost price, my gracious, they're nice,/So beautiful, lovely and new.

Refrain: Old clothes I buy and sell/Walk in the store, I'll treat you so well;
           Now, old clothes! when it's hard times/Come buy of Mordecai Lyons.

Verse: Alexander, my brother, he keeps a pawn shop,/Where the sports and gamblers all went,
           Mid vatches and diamonds, sealskin overcoats,/At six months, at forty percent;
           Three balls is the sign, The number is nine,/You can see his 'Terms Cash' on the wall;
           He's worth I am told just one million in gold,/He made in the Black Friday fall.
           [Refrain]

Verse: On Sunday I goes, I put on my new clothes/They cost me a five-dollar note,
           Go by the horse car I ride awfully far,/It's cheaper than wagon or boat;
           I do what I can, I'm not a mean man/I don't let a beggar go by,
           A penny I give, oh, the poor man must live;/I can't take it all when I die.[59] [Refrain]

* * *

During the late 1880s, New York City bookseller Judah Katzenelenbogen printed what was probably the first example of published Yiddish-American sheet music, Goldfaden's renowned lullaby "Rozhinkes Mit Mandlen" (Raisins and Almonds). Its success led to the issuance of a series of booklet songsters, called *Lider Magazin* (words only, no music), over the course of the next decade, beginning 1893 or 1897. (The inaugural year is difficult to ascertain since copyright notices were sometimes backdated to protect earlier printings.) Katzenelenbogen may have been emulating the example of William W. Delaney, who began publishing such songsters at the same time (1892) for general public consumption. Delaney's address, No. 117 Park Row, was also the home of the Variety Publishing Co., founded in 1886. Tin Pan Alley publisher Edward Marks recalled that Delaney "bought the privilege from the publisher of every successful song, and his presence at our office was always a sign we had a hit . . . His song sheets went all over the country, wherever people wanted cheap, sentimental reading matter."[60] It could be that Delaney, despite his apparent ignorance of the Yiddish language, was directly inspired by Katzenelenbogen or business associates. He might have read reports by Hutchins Hapgood, a non-Jewish chronicler of Lower East Side life.[61] Or he might have gotten wind of the merchandizing device through those ethnic dialecticians whose "Hebrew Yarn" routines he published. (see Illustration 3)

Whoever came first, Delaney's efforts opened the gates to ubiquitous American derivatives. An illicit Chicago publisher, who hid his identity, struck gold in the mid-1890s with unauthorized reprints of song lyrics. This crime of piracy came to trial, but the case backfired when the House of Witmark, the plaintiff publisher, was itself accused of being the culprit![62] Songsters lasted at least through 1955, in monthly periodicals such as *Songs That Will Live Forever* (issued by Charlton Publishing Corporation of Derby, Connecticut).

Contrary to the sobriquet of "Gay Nineties," popular songs of that decade lay sodden with sentimental tearjerkers such as the 1898 ballad by William B. Gray, "She Is More to Be Pitied, Than Censured":

> She is more to be helped than despised,
> She is only a lassie who ventured on life's stormy path, ill advised.
> Do not scorn her with words fierce and bitter,
> Do not laugh at her shame and downfall,
> For a moment just stop and consider that a man was the cause of it all.

Through Katzenelenbogen's efforts, better known to the Jewish population was a closely rendered Yiddish paraphrase by Isaac Reingold:

> *Zi iz mer tsum badoyern vi shuldik,/O, ver hot ir ere geroybt?*
> *O, mener, mit vos iz zi shuldik,/Ven zi hot gelibt un gegloybt?*
> *Tsit tsurik ayer shpot un farakhtung!*
> *A vayl zet, hot nor geduld,*
> *Batrakht es mit reyner batrakhtung,*
> *A man, nor a man hot di shuld!* [63]

> She is more to be pitied than guilty,/Oh, who robbed her of her honor?
> Oh men, of what is she guilty/When she loved and trusted?
> Oh take back your ridicule and hatred/Just stop a moment and be patient,
> Consider it with simple regard/A man, only a man did her in!

Delaney printed another lyric to this ballad by one Jere O'Halloran, who wrote a contrafact for a burning Jewish issue of the day about "Dreyfus an Innocent Man":

> He is more to be pitied than censured/He has suffered enough for all time,
> To confess, Esterhazy has ventured/Yet Dreyfus is blamed for the crime.
> I have heard of such justice in Ireland/Where a man gets no ghost of a chance,
> Let the French be ashamed of their sireland,/Till they do Dreyfus justice in France.[64]

The Dreyfus Affair was a convoluted miscarriage of justice. In 1894, Alfred Dreyfus, a Jewish Captain in the French army, was convicted of treason and court-martialed—the victim of a scheme to overthrow the French Republic. The villain of this travesty was a certain Major Walsin Esterhazy who had forged incriminating documents purported to be in Dreyfus's hand. It was not until 1906 that Dreyfus was exonerated from this web of collusion and conspiracy by the French government, although never directly by the army high command. Tin Pan Alley reacted to this mockery with the 1899 ballad "The Dreyfus Court Martial" (by Johnson & Stanley, first names unknown).

Translators hired by Katzenelenbogen to make Yiddish versions of Tin Pan Alley songs included Louis Gilrod and Isaac Reingold (who did most of them), Shlomo Shmulevitz (also known as Solomon Small), Isadore Lillian, Michal Aronson, Louis Kopelman, and David Meyerowitz. They were more consonant with the O'Halloran line of thought, rarely translating quid pro quo, but adapting the material to the more familiar terrain of Jewish life.[65]

In the Yiddish Theater, Shakespearean figures were metamorphosed into characters closer to home: King Lear, in Jacob Gordin's version, became a merchant; Gordin's *Mirele Efros*, a long-suffering Jewish mother, was also known as "The Jewish Queen Lear"; youthful lovers Raphael and Shaindele, from warring religious sects, in a previous existence are known as Romeo and Juliet (their "intermarriage" performed by Friar Tuck, as a Reform Rabbi!), and Hamlet became a rabbinical student.[66] There also was a Jewish Faust.

"Bake That Matza Pie,"an untraceable confection by Charles K. Harris, was probably written in the 1890s; but it was Harris's "A Rabbi's Daughter" of 1899 that really captured attention. A Jewish maiden, complying with her rabbi father's demand that "If you a Christian marry, Your old father's heart you'll break, You are a Rabbi's Daughter, and must leave him for my sake," is herself found dead of heartbreak. Michael Gold (b. Irwin Granich) writes about the song in *Jews without Money*, his exemplary fictionalized biography. He speaks of how his mother was emotionally taken in by the father who held a funeral rite for his estranged, but still living, daughter: "I know a cynic or Broadway clown must have written those songs, with tongue in cheek, maybe, for money."[67]

"Bedelia," a 1903 "Irish Coon [sic] Song Serenade" by William Jerome (W), an Irishman and Jean Schwartz (M), a Hungarian Jew, was one of many American tunes that underwent this transmogrification:

Bedelia, I want to steal ye,/Bedelia, I love you so,
I'll be your Chauncey Olcott [viz., Chancellor John Olcott, cowriter of enduring popular Irish songs]
If you'll be my *Molly O'.* [viz., title of a show by performer-author William J. Scanlan][68]

This was morphed by Louis Gilrod into a Yiddish lyric, sung by a biblically minded Jewish girl:

Gedalye, azoy makh nit kalye,	Gedalia, don't spoil everything,
Gedalye, azoy vart a vayl,	Gedalia, stay a while,
Oyb du bist mayn Shloyme hameylekh,	If you'll be my King Solomon,
Dan bin ikh dayn eyshes khayil.	I'll be your Woman of Valor.

Other metamorphoses included: "In Old Madrid," which became a song about Spanish Marranos; "On a Saturday Night," transformed into a song about Sabbath Eve; "Marching Through Georgia" became "Lift Zion's Banner High"; "All

Aboard for Broadway" opened with "Workers of the world, unite!"; "Break the News to Mother" became "The Jewish Volunteer"; "My Sweetheart's the Man in the Moon" became "The New World."[69] There also were parodies from mainstream America to Yiddish America. Harry Kennedy's waltz tune of 1892

> Molly, Molly, always so jolly,/Always laughing, chock full of glee,
> No one so happy, as happy as we,/Molly and I and the Baby.

was reconstituted by Harry Thompson into:

> Rachel, Rachel, Oh what a wife/She is so handsome, she's the joy of my life,
> And when I go out my carriage to drive,/I take Rachel and I and Abie.[70]

Around 1907, Delaney printed "Maid of Judah," a yearning for Zion that harkens back to the style of the medieval poet Yehudah Halevi:

> No more shall the children of Judah sing/The lay of the happier time,
> Or strike the harp with the golden string/'Neath the sun of an eastern clime.
> This was the lay of a Jewish maid,/Though not in her father's bowers,
> Land of my kindred, thou'lt ne'er be forgot,/While the ruins remain of thy towers.[71]

In "The Jewish Massacre," a Delaney song book offered a prescient song of hope about the Kissineff [sic, Kishinev, 1903] pogrom, "to be sung to the air 'In the City of Sighs and Tears'":[72]

> Out in that country so black and cold,/Down by the great Black Sea,
> Hebrews were murder'd right in their beds,/Before they had time to flee.
> Praying for someone to succor them,/Cut down in their youthful prime,
> The world stands aghast at this massacre,/For it was a terrible crime!
> . . . But there'll come a day of reck'ning,/Israel led by Zion's band
> Will return to Palestine/And the lovely Holy Land.[73]

Gerson Rosenzweig (1861-1914), a major interpreter of Hebrew in America, released his *Mi-zimrat Ha-arets* (Songs of the Land), American national songs in Hebrew, in 1898. "My Country, 'tis of Thee, Sweet Land of Liberty," became *Artzi bas d'ror no-e-mo,* with *Oschira loch rone-no,* one of the few lines that almost works. Neither Rosenzweig nor Katzenelenbogen were remotely in the same league as their publisher coreligionists on Tin Pan Alley. Obviously, their target audience was small in number and poor in income.

Whereas serious music publishing houses in America had originally excluded Jewish partners, popular music publishing was wide open territory. Actually the exclusion from "classical music" was an academic issue since the catalogs of standard houses were made up of church music, pedagogical methods, choral material, band and orchestra works, reprints of classics, and representations of catalogs from European houses, all requiring a large investment, not readily available to greenhorns. Max Winkler, of Belwin Music Co., was one of the first to break the barrier; and early on, Henri Elkan, a Jew, formed Elkan-Vogel Publishers with Adolph Vogel, his non-Jewish partner. In Europe, the Big Bs of music publishing houses—Bote and Bock, Breitkopf and Härtel, and B. Schott—were not under Jewish ownership; but Jews were (and still are) prominent in many of the other companies.

Their success was reinforced in no small measure by the replacement of Edison's cylinder recording contraption by the flat disc, invented by Emile Berliner (1881-1929). This not only ushered in the era of recordings for mass consumption, but it also stimulated sheet music sales.

* * *

Back on Tin Pan Alley, already well-entrenched German Jews had discovered the riches to be mined in the flatlands of Manhattan. It was a Jewish newspaper columnist who probably coined the Alley's appellation. All the stories about the provenance of the Alley's name involve the personage of Monroe H. Rosenfeld, a colorful character hailing from Richmond, Virginia—a philanderer, gambler, newspaper man, and songwriter who thought little about appropriating other composers' songs as his own. His 1896 "Those Wedding Bells Shall Not Ring Out," for instance, is a melodramatic *scena* almost worthy of Italian opera. Rosenfeld claims "the incidents in this song are based on upon a tragedy which occurred in a western city"; but it is suspiciously like the song "The Fatal Wedding" written three years earlier by a black songwriter, Gussie L. Davis. Same plot idea for the two of them. In Rosenfeld, it's a two-timing bride who is stabbed at the wedding altar by the jilted husband, who then commits suicide. In Davis, it is a two-timing husband who is confronted by the jilted bride at the altar with babe in arms; the child dies on the spot, prompting the dastardly father to do the same. Musically, don't ask: both have the same meter, key, harmonic style, motives, filler figurations, and verse length (65 bars). The only difference is that Davis begins with a quote from the Mendelssohn "Wedding March," while Rosenfeld adds an extra section of melodrama. On two editions of "Those Wedding Bells," Rosenfeld is acknowledged as author of words and music; on others, he is credited only as lyricist, further confirmation of his questionable business practices. (see Illustration 4)

At the turn of the century, West 28th Street, between Sixth Avenue and Broadway, was buffeted by pianos playing, their strings stuffed with newspaper to muffle sound in order to prevent theft from the likes of a Rosenfeld. In those days of no air-conditioning, the street sounded like "kitchen clatter," in the words of publisher-composer Harry Von Tilzer, who also laid claim to the title:

In 1899 I was sitting at the piano composing a song, and I wanted to get a banjo effect. So I cut up a newspaper and stuck it behind the keys next to the strings. While I was working the door to the outer office opened and in came Monroe H. Rosenfelt [sic]. "What are you doing, Harry?" Rosie called in to me. "Working on a tune." "What are the tin pans for?" I showed him how I fixed up the newspaper. "That gives me an idea," Rosie said. "I'm writing an article on the music business and I've been looking around for a name for it. I'll call it 'Down in Tin Pan Alley'."[74]

Rosenfeld supposedly first put the name into print in a 1900 *New York Herald* column of his.[75] But which column? The closest I have been able to trace are two Sunday *Herald* pieces by him, "How Popular Songs Are Made So" (18 February 1900), but no mention of Tin Pan Alley, and one on 'coon' songs and Von Tilzer (8 April 1900).[76] Or perhaps it was written for another newspaper, the *New York Clipper,* for which he was a columnist for more than fifteen years?[77] The actual article has yet to surface, if, indeed, it exists.

Another theory has the coinage credited to short story writer O. Henry, who passed it along to a lyric writer, Stanley Murphy, who, in turn, was a collaborator of Harry Von Tilzer, an early denizen of the Alley who was, as we have seen, frequently visited by Rosenfeld. Among the standards of Von Tilzer, are "Wait 'til the Sun Shines, Nellie," "A Bird in a Gilded Cage," and "I Want a Girl Just Like the Girl That Married Dear Old Dad." The last has been referred to, by a Jewish psychologist, as "the living out neurotically of an unresolved Oedipus complex."[78]

Harry's brother, Albert, ran the York Music Co. at No. 40, 28th Street. As composer, Albert was best known for writing the classics: "I'll Be with You in Apple Blossom Time," "Put Your Arms Around Me, Honey" and the anthem of the national pastime, "Take Me Out to the Ball Game."

The Von Tilzer brothers, German Jews from Detroit, were born with the surname Gumm (or Gumbinsky).[79] Harry used his mother's maiden name, adding the noble "Von" to give it cachet. He had originally formed a publishing troika with Maurice Shapiro (1873-1911) and Louis Bernstein (1879-1962), a former bookkeeper, but they came to a parting of the ways when Harry set up his own establishment.

In Kenneth Kanter's *The Jews on Tin Pan Alley*, a book riddled with inaccuracies,[80] other Jewish composer-publishers are profiled:

(1) The five Witmark Brothers: Isidore (1869-1941), Julius (1870-1924), and Jay (1872-1950)—later joined by brothers Frank (b. 1876) and Adolph S. (b. 1878)—who in 1893 had set up shop as M. Witmark & Sons on West 28th Street; but with their big hit of 1903, "Sweet Adeline," had moved uptown to 37th Street.

(2) Leopold Feist (1869-1930)—originally of Feist & Frankenthaler, founded in 1897—who coined the slogan "You can't go wrong with a Feist song" when Feist went into business for himself. He had begun his sales career with the W. and B. Corset Co., and went into music publishing because he viewed that as more of a "growth industry."

(3) Charles Kassel Harris (1867-1930), from Milwaukee, opened a New York branch at 29 West 28th Street and in 1892 became the first person to promote the unprecedented sale of five million copies of just one song, his "After the Ball."

(4) Joseph W. Stern (1870-1934) and Edward B. Marks (1865-1945), who penned a "Kaddish of My Ancestry." But these Jewish owned firms were hardly a monopoly presence on the Alley.

Among the non-Jewish enterprises, there were:

(1) T. B. Harms—but truth to tell, it was run by a Jew, Max Dreyfus (1874-1964), highly respected by his colleagues and the mentor, among others, of Will Cobb & Gus Edwards, authors of "School Days."[81]

(2) Paul Dresser (1857-1906), brother of novelist Theodore Dreiser, who opened his own company when the firm of Howley, Haviland & Dresser failed.

(3) Jerome H. Remick (1864-1931), originally Whitney-Warner Publishing Co.

(4) The Gotham-Attucks Music Co., publisher of songs by black entertainers such as Bert Williams. And still others: the Vandersloot Music Co., E. T. Paull

Music Co., Willis Woodward & Co., and Doty & Brill, whose name is on the Brill Building at 1619 Broadway, where the last vestiges of Tin Pan Alley reside.

Many Gaslight Era standards were in waltz time, which makes sense since waltzes were Germanic in origin. Three-four time is the least frequent meter used in Eastern Europe. Among others, dances such as the *bulgar, dobridyen, freylekh, hopke, hora, kozatska, krakoviak, volekh,* and *sher* are all two-steps. Of seventy-nine dances examined in the book *Old Jewish Music*, only ten are in three-four time, one-eighth of the total. Is it outlandish to suggest that triple meter connotes Trinitarian concepts of Christianity while duple meter is more symbolic of the Jewish one-on-one relationship of man and God (viz., philosopher Martin Buber's *Ich und Du*)? At the same time Jewish composers were grinding out waltzes on Tin Pan Alley, their counterparts in Eastern Europe were beginning to write songs indigenously their own; but out of nineteen examined songs by Polish-born, Yiddish folk poet Mordecai Gebirtig, only four are in three-four.

For the most part, music written by Jews in the United States for Jewish usage tended not to follow the assimilation route. Joseph Rumshinsky, for example, tried to introduce Americanisms into his Yiddish songs; but these remained paste-ons, not an organic integration. But in the 1940s, after the enormous success of "Bay mir bistu sheyn," many other Yiddish tunes were successfully subjected to swing treatment in recordings and on Yiddish radio. The grafting of popular idioms onto synagogue prayers began to take firm hold in the 1970s when the "folk-rock" idiom, along with guitar-strummers, hand-clapping, and campfire songs, increasingly became a preoccupation of some synagogue songwriters. It remains to be seen whether or not these ventures in a now outmoded style will eventually come to constitute a genuine American *nusakh* (tradition).

On the other hand, music written by Jews for non-Jewish consumption has blossomed naturally from the same breeding ground as music composed for Jewish listeners. America not only offered unprecedented opportunities, but released a collective longing which transcended isolationism and which plunged into hitherto unexpressed potentialities. No longer under the thumb of religious or state restrictions, it was possible, at long last, for frustrated aspiring musicians to participate in certain previously unavailable artistic endeavors. In East Europe, the musical talents of Jews had been buried under tablets of "thou-shalt-nots" from Jewish law and from ukases inflicted upon them by host countries. It was an inward culture forced to draw upon its own resources. Undoubtedly the centrality of learning instilled into Jewish populations over centuries, along with the ability to be critically detached and self-observant, were factors in fostering Jewish humor. But the need for upward mobility must have counted as much.

The Lower East Side of New York City produced many songwriters for similar reasons. An 1893 *New York Times* column described this area as "an eyesore . . . the filthiest place on the western continent. . . . Impossible for a Christian to live there. Getting out was the hallmark of success. The performing arts was a field open to young Jews."[82] Lyricist Sammy Cahn, a product of the Lower East Side, once observed:

The struggle to get out [of the ghetto] comes in waves with immigration . . . Irish, Jews, Italians, Blacks. I don't say I'm Margaret Mead, but that's how it always seemed to me.[83]

The struggle was dramatically symbolized by the 1911 Triangle Shirtwaist Factory Fire, a tragedy that may have instituted sweeping changes in occupancy law, but did not entirely stop abuses. In 1927, Fanny Brice recorded "The Song of the Sewing Machine" by Ballard MacDonald, Jesse Greer and her soon-to-be husband, Billy Rose. Her lament, "There is no song, there is no bird/And God is just another word," still resonates in the garment district of today where late twentieth-century newcomers, mostly Central Americans, now constitute the labor force.

At the same time, the Jewish population of New York increased with the new influx of middle-class Russian Jews, coming full circle with their counterparts of the early twentieth century. It is to the East European Pale of Settlement that we now turn our attention.

NOTES 1. A term from medieval Christian practice. Older and familiar tunes set to new words that might evoke associations to the primary source are known as contrafacts.

2. There is nothing new about this. Even Plato was discomfited by music. Religious authorities of many persuasions, east to west from past to present, have discredited music in general and women's voices in particular. In 1995 Barbra Streisand volunteered to perform at a Madison Square Garden memorial in New York City honoring the memory of slain Israeli Prime Minister Yitzhak Rabin, but was prevented from doing so by orthodox rabbis.

3. Velvel Pasternak, *Songs of the Chassidim,* Introduction. According to Jewish law, it is forbidden to inscribe the complete name of the Supreme Being in any language (*Kitzur Shulchan Aruch*: vol. I, chap. IV, vs. 3).

4. A letter from Max A. Tamir to the *New York Times* (5 February 1996) speaks of The Academy of the Hebrew Language being "stymied by conflicting opinions, not the least of which is the myth that to change the holy script of the Bible would amount to sacrilege." So venerated is the name of the Deity that it cannot be erased; and, what is more, burial services are held for worn-out or damaged Torah scrolls.

5. The usual form of the yellow badge was circular. For more than five centuries, the dress code was enforced only to be revived in 1939 in the form of a Star of David during the infamous Nazi era.

6. The intermingling continues today, with wedding combos at the ready to play anything from salsa to hora, from line dances to *freylekh*s.

7. Some observers have noted that this is the method of construction Gershwin used for

Rhapsody in Blue, wherein one section can be interchanged with another. All too often, however, it is forgotten that the *Rhapsody* was not written to be a symphonic piece.

8. Eric Werner, *The Sacred Bridge,* p. 362.

9. See Idelsohn, *Jewish Music,* Ex. 1, p. 40 and Ex. 5, p. 41. The Exodus passage of Ex. 1 is wrongly labeled. It is from 12:21, not 18:1-2. The same set of examples also can be found in *HOM,* II, p. 35.

10. An anonymous composer of the sixteenth century also used this monophonic melody as the cantus firmus for a polyphonic composition: Kyrie IV Toni, found in the Trent Codices, no. III. Hassler, who adapted the tune in 1601, may have known it from either source.

11. An indelicate innovation of early German Reform hymnals was the inclusion of various Bach church tunes. Among these was an adaptation of *O Haupt voll Blut und Wunden,* no. 16a of *Hebräische und Deutsche Gesänge* . . . (Hebrew and German Songs for Worship and Devotion, Firstly for the New Schools of Israelite Youth in Westphalia), compiled by Israel Jacobsohn (1768-1828) and published 1810 in Kassel. (See Idelsohn, *Jewish Music,* pp. 241 and 519, Chapter 12, n. 4.) As late as 1943, the American *Union Hymnal* used a melody by Georg Neumark (1621-1681) as harmonized by Bach (no. 89).

12. For first bringing these synagogue-church parallelisms to my attention, I am grateful for the insights of the musicologists Richard Neumann and Eric Werner.

13. Eric Werner, "Jewish Music," *Grove's Dictionary of Music and Musicians,* p. 632. *Mi-sinai* tunes are also known as "scarbove," a corruption of the Latin "sacra."

14. Alfred Sendry, *The Music of the Jews in the Diaspora*, p. 432.

15. Idelsohn, *Jewish Music*, p. 511.

16. See Werner, *A Voice Still Heard*, p. 90, for sources and p. 261, no. 2, for music examples—a most confusing layout! Or try Idelsohn, *Jewish Music*, pp. 171-174. Least confusing is Werner, "The Birth of a Tune," *The Jewish Layman* (December 1941): 12-15.

17. Wilhelm Tappert, *Musikalische Studien*, p. 7.

18. Eric Werner, *The Sacred Bridge*, p. 437.

19. Israel J. Katz, "Eric Werner, A Bibliography," *Musica Judaica* 10 (1987-1988):1-36.

20. Idelsohn, *HOM* (1973), combines the ten volumes into four with expanded versions in English of vols. I, II, and VI-X. In 1999, Tara Publications (www.jewishmusic.com) reprinted vols. VIII-X into one volume. Vols. III, IV, and V are in the original German (Leipzig) or in Hebrew translation (Jerusalem).

21. The Moors of northwest Africa, Mauritania, are descendants of Berbers and Arabs.

22. Moshe Beregovski (1892-1961), *Old Jewish Folk Music*, p. 524.

23. Ibid., p. 559.

24. Lazare Saminsky, *Music of the Ghetto and the Bible*, p. 121. If there is any validity to Saminsky's claim, it must be regarded as a fortuitous circumstance. Gershwin did not devise the wail-in-the-scale glissando, spawned as it was in rehearsal by the antics of clarinetist Ross Gorman, who first performed the *Rhapsody*.

25. Isaac Levy, ed., *Romanceros Judéo-Espagnole*. Recorded by the Salomone Trio (Maria Costanza, solo) on "Sacred and Profane," Titanic CD, TI-238. *Adio querida* can be heard as source music in Elia Kazan's 1963 film, *America, America*.

26. Nico Castel, Ladino song authority, conversation with author.

27. Beregovski, *Old Jewish Music*, p. 525.

28. Idelsohn, *HOM*, Introduction to vols. IX and X: "The Melodic Line," Eng. ed., p. xxvii. Edited quote.

29. In the Spanish-Judeo tradition, it is not unknown for secular tunes to be used for sacred purposes. The melody of the popular *La rosa enflorece* (The Rose Blossoms) is the same as the Hebrew Sabbath table hymn, *Tzur mishelo ahalnu* (Rock from Whose Store We Have Eaten). Yiddish culture tends to go in the opposite direction, with sacred elements used secularly.

30. See Idelsohn, *HOM*, vol. VIII, no. 313a, p. 108.

31. Joseph Rumshinsky, another Yiddish Theater composer who should have known better, identifies the quotation as coming from Handel's oratorio *Judah Maccabeus*, which either has to be gross ignorance or rank chauvinism. (In *Oisgeklibene Shriften: Avrom Goldfaden, Di Lieber Plagyator* [Selected Writings: Abraham Goldfaden, The Dear Plagiarist]: *Handel's Halleluyoh in der oratorie Yehuda Macabi*, Shmuel Rozhansky, editor, p. 274, reprinted from *Literarishe Bletter*, no. 464, Warsaw, 24 March 1933.) Idelsohn identifies Goldfaden's original sources for *Bar Kochba*, but nowhere mentions the Handel chorus. (Perhaps it was not published in the printed edition he examined.) Idelsohn also incorrectly ascribes *Dos pintele yid* (The Spark of Jewishness) to Goldfaden and assigns folk-song status to other theater songs whose authors must have been known to him. See Idelsohn, *Jewish Music*, p. 452-454.

32. Bar Kochba was also the subject of a 1913 film, *Bar Kochba, Hero of a Nation*, produced by William Fox.

33. Joachim Braun, "The Double Meaning of Jewish Elements in Dmitri Shostakovich's Music," *Musical Quarterly* 71 (1985): 68-80. For melody sources, see Mlotek, *Pearls of Yiddish Song*. Shostakovich studied at the St. Petersburg Conservatory with Maximilian Steinberg, the Jewish son-in-law of Rimsky-Korsakoff. See Holde, *Jews in Music*, p. 125.

34. Werner claims Rubinstein was born Christian. See *A Voice Still Heard*, p. 239.

35. Charles Wesley, a founder of Methodism, wrote the words for "Hark the Herald Angels Sing" in 1739. In 1855, W. H. Cummings, an English organist, set Wesley's text to a *Festgesang* by Mendelssohn.

36. Eric Werner, *Mendelssohn*, p. 471. For other possible Jewish source material in Mendelssohn's oeuvre, see Seroussi et al., "Jewish Music," *The New Grove Dictionary of Music*, 2nd ed., vol. 13, p. 94.

37. Avenary, meaning "Stone Lion," is the Hebrew equivalent of his original German name Lowenstein, "Lion Stone."

38. *Encyclopedia Judaica*, s.v. "music." Eric Werner, in *A Voice Still Heard* also refers to this Mahler passage as coming "close to cantorial technique" (p. 240). In an endnote, he

acerbically remarks: "Still worse, Dr. Avenary 'adorns himself with other scholar's plumes.'" (no. 27, p. 323).

39. Howard Pollack, *Aaron Copland*, pp. 146 and 332.

40. Lorenzo Da Ponte, Mozart's librettist, was born Jewish (as Emanuele Conegliano) and so were both of Richard Strauss's librettists, Hugo von Hofmannstahl and Stefan Zweig.

41. Richard Traubner, "With a 1-2-3, 1-2-3, 1-2-3, Vienna Honors a King," *New York Times*, Arts and Leisure, 27 June 1999.

42. Weinberger, a Czech Jew, was never able to duplicate the success of his opera after he emigrated to the United States and died a suicide in 1967.

43. As a radio, Yiddish film, and recording star, Moishe Oysher "blurred . . . boundaries between the sacred and the secular" (Hoberman, *Entertaining America: Jews, Movies, and Broadcasting*, p. 108). His sister Freydele contributed to this mixture as one of the early "chazentes," female cantors who could not officiate in a synagogue, but were participants in popular media. Marilyn Michaels, Freydele's daughter, is a well-known singer-mimic-entertainer.

44. Kenneth Aaron Kanter, *The Jews on Tin Pan Alley*, p. 79. Russell's song begins: "When the tempests fly o'er the cloudy sky/And the piping blast sings merrily,/Oh sweet is the mirth of the social hearth,/Where the flames are blazing cheerily/ Our way across the mountains, ho."

45. Both the "Song of the Hebrew Captive" (by B. Carr) and "The Sorrowing Jew" can be found in the Lester S. Levy Collection of Sheet Music at the Milton S. Eisenhower Library of Johns Hopkins University. Another early title in the Collection is "Hebrew Maiden" by Anthony Reiff (1869). An additional source for "The Sorrowing Jew" is the American Jewish Archive at Hebrew Union College-Jewish Institute of Religion, Cincinnati.

46. I use the terms refrain and chorus interchangeably, even though some writers make distinctions between the two. Verse is the song division that sets up either the refrain or chorus. Bridge and release are also equivalent terms for midsections of refrains or choruses.

47. Douglas Gilbert, *Lost Chords*, p. 180.

48. Arranged as a march and published by R. A. Saalfield. An etching of the hotel is on the cover of John Philip Sousa's "Manhattan Beach March," dedicated to Corbin. Corbin is buried in Woodlawn Cemetery, New York. The origin of the derogatory term "sheeny" may derive from the German *schön* (beautiful), heard as "sheen" when Jewish peddlers were selling wares.

49. William W. Delaney, ed., *Delaney's Song Book*, no. 2, p. 56. The lyrics of Alan Jay Lerner's "My Mother's Wedding Day" (from *Brigadoon*, 1947) describes a fracas something like that found at "The Hebrew Picnic."

50. Ibid., no. 5, p. 14.

51. Ibid., no. 53, p. 15. Music by Henrietta Bianke-Beicher, song published by Jerome H. Remick and Co.

52. Let the obvious be noted: "prejudice" is derived from "prejudge."

53. Danny Fisher, son of Fred Fisher, interview by author, New York City, 4 October 1983.

54. Among Jewish populations, Cohen is as numerous as Jones is elsewhere. The many derivatives of Cohen encompass Caan, Cain or Kane, Cahan, Cahane, Cahn (as in Sammy, the lyricist), Cohn, Cogan or Kogan (as in Leonid, the Russian violinist, the "h" in Russian is pronounced with a hard "g"), Cohon, Conn (as in the musical instrument company), Cowan (as in Lester, the theatrical producer), Coyne, Kahan, Kahana, Kahane, Kahanowsky, Kahanovitch, Kahn (as in Gus, the lyricist), Katz (from the Hebrew *Kohen tsedek*, righteous priest, and not as in the homonymic Andrew Lloyd Webber show), and Kohn. Levy becomes Lewis and there are scads of other derivatives, Moses becomes Moss, etc.

55. *Delaney's Song Book*, no. 89.

56. Also known as Michael Leoni, Meyer Leon appeared on the English stage, which led to his dismissal as cantor. But he remained a practicing Jew.

57. Roger Prior, "Jewish Musicans at the Tudor Court," *Musical Quarterly* 69 (1983): 264.

58. Braham's first child, Spencer (1790s), was illegitimate, from his mistress Nancy Storace, who was the first Susanna in Mozart's *The Marriage of Figaro*. Spencer, raised as a Christian, changed his last name to Meadows when he became precentor of Canterbury Cathedral, lest his Jewish origins became too clear. John then married Frances Bolton in 1816. Their offspring were: Hamilton, a bass singer; Charles, a tenor; Augustus, a sometime singer; Ward, active in theatricals—and

daughters: Frances, later Lady Waldegrave, and Josephine, involved in some mysterious scandal. In England, births since 1837 are registered at St. Catherine's House in London. There were a number of Brahams born in 1838 in various parts of the country, but no David. However, it turns out that birth registration was not compulsory until several decades later.

59. *Delaney's Song Book,* no. 57, p. 24. A plot summary and music can be found in Jon W. Finson, ed., *Edward Harrigan and David Braham, Collected Songs I.*

60. Edward B. Marks, *They All Sang*, p. 24.

61. Hutchins Hapgood, in *Spirit of the Ghetto*, p. 118, alludes to Katzenelenbogen's book store. Later prominent publishers of popular Jewish music include the Hebrew Publishing Co., Solomon Schenker Co., J. & J. Kammen, and Metro Music, founded by Henry Lefkowitch.

62. David Ewen, *All the Years of American Popular Music*, pp. 452-453.

63. A second version, translated by Isaac Reingold into Yiddish, appears in *Tsvey Hundert Lider.*

64. *Delaney's Song Book*, no. 23, p. 12.

65. Mark Slobin, in *Tenement Songs*, has amply demonstrated this process of interchange.

66. Lawrence Levine, *Highbrow/Lowbrow*, p.47.

67. Michael Gold, *Jews without Money.* Avon edition, 1965, p. 95.

68. The 1947 Warner Bros. pseudo biopic *My Wild Irish Rose*, starring Dennis Morgan as Chauncey Olcott and William Frawley as William Scanlan, has an extended sequence with Morgan in blatant blackface as a minstrel showman.

69. For an excellent overview of the Katzenelenbogen songsters, see Fred Somkin, "Zion's Harp by the East River."

70. *Delaney's Song Book*, no. 3, p. 13.

71. Ibid., no. 18, p. 26.

72. Pogrom is Russian for "riot." Kishniev is now known as Chisinau, Moldava.

73. *Delaney's Song Book*, no. 35, p. 8., words by Larry Levake.

74. Harry Von Tilzer, edited quote from Robert Bruce, "The Father of Popular Songs," *Popular Songs Magazine* (January 1935).

75. The year 1900 is also cited by author Tony Palmer in *All You Need Is Love: The Story of Popular Music* (New York: Viking, 1976).

76. Microfilm located at New York Public Library, Research Division.

77. Microfilm at Lincoln Center Performing Arts Research Division, New York City. Etymologist Barry Popik claims "A Visit to Tin Pan Alley, Where the Popular Songs Come," an article by Roy McCardell published in the *New York Times* of 3 May 1903, is the earliest identified mention. See the *New York Times,* 13 July 2003, Real Estate section, p. 7.

78. Dr. Nathaniel S. Lehrman, "Intermarriage: Abnormal or Normal," *The Psychological Implications of Intermarriage* (New York: Federation of Jewish Philanthropies, 1966), p. 45. Quoted in James Fuld, *The Book of World Famous Music*, p. 290, n. 2.

79. Judy Garland, raised as a Catholic, was also born Gumm. William Hyland, in *The Song Is Ended,* claims that Harry Von Tilzer was a cousin of Garland's, which would possibly make her Jewish. But I have not seen this validated elsewhere. In her memoir, Carol Channing, a lifelong Christian Scientist who is conversant with Yiddish, intimates that her mother was Jewish. See *Just Lucky I Guess*, p. 50.

80. Some of the more blatant Kanter bloopers: David Braham did not marry Edward Harrigan's daughter (Kanter's p. 13). It was the other way around, Harrigan married Braham's daughter. Abe Holtzman wrote "Smoky (not Smokey) Mokes," not Leo Feist, nor did Holtzman write it with the help of Harry Von Tilzer (p. 17); "Sweet Adeline" was not the last song in the Witmark catalog (p. 19); Gus Edwards did not discover the Marx Brothers (p. 33); Berlin's song is "Ragtime Violin," not "Violin Ragtime" (p. 35); Con Conrad was born Conrad K. Dober, not Konrad A. Dobert (p. 55). On p. 55 Conrad is credited with writing "Barney Google" with Billy Rose, but on the next page the same song is credited to Sammy Fain and Rose (the first team is correct); John Green wrote the music for "Body and Soul," not Arthur Schwartz (p. 65); "Yossel, Yossel" was not the Cahn-Chaplin title, but Casman and Steinberg's; "Joseph, Joseph" was the Cahn (born Cohen, not Cohn)-Chaplin adaptation; Don Raye wrote the lyrics for "This Is My Country," not Al Jacobs, who wrote the music (p. 71); Munroe H.

Rosenfeld could not have coined the term "Tin Pan Alley" for the *New York Herald Tribune* since no such paper existed in his lifetime (p. 91). The *New York Herald* was founded by James Gordon Bennett in 1835. Frank Munroe bought it in 1920 and merged it with the *Sun*. In 1924 it was again merged, this time with the *Tribune*, lasting until 1967. For his *Rhapsody in Blue*, Gershwin never reorchestrated Ferde Grofé's original version (p. 155); the Rodgers and Hart song "Any Old Place With You" is not a "reversal of the normal 16-bar verse, 32-bar chorus," since the 32 bars of the verse are in a fast 2/4, which is perceived as 16 bars of 4/4 (p. 184). And, furthermore, what did Rodgers and Hart have to do with Tin Pan Alley?

81. Gus Edwards, in turn, nurtured the young talents of George Jessel, Walter Winchell, Eddie Cantor, George Gershwin, and, of all people, the esoteric composer Milton Babbitt.

82. See William G. Hyland, *The Song Is Ended*.

83. Max Wilk, *They're Playing Our Song*, p. 187, edited quote. Cahn also stated his pride in the song "Call Me Irresponsible" since he came from a one-syllable neighborhood. New York Sheet Music Society meeting, 2 November 1991. Ernie Kovacs, playing a mean-spirited tycoon in the Columbia film *It Happened to Jane*, brags that no one could stand in his path once he had clawed his way out of the Lower East Side.

CHAPTER 2

The Lullaby of Brody—Childhood Experiences

Two Russian old-timers meet and get acquainted:
"Where are you from?"   "St. Petersburg."
"Where were you educated?"   "Petrograd."
"Where did you grow up?"   "Leningrad."
"Where would you like to be?"   "St. Petersburg."

DIMITRI TIOMKIN, *Please Don't Hate Me*, p. 84

There is more than sardonic humor in the above exchange, even though the citizen's last wish could have been fulfilled in 1991.[1] For the Russian-Jewish musician of the early twentieth century, St. Petersburg was the gateway to freedom. Five million Jews had been corralled within the Pale of Settlement[2] as a result of which they were "beyond the pale," in the catchphrase sense of being closed off to their greater surroundings. Actually, by this time some Jews had broken through quota systems and had begun participating in certain professions and living in urban populations. They had occupied the territory in the southwestern Russian empire since the mideighteenth century, and some restrictions had been relaxed; but they were not allowed to live in imperial St. Petersburg.

At the same time, the dictates of Orthodoxy fomented restrictions within Jewish communities. Creatively speaking, this tug of war of reaching out and being held back ultimately was a galvanizing force. Jewish-born Anton Rubinstein (1839-1894), the pianist-composer who founded the St. Petersburg Conservatory in 1862 and married into the Russian aristocracy, was able to do so only because he had been converted to Christianity at an early age. Hungarian-born violinist Leopold Auer (1845-1930) had an easier time of it, becoming an illustrious pedagogue on the strength of his musicianship alone, which would have been much harder if not for the groundwork laid down by Rubinstein. In fact, Auer was given the rank of nobleman. One of his Jewish child prodigies, Mischa Elman (1891-1967), was plucked out of the Pale of Settlement and resettled into the St. Petersburg Conservatory. The father of American pianist Gary Graffman, having used his gifts as a violinist to escape the Vilna ghetto, became Auer's teaching assistant.

Child prodigy Jascha Heifetz (1901-1987) had greater difficulty, trudging back and forth over the border of Poland into Russia with his father. The problem was solved when his father, who was Jascha's teacher, was himself enrolled as a student, making it all legitimate. In whatever way special dispensation was achieved, including the act of bribery, much sacrifice was required of both parent and child before residence could be, and after residence was, taken up in St. Petersburg.

The effort must have been well worth it because a certificate of graduation from the prestigious conservatory potentially was more than a meal ticket for the budding concert artist. While it did not work for every graduate (anti-Semitic policies confined conductor Ilya Musin, 1904-1999, to the conservatory as a teacher for sixty years), it also became a dwelling permit for Jascha Heifetz's family. In effect, such a diploma meant that Jews with gifted children could then reside elsewhere in Russia, and the young-blood was given liberties unheard of for other Jews. Is it any wonder, then, that a preponderance of renowned Jewish violinists was spawned by Mother Russia? As violinist Nathan Milstein (1904-1992) allegedly put it: "a fiddle was easier to pick up and run with than a piano." In the more poetic words of Yehudi Menuhin (1916-1999): "the piano stands immovable . . . but the violin is as mobile as the violinist's heart, as flexible and as adjustable."[3] This circumstance helps to deflate notions of Jewish specialness, that artistic gifts are due to inherited traits or genetic predisposition or other 'racial' malarkey. In America, where flight was no longer a concern, the weighty piano became the instrument of choice. According to an anecdote, Arthur Gershwin, George's younger brother, gave up learning how to play the violin because George got to sit at the piano while he, Arthur, had to stand.[4] (see Illustration 5)

In addition to *Mischa* Elman and *Jascha* Heifetz, other Auer disciples included *Sascha* Jacobsen (b.1895*)* and *Toscha* Seidel (1899-1962).[5] They unite forces in "Mischa, Yascha, Sascha, Toscha," a song written by the Gershwin brothers for a party hosted by Jascha Heifetz in 1921 (see Illustration 6):

Ex. 2-1

"Mischa, Yascha, Sascha, Toscha"
Arthur Francis (pseudonym for Ira Gershwin) & George Gershwin

When we be-gan,   our notes were sour,__   Un-til a man,   Pro-fes - sor Au- er, __

In this novelty number, there is a simulation of a violinist playing on open strings and possibly a musical allusion to the Yiddish song "Dem milners trern" (The Miller's Tears), a song about Jewish expulsion from Czarist regimes. In Ira Gershwin's lyric, the fiddlers were born "in darkest Russia," an expression that has become a figure of speech in a number of languages. The violin is referred to as "fiddle-le," a diminutive Yiddishism, and the quartet sings, "Outside of dear old Fritz [i.e., Fritz Kreisler[6]]/All the fiddle concerts hits" are performed by themselves.

A 1927 Broadway show tune by the Gershwin brothers was derived, unbeknownst to them, from a Russian lullaby:[7]

Ex. 2-2

"Spi mladyehnits"

Spi mla - dyeh-nits, Moy pri - kras-ni,   Ba - yush-ki, ba - yu.
(Sleep, my beautiful baby, hushaby, hush.)

Ti - kha sma - triht, Myes-itz yas - ni f' - ka - li - byel tva - yu.
(The serene moon quietly keeps watch over your cradle.)

The words, written by Mikhail Iur'evich Lermontov (1814-1841), are from a poem entitled "Kazach'ia kolybel'naia pesnia" (Cossack Lullaby). Lermontov was exiled to the Caucasus for a poem he had written in which he blamed Czar Nicholas I for the death of the poet Pushkin.[8] It is not clear if Lermontov was favorably disposed toward the Jews, but we do know that in 1827 Nicholas issued a ukase demanding conscription of Jewish boys for twenty-five years, during which time a few of them became skilled musicians in military bands. This one act, however, along with systematic pogroms, triggered the eventual departure of whole Jewish populations from the Russian empire. The sad legacy of a lost generation is woven into folk songs about *Nikolaevske-soldaten* (Nicholas's soldiers).[9] Whatever the circumstances, the composer of the lullaby is unknown; it is probably a pirated tune. Actually, more than fifty songwriters wrote settings or arrangements of the poem, including the poet himself. Among them was Abraham Goldfaden, who took Lermontov's lullaby, passed it through a Jewish filter and out came (Ex. 2-3):[10]

Ex. 2-3   "Shlof in freydn"

Shlof   in   frey - dn, Du veyst kayn ley - dn, Shlof - zhe, shlof mayn   kind.
(Sleep in happiness, you should not know suffering. Sleep, my child, sleep.)

Shlof   mayn fey - ge - le, ___ Makh tsu dayn ey - ge - le, ___ Shlof - zhe, shlof ge - zint.
(Sleep my birdie, Close your eyes, Sleep in good health.)

A choral arrangement of the lullaby by Leo Low[11] states that the melody is a folk song, which suggests Goldfaden's words were adapted to the original Russian version.[12] Whatever its origin, the lullaby became Judaicized in its progression from the Russian to the Yiddish.[13] (see Illustration 7)

Somewhere along the line at least two Hebrew variants of the Yiddish lullaby cropped up. One of them was:[14]

Ex. 2-4   "Numa ferach"

Nu - ma fer - ach, B' - ni ma - cha - ma - di,   Ar - sach ki   a - ni - ya.

Me - cha - ye - cha ha - a - ti - dim Si - chot lach_ a - bi - a.
(Sleep my flower, my beloved son, while I rock you. May you have a long life, this I wish you.)

Unlike its Yiddish counterpart, the first bar of the Hebrew example[15] duplicates the Russian original. The second bar, however, presents a new wrinkle, one that comes closer to the sound of the Gershwin song. By which route does a Russian lullaby travel to Broadway?

The staging area for Jews spilling out of Ukraine on their way to northern European seaports (Hamburg, Rotterdam, etc.), and from there to the United States and elsewhere, was the Galician (Austrian, at that time) town of Brody. This was the home base of an important group of folk singers named after the town, the Broder Zinger (1840-1850). The Broders settled in Jassy, Romania, and together with Goldfaden[16] molded the beginnings of the Yiddish theater (1870s). This could have been one possible itinerary for the tune's journey, as it were, from Brody to Broadway. (see Illustrations 8 and 9)

Is "My One and Only"[17] a Jewish tune? After all, there are inevitable accidental concurrences throughout song literature. For example, the last phrase of Sholem Aleichem's poem, the beloved Yiddish lullaby *Shlof, mayn kind* (Sleep, My Child, with music by David Kovanovsky[18]), is very much like the opening of "The Kerry Dance," an Irish jig, but it is improbable such jigs were heard in Ukraine. Gershwin, however, must have been aware of Goldfaden's lullaby, although it is doubtful he was familiar with its Hebrew transformation. In fact, Molly Picon, star of the American-Yiddish theater, did inform me that Gershwin had told her "My One and Only" was consciously based on the Yiddish lullaby;[19] and it is conceivable that Gershwin heard a 1919 recording of it by Cantor Pinchos Jassinowsky. Composer Lazare Saminsky avers that he heard Gershwin confess:

While I actually do not know much about Jewish folk song, I think that many of my themes are Jewish in feeling although they are purely American in style.[20]

Annotator Nathan Ausubel, without attribution, quotes Gershwin somewhat differently:

Even though I know practically nothing about the poetic content of the Yiddish folk song, nevertheless, I believe that many of the melodies I use in my works are Jewish according to the internal, deep emotional element that flows in them, regardless of the fact that they are purely American in style.[21]

Since much of Jewish music itself is based on oral transmission, rather than on written documentation, this word-of-mouth evidence will have to suffice. But for those who are not convinced, perhaps more potent evidence is to be found in another lullaby configuration, first from Southern Russia:[22]

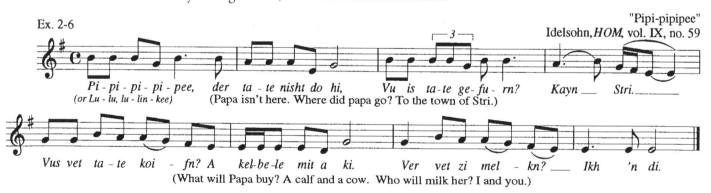

Then from Catfish Row, South Carolina, as depicted in Gershwin's *Porgy and Bess,* where "it is well known among black-music scholars that 'Summertime' . . . is an adaptation of the Afro-American spiritual 'Sometimes I Feel Like a Motherless Child.'"[23] There is no surprise in this observation since African-American and Russian (i.e., Jewish) music materials, consciously or not, are elements of this "folk opera." But to call it an adaptation, a conscious retooling of previous material, is an unjustified judgment.[24] Both the Yiddish and Gershwin lullabies are in the dorian mode, using a lowered seventh step (plain D), whereas the spiritual, in the more conventional minor mode, raises the 7th step to D-sharp. In the Ex. 2-7 schematic representation, "Summertime" may be viewed as an amalgamation of Jewish- and Black-based components.

Ex. 2-7

Yiddish lullaby

"Summertime" George Gershwin

"Sometimes I Feel Like a Motherless Child"

Lullaby

Gershwin

Spiritual

According to film composer Bernard Herrmann, Gershwin had misgivings about "Summertime":

He was very worried about it. "Do you think it sounds colored?" he asked me. . . . I said, "What difference does it make? Negro music, Jewish music, they're all quite alike." George said, "I'm still worried. It starts my *Porgy and Bess*. People may think it sounds too Yiddish."[25]

Just as cradle songs were maternal kin to Gershwin theater songs, so a famous lullaby from *Shulamis* (Shulamith), an 1880 Yiddish operetta by Goldfaden,[26] could have been one of the parents of a 1927 Irving Berlin tune, which Berlin unknowingly turned into the opening strain of what became an instant classic:

Ex. 2-8a: Refrain

"Roszhinkes mit mandlen" Abraham Goldfaden, *MTAG*, p. 4

Un - ter Yi - de - les vi - - ge - le_____
(Under Yidele's cradle)

Ex. 2-8b: Refrain

"Blue Skies," Irving Berlin

Blue Skies,_____ smi - ling at me,_____

Another phrase from the verse of "Raisins and Almonds," that same Goldfaden lullaby (Ex. 2-9a), was also unknowingly transformed by Berlin (Ex. 2-9b).[27] It is no accident that the cantor's son, played by Al Jolson in *The Jazz Singer*, chooses to sing "Blue Skies" to his screen mother, Eugenie Besserer (in Yiddish *beser* means "better").[28] The lullaby connection becomes even clearer.

Commenting upon "Blue Skies," one authority feels that "the apparent dichotomy between the minor melody and the sunny outlook of its lyric has had song analysts wagging their heads for decades."[29] But the Jewish view of minor is not incompatible with merriment; and, in fact, the release section of Berlin's 1926 classic springs from yet another Goldfaden tune, one filled with jollity, even though it is in minor.[30] It was in a Yiddish comedy of 1878 called *Nibe ni-me ni-kukeriku oder der kampf zwischen bildung und fanaticizm* (Neither This, That Nor Cockadoodle-doo or The Struggle Between Education and Fanaticism) that Goldfaden fashioned this ditty (Ex.2-10a) which soon passed into Yiddish folklore. Indeed, it is titled *Der Rebe hot geheysn freylekh zayn* (The Rabbi Bids Us Be Merry); and it could have been the involuntary progenitor of the bridge section to "Blue Skies" (Ex. 2-10b):[31]

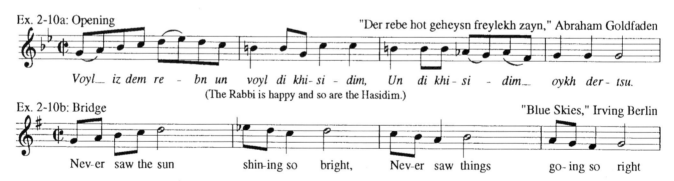

There is no direct evidence that Berlin was making allusions to Jewish sources. Compared to a similar tune written after "Blue Skies," the Yiddishisms do stand out more clearly. Both the 1929 "Deep Night"—words by Rudy Vallee* and music by Charles Henderson*—and "Blue Skies" are in minor, and both begin with an open 5th followed by a triplet rhythm; but whereas Berlin's melody vacillates between minor and its relative major, in typical Jewish music fashion, "Deep Night" begins in E minor to resolve in C major, a more distant key. Nevertheless, Berlin's "never saw the sun," draws upon a reserve of idiomatic memories without any calculated effort to borrow phrases. Trying to prove so-called plagiarism would have to take into account more than coincidental musical phraseology. For example, the first four bars of a 1970 prize-winning Israeli song by David Weinkranz (Ex. 2-11a) is virtually a replica of an earlier Yiddish lullaby by Mordecai Gebirtig (Ex. 2-11b):

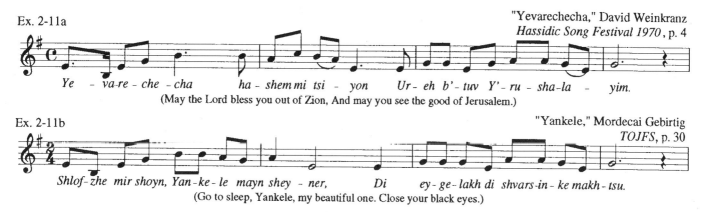

Ex. 2-11a
"Yevarechecha," David Weinkranz
Hassidic Song Festival 1970, p. 4

Ye - va-re -che -cha   ha - shem mi tsi - yon   Ur- eh b'- tuv Y'-ru - sha-la - yim.
(May the Lord bless you out of Zion, And may you see the good of Jerusalem.)

Ex. 2-11b
"Yankele," Mordecai Gebirtig
TOJFS, p. 30

Shlof-zhe mir shoyn, Yan-ke- le mayn shey - ner,   Di   ey-ge-lakh di shvars-in- ke makh-tsu.
(Go to sleep, Yankele, my beautiful one. Close your black eyes.)

Although the purpose of the song competition, for which Weinkranz placed first, was to popularize Hasidic religious music, Weinkranz did not set out to update the Yiddish lullaby by putting it into a march tempo. But, still, it may have been a tune lodged in his subconscious from childhood.

* * *

In the movie *Stalag 17*, Otto Preminger (who was Jewish) played a Nazi commandant and addressed his American prisoners while contemptuously dismissing the song "White Christmas," written, he says "by one of your composers who stole his name from our capital!" An ironic remark since Berlin grew up in an east European milieu as opposed to the West European zeitgeist of the so-called uptown Jews of New York City. That's a crucial difference in characterizing Jewish musical over- and under- tones in American popular music. You will not find them among the songs of Jerome Kern, one of those Germanic uptowners, despite a ditty he once dashed off called "Keep Your Rabbits Rabbi, We've Got Rabbits of Our Own."[32] One could argue that there is a kernel of the cantorial in Kern's distinguished song "Yesterdays":[33]

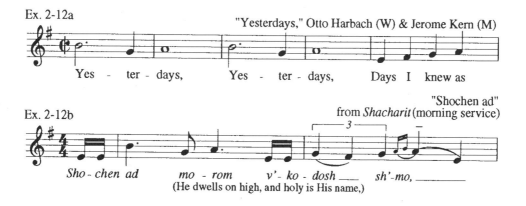

Ex. 2-12a
"Yesterdays," Otto Harbach (W) & Jerome Kern (M)

Yes - ter - days,   Yes - ter - days,   Days I knew as

"Shochen ad"
from *Shacharit* (morning service)
Ex. 2-12b

Sho- chen ad   mo - rom   v'- ko - dosh ___ sh'-mo, ___
(He dwells on high, and holy is His name,)

It may be *mittel-Europa* operetta, but it is also pure Sabbath morning *nussakh*—traditional synagogue chant; but this is a fluke. Just because Rodgers and Hart's "My Funny Valentine" happens to be a pensive ballad in minor, no Jewish label need be ascribed to it. Dorothy Rodgers, the composer's wife, once stated: "Dick was, and still is, an atheist."[34] That does not necessarily mean Jewish sounds did not enter the Rodgers domicile as he was growing up. Indeed, early on, with Hart he wrote songs such as "Jake the Baker" and "Madame Esther, Queen of Hester Street."[35] Their show *Betsy* (in which Berlin's "Blue Skies" had been interpolated for Belle Baker) had two Yiddish name songs, "Stonewall Moskowitz March" and "Six Little Kitzels."[36] Later, with Hammerstein, Rodgers hints at a Yiddish folk song,[37] in "My Favorite Things." But again it is pure happenstance:

Or, to take another pairing, there is a correlation between a 1924 Yiddish-theater tune, "Mayn goldele" (My Golden One) by Joseph M. Rumshinsky and Max Steiner's 1939 "Tara Theme" from *Gone with the Wind*:

Viennese-born Max Steiner was hardly a Yiddishist, but he did write a set of four very Jewish-sounding character pieces called "The Cohen Family" (Sam Fox Pub. Co., 1933). Before he went, in the words of Milton Babbitt, to "Hollywood and Wien," Steiner made a living playing violin in the movie palaces of New York City, where he might have frequented the Yiddish theater.

In the annals of American film, Steiner's significance runs deeper than his accomplishment on *Gone with the Wind*. In 1932, he tried to convince producer David O. Selznick that the then current practice of filling nondialogue moments with swatches of concert orchestral repertoire and popular works, mixed in with standard musical stock formulas, was not as effective as original music could be. Arguing for the underscoring of dialogue, Steiner reasoned that background music would heighten the emotional content of scenes. Selznick feared that audiences would wonder where the music was coming from, but ultimately he was persuaded to allow Steiner to have a go at it. The film was *Symphony of Six Million* (also known as *Melody of Life*), a melodrama about a Jewish family on New York's Lower East Side, with screenplay by novelist Fannie Hurst, based on a story by an undisclosed author, the pseudonymous John Adams. Starring Irene Dunne, Ricardo Cortez (born Jacob Krantz, a Viennese Jew), Gregory Ratoff, and Anna Appel (both of the Yiddish theater), its plot concerned Dr. Felix Tauber, one of three children, who in his own words "sold my soul for a mess of pottage" by leaving behind the work he had accomplished in a downtown "ghetto" clinic and moving uptown to Park Avenue where he becomes a successful surgeon.

Symphony of Six Million (a figure based on the then current population of New York City, but in retrospect, an ironic title in view of the Holocaust a short decade later) was a groundbreaker, even though only 35 percent of the film had underscoring. But it permitted Steiner's next film, *Bird of Paradise*, to be musically covered virtually 100 percent. Then, in 1933, Steiner hit his stride with his milestone score for *King Kong*.

His score for the 1932 *Symphony* film has been described by some observers as original, but it actually is based on touchstone Jewish melodies, an opening *freylekh*, the Hebrew "Kol nidrei" and "Hatikvah," and the Yiddish "Oyfn pripetshik," "Khosn kale mazl tov," and "Eli, Eli." Although these themes are treated lugubriously, they are countered by a lively tune played at a scene of a *pidyon habeyn* (redemption of the son) that may be based on another Yiddish song. At first, it seems that Steiner uses these melodies willy-nilly, placing them throughout the film indiscriminately. It may well be, however, that his choices were symbolic. "Kol nidrei" (All Vows) is indicative of vows taken or broken; "Eli, Eli" (My God, a threnody of abandonment), and "Hatikvah" (The Hope) exhibit a yearning for redemption; "Oyfn pripeshtik" (By the Fireplace, a children's learning song) pointing toward future generations—all pertinent to the drama.

Whereas "Kol nidrei," in the earlier landmark talkie *The Jazz Singer*, was appropriately sung at a Yom Kippur service, and therefore limited by its specificity, Steiner's innovative approach swept up audiences and pointed the way for all future movie music. The same sacred melody now becomes universalized, and its use in other films goes beyond ethnic identification, elevating moviegoers' sensitivity and empathy.

* * *

Jerome Kern was an idol of both Richard Rodgers and George Gershwin; but there was a world of difference in how those geniuses displayed their admiration. Rodgers, whose paternal grandparents were Russian (the name either was Rodzinski or Rogozinsky[38]), continued to wear the white-collar mantle of Kern, while Gershwin, with his thoroughbred Russian parents, refitted it with a blue collar. Unlike Rodgers, Gershwin was a first-generation American Jew. What is more, Kern and Rodgers did not wear their Jewishness as comfortably as did Gershwin.

In contrast, Harry Von Tilzer was of German-Jewish stock. Although he wrote everlasting standards (e.g., "Wait 'til the Sun Shines, Nellie"), he also wrote the ever-to-be-forgotten song: "In a Garden of Y'Eden for Two." This 1908 novelty may have inspired the title of a 1913 song: "In My Garden of Eden for Two" (from *All Aboard*) by E. Ray Goetz. Nevertheless, Von Tilzer's effort is no catalyst for induction into the Jewish pantheon.

German-born tunesmiths Fred Fis[c]her and Gus Edwards, in their respective curios "Mighty Like a Rosenbloom" and "Casey's Wedding Night" (a Jewish-Irish contretemps), also wrote other such instantly disposable novelties. But none of them is a conduit of Jewish musical content either, even though the Edwards song quotes the Jewish wedding march "Khosn kale mazl tov" (Groom and Bride, Congratulations).

* * *

There is a German table song, one of the *zemirot* sung at Sabbath meals, which resembles, of all things, a tune from *My Fair Lady* by Frederick Loewe:[39]

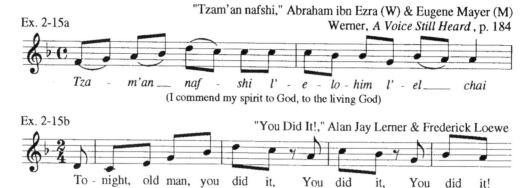

Ex. 2-15a
"Tzam'an nafshi," Abraham ibn Ezra (W) & Eugene Mayer (M)
Werner, *A Voice Still Heard*, p. 184

Tza - m'an __ naf - shi l' - e - lo - him l' - el __ chai
(I commend my spirit to God, to the living God)

Ex. 2-15b
"You Did It!," Alan Jay Lerner & Frederick Loewe

To - night, old man, you did it, You did it, You did it!

Loewe's parents were Viennese Jews. His father, Edmund, as a tenor famous for creating the role of Prince Danilo in Franz Lehár's* operetta *The Merry Widow*.[40] But it's implausible for Fritz Loewe to have heard *zemirot* in his youth. There is nothing else in his life and work to indicate an interest in *materia Judaica*; and in the world of his worldly father, who was an inveterate gambler, it's improbable there was a household Sabbath table.[41]

Fritz studied piano with the great Ferruccio Busoni* in Berlin. Another protégé of Busoni[42] was the Russian-born Dimitri Tiomkin, later an illustrious Hollywood composer. Tiomkin, in a well-known song of his, could have been affected by the Yiddish song "Dem milners trern" (referred to earlier in the Gershwin song about Russian fiddlers). Mill wheels from Russia subsequently turn into wagon wheels in the dusty American plains:

Ex. 2-16a
"Dem milners trern," Mark Warshavsky
MTAG, p. 120

Oy, vi - fl yo - rn zay - nen far - fo - rn, Zayt ikh bin mil - ner o - to do; Di re - der
(Oh, how many years have flown by since I have been a miller here)

drey - en zikh, Di yo - rn gey - en zikh, Ikh bin shoyn alt un grayz un gro.
(The wheels turn, the years pass, I am already old and grizzled and grey.)

Ex. 2-16b
"High Noon"
Ned Washington (W) & Dimitri Tiomkin (M)

Do Not For - sake Me, Oh my dar - ling, __ On this our wed - ding day, __

Do Not For - sake Me, Oh my dar - lin', Wait __

East goes Western in the movie *High Noon*. But why should that example be any less coincidental than the table song with *My Fair Lady*? "Dem milners trern" was written by Mark Warshavsky, born in Ukraine. A popular balladeer,[43] he toured widely with lecturer Sholem Aleichem, on the original "borscht circuit" in Russia, as opposed to its later reincarnation in the Catskill Mountains of New York State. Kiev (where Warshavsky died) is equidistant to Zhitomir (where he was born) and Poltava, which is the birthplace of Dimitri Tiomkin. Leaving Poltava for St. Petersburg at age seven, Tiomkin could "recall peasant women laundering in the river, beating cloth and singing songs in rhythm—melodies beautiful and sad."[44] The odds are favorable that some of the melodies were by Warshavsky.

Fiddler on the Roof, based on stories of Sholem Aleichem, the pen name of Solomon Rabinowitsch, was choreographed and directed by Jerome Robbins, born Jerome Rabinowitz. Jerry Bock admits he drew upon childhood memories of the music in composing the score for *Fiddler* (Ex. 2-17a). In fact, he has said: "I could still be writing it today. I'm not sure of the reason, but I think it has everything to do with my background. I'm a Russian-Hungarian-German Jew, mostly Russian."[45] Case in point: take one song from *Fiddler on the Roof*, then go back some thirty years before it to a Yiddish variety song by Herman Yablokoff (Ex. 2-17b) or to one by the team of Abe Ellstein and Molly Picon (Ex. 2-17c):

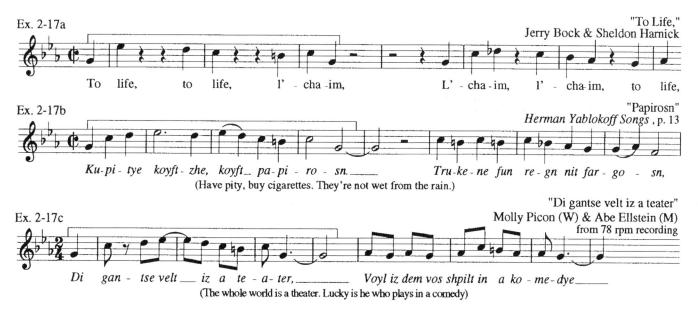

Ex. 2-17a

"To Life,"
Jerry Bock & Sheldon Harnick

To life, to life, l'-cha-im, L'-cha-im, l'-cha-im, to life,

Ex. 2-17b

"Papirosn"
Herman Yablokoff Songs , p. 13

Ku-pi-tye koyft-zhe, koyft_ pa-pi-ro-sn.____ Tru-ke-ne fun re-gn nit far-go-sn,
(Have pity, buy cigarettes. They're not wet from the rain.)

Ex. 2-17c

"Di gantse velt iz a teater"
Molly Picon (W) & Abe Ellstein (M)
from 78 rpm recording

Di gan-tse velt__ iz a te-a-ter,_____ Voyl iz dem vos shpilt in a ko-me-dye_____
(The whole world is a theater. Lucky is he who plays in a comedy)

Yablokoff's song became the best known of several texts sung to the same melody: "Nemele" (A Name) and "Drey iber dem redl" (Turn over the Wheel). Although Yablokoff wrote the words, his melody was derived from one of two Russian songs: "U nas v Matushke Rossiya" (In Our Mother Russia) and "Po kartotshnoy sisteme" (According to the Ration Card System). Moreover, there is a Bulgarian song from the same melodic family: "Az sim Dosho khubevetsa" (I Am Dosho the Handsome One).[46]

Jerry Herman, composing the score for *Milk and Honey*, "soaked in the Jewish flavor" and stated that "it was no trouble to write in a Yiddish idiom."[47] His song "I Will Follow You" not only alludes to the famous biblical phrase of Ruth, but the melody hints at one setting of "Ani maamin" (I Believe), the Hebrew credo song. In fact, his work was so convincing that producer David Merrick at first thought

Herman was too "ethnic" to write the score for *Hello, Dolly!*[48] Herman then went on to create Jewish characters in *The Grand Tour*; and in a later effort, the 1996 television musical *Mrs. Claus*, much of the action is set in the Lower East Side of 1910, replete with dancing Hasidic Jews on Avenue A.

On Tin Pan Alley, Gerald Marks, composer of "All of Me," writes about the influence of his grandmother:

Years ago I had a hit called "Night Shall Be Filled with Music." Kate Smith introduced it on the radio and I immediately began hearing from rabbis around the country blasting me for using *Got un zayn mishpet iz gerecht* (God and His Judgment Is [sic] Righteous). I had heard my grandmother hum it, and naively believed she wrote it.[49]

The Yiddish song, a warhorse introduced by the mighty actor Jacob Adler, was written by Louis Gilrod (W) and David Meyerowitz (M) in 1921. Set alongside Marks's 1932 transformation there are striking differences, a fascinating instance of how vocal music travels from year to year as well as from ear to ear:

The songwriter recalls his grandmother's recollection of a tune, like the children's game of telephone wherein words are whispered from one person to the next, ending up with no resemblance to the original input. That, in microcosm, is what happens in the evolution of so-called folk music. Folk songs have wings. One person, not always anonymous, gives birth to it, and others subtly nurture it along, "a wrinkle here, a curlicue there,"[50] into folk-song status.

On Broadway, Fanny Brice introduced a number of ethnic tunes in the Jewish vein, including "Rockaway Baby," an atypically acerbic lullaby that captured the immigrant experience in the outer reaches of Brooklyn.[51]

In Hollywood, comedienne Brice was probably the first to introduce a Yingish tune, entitled "Sasha, the Passion of the Pascha," to the movies. Like "Rockaway Baby," it was also by Ballard MacDonald (along with Jesse Greer & William Rose) and appeared in the film *Broadway Nights* (1928). But all these Yiddish-inflected tunes remained specialty material with a limited shelf life.

This is not so, however, in the case of "Chim Chim Cher-ee," a kind of lullaby from the 1964 Walt Disney film *Mary Poppins*. Written by Richard M. and Robert B. Sherman, this London chimney sweep's song appears to have Yiddish antecedents. Although the Disney Company[52] did not grant permission to reproduce an excerpt from the song, claiming it had no basis in Yiddish or synagogue music, readers may draw their own conclusions from the following two examples. The first, by Itsik Manger, shows a melodic affinity with "Chim Chim Cher-ee." The second, from a 1927 collection of *Yiddish Folk Songs* by Sarah Pitkowsky Schack and Ethel Silberman Cohen, reveals the descending chromatic line of the accompaniment shared with the Disney song. Although folk songs would not have been performed originally with piano accompaniment in Eastern Europe, the Schack-Cohen collection did find a niche in American-Jewish households, including, perhaps, the Sherman family. Al Sherman, the father, was also a tunesmith and he was born in Minsk, Russia.[53] (see Illustration 10)

Ex. 2-19 "Vaylu," Itsik Manger / *POYS*, p. 190

Chim chim-in-ey   Chim chim cher-ee,

Shpil mir tsi - gay-ner   Shpil mir a   lid,   Shpil mir un   shpil mir   Un ver gor nit mid.
(Play for me, gypsy, play. Play and don't get tired.)

Ex. 2-20 "Undzer rebenyu," Joseph Rumshinsky? / *POYS*, p. 125

Un-dzer re-ben-yu,   re-ben-yu, re-ben-yu,   Oy vey, re-ben-yu,   re-ben-yu, re-ben-yu,   Oy vey, re-ben-yu!
(Our dear Rabbi, Oh, Rabbi!)

NOTES

1. Czar Peter I's Sankt-Peterburg was founded in 1701. Although of Dutch origin, its German-sounding name was changed to Petrograd in 1914. Then in 1924, after the Bolshevik revolution, it was renamed Leningrad.

2. Established 1791 by Catherine the Great, the Pale of Settlement [*tchertan* in Russian] contained fifteen *gubernias* (states) that extended south from the Baltic to the Black Seas. The word Pale derives from "stake" (as in "impale"), setting boundaries.

3. For Menuhin quote, see Douglas Villiers, ed., *Next Year in Jerusalem*, p. 334.

4. See Nathan Milstein, *From Russia to the West*, p. 83.

5. Efrem Zimbalist (from cimbalom) was another Auer student. The first Jewish student to attend the St. Petersburg Conservatory (from 1867 to 1870) was cantor-composer Baruch Leib Rosowsky (1817-1919), father of musicologist Solomon Rosowsky. Other Jewish musician surnames, all of which can be found in the 2003 New York City phone book, include Bass, Cantor, Feiffer, Fiedler, Freilich, Geiger, Hazan,

Kapell (from Kapellmeister), Musiker, Schulsinger (alternate name for Cantor), Spielberg, Singer, and Tanzman.

6. Actually, Kreisler was half-Jewish on his father's side. See Biancolli: *Fritz Kreisler*.

7. From two oral sources: Vera Rosanka and Emil Gorovets, Russian-Jewish singers. Also see Idelsohn, *HOM*, vol. X, p. xxiv, English edition, for a related Ukrainian tune, *Bolit mene golovonka vid samogo tshola, ne batshila milencogo* ("I have a headache, a pain in my brain. I did not see my lover.").

8. Letter from Dr. Robert A. Rothstein, Univertsity of Massachusetts, Amherst, 5 July 1987.

9. See Ausubel, *The Book of Jewish Knowledge*, p. 344.

10. Goldfaden's lyric, here edited, first appeared in *Di Yudeneh* (The Jewish Woman) (Odessa, 1869) and, later, in *Di yidishe bine* (The Jewish Stage), pp. 171-73, (New York: J. Katzenelenbogen, 1897), pp. 171-173; see Illustrations 7 and 9.

11. Published by Transcontinental Music, New York City, in 1940. A variant of the melody may be found in Janot S. Roskin's, *Jüdische Folkslieder*, no. 35.

12. For other derivatives, see "Shlof Oleska" in *Old Jewish Music*, p. 134 and "Hulyet, hulyet, beyze vintn" in *Pearls of Yiddish Song*, p. 67.

13. The arrows, in Ex. 2-3, indicate the "Jewish interval" of the augmented second.

14. Found in Idelsohn, *HOM*, vol. X, no. 433. The other Hebrew variant is a Palestinian children's song for Passover: *Dunam tzafa teiva k'tanah/Al hay'or hazach/Uvateiva Moshe hakatan/Yeled yafe varach* (The small basket silently floats on the clear Nile. And in the basket is little Moses, a beautiful young boy). The translation continues: "From above, the brightness of the blue skies, and from below, the waves of the Nile. And the sun pours down great light from the skies. Softly, you mischievous waves, Little Moses is resting. He will not die, but he will live, this young Moses."

15. Idelsohn, *HOM*, vol. X, no. 433, p. 123. Is *ferach* a misprint for *terach*? A printed 1912 version ascribes the words to A. D. Lifschiz, but they are set to different music (Gesellschaft für Jüdische Volksmusik, St. Petersburg).

16. Goldfaden is a classic example of the so-called Wandering Jew—an unfortunate term invented by anti-Semites who claimed the wandering was imposed upon the Jew by divine retribution for not having accepted Christ. Another tale has it that a Jew assailed Christ on his final journey, and therefore all Jews are destined to wander forever. From his native Russia, Goldfaden moved to Romania, thence to Poland and England before he emigrated to America.

17. The 1985 show *My One and Only* was based on the 1927 show *Funny Face*.

18. See Mlotek, *Mir Trogn a Gezang*, p. 153.

19. Interview, summer 1972, Dayton, Ohio, where Picon was appearing in *Milk and Honey*.

20. Saminsky, *Music of the Ghetto and the Bible*, p. 120.

21. *A Treasury of Jewish Folklore*, p. 654. On p. 650, Ausubel also quotes Maurice Ravel's attraction to "the strange and haunting beauty of Jewish music." According to Arbie Orenstein, Ravel's biographer, this is spurious, and is based on an inept study of Ravel by Victor Serov. The false attribution is perpetuated elsewhere: *Pearls of Yiddish Song* (p. ix), 1988, which cites as its source an article by David Ewen: "Maurice Ravel on Jewish Music," *Hadassah Magazine* (January 1936). Despite this, Nathan Milstein has observed: "They call Ravel's Sonata for Violin and Piano the *Blues Sonata*, but I hear more Jewish motifs in it then blues," in *From Russia to the West*, p. 83.

22. Idelsohn, *HOM*, vol. IX, no. 59 (with slight word change).

23. Samuel A. Floyd, Jr., in *Black Music in the Harlem Renaissance*, p. 22. Gershwin biographer Deena Rosenberg goes a bit further "the melody, harmony, and subject matter of 'Summertime' are related to the spiritual," *Fascinating Rhythm*, p. 281. Melody, yes; but harmony, no. As for subject matter, I am not convinced there is anything beyond the cognates between Sum(mer)time and Sometimes.

24. Author Jeffrey Melnick, in *A Right to Sing the Blues*, does not acknowledge either Floyd or Rosenberg in his attempt to prove that Gershwin commandeered the spiritual.

25. "Tin Pan Alley Wits" by Max Wilk, in *Variety*, 8 January 1986, p. 239.

26. Five years later, *Shulamith* was performed on the London Yiddish stage, starring a teenaged Anna Held (1872?-1918). Later the toast of Broadway–in a career shaped by Florenz Ziegfeld, Jr.–she was born Hannah Held in Warsaw, Poland.

27. The service held on 28 October 2001 at ground zero in memory of the World Trade Center victims, and attended by over nine thousand people, included a rendition of "Raisins and Almonds."

28. Jolson does not sing the melody exactly as written. It is generally unknown that Jolson had appeared in blackface and sang in an even earlier Warner Bros. talking picture, *April Showers*, a 1926 Vitaphone short which utilized a process of synchronization with a prerecorded disc.

29. Sheila Davis, *The Craft of Lyric Writing*, pp. 244-245. According to ragtime pianist Max Morath, "Blue Skies" is atypically a happy song since it is slow and in a minor key and uses the color blue, *New York Times*, 21 October 1983. Mark Slobin, however, makes the absurd claim that although Berlin's music "was understood to bubble up from an almost genetic source" of ethnicity, "Blue Skies" is "like most of [Berlin's] work . . . remarkably generic." Hoberman, *Entertaining America: Jews, Movies, and Broadcasting*, p. 96.

30. Goldfaden's cheerful tune was incorporated into or used as the basis for other songs: "Yoshke, Yoshke shpan dem loshke" (Coachman, Crack the Whip) and in French Canada as "Tire l'aiguille" (Pull the Needle). It became a cliché of Jewish stereotyping in

movies. The opening montage of Mae West's film *She Done Him Wrong* (1933) uses it as background music for a Jewish peddler. In 2002 it was heard mockingly as source music in Roman Polanski's holocaust film *The Pianist*, where the end credits list it as "Tants, Yiddelach, Tants" (Dance, Little Jews, Dance).

31. Writing under a deadline, Berlin was drafted by producer Florenz Ziegfeld, Jr., to come up with a hit for *Betsy*, a Rodgers & Hart show. It was this bridge section of eight bars that gave him the most trouble. The story goes that he finished it with the breaking of daylight, appropriately with the lyric: "Never saw the sun shining so bright."

32. Words by Franklin P. Adams, written after both writers overheard a family story at the home of Rabbi Stephen S. Wise. Privately printed, T. B. Harms, 1920.

33. In the film *Roberta* it is sung by a Russian emigrée princess (Irene Dunne), to the dying dress designer Mademoiselle Roberta.

34. See Dorothy Rodgers, *A Personal Book*, p. 32. Rodgers was not noted for Jewish philanthropy; but in 2002, following the deaths of his brother and sister-in-law, Hart's income from his valuable copyrights went to the UJA-Federation of New York, due to the machinations of his money manager, William Kron. See Secrest, *Somewhere for Me*, p. 236.

35. "Esther from Hester Street" opens the song "My Little Yiddisha Queen" (see Chapter 6).

36. The plot was about a Jewish mother who would not permit her other children to marry until daughter Betsy found a husband. "Moskowitz, Gogelach, Bebelkroit, and Svonk," from the show *Merry Go Round* by Jay Gorney and Howard Dietz, is a 1927 novelty about lawyers. Mr. Kitzel (Artie Auerbach), on the Jack Benny radio show, sang the jingle: "Pickle in the middle and the mustard on top."

37. There are at least two versions: *A Treasury of Jewish Folklore*, p. 674 and the one quoted, which is from *A Treasury of Jewish Folk Song*, p. 80 (a "Bessarabian variant").

38. Interview with Mary Rodgers Guettel, Rodgers's daughter, 2 December 1984. But also see Secrest, *Somewhere for Me*, p. 16.

39. Cited in *A Voice Still Heard* by Eric Werner, p. 184.

40. Like Johann Strauss, Lehár had a Jewish wife and all his librettists were Jewish. Despite these *verboten* affiliations, Adolf Hitler adored the operettas of both Strauss and Lehár.

41. *The Street Where I Live* by Alan Jay Lerner, pp. 27-28.

42. Kurt Weill was also a Busoni student.

43. Warshavsky's best-known song is "Oyfn pripetshik" (By the Fireplace).

44. Tiomkin and Buranelli, *Please Don't Hate Me*, p. 79. At the Paris Opera House on 29 May 1928, Tiomkin became the first pianist to perform Gershwin's *Concerto in F* after its initial flurry of performances by the composer at the piano.

45. *The Making of a Musical* by Richard Altman, p. 35.

46. See *Pearls of Yiddish Song*, p. 267.

47. *Notes on Broadway*, p. 175.

48. Ibid., p. 177. A few years later, Merrick dismissed *Fiddler on the Roof*, even after it had opened, as "a Jewish show . . . no one will go." Cited in *Dance with Demons, The Life of Jerome Robbins* by Greg Lawrence, p. 336.

49. Letter to the author, 21 January 1984.

50. Chaim Kotylansky in *Folks-Gezangen*, p. 12.

51. Refrain:

> Rockaway Baby, the hocean breeze blows,
>
> My little Abie, my Yiddisha rose.
> Don't cry, for papa, he only goes to New York just a few miles,
> Laying out the new styles, making money from the fancy gentiles.
> Rockaway Baby, some day you'll grow hop,
> Then like the papa, baby'll own a clothing shop.
> Take advice, don't try the marriage game,
> Bring your children up to do the same,
> Oh! Rockaway Baby, Papa's on the five-fifteen.

Written by Ballard MacDonald (W), Harry Piani & Sammy Stept (M) for the *Ziegfeld Midnight Frolic of 1920*, the opening musical motive for "Rockaway Baby" quotes "Rock-a-bye Baby" by Effie J. Canning.

52. "Disney's legacy is that only cute animals can survive," Peter Stone, ASCAP Workshop, 31 October 1989. Disney, by most accounts, was anti-Semitic; but in 1955 B'nai B'rith researched and rejected these reports, granting him its Man of the Year award.

53. Among other hits, Al Sherman wrote (with Al Lewis) "Now's the Time to Fall in Love," a 1931 Depression song that bears some semblance to the earlier Mexican folk song, *La Cucaracha*.

CHAPTER 3

Pathways of Americanization

As a Jew, you will always have to be twice as good to get ahead in life.

KIRK DOUGLAS, *The Ragman's Son*, p. 22

The inroads made by Jewish song idioms into American popular music were mapped out by four different "A" routes: Adaptation, Adoption, Absorption, and Acculturation. Both Adaptation and Adoption function out in the open as conscious procedures on the part of authors. Absorption and Acculturation may or may not be conscious methods, but the Jewish materials they employ are hidden, resulting more in a synthesis than a mixture. Rhythmic disparities can dramatically transform the bonds between two melodies otherwise related by similar note patterns. As illustration, consider the pitch congruities between a simple motive of four notes built out of two intervals of the 4th and then observe the rhythmic divergences. The motto from the opening of the Sibelius Fifth Symphony, with its accent on the third note, is a clarion call (Ex. 3-1a). Bernstein, by shortening the third note and punching the last one, turns the same notes into a sassy shout in *On the Town* (Ex. 3-1b). The Andante theme from the Brahms *"Double" Concerto* (Ex. 3-1c) condenses the four-notes into ravishing lyricism, while the theme of *The Eternal Light*, a radio show on Jewish topics (1944-1981, Ex. 3-1d), expands it into a majestic pronouncement. Earlier than any of these, a synagogal version of the priestly "Three-fold Benediction" from midnineteenth-century southwestern Germany denatures the motive of any rhythmic pulse (Ex. 3-1e):

Ex. 3-1a — *Symphony No. 5*, Mvt.1 / Jean Sibelius

Ex. 3-1b — "New York, New York" / Leonard Bernstein

Ex. 3-1c — Andante from *"Double" Concerto* (transposed) / Johannes Brahms

Ex. 3-1d — "Shomer Yisrael," Theme from *The Eternal Light* / Morris Mamorsky

Ex. 3-1e — "Three-fold Benediction" by M(oses?) Levi / Werner, *A Voice Still Heard*, p. 178

Ye-vo-re-khe-kho Adonoy ve-yish-me - re - kho; Yo-er   Adonoy ponov elekha vi-hu - ne - kho;
(May the Lord bless you and keep you; May the Lord shine upon you and be gracious unto you;)

Rhythmic alteration of larger phrases also changes the character of a melody. "Among My Souvenirs," a woebegone 1927 ballad, becomes the lively "Dayeinu" (It Is Enough), a popular "folk tune" (probably derived from a drinking song) sung at family Passover seders. Recalling events in Jewish history, even some words from the seder tune faintly suggest the ballad's lyrics: e.g., "Had [God] done nothing more than take us out of Egypt, that would have been enough."

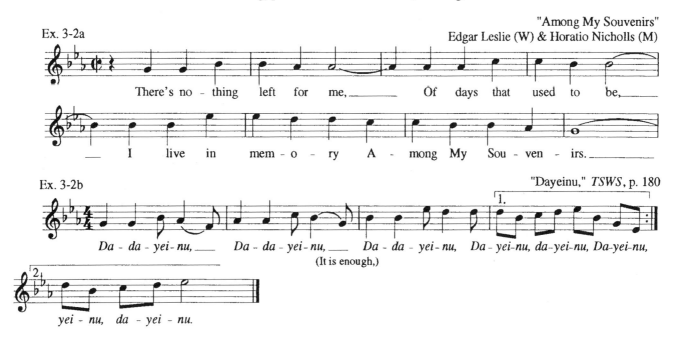

Both have the same sequences of notes, one with snappy syncopes, the other with a steady quarter-note beat, and both are concerned with memories of the past. These two analogous tunes may be harmonized the same way, but such concurrences are irrelevant to my investigations since the basic nature of Jewish music is linear and monophonic, not vertical or polyphonic.

Adaptation—Musical Transformations

Song adaptors are ruled by the axiom "make it singable to be saleable and playable to be payable." Of course, Yiddish melodies were not the only foreign-language songs to be so treated. To cite only a few representative examples from various languages:[1]

"Autumn Leaves" (1950): Johnny Mercer's adaptation from Jacques Prévert's French poem "Les Feuilles Mortes," music by Joseph Kosma

"The Girl from Ipanema" (1963): Norman Gimbel's adaptation from the Portuguese (Brazil) "Garota de Ipanema" by Vinicius De Moraes, music by Antonio Carlos Jobim

"Mack the Knife" (1952): Marc Blitzstein's adaptation for *The Threepenny Opera*, from Bertolt Brecht's German-lyric "Moritat," music by Kurt Weill

"Never on Sunday" (1960): Billy Towne's adaptation of the Greek "Ta Pedia Tou Pirea" (The Children of Piraeus) by Manos Hadjidakis

"Now Is the Hour" (1946): Maewa Kaihan's and Dorothy Stewart's adaptation of the

Hawaiian "Haera Ra" (Maori Farewell Song), music by Dorothy Stewart and Clement Scott (a tune that begins the same as Salomon Sulzer's setting of the Jewish monotheistic creed, *Sh'ma Yisrael*)

"Without You" (1945): Ray Gilbert's adaptation from the Spanish (Mexican) "Tres Palabras" (Three Words), words and music by Osvaldo Farrés

It almost goes without saying that American songs have returned the favor, often having been adapted to foreign-language settings worldwide.

Italy is a special case. Since opera is the Italian equivalent of baseball, the American national pastime, many Italians may well be frustrated opera singers. The preponderance of Italian male singers who popularized adaptations from Italian opera and folk song include such crooners and belters as: Frankie Avalon, Tony Bennett, Perry Como, Alan Dale, Vic Damone, Bobby Darin, Sergio Franchi, Mario Lanza, Julius La Rosa, Frankie Laine, Dean Martin (but not Tony Martin, born Alvin Morris, who was Jewish), Al Martino, John Pizzarelli, Louis Prima, Johnny Ray, Tony Rosetti, Steve Rossi (partner of Marty Allen[2]), Frank Sinatra, and Jerry Vale.

And the songs include:

"Don't You Know" (1959), Bobby Worth's adaptation of "Musetta's Waltz" from Puccini's *La Boheme*

"Vesti la giubba" from Leoncavallo's *I Pagliacci*, under the ministrations of Sammy Kaye, became "Tell Me You Love Me" (1951)

"Here" (1954), the Dorcas Cochran and Harold Grant adaptation of "Caro Nome" from Verdi's *Rigoletto* (In 1952, Verdi's *Aïda* was turned into the Broadway show *My Darlin' Aida*, adapted by Hans Spialek and Charles Friedman[3])

"O Sole Mio," the Neopolitan song by G. Capurro (W) and Eduardo Di Capua (M) was converted twice; in 1949 as "There's No Tomorrow," by Al Hoffman, Leo Corday and Leon Carr, and in 1960 as "It's Now or Never" by Aaron Schroeder and Wally Gold

"Torna a Surriento" by brothers Giovanni Battista de Curtis (W) and Ernesto de Curtis (M), adapted by Doc Pomus and Mort Shuman into "Surrender" (1960)

Italians also performed Jewish material. "My Yiddishe Momme" and "Oy, der Rebbenu" were recorded by Pietro Gentile and Joe Venuti (on UK 63236); "Eli, Eli" and "Kol Nidrei" by Perry Como (see Chapter 7). Connie Francis (b. Concetta Franconero) did an album of Yiddish songs. Louis Prima recorded "Mahzel Means Good Luck" (1947) and "Mashuga" (1959) and his "Sing, Sing, Sing" sounds as if it could be a Jewish tune.

The Andrews Sisters, the popular singing trio, had a minor hit with the Jimmy Dorsey Orchestra in "Sha Sha Yasha"—1938, an adaptation by Jimmy Van Heusen* & Manny Kurtz of "Oy iz dus a rebetsn"(Wow, Is This a Rabbi's Wife) a Yiddish comic song by Adolf King[4] which, in turn, was an adaptation of a Polish Hasidic tune, "Es zol zayn shtil, der rebe geyt" (Quiet!, The Rabbi Is Taking a Stroll). King changed the original expression of folk piety to a gentle poke at a pompous Rabbi and his aristocratic wife returning home from the synagogue. All traces of reverence were gone by the time movie composer Van Heusen and Kurtz, his lyricist, got their hands on it.

Other adaptations recorded by the Andrews Sisters include "Joseph! Joseph!" (from "Yossel, Yossel")[5] and "The Wedding Samba" (originally, "Der naye sher"). But these were in the afterglow of having come into the big time with their 1938 hit record of the Sammy Cahn-Saul Chaplin adaptation of the Jacob Jacobs-Sholom Secunda "Bay mir bistu sheyn" (To Me You Are Pretty). This, the major song success of 1938, originally appeared in a Yiddish musical of 1932:

Ex. 3-3

"Bay mir bistu sheyn"
Jacob Jacobs (W) & Sholom Secunda (M)

Bay mir bis-tu sheyn, Bay mir hos-tu kheyn, Bist ey-ne bay mir oyf der velt. Bei

(To me, you are pretty. To me, you have charm. To me, you're the only one in the world.)

The contrary stories of how "Bay mir bistu sheyn" ("BMBDS") journeyed from the Rolland Theater in Brooklyn to the Decca Recording Studios in Manhattan, do not mention the musical changes that occurred after that trip over the bridge.[6] Cahn, commenting on the rhyme of the Yiddish *git* (good) with the English "It" (for the "It Girl," Clara Bow), says the coupling: "shows a curious way Yiddish writers would rhyme any kind of word." But he fails to mention that he followed the same "curious way" himself by rhyming the Yiddish *sheyn* with the English "explain." He then tells us he borrowed the Italian and German words *bella* and *voonderbar* [sic] from the words of songs current in the late thirties.[7] In other words, Cahn followed Yiddish song tradition by mingling languages, a linguistic practice known as "macaronics" (i.e., to break apart into bits and pieces, like macaroni). Yiddish in and of itself is, of course, an entangled pasta.

Cahn then claims he and Chaplin doubled the length of Secunda's verse; but comparison shows the Yiddish verse is in 2/4 time, while Cahn's is in cut time. Yes, two beats to a bar have visually been doubled, but they are played twice as fast. The end result is the same. In fact, the verse was not doubled, while four bars of the original were excised; twenty bars were reduced to sixteen. Two kinds of adaptation are operating here. The first is cut time, the prototype meter of the Swing Era, and the second is the construct of sixteen bars, the standardized length for pop-song verses of that period.

Besides differences between meter and length, the key was lowered a third, to make it easier to sing; square rhythms were made groovy; a thuddy "oom-cha" accompaniment was turned into a Big Apple beat; and, above, the klezmer tootling—Jewish riffing—was eliminated altogether:

Ex. 3-4

"Bei Mir Bist Du Schoen"
Saul Chaplin, Sammy Cahn, Jacobs & Secunda

"Bei Mir Bist Du Schoen,"___ Please let me ex - plain, ___ "Bei

Mir Bist Du Schoen"___ means that ___ you're grand. ___ "Bei

In an obvious effort to capitalize on their freak success with Secunda's tune, Cahn and Chaplin adapted two other well-known Yiddish theater songs. The first endeavor slangily altered David Meyerowitz's three-quarter time "Vos geven iz geven" (What Was, Used to Be and Is No More) of 1926 into common-time as "What Used to Was, Used to Was, Now It Ain't!" (1939):

Ex. 3-5a (compare with Ex. 3-7)

"Vos geven iz geven," David Meyerowitz
POYS, p. 274

Vos ge - ven iz ge - ven un ni - to, ___ Shoyn a - vek ye - ne yor, ye - ne sho ___
(What was, used to be and is no more. Gone are those years, those hours)

Ex. 3-5b

"What Used to Was"
Chaplin, Cahn & Meyerowitz

What Used to Was, Used to Was, ___ Now it ain't! ___ You had your

chance, So what good's ___ your com - plaint? ___

More blatant than their purposeful grammatical distortions, was the adapters' decision to cannibalize the instrumental introduction of "BMBDS" for the vocal line of the verse to "What Used to Was." If they had hoped that subliminal recall would somehow help this newfangled version rival the proportions of the earlier megahit, they were surely disappointed.[8]

Ex. 3-6a: Verse — "What Used to Was" — Saul Chaplin & Sammy Cahn

Lis - ten, lo - ver, our love is o - ver, it's end - ed,

Ex. 3-6b: Piano Introduction — "Bei Mir Bist Du Schoen" — Chaplin & Cahn

Allan Roberts and Doris Fisher had better luck with a 1940s movie torch song that relates to the Meyerowitz melody, although it is not purposeful and certainly is not an adaptation:

Ex. 3-7 (compare with Ex. 3-5a) — "Put the Blame on Mame" — Doris Fisher (W) & Allan Roberts (M)

a varied

Put the Blame on Mame, boys,_____ Put the Blame on Mame.

b varied

Mame kissed a buy -er from out of town,_____ That kiss burned Chi - ca - go down,_____

There are also pitch changes in "BMBDS." In bar three of the Secunda verse, an ascending leap of a 5th—on the words *a toter*, a Tartar—is modified downward by Cahn and Chaplin to the interval of a 4th—on the words "I've known some." That's the musical equivalent of a nose job! How much more American can one get?[9]

Ex. 3-8a — "Bay mir bistu sheyn" — Original

5th

Ven du zolst zayn shvarts vi a to - ter,
(If you were as black as a Tartar,)

Ex. 3-8b — Adaptation

4th

Of all the girls I've known,_____ And I've known some,_____

Another musical change in "BMBDS" concerns the Jewish-sounding sob (i.e., the interval of an augmented 2nd in bar seven of the Yiddish verse) which is wiped away by the adapters. Ironically, the lyrics have more macaronics in the copy than in the model. But Cahn does not attempt to translate the Yiddish. In this respect, note the title of the 1932 musical in which "BMBDS" made its debut: *M'ken leben nor mir lost nit* (One Could Live But They Don't Let You), rendered on the theater sheet music as "I Would If I Could."

Translation from the Yiddish	*English Adaptation*
If you were as black as a Tartar,	Of all the girls I've known,
If you had cat eyes,	And I've known some,
And if you limped	Until I first met you I was lonesome.
And had a wooden foot,	And when you came in sight, dear,
I would say it does not matter.	My heart grew light,
And this old world seemed new to me.	
And if you had a moronic smile,	You're really swell, I have to admit
And if you had Vayezusu's* brain,	You deserve expressions
If you were as wild as Indians,	That really fit you
Even if you were a Galizianer,**	And so I've racked my brain
I'd say it does not matter.	Hoping to explain
She: What are you talking about?	All the things you do to me.
He: I'm about to tell you.	

Refrain: To me you are pretty,	*Bei Mir Bist Du Schön,*
To me you have charm,	Please let me explain,
To me you are one in a million,	*Bei Mir Bist Du Schön*
To me you are good,	Means that you're grand.
To me you have "It,"	*Bei Mir Bist Du Schön,*
You are dearer to me than money.	Again I'll explain,
Lots of pretty girls	It means that you're
Have wanted me,	The fairest in the land.
Out of them all	I could say "*Bella, Bella,*"
I chose only you.	Even say "*Voonderbar.*"

*from Purim story, Haman's dumb son   Each language only helps to tell you

**a bumpkin, from Galicia   How grand you are.

Finally, witness the authors' mutually divergent name changes. The copyright notice of the 1932 sheet music registers Secunda's first name as Samuel, later refined, for "dignity and good luck," to the Hebraic Sholom.[10] But Samuel Cahn, born Cohen, later modified his moniker to Sammy.

The Yiddish original was written to be performed as a duet. The adaptation, although written for a single voice, was taken to the top of the charts by the Andrews Sisters in an arrangement by their subsequent music director, with the name of–fortuitously–Vic Schoen. Cahn says that Patti Andrews, on first hearing the tune, asked if it were of Greek origin, a not-so-strange question since the sisters were half Greek, as well half Catholic. Patti could not have known, however, that "BMBDS" had an ancestry in a number of Yiddish folk songs whose lyrics sing the praises of maidens who are *shvarts* (black), and who also have *kheyn* (charm). This can be seen in Ex. 3-9 where Yehuda Leib Cahan, an ethnomusicologist, transcribed the following folk song for posterity:[11]

Ex. 3-9

"Shvarts, bist du shvarts"
Y. L. Cahan, *Yidishe folkslider*, arr. by J. Gottlieb

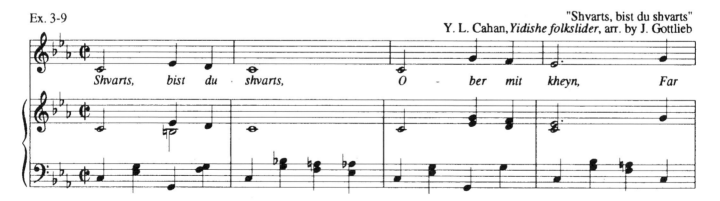

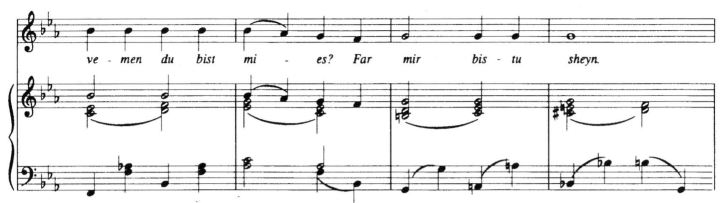

(Black, you are black, but you have charm. For others you may be ugly, but to me you are pretty.)
The lyric continues: "If you love me, if you don't love me, Let's at least go for a walk."

"Bay mir bistu sheyn" evolved, as it were, from shtetl to stage door. A recording—"Bei Mir Twist Du Schoen"—was a double pun, referring both to the dance craze of the 1960s and to the braided (twisted) Sabbath bread known as chalah. A more unusual twist is Judy Garland's cantorial rendition in a scene deleted from the 1938 film *Love Finds Andy Hardy*.

In the 1980s "BMBDS" became a music video from France entitled *Sonnifere*, and a parody, "The Fare Missed the Train," was recorded. In the 1990s it became the rage in Japan and was featured in a Paul Taylor ballet score called *Company B*; and in 1993, it was used as part of the background score for the BBC-TV film of Romain Gary's 1968 novel *The Dance of Genghis Cohn*. The beat still goes on and on.

Sammy Cahn said in 1991 that the song made his mother finally comprehend what he did for a living. She then suggested he (actually, in partnership with Chaplin) convert the Yiddish variety song "Yossel, Yossel" since his sister, Pearlie, was dating a fellow named Joseph.[12] This was an adaptation of a 1923 song by Nellie Casman and her director-husband Samuel Steinberg:[13]

Ex. 3-10

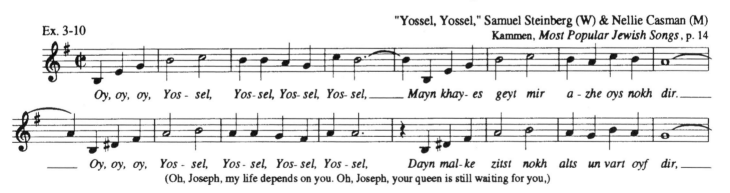

(Oh, Joseph, my life depends on you. Oh, Joseph, your queen is still waiting for you,)

Unlike "BMBDS," however, "Yossel" was barely scratched when it was recast to become:

Ex. 3-11

Musically, that Yankee still has a Jewish accent. But in 1934, eleven years after Yossel was born, a Jewish composer named Wil Grosz might have kidnapped him, putting him under wraps in a major mode:

Ex. 3-12

"The Isle of Capri"
Jimmy Kennedy (W) & Will Grosz (M)

'Twas on The Isle Of Ca-pri That I found her, Be-neath the shade of an old ap-ple tree,____ Oh, I can still see the flow'rs blooming 'round her, Where we met on The Isle of Ca - pri,_____

Wilhelm Grosz was born in Vienna, lived in the United States, where he made arrangements of Yiddish folk songs and, under the pseudonym of Hugh Williams, wrote the hit song "Red Sails in the Sunset."[14] The American selling agent of "The Isle of Capri" is Harms Music, the publisher of "Joseph, Joseph" (1938). Other than these inferences, there is no documentation that Grosz made a gloss on the Yiddish song. Nellie Casman brought a plagiarism suit against Grosz, but nothing came of it.[15] To cloud the issue even further, composer Paul Reif is said to have written the original tune of "The Isle of Capri" to a German text: "Ich bin ein kleiner Strassensinger" (I Am a Small Street Singer).

As already seen in the conversion of "Vos geven" to "What Used to Was," another possible way to camouflage a tune is to take something written in three-quarter time and put it into common time (i.e in a four-quarter meter) or the other way around. For example, "The Star-Spangled Banner," which is in triple time, is an acceptable tune when put into duple time. When squared into a matrix of four, a Yiddish tune in a triple meter (Ex. 3-13a) becomes a tune made popular by Doris Day in the early 1950s (Ex.3-13b):

Ex. 3-13a

"Der becher," Mark Warshavsky
POYS, p. 203

Tay - e - re Mal - ke, ge - zunt zol - stu zayn, Gis on dem be - kher, dem be - kher mit vayn
(Dear Malke, may you be well. Fill up the goblet with wine)

Ex. 3-13b

"A Guy Is a Guy"
Oscar Brand

I walked down the street like a good girl should, He fol- lowed me down the street like I knew he would, Be-cause A Guy Is a Guy

But, surprise!—the pop song is an adaptation of an entirely different folk ballad, known in World War II as "A Gob Is a Slob."[16] Oscar Brand, the author of "A Guy Is a Guy," not only wrote the score for *The Education of H*Y*M*A*N K*A*P*L*A*N* (in tandem with Paul Nassau), but is also a folk-song specialist. It is conceivable the tune by Warshavsky could have antedated the other folk ballad that became the "Gob-Slob" contrafact. But it is more likely that the form of the tune is so basic that it can be found in many different cultures.[17]

A closely related pattern opens a novelty song of 1929 in triple meter (Ex.3-14a); and, in common time, a tune sung at campfire hootenannies (Ex.3-14b), as well as two traditional synagogue responses (Exx. 3-14c and 3-14d). Gerald Marks also used the sequence as the first four bars of his "That's What I Want for Christmas." He reminisced about how he had heard another tune which began the same way and threatened to sue. In response, the publisher of the other song sent back a list of twelve other songs dating back to the American Revolution, using the same four-bar configuration! Mr. Marks kept mum after that.[18]

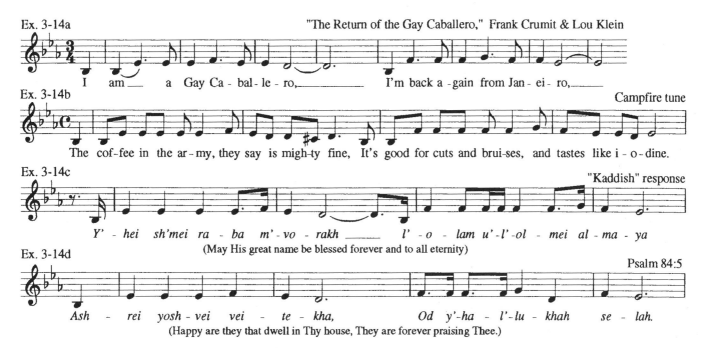

In 1950, Harry Coopersmith, then head of music at the New York Board of Jewish Education, edited and composed songs for a collection called *The Songs We Sing*. A Chanukah song, written in common time by Coopersmith (Ex. 3-15a) has an uncanny resemblance to Harold Rome's three-quarter time "Bar Mitzvah Song" (Ex. 3-15b) from the 1962 show *I Can Get It for You Wholesale*. Note how both songs refer to raised tools, a sword, and a wand.

The Israeli toe tapper, "Tzena, Tzena," turned into an American hit by The Weavers in 1950, has a thorny history of authorship.[20] But for all that, it has been suggested that the tune was probably of Polish origin, dating from World War II.[20] Israel plays an indirect but powerful role in American musical theater since shows with Jewish subject matter (including Bible stories) almost all came to the fore after the creation of the State of Israel in 1948, as if that milestone legitimized Jewish topics for musical comedy. Arising after the heyday of the Yiddish Theater of New York, the assimilated theatergoer had the best of the old and new worlds, *Yiddishkayt* (Jewishness) wrapped in nostalgia.

More prevalent are the mainstream shows that have incidental Jewish songs, idioms, characters and/or scenes. They include: *Cabaret, Candide, A Day in Hollywood/A Night in the Ukraine, Fiorello!, Guys and Dolls, Gypsy,* and *Little Shop of Horrors*. Is Thornton Wilder's Dolly Gallagher Levi in *The Matchmaker* (trans-

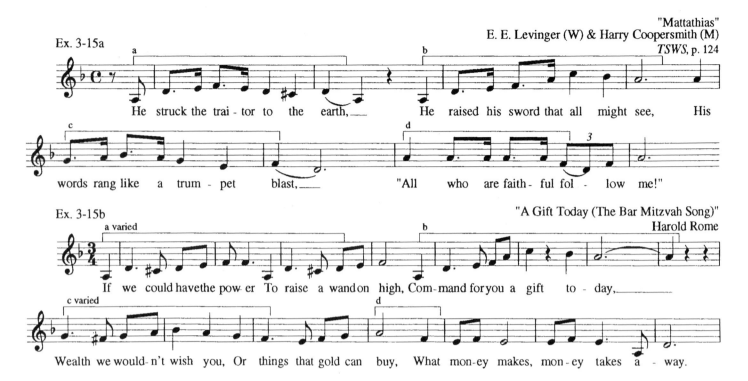

Ex. 3-15a

"Mattathias"
E. E. Levinger (W) & Harry Coopersmith (M)
TSWS, p. 124

He struck the trai-tor to the earth,___ He raised his sword that all might see, His words rang like a trum-pet blast,___ "All who are faith-ful fol-low me!"

Ex. 3-15b

"A Gift Today (The Bar Mitzvah Song)"
Harold Rome

If we could have the pow-er To raise a wand on high, Com-mand for you a gift to-day,___ Wealth we would-n't wish you, Or things that gold can buy, What mon-ey makes, mon-ey takes a-way.

formed by Jerry Herman into *Hello, Dolly!*) more a Levi and less a Gallagher in her role as a *shadkhen* (matchmaker)?

Even shows with western settings have Jewish-based interludes. In "Goldfarb, That's I'm" (the so-called Finaletto from *Girl Crazy*), Gershwin makes a sly reference to the character's ethnicity in the phrase "Goldfarb, he's all right." A crossrelation is set up between melody's B-flat on the word "he's" (referring to Goldfarb) and the harmony's B-natural on the word "right," indicating Goldfarb is acceptable despite his ethnic origin. It has also been argued that in *Oklahoma!* the peddler's song "It's a Scandal, It's an Outrage" represents Jewish hopes of assimilation.[21]

There is a lineage of vaudeville encounters between Jewish peddlers and Native Americans, ranging from Yiddish skits to the Broadway stage (*Whoopee!*) to films (*Blazing Saddles*).[22] These comic unions are also to be found in early novelty songs: "I'm an Indian" (a Fanny Brice specialty), "I'm a Yiddish Cowboy," "Yonkel, the Cowboy Jew," and "Big Chief Dynamite." Apparently, there were actual Jewish-Indian alliances, peddlers marrying into tribes, others doing business with natives.[23]

A counting-song in Yiddish "Tsen brider" (Ten Brothers) may have been inspired by "Ten Little Injuns," a popular American minstrel show jingle of 1869. Is it possible that a midnineteenth-century American ditty could have reached out to Eastern European Jewry? The words by Septimus Winner had many spin-offs (most notably, "Ten Little Niggers"), while the music by Mark Mason became the basis, by way of England, for the 1891 folkish "A Drunken Sailor."[24] But whereas the Indians die off one by one from drowning, bee stings, assaults, etc., until "there were none," the manner in which the Jewish brothers die is not mentioned. Instead, it is the brothers' prosperity that decreases each time they diminish in number. They begin by trading in flax (*layn*, and then there are *nayn*, "nine") and are forced to adopt new trades, going from cargo to candles to hay to bones until the last one is utterly impoverished: "I die every day/I have nothing to eat." The refrain of the song (Ex. 3-16a) was appropriated by Itzik Manger (W) and Abe Ellstein (M) and put into the Yiddish film song "Yidl mitn fidl" (Little Jew with a Fiddle) which ends "life is a joke" (Ex. 13-6b). It may also have been a stimulus for the fiddler's theme in *Fiddler on the Roof* (Ex. 3-16c). Less than a decade later, the light-hearted tune became a dirge as the word *gas* (street) was changed to *gaz* (gas) and the brothers are smothered to death in the Nazi concentration camps.[25]

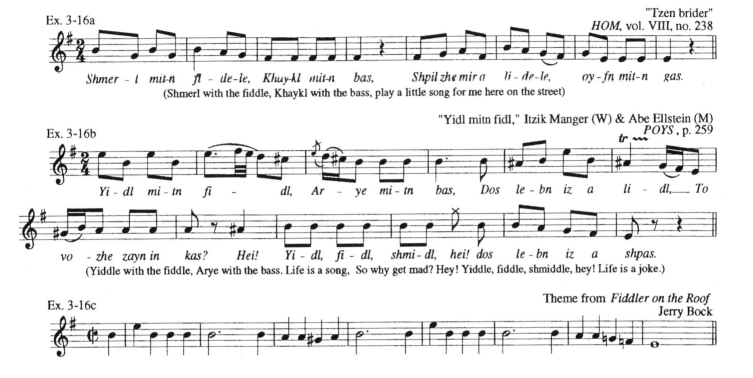

Ex. 3-16a

"Tzen brider"
HOM, vol. VIII, no. 238

Shmer - l mit-n fl - de-le, Khuy-kl mit-n bas, Shpil zhe mir a li - de-le, oy-fn mit-n gas.
(Shmerl with the fiddle, Khaykl with the bass, play a little song for me here on the street)

Ex. 3-16b

"Yidl mitn fidl," Itzik Manger (W) & Abe Ellstein (M)
POYS, p. 259

Yi - dl mi - tn fi - dl, Ar - ye mi - tn bas, Dos le - bn iz a li - dl,___ To
vo - zhe zayn in kas? Hei! Yi - dl, fi - dl, shmi - dl, hei! dos le - bn iz a shpas.
(Yiddle with the fiddle, Arye with the bass. Life is a song, So why get mad? Hey! Yiddle, fiddle, shmiddle, hey! Life is a joke.)

Ex. 3-16c

Theme from *Fiddler on the Roof*
Jerry Bock

A Young Wife's Tale–"Love Me to a Yiddisha Melody"

Another geographic journey took place with a song from a Chicago Yiddish operetta of 1899, *Khokhmes noshim* (Women's Wisdom), music by David Hirsch and book by "Professor" Moshe Hurwitz, adapted from a German play *Die Hexe* (The Sorceress). Originally, a Hasidic tune called "Der rebe's nigele" (The Rabbi's Little Song, Ex. 3-17a), it was adapted in 1911 for a Yiddish theater song (Ex.3-17b) by Isaac Reingold. This transcription was then swallowed whole hog—if one can use that expression in this context—to become the verse for a brand new ragtime tune. But, unlike "BMBDS," the words of this adaptation bore no resemblance to the Yiddish song. Quite the opposite. In Reingold's adaptation, a wife, subjected to her husband's tyranny, bitterly concludes she should have stayed an old maid (Ex.3-17c). Hers is a sad tale of woe:

A yor ersht nokh mayn khasene	Only one year after my wedding,
Zet vi kuk ikh oys, taynet a yung vaybele	See how I look!, a young wife complains
Un khlipet shtark.	Crying all the time.
Oy gute libe shvesterlakh	Oh good, dear sisters,
Dem sod zog ikh aykh oys,	I'll let you in on a secret;
Az a man iz nor a tsore oyfn kark.	A man is a pain in the neck.

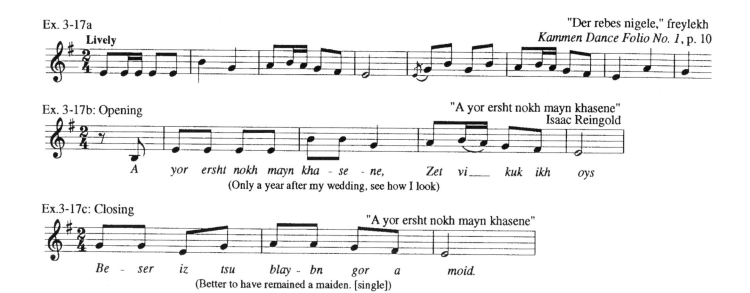

Ex. 3-17a
Lively
"Der rebes nigele," freylekh
Kammen Dance Folio No. 1, p. 10

Ex. 3-17b: Opening
"A yor ersht nokh mayn khasene"
Isaac Reingold

A   yor ersht nokh mayn kha - se - ne,   Zet vi___ kuk ikh   oys
(Only a year after my wedding, see how I look)

Ex.3-17c: Closing
"A yor ersht nokh mayn khasene"

Be - ser iz tsu blay - bn gor a   moid.
(Better to have remained a maiden. [single])

Geven bin ikh a meydl a freylekhe,	I was a happy girl,
Gor-moyredik geshtift	God-fearing,
Mit yunge-layt lakhn hob ikh dan	Laughed with young people.
Un haynt bin ikh a yidene,	Today I'm an old woman,
Shvakh un more shkhoyredik,	Weak, fearful and scared,
Un ales vayl ikh hob gevolt a man.	And all because I wanted a man.
Er darf a lebn makhn bloyz, oy!	All he has to do is make a living, oh!
Un ikh, oy vos bin ikh nit in hoyz, oy!	And me? What am I not in this house?, oh!
A vayb un a damele,	A wife, a woman,
A dinst un oykh a mamele,	A maid and also a mother.
Ales, ales kumt dokh on mit shverer noyt.	Everything's a burden.
Oy es iz an kleynikayt,	Oh, it's not a little thing,
Ikh shver aykh bay a reynikayt,	I swear with all my heart,
Az beser is tsu blaybn gor a moyd.	It's better to have remained single.[26]

Subsequent verses paint her picture in even darker colors. However, in the adaptation, "Love Me to a Yiddisha Melody," Joe Young and Edgar Leslie[27] (see Illustration 11) turn the tables. The wife becomes a *balabusteh*—not a "ball buster," but close enough since it does mean "bossy woman." She is the one who now wears the pants in the family. In a delightful about-face, the Yiddish song verse is allied with the Irish fellow, while the chorus, in a ragtime beat, is reserved for the Jewish tootsie!

"A yor ersht nokh mayn khasene" had still further adventures. Though written in America, it traveled to Europe where it was appropriated, not untypically, as part of Yiddish folk-song literature. A dance tune, which was based on it, can be heard in the 1982 film of Chaim Potok's *The Chosen* where it is used for a Hasidic wedding scene. Thus, an American theater song about a disillusioned wife travels overseas to Poland, where it may have first originated, to become a happy instrumental tune for a wedding that takes place in Brooklyn! (see Illustrations 12a & 12b, with Exx. 3-18 & 3-19)

But Reingold's piece was not the only one to travel back and forth over the Atlantic. Other popular Yiddish theater songs made in America, but expropriated as "folk music" in Europe, included such hits as "Eli, Eli," "Mayn shtetele Belz," "Got un zayn mishpet iz gerekht" and "Dos pintele yid." Tangos imported to

Poland in the 1910s were similarly transmogrified, and this led to the creation of new tangos by Jews.

The process could work in both directions. Khona Wolfstahl, a Romanian composer who never came to the United States, wrote the score for a play that was pirated in New York by the team of Arnold Perlmutter and Herman Wohl, giving Wolfstahl no credit. Without realizing that Wolfstahl was the author, Perlmutter and Wohl naively forwarded it to him so that he might consider producing his own score in Romania. The word chutzpah takes on a new dimension.

Ex. 3-18: Verse

"Love Me to a Yiddisha Melody"
Joe Young & Edgar Leslie

Pa- trick J. O'-Brien met Sa-die__Katz-en-stein, At a mas-quer-ade brought her wine, So fine, Oy!

Ex. 3-19: Refrain

"Love Me to a Yiddisha Melody"
Joe Young & Edgar Leslie

Oh! you Kid – di-sha, Love Me to a Yid-di-sha __ Mel – o – dy.

A more recent example of international exchange took place in 1996 on the PBS television documentary *Shtetl*. Both the American-made songs "Belz" and "Bay mir bistu sheyn" were heard in the Polish town of Bransk, where all traces of Jewish life had been eradicated. Sadly and most ironic of all, the town celebrated its 500th anniversary with the local band playing "If I Were a Rich Man" from *Fiddler on the Roof*.

Adoption–Musical Quotations

Adoption, the second process of Americanization, utilizes material not naturally one's own, but put into practice as if it were. Unlike adaptation, adoption does not embrace a complete song, only a distinctive part of one. Musicologically known as quodlibet (Latin for "as you please"), this technique of quoting is often done for comic effect. The song "Rebecca," from the 1908 production *Nearly a Hero*, illustrates this engagingly. The authors, Harry Williams* and Egbert Van Alstyne,* who wrote the memorable "In the Shade of the Old Apple Tree," adopted a potential Jewish bride (Ex. 3-20).

At the beginning of the last staff there is a quote from a Jewish wedding march (Ex. 3-21a) composed by Sigmund Mogulesko for his 1894 operetta *Blihmele di perl fun Varsha oder graf un Jude* (Little Flower, the Pearl of Warsaw—or the Count and the Jew, book by Joseph Lateiner).

"Khosn kale mazl tov" became a well-known signature tune and was used in many different contexts. Composer Victor Young,* for example, turns it into a tango rhythm for a party scene in the 1933 film *Folies Bèrgere*. Al Jolson and Bernie Russell adapt it in a 1948 Decca recording celebrating the birth of the State of

Ex. 3-20

"Rebecca"
Harry Williams (W) & Egbert Van Alstyne (M)

Oui my Re - bec - ca, _____ Oui yoi! Re - bec - ca, _____ I've got _____ a love for you, _____
(Oy)   (Oy)

You say _____ dot you're for bus - 'ness, _____ I'm out _____ for bus-'ness, too. _____

Tink of _____ de ved-ding pres - ents, _____ And, dear, _____ if you'll be mine, _____

Dey vill all say "Moz-zle-toff" _____ Ven you are Miss-es Ros-en - stein. _____

Israel, mangled by Jolson as "Is-ree-el." It has been suggested that the precursors of the melody include a Serbian folk song and, of all things, the main theme of Tschaikovsky's *Marche Slav* (Ex. 3-21b).[28] The musical habitat for these Jewish and Slavic tunes is the Ukrainian Dorian mode. More on this in Chapter 12.

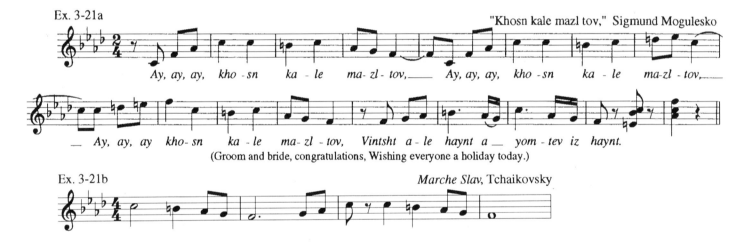

Ex. 3-21a

"Khosn kale mazl tov," Sigmund Mogulesko

Ay, ay, ay, kho - sn ka - le ma-zl - tov, _____ Ay, ay, ay, kho - sn ka - le ma-zl - tov, _____

_____ Ay, ay, ay kho - sn ka - le ma-zl - tov, Vintsht a - le haynt a _____ yom - tev iz haynt.
(Groom and bride, congratulations, Wishing everyone a holiday today.)

Ex. 3-21b

Marche Slav, Tchaikovsky

Absorption–Musical Anagrams

With song adoption and adaptation, original source materials are clearly discernable. Not so with the third process of Americanization, absorption, which soaks up materials like a blotter, leaving an imprint of some kind. This is a sticky wicket since it concerns the trap of musical permutations or anagrams. If a motive consisting of notes 1 2 3 4 3 2 is reordered as 3 2 1 3 4 2, and retains the same basic rhythmic profile, is it a new pattern or a related variant?

There is a children's song in *mameloshn* (mother tongue)[29] by Zalman Rozental that extols the charms of the shtetl, a word loosely translated as "little town," but generically associated with villages of Jewish Eastern Europe. Yiddish Theater composers in New York City would wax nostalgic about their Old World home towns. One such romanticized reminiscence was recalled by the team of Aaron Lebedeff and Herman Wohl, about Slutzk, a real town in Belarus (White Russia). Superimpose Slutzk above the children's song, and they make—as the saying goes—beautiful music together:

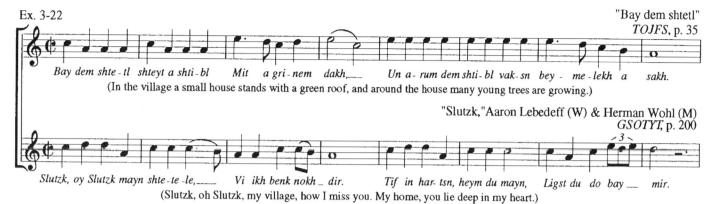

Ex. 3-22

"Bay dem shtetl"
TOJFS, p. 35

Bay dem shte-tl shteyt a shti-bl Mit a gri-nem dakh,___ Un a-rum dem shti-bl vak-sn bey-me-lekh a sakh.
(In the village a small house stands with a green roof, and around the house many young trees are growing.)

"Slutzk," Aaron Lebedeff (W) & Herman Wohl (M)
GSOTYT, p. 200

Slutzk, oy Slutzk mayn shte-te-le,___ Vi ikh benk nokh_ dir. Tif in har-tsn, heym du mayn, Ligst du do bay__ mir.
(Slutzk, oh Slutzk, my village, how I miss you. My home, you lie deep in my heart.)

Voila!, one song has been absorbed by the other.

Still another team, Jacob Jacobs and Alexander Olshanetsky, became the architects for "Belz,"[30] (another Bela[Byelo-]Russian town), probably the best known of all shtetl songs:

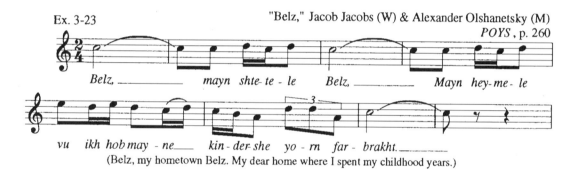

Ex. 3-23

"Belz," Jacob Jacobs (W) & Alexander Olshanetsky (M)
POYS, p. 260

Belz,___ mayn shte-te-le Belz,___ Mayn hey-me-le vu ikh hob may-ne___ kin-der-she yo-rn far-brakht.___
(Belz, my hometown Belz. My dear home where I spent my childhood years.)

Written for a 1932 play, *The Song of the Ghetto*, this famous ballad was introduced by Isa Kremer; and the fact that it was meant to be a woman's song is confirmed by the lyrics (see Ex. 3-24a). A 1929 torch-song by Harburg and Gorney: "What Wouldn't I Do for That Man?" performed by song stylist Helen Morgan in two different movies (*Applause* and *Glorifying the American Girl*) begins with a verse that presages the bridge section of "Belz" (Ex. 3-24b). Here was an instance where a Yiddish song could well have been activated by an American source. Did Olshanetsky recall the earlier film song and associate it with the female gender?

Olshanetsky's song is better known than Gorney's, so much so that two English pop songs were adapted from it. The verse to the first version, called "That Wonderful Home Town of Mine," curiously begins with an adaptation of the verse to "Bei mir bistu sheyn." This had to be another example of plundering one song's notoriety to promote another. Although both the original Yiddish "Belz" and "BMBDS" have Jacob Jacobs in common as lyricist, how is it that a gloss was made on Sammy Cahn's lyric? "Of all the girls I've known, and I've known some" in "BMBDS" becomes: "Of all the towns I've known, and I've known some/When I hear Belz/It makes me so lonesome . . ." The chorus, however, is more faithful to the Yiddish original: "I long for Belz/My hometown Belz . . ." But no doubt that was still too ethnic for sales appeal, and so in 1949 "Belz" was again adapted into

Ex. 3-24a: Bridge

"Belz"
Jacob Jacobs (W) & Alexander Olshanetsky (M)

Ye - dn sha - bes fleg ikh loy - fn dort mit der t'khi - ne glaykh. Tsu

zi - tsn un - ter dem gri - nem bey - me - le ley' - nen bay - dem taykh.

(Every Sabbath I'd run to read the woman's prayerbook by the river, sitting under the green trees.)

Ex. 3-24b: Verse

"What Wouldn't I Do for That Man?"
E. Y. Harburg (W) & Jay Gorney (M)

Life   was   blind to me,   Now   it's   kind to me,   Love   has   o - pened   my   eyes.

Since   it   came   to me,   Life's   a   game to me   with   the   sweet -est   sur -   prise.

"That Wonderful Girl of Mine," words by Sammy Gallop. His lyric had nothing to do with the shtetl, but everything to do with getting a financial slice of the Tin Pan Alley pie.

A good illustration is the 1940 conversion of the Olshanetsky-Chayim Tauber Yiddish tango "Ikh hob dikh tsu fil lib" of 1934. In its English adaptation by Don Raye, this quite naturally became "I Love You Much Too Much," and with it the composer's name was reduced to Alex Olshey. Here is a sampling of original releases by name artists (some rereleased under other labels):

Ames Brothers (Vocalion, 1967), Andrews Sisters (Vocalion, 1958), Pat Boone (Dot, 1960), Carmen Cavallaro (Decca, 1967), Emery Deutsch (ABC Paramount, 1958), Helen Forrest (Capitol, 1957), Connie Francis (MGM, 1960), Jackie Gleason (Capitol, 1957), Gordon Jenkins (Time, 1961), Mickey Katz (Capitol, 1962), Morgana King (Ascot, 1966), Gene Krupa (Columbia, 1940), Dean Martin (Capitol, 1960, incongruously remastered in 1997 by EMI under the title *Italian Love Songs*), Jan Peerce (Everest, 1970), Carlos Santana (Columbia, 1981), Jerry Vale (Columbia, 1963), Bobby Vinton (Epic, 1964), and Fred Waring (Decca, 1949).

Getting back to the shtetl songs, the three towns can be mixed into a kind of layer cake: "Bay dem shtetl" on the bottom, "Slutzk" in the middle, and "Belz" on top:

Ex. 3-25

"Belz"

"Slutzk"

"Bay dem shtetl"

The cake is tasty, but it lacks an icing. Decades after "Belz," Jerry Bock and Sheldon Harnick, in *Fiddler on the Roof*, built a shtetl called "Anatevka" on an American stage, but based on European blueprints:

Ex. 3-26   "Anatevka," Bock & Harnick

All four songs share a common prepackaged mix. They begin on the mediant (third note of the key), virtually using it as a reciting tone for two or three bars. The first eight bars of each phrase utilize the same five-note range. Each has a pitch pattern of C-B-A. In "Belz" and "Anatevka" there is a rhythmic motive of two eighths and a quarter note, which appears in the penultimate bar of "Slutzk" (not illustrated). The B sections of "Slutzk" and "Belz" (also not shown) ascend in parallel motion and end on the mediant. In "Belz" and "Anatevka" the midsections diverge in contrary motion, but come together on the dominant (fifth) tone. And finally, the texts of three of the songs evoke the joys of Sabbath.

To prepare the layer cake in a Broadway oven, the recipe calls for the following ingredients: first, combine a cup of "Belz" with an equal amount of "Slutzk." Next, fold in a dollop of the children's song for enrichment. Finally, add the icing of "Anatevka," which spreads smoothly on top of the layers until the seventh bar, where a lump of dissonance appears. Even though the final notes of the layers have to be altered to accommodate the icing, this cake is no half-baked idea:

Ex. 3-27

NOTES   1. Songs adapted from the standard classical repertory, such as the works of Tchaikovsky, Rachmaninoff, and company, are a whole other way to go.

2. Like Jerry Lewis, Dean Martin's former partner, Marty Allen is Jewish.

3. The 1989 musical *Miss Saigon* (music by Claude-Michel Schönberg, words by Alain Boubil and Richard Maltby, Jr., was loosely based on Belasco's drama *Madama Butterfly*, but not on Puccini's music.

4. The original Yiddish version had been recorded by Aaron Lebedeff, known as "The Litvak Comedian." (More recent is the recording of "Sha Sha" made by the Kapelye Ensemble.) Lebedeff's tongue-twister routines must have influenced Danny Kaye.

5. "Joseph! Joseph!" was recorded by the Andrews Sisters in 1938 on the Decca label 23605.

6. Sammy Cahn, *I Should Care*, pp. 63ff; Victoria Secunda, *Bei Mir Bist Du Schön*, pp. 129ff; Saul Chaplin, *The Golden Age of Movie Musicals and Me*, pp. 35-37; and Sholom Secunda, "From the Melody Remains: The Memoirs of Sholom Secunda, as told to Miriam Kressyn," in *Memoirs of the Yiddish Stage*, Joseph Landis, ed., excerpt pp. 140-150. For an especially fine overview, see Marvin Caplan, "*The Curious History of Bei Mir Bist Du Schon*," *Congress Monthly* 62, no. 1 (January/February 1995), published by the American Jewish Congress.

7. Cahn says that "Bella" comes from "The Umbrella Man," but if this refers to the 1938 song of that title by Cavanaugh, Rose and Stock, there is no such word in the printed sheet music.

8. In his memoirs, black pianist Willie "The Lion" Smith claims to have written a Yiddish song entitled "Wus Geven Is Geven" in collaboration with a certain Cantor Goldman. Written in memory of his mother, Smith translates the title as "Gone, Never to Return." Given the vague looseness of his other Jewish connections, this probably was confused (and fused) with the original Meyerowitz melody. See Smith, *Music on My Mind*, p. 245.

9. Another lyricist reports on two life changes on the same page of her memoir: Betty Cohen becomes Betty Comden and a rhinoplasty is performed on her physiognomy. See Betty Comden, *Off Stage*, p.104.

10. Joseph Landis, ed., *Memoirs of the Yiddish Stage*, p. 113.

11. "Shvarts bist du shvarts," from Y.L. Cahan, ed., *Yidishe folkslider* (Yiddish Folk Songs), no. 247. Another collection containing similar sentiments is Peysakh Marek and Saul Ginzburg, eds., *Evreiskiya narodniya pesni v' Rossii* (Yiddish Folk Songs from Russia), nos. 203, 229, and 235. The disdain for swarthiness expressed in these songs implies that biases were endemic to minority Russian Jews as much as to majority Russian Christians.

12. New York Sheet Music Society meeting, 2 November 1991.

13. Cahn and Chaplin rhythmically altered the original verse in such a way that it resembles the Russian folk song *Bublitchki* (Pretzels), as if they were giving us two adaptations for the price of one. The Russian song, popular among Jews as *Baigelach* (Bagels) was recorded by the Bagelman Sisters, later known as the Barry Sisters. Their swing, up-tempo versions of English pop songs performed in Yiddish were all the rage on radio, recordings, and stage from 1939 to 1953.

14. Artur Holde, *Jews in Music*, p. 108.

15. Dorothy (Mrs. Bernard) Etkin, Nellie Casman's niece, interview with author, November 1984.

16. David Ewen, *All the Years of American Popular Song*, p. 484.

17. Vivaldi's Cello Sonata in E minor, op.14, no. 5 (F14, RV 40) begins with the theme. The seminal study of wandering melodies, showing analogues among folk-song, church, and concert repertoires, is *Musikalische Studien*, by Wilhelm Tappert.

18. Not knowing the twelve titles the publisher specified, three of them might be the folk tunes: "I see the moon, the moon sees me/Shining through the banana tree"; "Papa's gonna buy you a mocking bird"; or "Pineapples, Peaches and Cherries" (recorded by Peggy Lee). Marks spoke at the New York Sheet Music Society meeting, October 1984.

19. Music by Issachar Miron (b. Michrovsky) and Julius Grossman, words, variously, by Gordon Jenkins and Mitchell Parish, arranged by Spencer Ross.

20. According to Dan Almagor, Israeli poet, professor of Hebrew literature and a TV host.

21. Scholar Andrea Most contends that peddler Ali Hakim (a role originated by Yiddish theater actor Joseph Buloff) represents "Jews' hopes of moving into white America," while "Jud (described in the stage directions as singing like a Negro) personifies the qualities that Jews feared would make them black." See Scott Heller, "The Several Roads to Respectability: Scholars Examine How Jews Fit into America," *The Chronicle of Higher Education* 29 (January 1999): A23. See also Andrea Most, *Making Americans: Jews and the Broadway Musical* (Cambridge: Harvard University Press, 2004).

22. Cantor repeated his Yiddish-Indian "shtick" in the 1931 screen version of *Whoopee*. See Mark Slobin, *Tenement Songs*, pp. 108ff.

23. See Leon Harris, *Merchant Princes*, p. 261.

24. The Ukrainian folk song called "The Cossack" is rather similar to "Drunken Sailor." See James Fuld, *The Book of World-Famous Music*, p. 206.

25. Seroussi et al., "Jewish Music," *The New Grove Dictionary of Music*, 2d ed., p. 96.

26. Music for this song may be found in Mlotek, *Songs of Generations: New Pearls of Yiddish Song*, p. 253.

27. Joe Young wrote "Five Foot Two, Eyes of Blue" and "I'm Sitting on Top of the World." Edgar Leslie's songs included "Among My Souvenirs" and "For Me and My Gal."

28. James Fuld, op. cit., p. 348.

29. The expression *mameloshn* can be taken quite literally since Yiddish in its infancy was the language of domesticity (of women), while Hebrew, *loshn hakodesh* (the holy tongue), was the language of the synagogue (of men).

30. *The ASCAP Biographical Dictionary*, 4th ed., 1980, p. 246, gives the title as "My Shtellelo Betty," and that of Jacob Jacobs's other famous song as "Bie Mein Bistu Shain." Jacobs's colleagues are listed as Mshanetsky, Abe Eilstien, and Rumshensky— for which, read: Olshanetsky, Ellstein, and Rumshinsky. Hmm!

CHAPTER 4

"Writes" of Passage

Marching backward into the future.

THEODORE BIKEL describing his career in a 1988 radio interview (WNEW, New York City)

Accent-Free Adaptations–"And the Angels Sing"

Thus far the examples of adaptation, adoption, and absorption have been loaded. Jewish material has not been so much converted as it has been recycled.[1] Although stylized for Yankee audiences, these selections retain a recognizably Jewish inflection. But it's equally possible to adapt, adopt, and absorb Jewish song-stuff without leaving any accent. In 1939, a Jewish dance (Ex. 4-1a) was so gussied up by Ziggy Elman, the jazz trumpeter, it was hardly recognizable (Ex. 4-1b)—despite its original title of "Fralikh in Swing." *Freylekh*, from the German *freulich*, means happy; the tune is a.k.a. "Der shtiler bulgar" (The Quiet Bulgar):

Ex. 4-1a

Romanian-Serbian *freylekh*
Kammen Dance Folio No. 1, p. 19

Ex. 4-1b

"And the Angels Sing"
Johnny Mercer (W) & Ziggy Elman (M)

We meet ____ And The An-gels Sing, ____ The an-gels sing the sweet-est song I e-ver heard,

With words by Johnny Mercer,* the bridge section of the adaptation shows vigorous assimilation:

Ex. 4-2a: Bridge

"And the Angels Sing"

Sud-den-ly the set-ting is strange,____ I can see wa-ter and moon-light beam-ing,

Ex. 4-2b: Bridge

"Freylekh"

Ziggy Elman (1914-1968) was one of several jazz musicians who were also adept at playing klezmer music, among them: trumpeters Mannie Klein (1908-1994) and the African American Charlie Shavers (1913-1917), fiddler Abe Schwartz (1881-1963), and trombonist Sy Zentner (1917-2000). Others were destined to build international careers known for the most part only to those of the same ethnic background, including clarinetists Naftule Brandwein (or Brandwine, 1884-1963), David Tarras (1897-1989), and his son-in-law Sam Musiker (1916-64), whose name bespoke his profession. Better known to the public at large was clarinetist Mickey Katz (1909-1985). Far less a purist than the others, he was influenced by the antics of Spike Jones (1911-1965), in whose band he played from 1943 to 1947. Among Tin Pan Alley tunes Katz targeted there were "Shrimp Boats," which—to keep it kosher—he turned into "Herring Boats," and "Davy Crockett," converted to "David Crockett." In the 1990s, African-American clarinetist Don Byron revived Katz's repertoire in live performance.

Returning to Elman's swinging angels, the *freylekh* on which he based his tune, originates from Romania; but Russia was generally the more likely source for adaptations. Witness the following examples, decade by decade.

In the 1920s, Gershwin and Herbert Stothart adapted two Russian songs for the musical *Song of the Flame*: "Cossack Love Song," based on "Minka, Minka," and the title song (Ex.4-3a) from "Kazbeck" (Ex. 4-3b):

Ex. 4-3a

"Song of the Flame"
Herbert Stothart & George Gershwin

What's that light that is beck-on-ing?_____ Come, come, come, come! Take
Through the night it is beck-on-ing;_____

Ex. 4-3b

"Kazbeck"

Yest u nas le-gen-dee skaz-kee, Adzhan! Ee o bee tchai nash kav-kaz-kee, Adzhan!
(We have legends and fairy tales of our own, friend! And our Caucasian tradition, friend!)

In the 1930s, Jack Lawrence, author of the hit ballad "All or Nothing at All," combined a Ukrainian folk song with a paraphrase of an old English rhyme into a blockbuster smash for Dinah Shore. In the Russian original, a mother exhorts her son not to be enticed by pretty girls (Ex. 4-4a); but Lawrence has it as a daughter, not a son, receiving mama's advice about the opposite sex (Ex. 4-4b):[2]

Ex. 4-4a

"Oi, nie khody, Hrytsiu"

Oi, nie kho - dy, Hry - tsiu, ____ Na ve - cher - ny - tsi.
Bo na ve - cher - ny - tsi - akh,____ Div - ki cher - iv - ny - sti.
(Do not go, Gregory, to the dance, Because at dances girls will enchant you.)
The lyric continues: "The girl with black eyebrows is the most enchanting. And, my son, if you get married,
Don't marry a widow, God forbid! Because a widow has a heart like a winter sun. Though it shines, a cold wind blows!"

Ex. 4-4b

"Yes, My Darling Daughter"
Jack Lawrence

Mo - ther, may I go out dan - cing? Yes, My Dar - ling Daugh - ter, _
Mo - ther, may I try ro - man - cing? Yes, My Dar - ling Daugh - ter, _

In the 1940s, Sholom Secunda's Yiddish tune "Dona, Dona"[3] (Ex. 4-5a), later popularized in English by Theodore Bikel, Joan Baez, and others, is a partial absorption from the main theme of Tchaikovsky's *Swan Lake* ballet (Ex. 4-5b). But unlike the Jack Lawrence adaptation, this was not a willful borrowing. If anything, Irving Berlin's "Russian Lullaby" is more consonant with the *Swan Lake* strain (Ex. 4-5c):

Ex. 4-5a — "Dona, Dona" Aaron Zeitlin (W) & Sholom Secunda (M)

Oy - fn fu - rl ligt dos kel - bl, Ligt ge - bun - dn__ mit a shtrik.
(In a wagon lies a calf tied up with a rope.)

Ex. 4-5b — Theme from *Swan Lake* (transposed from B minor) Tchaikovsky

Ex. 4-5c — "Russian Lullaby" Irving Berlin

Ev - 'ry night __ you'll hear __ her sing __ A Russ - ian Lull - a - by.__

In "Somewhere" (from *West Side Story*), Leonard Bernstein shows an affinity for the succeeding phrase of Tchaikovsky's ballet theme. Like the Secunda melody, Bernstein's also is an inadvertent analogue, despite its rhythmic allegiance to Tchaikovsky:

Ex. 4-6a: continuation — *Swan Lake* (transposed)

"Somewhere," Stephen Sondheim (W) & Leonard Bernstein (M)
Ex. 4-6b — (transposed from E major)

us.   Hold   my hand and we're half - way there.   Hold   my hand and I'll   take   you there

"Dona, Dona" and "Russian Lullaby" are not so much Tchaikovsky-inspired as they are recollections of Mother Russia refined through a Jewish sensibility. "Somewhere," on the other hand, is more Tchaikovsky-oriented as processed through an American sensibility.

With the latter two examples, we depart from opening melodic statements to interior and to penultimate phrases. In these regions also, there are examples of Russo-American crossover. One such illustration is a secondary phrase from the sultry "Amado Mio," performed by Rita Hayworth (but dubbed by singer Anita Ellis) in the film noir classic *Gilda* (Ex. 4-7a). These notes are virtually a retrograde version of an interior section from a 1934 Tin Pan Alley tango, "The Moon Was Yellow"(Ex.4-7b). Play the notes of Ex. 7a backwards and you can almost reproduce Ex. 4-7b. Whatever the lineage might have been between the two, both the Hollywood and the Tin Pan Alley songs had a comrade overseas in the Russian folk song "Kirpitchiki" (Little Bricks, Ex. 4-7c).

Continuing our decade-by-decade survey, in the 1950s, Eddie White, Mack Wolfson and Sid Danoff rolled over another kind of dance. This time it was a Ukrainian *kazatsky/kazatska* (Exx. 4-8a and 4-8b), a dance which received a fully realized treatment in the 1943 Warner Bros. film *Mission to Moscow*.

Ex. 4-7a
Bar 22
"Amado Mio"
Allan Roberts (W) & Doris Fisher (M)

It was just ___ a phrase that I'd heard ___ in plays, I was act - ing a part.

Ex. 4-7b (Ex. 4-7a in modified retrograde)
Bar 5
"The Moon Was Yellow"
Edgar Leslie (W) & Fred Ahlert (M)

A smile brought us to - ge - ther, And I was won-d'ring whe-ther We'd meet a-gain some day, ___

Ex. 4-7c
"Kirpitchiki" (Little Bricks)
from Gypsy Memories

Gor - ye mi - ka - ya, let' pyat - nad - tsa - ti, Na kir - pich - ny za - vod nan - ya - las. ___
(Fifteen years were sad, many fears I had ere I knocked at the factory door.)

Ex. 4-8a
Ukrainian Kazatsky
Kammen Dance Folio No. 1, p. 27

Ex. 4-8b
"Mashuga"
Eddie White, Mack Wolfson & Sid Danoff

I'm Ma-shu - ga for my su - gar, And my su-gar's Ma - shu-ga for me. ___
Means I'm cra - zy for my ba - by, And my ba-by's cra - zy for me. ___

In 1968, a Russian tune (known in English as "Dear for Me") was adapted by
Gene Raskin—

Ex. 4-9a
"Dorogoy dlinoyu"
Boris Ivanovich Fomin (M) & Konstantin Podrevskii (W)

Dor - o - goy dlin-no - yu, Da noch-yu lun - a - yu, Da's pes - nei toy, shto vdal le-tit zven - ya,

I stoy star - in - na - yu, Da se - mist - ru - na - yu, Shto pa - na - cham tak mu - cha la men - ya.
(On that distant road in the moonlit night, with that song that echoes far and wide,
And with that seven-stringed [guitar] which tormented me at night.)

Ex. 4-9b
"Those Were the Days," Gene Raskin

Those Were the Days, my friend, ___ We thought they'd ne - ver end, ___ We'd sing and dance For - e - ver and a day;

—a bull's-eye example of how Jews have exported Russian tunes to the rest of the
world. Moreover, they often were the creators of those goods, labeled "made in
Russia," but never "Jewish." According to music archaeologist Joachim Braun,
"forty-five percent of Russian song composers mentioned in the *Encyclopedia of
Slovak Music* are Jewish. Eight of the seventeen most popular Russian songs were

written by Jews."[4] Red Army songs of World War II were authored, for instance, by the Russian Jews Isaac Dunayevsky, brothers Dimitri and Daniel Pokrass and others.

Accent-Free Adoptions–"Nature Boy"

In adoption cases, songwriters are limited in the number of Jewish foundlings they can select. Often the adoption agency puts up a tune that has already gone from one foster song to another, not that it is unwanted, but because evidently there are fewer Jewish orphans available to meet the demand. For example:

This "Nature Boy" of 1948 has a Yiddish counterpart in a *yingele* (youth) of 1935, who suffered in "Russland" and who also wandered until he settled in America, where he had fleeting contentment. Now hear him cry:

Was "Nature Boy" made with conscious knowledge of its Yiddish antecedent? This is not simply a matter of tune detection. Just because a song in some way resembles an earlier one does not make it, pro forma, unworthy of a performer, or, worse yet, stolen goods. Still, if it helps to assuage doubting Thomases, some degree of guilt can be established in this case.

Herman Yablokoff, composer of "Shvayg mayn harts," relates in his memoirs that he brought suit against Eden Ahbez, author of "Nature Boy," for plagiarizing his song. Ahbez, born Alexander Aberle, was a Jew who as an adult acquired a Yogilike demeanor and repute. Yablokoff tells us Ahbez telephoned him to proclaim his innocence, that he

had heard the melody as if angels were singing it . . . in the California mountains. He offered me $10,000 to withdraw the suit. I said the money was not important, but I wanted him to admit the song was *geganvet* [stolen]; and if he heard angels, they must have bought a copy of my song.[5]

Both litigants must have thought it over for eventually Ahbez's lawyers offered, and Yablokoff accepted, $25,000 for settlement. Next case? There is none—although Antonin Dvořák could have been a party to the suit since the opening strain of the slow movement of his Piano Quartet in A, op. 81 matches that of "Nature Boy." The DAs of the world, by which I mean District Attorneys, Devil's Advocates, or Doubting Amoses, may be thinking: "that may have been the situation with an oddball composer like Eden Ahbez, but what did big-time Broadway composers know about Yiddish Theater composers?"

Accent-Free Absorptions

E. Y. Harburg reminisced:

on many a Saturday, after services, my father packed me up and told my mother we were going to *shul* to hear a *magid* [i.e., itinerant preacher] . . . but somehow . . . we always arrived at the Thalia Theater . . . we never told the mama. As far as she knew, it was the holy Sabbath, we were out soaking up the divine wisdom of a *magid*.[6]

Entertainment was a precious commodity on the Lower East Side. The socialist work ethic of Harburg's father, forged in sweatshops, left little time for religious observance or relaxation, all of which left an indelible mark on the son. Yiddish theater composer Joseph Rumshinsky, known as *Yoshke der notnfresser* (Joe, the note-eater), said:

Upon my coming to America, I found a perceptible rivalry between the synagogue and the theatre. In the synagogue, hopping ditties are sung, flutes, trombones, clarinets are imitated, there is much falsetta singing, there is a stamping of feet, tunes without words are indulged in,—after every *Shma Yisroel* a little excursus in dance music—in a word, theatrical effects. In the theatre, on the other hand, I encountered everywhere choirs garbed in prayer shawls and skullcaps, Jews bearded, Jews bearing scrolls of the Law, and a great deal of singing of the accepted liturgical pieces—just as if it were a synagogue![7]

In fact, the theater stage replaced the synagogue *bimah* (platform) for many Lower East Siders. It helped perpetuate the joys of Yiddish for immigrants, who were relatively fluent in various other languages: Hebrew, Polish, Russian, etc.; but it did not help them overcome the vagaries of English. Their children, however, took delight in the language of the school and of the streets and reveled in its word play. Compared to the arcane lingo heard at home and in the theater, the English vernacular was fresh and exciting. "Words are . . . for Jews not mere playthings, but a means of survival and transcendence, of achievement and strength."[8]

In his memoirs, Rumshinsky also informs us that Irving Berlin attended a performance of Rumshinsky's operetta *Di goldene kale* (The Golden Bride) in 1923, after which Berlin introduced Rumshinsky to his golden bride-to-be, Ellin McKay.[9] Did Berlin subconsciously sponge up some of Rumshinsky's musical ideas? Here is the first phrase of "The Morning Star" from Rumshinsky's 1919 operetta *Dem rebns nign* (The Rebe's Tune, Ex.4-11a). Eight years later (1927), Berlin came out with something like it (Ex. 4-11b):

Ex. 4-11a

"Der morgn shtern," Joseph M. Rumshinsky

KJTS, vol. 2

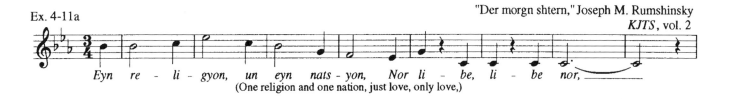

Eyn re - li - gyon, un eyn nats - yon, Nor li - be, li - be nor, ____
(One religion and one nation, just love, only love,)

Both songs are in the pentatonic scale, beginning with the archetypical motive of "Ol' Man River," a whole step and a minor third. Plunging into the river on the opposite side, however, could Rumshinsky have benefitted from a model of Berlin's? Look at a song from his 1922 production *Berele tremp* (Little Berel the Tramp). With words by Sam Lowenworth, it's so full of macaronics, it's virtually a *lukshn kugel* (noodle pudding).

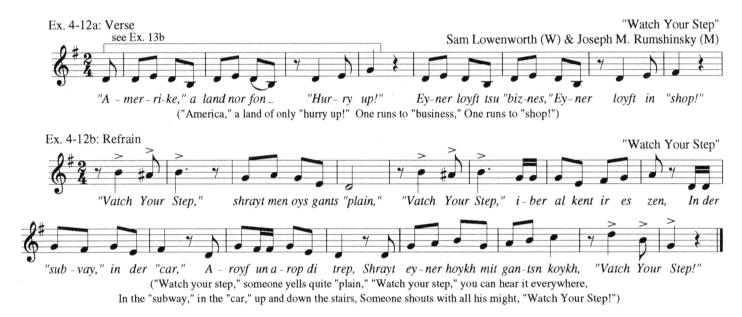

In 1914, eight years before Rumshinsky's show, Berlin wrote his first complete show score, *Watch Your Step*. There are more tangential connections than those in Exx. 4-12a and 4-12b, but they are not worlds apart (Exx. 4-13a and 4-13b).

Berlin was not the only big-timer to step inside a Second Avenue theater. Sometime in the 1920s Rumshinsky was rumored to be leaving Thomashefsky's National Theater. Sholom Secunda tells the story of how Thomashefsky then tried to get the young diamond-in-the-rough Gershwin and the older, more experienced Secunda to form a team, replacing Rumshinsky. Gershwin had, in Secunda's words, "no knowledge of music at all,"[10] and so Secunda was turned off; but, in theory, the partnership of a Tin Pan Alley neophyte and one "steeped in *Yiddishkeit*" could have been a working combination. The name Secunda, coming from klezmer terminology, means "second fiddle," which had to be a presentiment of things to come. Not only was Secunda destined to play second fiddle to Gershwin, but also, when it became part of the American mainstream, to his own best-known song, "Bay mir bist du sheyn." Elsewhere, Secunda claimed that "Gershwin never denied 'borrowing' from the old Goldfaden melodies."[11]

The proofs we do have of Gershwin's direct Jewish musical experience are: (1) the knowledge that he attended musical shows at the Yiddish theater, a venue steeped in Hasidic, klezmer, and cantorial music;[12] (2) his older brother's Bar Mitzvah training, which meant that George could have been privy to Ira's chanting lessons, and, at the least, that he must have attended the synagogue ceremony; (3) that he signed a contract to write an opera based on the venerable Yiddish play *The Dybbuk* for the Metropolitan Opera, but abandoned the project when he learned that the Italian composer Ludovico Roca had secured the rights. Gershwin biographer Isaac Goldberg asserts that he heard sketches for this opera (never found), and that of "Jewish folk music . . . [Gershwin] must have heard a-plenty." (4) A guest at a Passover seder is quoted as saying she heard "Gershwin and . . . Oscar Levant improvise . . . jazz versions of the traditional holiday melodies;[13] and (5) scattered amorphous statements by the composer, in tandem with some biographical claims that Gershwin's use of "blue" notes and minor thirds were Jewishly derived.

Furthermore, Rumshinsky says that he heard in the Catskills, circa 1916, the young Gershwin play selections from Rumshinsky's *Dos tsebrokhene fidele* (The Broken Fiddle). Apparently, George was so taken with the songs that he played them from memory. He told Rumshinsky that his parents often took him on their jaunts to Yiddish musicals. "Ten years later," Rumshinsky's account continues, "I met him again at a performance of my *Oy, iz dus a meydl*."[14] Although the title song (Ex. 4-14a) from this 1927 Molly Picon showcase may not resonate in any Gershwin song, it does ring bells in later pop songs. First, there is a 1953 jazz instrumental by Bernie Miller set to words, two years later, in collaboration with Mike Stoller and Jerry Lieber (Ex. 4-14b). Then, in that same year of 1955, Jerry Ross and Richard Adler unleashed a femme fatale from *Damn Yankees* (Ex. 4-14c), followed, one year after that, by Alfred Newman's title song from a film about another female (Ex. 4-14d).

At one end a *Yiddishe meydl* extolled by a Russian-born composer—Rumshinsky—and at the other, a Hollywood tribute by Newman to a Russian czarina. In between, a Tin Pan Alley guy and a Broadway doll—songs that all, in some way, feed each other. Absorption! A layer cake could be made of them, too. Newman had to be aware of "Lola," a smash hit. "Bernie's Tune" might have been known to Ross and Adler. But more fascinating is the backward glance Ross might have given to the *meydl* song. He was born (1926) Jerold Rosenberg in the Bronx, New York, and he was a child performer in the Yiddish theater, most likely Rumshinsky's.[15]

Ex. 4-14a
"Oy iz dus a meydl"
Molly Picon (W) & Joseph M. Rumshinsky (M)

Oy, iz dus a mey - dl,_____ A - za yor oyf mir,_____ Oy, iz dus a

mey - dl,_____ _____ Kh'bin far - libt in dir. _____
(Wow, what a girl. Such a year on me. [It should only happen to me.] Wow, what a girl, I'm in love with you.)

Ex. 4-14b
"Bernie's Tune"
Bernie Miller, Mike Stoller & Jerry Lieber

In the park, In___ the dark, Un-der-neath the moon,_____ Heard a boy and

___ a girl Hum - min' Ber - nie's Tune, _____

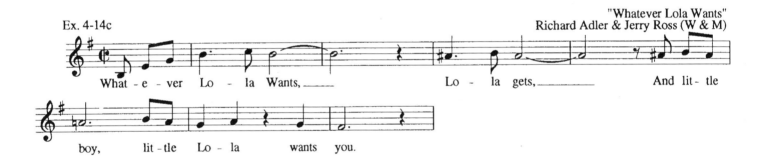

Ex. 4-14c
"Whatever Lola Wants"
Richard Adler & Jerry Ross (W & M)

What - e - ver Lo - la Wants,_____ Lo - la gets,_____ And lit - tle

boy, lit - tle Lo - la wants you.

Ex. 4-14d
"Anastasia"
Paul Francis Webster (W) & Alfred Newman (M)

A - na - sta - sia,_____ tell me who you are._____ Are you

some - one _____ from a - no - ther star ?_____

Jury members, are these songwriters to be held accountable to "Jewish-pru-dence"? The parallelisms cannot be regarded as conscious borrowings. Chasing the authorship of tunes, with all its twists and turns can sometimes be like getting lost in a maze.

Frank Sinatra was one of three authors of a 1951 potboiler that is almost a dead ringer for a tune about a Russian coachman—written by Y. L. Feldman—and sub-sequently translated into Yiddish as "Ferdele fli" (Fly Horsey):

A Yiddish folk song also uses the same configuration, but fuses the first phrase with the second phrase, placing the latter in the lower octave:

In Yiddish theater, the sequence was incorporated into the verse of a Rumshinsky love song about the moon (Ex. 4-17a), and in the Broadway theater it was transmuted into a haunting melody about the sun (from *Fiddler on the Roof*, Ex. 4-17b), both with the same sequential relationship, though the pitches vary from the Russian song:

In films, the sequence was the basis for yet another "fool" song, this time, "A Day in the Life of a Fool"—Carl Sigman's English version of the original Portuguese song by Antonio Mariz (W) and Luiz Bonfa (M) in the Brazilian movie *Black Orpheus*—and also for pinup movie stars Rita Hayworth and Betty Grable who warbled the same phrases in "I've Been Kissed Before," a tune by Bob Russell and Lester Lee from, respectively, *Affair in Trinidad* (1951) and *Three for the Show* (1955). In the 1956 film noir thriller *Nightmare*, actor Kevin McCarthy plays the part of a jazz musician who has a dilemma: did he or did he not commit murder? Herschel Burke Gilbert's use of the sequence in his background score helps McCarthy solve the mystery when it becomes a musical clue.

It is probable Sinatra was named an author of the 1951 pop song not because he offered something substantial to its creation, but because he promoted it into a hit, a practice fine-tuned into a science by Al Jolson.[16] The other two authors, Joel Herron and Jack Wolf, were more likely to have known the Russian and/or the Yiddish songs.[17] The middle section of "I'm a Fool to Want You" breaks out into another almost exact twin, but this time to the bridge section of the "Anniversary Song":

The correlation between the two bridge sections from these two songs cannot be dismissed as accidental. How common are such downward minor scale phrases in popular songs? Not very; and if they were, would they appear in midsection? An ethnic impulse of some kind is at work during the incubation period, even if only on a subliminal level.

"Anniversary Song" actually is an adaptation, made by Al Jolson and Saul Chaplin for the 1946 movie *The Jolson Story*, from a Romanian waltz called *Valurile Dunaril* (The Waves of the Danube) composed by Jon (Ian) Ivanovici.[18] This waltz was a perennial favorite with Jewish populations, Ivanovici's adapted melody is sung in honor of Cantor Yoelson and his wife, Al's parents, in the very popular Columbia motion picture and therefore was perceived to be a Jewish tune. One section from "The Waves of the Danube," not used in the "Anniversary Waltz" or in "I'm a Fool to Want You," was incorporated into the well-known Yiddish folk song "Tum-balalayke":

All this is a maze, to say nothing of amazing. It seems, then, that "I'm a Fool to Want You" is a synthesis of Russian-Romanian-Jewish sources. Further corroboration of such synthetic writing is found in a tune called "Take My Love" (1950) written by the same trio of authors, Sinatra, Herron and Wolf.[19] The fact that it was an adaptation of the slow movement theme from Brahms's Third Symphony was not acknowledged by them or the publisher.

The year cited in a copyright notice is not a reliable index to the date of composition. A song can go into print long after its completion in manuscript. Therefore the question of which of two songs came first can be a chicken versus egg puzzlement. What is more, access to, or knowledge of prior materials has to be proven in order to decide who is the borrower or the lender, virtually an impossible task.

While we are on the subject of Brahms, a vivid illustration of how this nettlesome problem can—or cannot—be pursued is to be found in the world of symphonic music. On a 1968 Young People's Concert, during a musical quiz with the New York Philharmonic, Leonard Bernstein at the piano asked his listeners to answer true or false to the statement: "The following two phrases are absolutely identical":

Ex. 4-20   From Young People's Concert No. 43: "Quiz, How Musical Are You?"

Did Bernstein pick these notes out of thin air or was he making a reference to Mozart's C-minor Piano Concerto, K491 (Ex. 4-21a).[20] Then, in his *Songfest* of 1977, was Bernstein making an allusion to the Mozart phrase in his setting of an Edna St. Vincent Millay poem (Ex. 4-21b)? Almost a decade later, in his last large work *Arias and Barcarolles* (1988), Bernstein again draws upon a variant of the same phrase, this time more completely (Ex. 4-21c):

These allusions by Bernstein to Mozart might be traceable to the Philharmonic quiz or to one of his symphonic concerts or to neither. A deliberate reference or an homage? Let us presume that it was conscious; but then must we hold Mozart himself accountable for the affinity between his Piano Concerto phrase and the opening of Haydn's *Symphony No. 78*, written four years earlier than Mozart's work?

Ex. 4-22   *Symphony No. 78*, Mvt. I
                                                                                         Haydn

The evidence is thorny, albeit fascinating. All that matters, really, are the common links from Haydn to Mozart to Bernstein; and, for that matter, from "Oy, iz dus a meydl" to "Anastasia," connective links that inherently appealed to the composers. This brings us to the fourth and final process of Americanizing ethnic materials, acculturation, which Eric Werner has defined as two cultural elements treated with equal value—as opposed to "assimilation," which he considers to be one of two cultures that is a priori higher. However, the buzz words "value" and "higher," confuse quantity with quality. No matter how small the Jewish cultural element may be, it still colors the import of the larger American context. More convincing is Patricia Erens's definition of acculturation as "the absorption of the dominant culture without the . . . loss of ethnic specificity."[21] Acculturation may be regarded as the stirring of ethnic fruit into American yogurt and the blending of both so that specific quotations are no longer distinguishable as much as they are recurring melodic patterns.

NOTES

1. A Yiddish song by Molly Picon and Joseph Rumshinsky called "Gilgl" (Wandering Soul) treats a wordless Hasidic *nign* as a theme for Russian trepak, American Charleston, and Israeli hora variations.

2. John Bartlett, *Bartlett's Familiar Quotations*, p. 924, no. 17. Perhaps "Yes, My Darling Daughter" was inspired by the 1937 Broadway play by Mark Reed of the same name, then a Warner Bros. film (1939). Textual equivalents can be found in folk songs from England: "Lazy Mary, Will You Get Up"?, France: "Maman, si veux-tu un bouquet," and in the Yiddish "Yome, Yome." The Lawrence adaptation was recorded in Yiddish by the Barry Sisters.

3. "Dona, Dona" came from the Yiddish musical *Esterk*, and was originally called "Dana, Dana, Dana."

4. Joachim Braun, *Jews and Jewish Elements in Soviet Music*, p. 80. See also *Entsiklopedicheskiy Muzykal'niy Slovar* [Encyclopedia of Slovak Music], 2nd ed. (Moscow, 1966).

5. Herman Yablokoff, *Der Payatz*, p. 469.

6. Bernard Rosenberg and Ernest Goldstein, eds. *Creators and Disturbers*, p. 139.

7. Joseph Rumshinsky, *Klangen fun mayn lebn*, p. 547. Quoted in Israel Rabinovitch, *Of Jewish Music*, p. 227. Rumshinsky's papers are housed at the UCLA Music Library.

8. E. Anthony Rotundo, "Jews and Rock and Roll: A Study in Cultural Contrast," *American Jewish History* 72 (no. 1,1982): 82-107.

9. "When a Kid Who Came from the East Side Found a Sweet Society Rose" (1926) by Al Dubin (W) and Jimmy McHugh (M) was a tribute to their (inter)marriage over the objections of her father, millionaire Clarence H. McKay, an anti-Semite.

10. Joseph Landis, ed., *Memories of the Yiddish Theater*, pp. 122-128.

11. Sholom Secunda, letter to the author dated 31 August 1971.

12. A letter dated 15 April 1933 from Gershwin to Milton Weintraub, Esq. relates he had seen the classic Yiddish play *Yoshe Kalb* at the Yiddish Art Theater.

13. Re *Dybbuk* sketches, see Isaac Goldberg, "What's Jewish in Gershwin's Music?," *B'nai B'rith Magazine* (1936): 226. Seder observation was reported by Kitty Carlisle Hart, in

"Embraceable Jew," *The Jewish Week*, 8 June 2001, p. 36.

14. Rumshinsky, *Klangen fun mayn lebn*, p. 674.

15. The rise and fall of the melodic curve in Joseph Achron's wistful *Hebrew Melody* for violin and orchestra haunts Jerry Ross's melancholy ballad, "Near to You" from *Damn Yankees*.

16. In all fairness, however, it should be noted that Jolson donated his ASCAP song royalties to a rest home for show business folk in Northbrook, New York. Mentioned on radio station WNEW, 4 January 1990, *Les Davis Show*.

17. Herron also wrote a tune called "Sh'lom Bait" [sic, Household Peace], a Hebrew expression.

18. A Yiddish version of "Anniversary Song," called "Nokh eyn tantz" (One More Dance, words by Chaim Towber) claims the melody to be by Emil Waldteufel, composer of "The Skater's Waltz."

19. "Take My Love" is not to be confused with the 1954 song of the same name by Helen Deutsch (W) and Bronislau Kaper (M).

20. Bernstein conducted the Mozart Piano Concerto three times at New York Philharmonic concerts, with soloists Rudolf Firkušnỳ (1956), Glenn Gould (1959), and Daniel Barenboim (1973).

21. Patricia Erens, *The Jew in American Cinema*, p. 10.

CHAPTER 5

The Wandering Gypsy

Rose: "You name a big city and we've played it!" Louise: "Grandpa says we've covered the country like Gypsies!"

ARTHUR LAURENTS, *Gypsy*, Act II

Acculturation–By Way of an Idiomatic Musical Formula

Lola's siren song from *Damn Yankees* (see Ex. 4-16c) contains a cluster of notes that rotate on the dominant axis of the key—that is, on the fifth note: "Whatever Lola wants Lo. . . ." This inverted S turn (~) is a seductive swivel, and, in fact, is a cliché in Slavic and Russian-Gypsy music. To wit, from Dvořák's Second Slavonic Rhapsody:

Ex. 5-1

Slavonic Rhapsody No.2
Antonin Dvořák

"Otchi chorniya" (Dark Eyes, Ex. 5-2a), the Russian-gypsy ballad—derived from a waltz possibly written by a Jew (not clear)[1]—begins with this motif. Originally a cabaret number, "Dark Eyes" became so widespread that songwriters could not resist taking potshots at it (Ex.5- 2b):

Ex. 5-2a

"Otchi chorniya"

O - tchi   chor - ny-ia,   O - tchi strast - ny-ia,   O- tchi zhgu -tchi-ya,   Yi   pre - kras - ni-ya,
(Dark eyes, passionate eyes, burning eyes, and so beautiful,)

Ex. 5-2b

"Leonora", Abner Silver

Le - on - or - a,   Le - on - or - a,   I   a - dore   ya,   Le - on - or - a!

In 1940, Russian-born L. Wolfe Gilbert, author of "Waiting for the Robert E. Lee," wrote a parody of "Di Greene Koseene" [sic] that had *Otchi chorniya* in its lyric, further proof that Russian sources were often identified with Yiddish exporters:

> Can she sing that Greene my *koseene?*/*Orchy chornya* [sic]with a concertina,
> Dances very light just like a feather,/Lots of times we finish both together.
> Can she cook that Greene my *koseene?*/Anything excepting pork and beene,
> She can make a noodle soup with *luckshn*,/Looking like an M.G.M. production.

In "Could You Use Me?"—from Gershwin's *Girl Crazy* (1930)—the leading lady envisions an ideal suitor, "There is one *in Cal-i-for*-ni-a/More roman-*tic far than you*/When he sings 'Ha-cha-cha-chor-ni-a'/I often think he'll do."[2] The music uses the motive of "Otchi Chorniya" on the italicized syllables, but not on the dominant pivot of the key. The film world was particularly enamored of "Otchi Chorniya," quoting it extensively in movies ranging from Paul Whiteman's band in *King of Jazz* (1930) to Gloria Jean's girlish warbling in *Never Give a Sucker an Even Break* (1941) to Kathryn Grayson's patrician coloratura in *It Happened in Brooklyn* (1947). As recently as 1999, the durable ballad appeared in *Taxman*, another Brooklyn film, this one about the Russian mafiosi in the Brighton Beach quarter. Spike Jones did "Hotcha Cornia," a zany spoof in *Thank Your Lucky Stars* (1943). Fred Astaire, playing a pretender-Russian, greets Ginger Rogers in the 1937 Gershwin film *Shall We Dance?* with a thick-accented salutation of "Otchi chorniya." As a music box tune, the ballad supplies an important plot point in the classic 1940 Ernst Lubitsch film comedy *The Shop Around the Corner*.[3] Even Louis Armstrong got into the act and recorded it Dixieland style, rhyming *chorniya* with *caldonia* (the latter alluding to Fleecie Moore's 1945 hit title).

A doleful Russian ballad from the repertoire of "Harry Horlick and His A & P Gypsies"—a radio performing group from the late 1920s to the mid-1930s—also toys with this twisting figuration. (An English version of this ballad was sung by Marina Koshetz in the 1946 film *No Leave, No Love*.)

(The highpoint of Ex. 5-3 corresponds to a cadential leitmotif—the interval of a descending 4th followed by the step of a 2nd—prominently associated in synagogue music with the High Holy Days and other major Jewish holidays.[4])

The gypsy motif traveled from Moscow to Berlin, where Kurt Weill embraced it in a song from *The Threepenny Opera*, which also peaks with the Jewish leitmotif (Ex. 5-4a). In another *Threepenny Opera* number, Weill inverts the order of the two groupings, first the Jewish holiday leitmotif and then, five bars later, the gypsy motive (Ex. 5-4b):

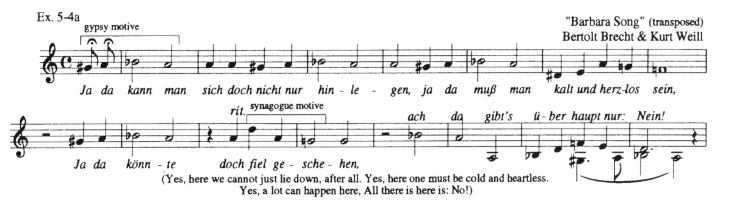

Ex. 5-4b · synagogue motive

"Anstatt-daß"
Bertolt Brecht & Kurt Weill

An - statt daß   an - statt daß,   sie zu Hau-se blei-ben und im war-men Bett,

gypsy motive

brau-chen sie Spaß,   brau-chen sie Spaß,   grad als ob man ih - nen ei - ne Ex-tra-wurst ge-bra-ten hätt'.

(Instead of this, you're staying home in your warm bed,
You need fun, just as if someone had cooked up a special wurst for you.)

From the city of Berlin the gypsy peregrinator journeyed to Paris where it made camp in a song by Norbert Glantzberg that was popularized by Edith Piaf:

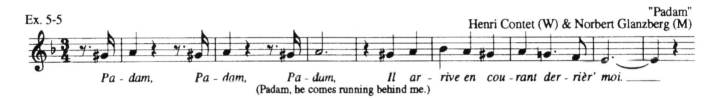

Ex. 5-5

"Padam"
Henri Contet (W) & Norbert Glanzberg (M)

Pa - dam,   Pa - dam,   Pa - dum,   Il ar - rive en cou - rant der - rièr' moi. ___
(Padam, he comes running behind me.)

A partial echo of all this wandering from country to country can be heard as far back as the so-called *Tonus Peregrinus* (Wandering Tone) of the Roman rite:[5]

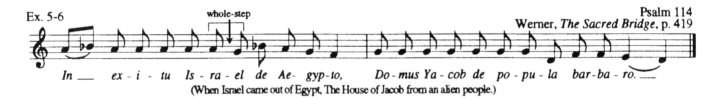

Ex. 5-6   whole-step

Psalm 114
Werner, *The Sacred Bridge*, p. 419

In ___ ex - i - tu Is - ra - el de Ae - gyp-to,   Do - mus Ya - cob de po - pu - la bar - ba - ro. ___
(When Israel came out of Egypt, The House of Jacob from an alien people.)

A documentary filmmaker points out: "Gypsies and Jews [in the Carpathian mountains of Ukraine] were treated like pariahs . . . Gypsies learned Yiddish and Jews learned the Gypsy language, *Romani*. And there was plenty of cross-fertilization musically."[6] Jewish Middle Eastern modes coupled with dance rhythms of Romania, Russia, and Poland interacted with the Northern India modes of Gypsies. In Spain, both Sephardic and Gypsy musical materials stimulated the development of Flamenco music; and in all likelihood the *fados* of Portugal, the *tangos* of Argentina and the *amanes* of Greece all, in some way, were impregnated by Gypsy-Jewish sonorities.

Through sheer usage by Jewish composers, the gypsy motive became acculturated as a *meydl dreydl* (loosely, twisting girl). Going abroad, she was displayed on Tin Pan Alley in songs like "Play Fiddle Play" and "When a Gypsy Makes His Violin Cry" (Ex. 5-7), both by Emery Deutsch:

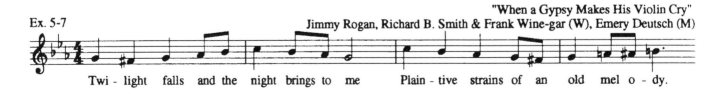

"When a Gypsy Makes His Violin Cry"
Ex. 5-7   Jimmy Rogan, Richard B. Smith & Frank Wine-gar (W), Emery Deutsch (M)

Twi - light falls and the night brings to me   Plain - tive strains of an old mel o - dy.

A 1930 musical joke by Walter Doyle (Ex. 5-8a) has the gypsy motive serving as a commentary on a college song popularized by Rudy Vallee (Ex. 5-8b), but here put into minor and inverted:

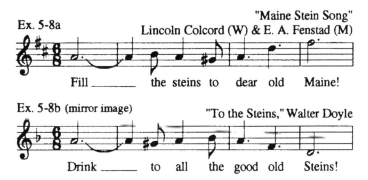

It continues, "Drink to Bernstein, Bornstein, Braunstein, and Eisenstein. . . ." You get the point.

On Broadway the gypsy sound was featured as early as the late nineteenth century in "Mister Dooley," from *A Chinese Honeymoon*, by William Jerome (W) and Jean Schwartz (M), and in the *czardas* "Romany Life," from *The Fortune Teller* by Victor Herbert. But these were merely warm-up exercises for this lofty gent in *Fiddler on the Roof*:

The gypsy benchmark thus achieves *yikhes* (pedigree) and is imbedded elsewhere in the musical in Tevya's "If I Were a Rich Man" on the words "Posing problems that would cross a Rabbi's eyes."

In the Yiddish theater, all the music makers fell under the gypsy's alluring spell—Itzik Manger in *An oreme tsigaynerl* (A Poor Little Gypsy), Adolph King in *Der yidisher vanderer* (The Jewish Wanderer), Abe Ellstein in *Ikh viles hern nokhamol* (I Want to Hear It Again), and *Mazl* (Luck) and Sholom Secunda in *A sheyner kholem* (A Beautiful Dream). Alexander Olshanetsky also used the gypsy motive in "Azoy vi du bist" (Just As You Are), a 1943 song written in the same vein as the 1943 Latin-American tango "Besame Mucho"[7] (Ex. 5-10a). It could be that the popularity of the latter influenced Olshanetzky. Near the end of their respective bridge sections, even the sentiments of the Spanglish and Yiddish songs converge (Ex. 5-10b).

Joseph Rumshinsky and Molly Picon were also bitten by the gypsy moth, first in *Dos tsigayner meydl* of 1925 (The Gypsy Girl, book by Joseph Lateiner) and then one year later in a song from yet another show, *Der kleynem mazik* (The Little Devil, book by A. Nager), produced at Kessler's Second Avenue Theater (Ex. 5-11).[8]

Traveling west to America, the gypsy was to be found in the café scene of Charlie Chaplin's *Modern Times* (1938); and then, in the eponymous song for the 1946 movie *Golden Earrings*, a Paramount Pictures vehicle for Marlene Dietrich. But now the lower neighbor-note to the pivot-note of G is F, not F sharp (Ex. 5-12).

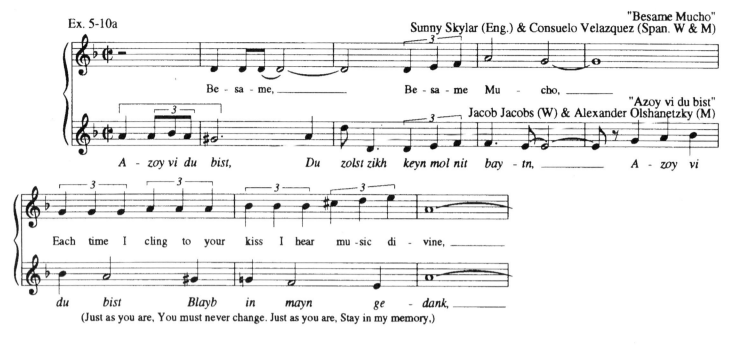

Ex. 5-10a

"Besame Mucho"
Sunny Skylar (Eng.) & Consuelo Velazquez (Span. W & M)

Be - sa - me, _____ Be - sa - me Mu - cho, _____

"Azoy vi du bist"
Jacob Jacobs (W) & Alexander Olshanetzky (M)

A - zoy vi du bist, Du zolst zikh keyn mol nit bay - tn, _____ A - zoy vi

Each time I cling to your kiss I hear mu - sic di - vine, _____

du bist Blayb in mayn ge - dank, _____
(Just as you are, You must never change. Just as you are, Stay in my memory,)

Ex. 5-10b: Bridge

"Besame Mucho"

Who e - ver thought I'd be hold - ing you close to me, Whis-p'ring it's you I a - dore.

"Azoy vi du bist"

Ver hot zikh den ge - gloybt az ikh zol a - za glik gor der - kri - khn. _____
(Who would have thought I would have such happiness come to me.)

Ex. 5-11

"Vu iz mayn zivig?"
Molly Picon (W) & Joseph M. Rumshinsky (M)

"Vu iz mayn zi - vig?" _____ fregt ye - des mey-de-le, _____ "Ver vet mikh

ru - fn _____ zayn ersh - te ley-de-le?" _____
("Where is my intended?," asks every girl. "Who will call me his First Lady?")

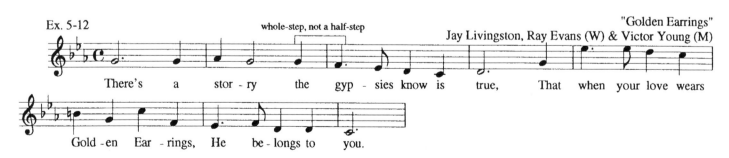

Ex. 5-12

whole-step, not a half-step

"Golden Earrings"
Jay Livingston, Ray Evans (W) & Victor Young (M)

There's a stor - ry the gyp - sies know is true, That when your love wears

Gold - en Ear - rings, He be - longs to you.

The movie song comes some twenty years after the Yiddish theater song, but Molly could have easily switched places with Marlene, an act no more ridiculous than a heavily made up Dietrich impersonating a gypsy. With some finagling of the

rhythms to accommodate the syllabification, and with the restoration of the half
step to F sharp, here is how Molly might have sung "Golden Earrings" in Yiddish:

In 1934, Howard Dietz and Arthur Schwartz in their revue *Revenge with Music*,
introduced the gypsy, now utterly absorbed into high society. The pitches, instead
of being ordered 1-2-1-3, are anagrammed as 1-2-3-1. Schwartz additionally
evokes the High Holy Day cadence on the words "flaming desire":

The gypsy can be a fortune teller (Ex. 5-12) or a fortune hunter (Ex. 5-14), a
quick change artist who changes her tune with the territory. She seems also to
materialize in the opening of Nacio Herb Brown's "Love Is Where You Find It"
(see Chapter 11) and Irving Berlin's "White Christmas." But they do not qualify
since Brown's impersonator-gypsy pivots on the tonic (first) note of its key and
Berlin's rotates on the mediant. A bona fide gypsy revolves on the dominant step,
after the fashion of a famous cadence:

There are numerous examples of tunes which begin by twirling on the dominant, but they also cannot be considered legitimate gypsies. They range from F. E.
Bigelow's 1895 march "Our Director" to Euday Bowman's "Twelfth Street Rag"
of 1919 to later pop songs:[9]

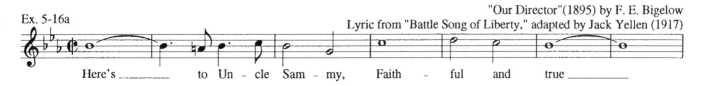

Ex. 5-16b — "12th Street Rag" (Trio) by Euday L. Bowman (1919)

Ex. 5-16c — "Roll out the Barrel"
Lew Brown, Władimir A. Timm, Vaclav Zeman & Jaromir Vejvoda (1939)
Roll out The Bar-rel, _____ We'll have a bar-rel of fun, _____

Ex. 5-16d — "A Gay Ranchero"
Francia Luban, Abe Tuvim (W) & J. J. Espinosa (M) (1936)
A _ Gay Ran-cher-o, a _ cab-al-ler-o, Can _ al-ways find some-one to pet, _____

Ex. 5-16e — "With a Song in My Heart"
Richard Rodgers & Lorenz Hart (1929)
With a Song in My Heart, _____ I be-hold your a - dor - a - ble face,

Ex. 5-16f — "Mona Lisa"
Jay Livingston & Ray Evans (1949)
Mo - na Li - sa, Mo - na Li - sa, men have named you

Ex. 5-16g — "Some Enchanted Evening"
Richard Rodgers & Oscar Hammerstein II (1949)
Some En-chant-ed Eve - ning _____ You may see a strang - er, _____

The twirling also occurs on secondary phrases of other songs—all of them built on
the half step below the fifth, but with a whole step above it:

Ex. 5-17a — "Whispering"
Malvin & John Schonberger (1920)
Whis - per-ing while you cud-dle near me, Whis - per-ing so no one can hear me,

Ex. 5-17b — "Ain't We Got Fun?"
Gus Kahn (W) & Richard A. Whiting (M) (1921)
Ev' - ry morn - ing, ev' - ry eve - ning, Ain't We Got fun? Not much mon -ey,
Oh, but hon - ey, Ain't We Got Fun? The rent's un - paid, dear, _____

Ex. 5-17c — "Side by Side," Harry Woods (1927)
Oh! we ain't got a bar-rel of mon - ey, May-be we're rag-ged and fun - ny,

Or take the Notre Dame *team* song and Rudy Vallee's *theme* song, both of which begin by twirling their batons on the third step:

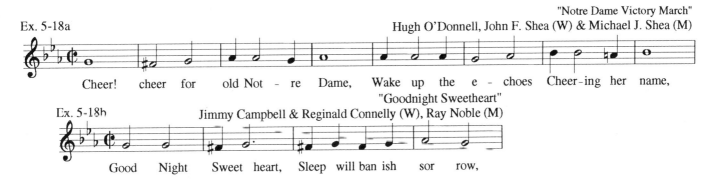

But look what happens when the same half-step pattern of the opening is transferred to the subsequent passage on the fifth step:

Obviously, neither song veers off into *mittel-Europa* by going to C-flat (the note with the x inside in the above-cited musical examples). No, they stay comfortably put, middle-American with C-natural.

The Charm of the Flatted Sixth–Jewish Coloration

That whole step, on the sixth note of the scale, makes all these examples sound "WASPy." When the sixth step (a.k.a. the submediant, but don't ask why) in a major key is flattened, the music takes on a beguiling quality, major in the bottom half—called tetrachord in theoretical terminology— and minor in the top half. But when the submediant of the last five excerpts that make up Ex. 5-16 are lowered a half-step, the gypsy emerges: half steps both below and above, which is to say, the fourth step is raised and the sixth step is flattened:

Broadway writers also have been bewitched by the gypsy, viz., Bock and Harnick in their Hungarian-flavored score for the show *She Loves Me*, Kurt Weill and Ira Gershwin in "Tchaikovsky (and Other Russians)" from *Lady in the Dark*; but these examples of acculturation are ethnically specific.

Irving Berlin, on the other hand, acculturated the gypsy so that all traces of her European origins were erased. In the 1947 movie *Easter Parade*, he Americanized these foreign elements in a dance number for Ann Miller and Fred Astaire. The first phrase starts on the third step of the scale; the subsequent phrase begins on the fifth (Ex. 5-21). Try the example with the sixth step not flatted (i.e., C-natural instead of C-flat), and poof, the gypsy sound is eliminated! That little half step of the lowered sixth step makes all the difference in the (New) world. That difference is the Jewish connection, albeit a highly acculturated one.

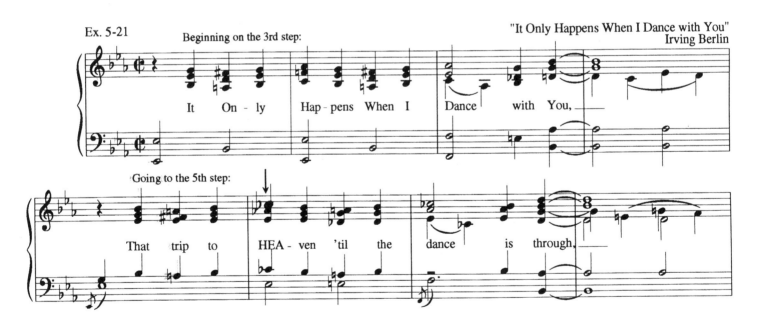

Latin-American composers have also exploited the gypsy for exotic coloration as in, for example, the Brazilian "Tico-Tico," (Ex. 5-22a) and the Argentinian "Dream Tango" (Ex. 5-22b). Although it was not typical of Vincent Youmans to write in the gypsy mode, he did something like it in the verse of "Carioca," for the film *Flying Down to Rio*. (However, the half step lower neighbor tone, A-natural in this instance, is missing). The minor mode of the "Carioca" opening turns to major in the chorus, a typical device of Jewish novelty songs. Perhaps Youmans was influenced by his Jewish collaborators, and/or the fact that the number was danced by blacks in an otherwise all-white cast, including the then new dance partnership of Fred Astaire and Ginger Rogers.

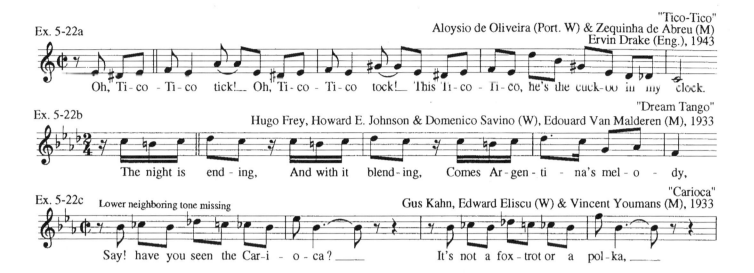

Similarly, there is something off center when the very non-Jewish Noël Coward (1899-1973) spoofs "The Stately Homes of England" by using the gypsy motive. One of his verse couplets in this number goes: "Our homes extend extensive views/ . . . with the assistance of the Jews." But the gypsy sound is not such an odd tack when wielded by the non-Jewish Hollywood composer Harry Warren in a production number for the 1933 film *Moulin Rouge* (Ex. 5-23a). Seven years earlier, Alexander Olshanetsky, in his score for a Yiddish operetta, *In gartn fun libe* (In the Garden of Love), includes a song (Ex. 5-23b) that is a kissing cousin to the acculturated gypsy strain in Warren's dirge for down-and-out losers. Contrast the two:

Harry Warren, born in Brooklyn of Italian parents as Salvatore Guaragna (literally, Meritorious Savior) once pointed out that his song "Would You Like to Take a Walk?"— from the show *Sweet and Low*—was subconsciously "stolen" from a *Laudaumus Te* he sang as a choir boy in church. It follows that other sounds from his early years must have entered his memory bank. He "worked [as a vendor] at the Liberty Theater in Brownsville when the great Jacob P. Adler ran the Yiddish stock company there."[11] From that experience alone, sounds of Yiddish songs must have lodged in his inner ear. Catholic-Italian by descent, he became Jewish-American by association. In fact, he spoke a smattering of Yiddish, and before his Hollywood days, he even wrote a song in Yiddish (see Chapter 6).

In addition to "The Boulevard of Broken Dreams," idiomatic contours of Jewish melody can be detected in other movie songs of his, tunes such as "At Last" (from the film *Orchestra Wives*, 1942) and the title song for the 1932 movie *Forty-Second Street*. Perhaps Warren, consciously or not, was making commentary on the fact that, in its heyday, the street was chock-full of legitimate theaters run by Jews. Put the song up against the Jewish camp song "Shalom chaverim" (So Long, Friends) and the kinship is unmistakable:

Ex. 5-24

Strange bedfellows? Not when you consider that "Shalom chaverim" has leapt over other unexpected national borders. A popular singing star from Venezuela, Jose Luis Rodriguez—better known as El Puma—adapted it into Spanish, adding a verse. In the song, known simply as "Shalom," the singer bids adios to Jezebel, his Jerusalem lover, as he goes off to war (presumably in Israel).

Composer-theorist Milton Babbitt has said that Harry Warren was the most "non-Jewish Jew" he ever met.[12] Confirmation of this oxymoron is easily obtained by viewing the finales of two 1933 movie musicals with songs by Warren and Al Dubin: "Shangai Lil" from *Footlight Parade* (in which a bit player with a Yiddish inflection says: "Looking for mine in Palestine") and "My Forgotten Man" from *Gold Diggers of 1933*, a classic social commentary on World War I veterans down on their luck because of the Depression.

* * *

The poignant charm of the flatted 6th is revealed in the following mainstream examples from American pop music. First, a Tin Pan Alley song by George Fragos and Jack Baker, then from Broadway, in Cole Porter's show *Kiss Me Kate*, and

Illustration 1
Abraham Zvi Idelsohn (left) and Eric Werner

Illustration 2
"The Sorrowing Jew," (below) Song Cover.
(Courtesy of the American Jewish Archive,
Cincinnati, Ohio)

Illustration 3

Advertisement from a *Delaney Songster*, 1906

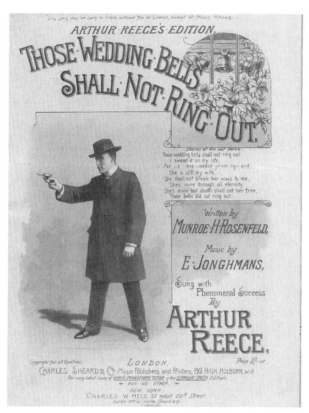

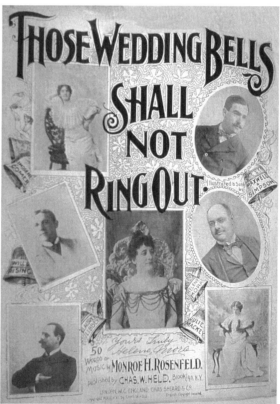

Illustration 4
Monroe H. Rosenfeld and three covers of "Those Wedding Bells Shall Not Ring Out."
(Cover of man with gun from the Lester S. Levy Collection of Sheet Music, Johns Hopkins University)

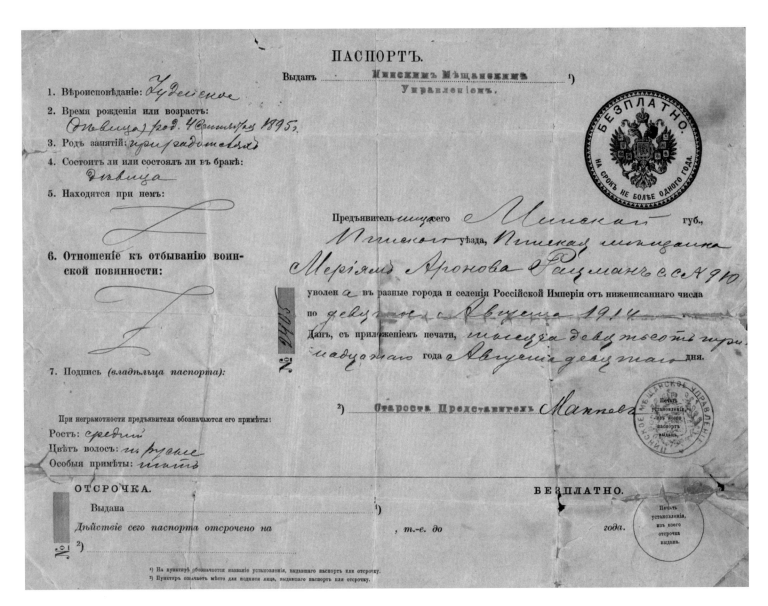

Illustration 5
A Russian passport issued to my mother's sister,
Miriam Aronova Ratzman, age 19 in 1913, who died in 1990,
age 95. It allowed my Aunt Minnie restricted travel
from Pinsk to other parts of Russia for
a period of one year. To be sure,
her religion is the first item cited.

Leopold Auer

Illustration 6
Leopold Auer, the teacher
and his students
who are the subject of
the Gershwin brothers'
song "Mischa, Jascha,
Sascha, Toscha."

Mischa Elman

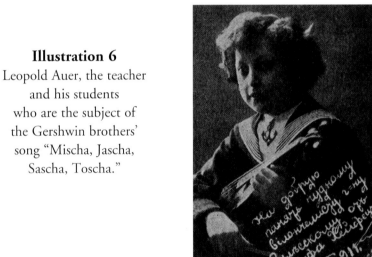

Jascha Heifetz

Sascha Jacobsen

Toscha Seidel

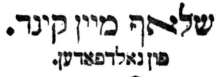

1.

שלאָף אין פריידען

דיא ווייסט קיין ליידען

שלאָף=זשע שלאָף מיין קינד

שלאָף מיין פּינעלע

מאך צו דאָס איינעלע

שלאָף=זשע שלאָף געזונד.

2.

דער שלאָף דער גיטער

וויא אַ היטער

שטעהט ביי דיר ביז פריה.

מיט זיין פליגעלע

אויף דיין ווינעלע

דעקט ער שטיל דיך צ׳א.

3.

וועסט נאָך אויך נעפּעלללען

צווישען אלע מאמזעלען

וועסט זיך רערהען אהער און אהין

Illustration 7

The original Yiddish text for "Shlof mayn kind" by Abraham Goldfaden corresponds to Ex. 2-3.
From *Di Idishe Bihne* (The Jewish Stage) (New York: J. Katzenelenbogen, 1897), p. 171.

Form 2203
Department of Commerce and Labor
NATURALIZATION SERVICE

No. ....

M-124-117.

TRIPLICATE
[To be given to the person making the Declaration]

UNITED STATES OF AMERICA

DECLARATION OF INTENTION

(Invalid for all purposes seven years after the date hereof)

State of New York, }
County of New York, } ss.:

In the Supreme Court of New York County.

I, Morris Gottlieb ...., aged ...22... years,

occupation ...Tailor......................................, do declare on oath that my personal

description is: Color ...white..., complexion ...fair..., height 5 feet 7 inches,

weight ...140... pounds, color of hair ...brown..., color of eyes ...gray...

other visible distinctive marks ...none...

I was born in ...Pinsk, Russia...

on the ...12th... day of ...June..., anno Domini 1.890.; I now reside

at ...255 Broome Street... (Give number and street.), New York City, N. Y.

I emigrated to the United States of America from ...Rotterdam, Holland...

on the vessel ...Noordam... (If the alien arrived otherwise than by vessel, the character of conveyance or name of transportation company should be given.); my last

foreign residence was ...Pinsk, Russia...

It is my bona fide intention to renounce forever all allegiance and fidelity to any foreign

prince, potentate, state, or sovereignty, and particularly to ...Nicholas II,...

...Emperor of all the Russias..., of which I am now a subject; I

arrived at the port of ...New York..., in the

State of ...New York..., on or about the ...10th... day

of ...July..., anno Domini 1.909.; I am not an anarchist; I am not a

polygamist nor a believer in the practice of polygamy; and it is my intention in good faith

to become a citizen of the United States of America and to permanently reside therein:

SO HELP ME GOD.

Morris Gottlieb
(Original signature of declarant.)

Subscribed and sworn to before me at New York City, N. Y., this

[SEAL]

...7th... day of ...January...

anno Domini 1913.

WILLIAM F. SCHNEIDER,
Clerk of the Supreme Court.
DEPUTY

By *Philip Schneider*, Special Clerk.

11—3778

Illustration 8

Certificate of my father's intention to become a U.S. citizen in 1913. Note
the oath of renunciation to Czar Nicholas II. In 2000, the Moscow-
based Russian Orthodox Church canonized Nicholas and his family as martyrs.
In the 1920s, the church outside of Russia had already canonized him.

Illustration 9

Frontispiece from *Oisgabe Yubilatum: Di Idishe Bihne* (Jubilee Edition: The Jewish
Stage, 1897). A celebration of Abraham Goldfaden's founding of the Yiddish Theater
(1876). Goldfaden's portrait appears at middle top. Operettas in clockwise order:
Bar Kochba, Bhlimele,* The Yiddish King Lear,* and *Shulamith.**
Asterisked titles are discussed in this book. Note the view of the world, which consists of
Russia, Romania, Galicia, and Africa on the left, and North America on the right.

Illustration 10
As they say in French, *Chacun* [Schack-Cohen?] *a son goût.*

Illustration 11
Willie and Eugene Howard, vaudeville stars.

Illustration 12a
From a set of sixteen illustrated song slides (no. 2) for
"Love Me to a Yiddisha Melody" (1911)
and the musical phrase to which it corresponds.

Ex. 3-18: Verse

"Love Me to a Yiddisha Melody"
Joe Young & Edgar Leslie

Pa- trick J. O'-Brien met Sa -die__ Katz- en - stein, At a mas- quer -ade brought her wine, So fine, Oy!

Illustration 12b

From a set of sixteen illustrated song slides (no. 6) for
"Love Me to a Yiddisha Melody" (1911)
and the muscial phrase to which it corresponds.
Note Sadie holding a copy of "Kol nidrei."

Ex. 3-19: Refrain

"Love Me to a Yiddisha Melody"
Joe Young & Edgar Leslie

Oh! you Kid - di - sha, Love Me to a Yid-di-sha __ Mel - o - dy.

Illustration 13
From a set of fifteen illustrated song slides
(this one is no. 10)
for Irving Berlin's "Yiddle, On Your Fiddle, Play
Some Ragtime."

Illustration 14a
From the verse of "Yiddle, On Your Fiddle, Play Some Ragtime."
From a set of fifteen illustrated song slides (no. 2)
and the musical phrase to which it corresponds.

Ex. 6-5

"Yiddle, On Your Fiddle, Play Some Ragtime"
Irving Berlin

Ev' - ry - one was sing - ing, dan - cing, spring - ing, At a wed - ding yes - ter - day,

Yid - dle, on his fid - dle, played some rag - time, And when Sa - die heard him play,

Illustration 14b
From the chorus of "That Swaying Harmony."
From a set of sixteen illustrated song slides (no. 3),
a composite that uses "Yiddle, On Your Fiddle" on the right side
and the musical phrase to which it corresponds.

Ex. 6-6

"That Swaying Harmony"
Charles K. Harris

That Sway - ing Har - mon - y, ____ It's sweet mu - sic's so en - tran - cing, ____ That

Illustration 15a

From the chorus of "The Band Played On."
From a set of four illustrated song slides (no. 3). The song was written in 1895,
but the slides, incorporating "Yiddle, On Your Fiddle" in the background
(image reversed!), was made after 1909. The lyrics of the musical phrase to which it
corresponds also were later altered to:

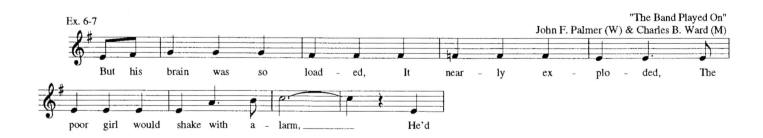

Illustration 15b
From the verse of "Yiddle, On Your Fiddle, Play Some Ragtime."
From a set of fifteen illustrated song slides (no. 6)
and the musical phrase to which it corresponds.
This was the background in Illustration 15a.

Ex. 6-8

"Yiddle, On Your Fiddle, Play Some Ragtime"
Irving Berlin

Yid - dle, in the mid - dle of your fid - dle, play some rag - time, Get

bu - sy, I'm diz - zy, I'm feel - ing two years young, Mine choc' - late

Illustration 16
Note the sheet music cover on the stand—a promotional selling point.
From a set of fourteen illustrated song slides (no. 12)
for "My Little Yiddisha Queen" (1909)
and the musical phrase to which it corresponds.

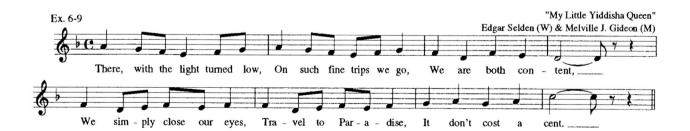

Ex. 6-9

"My Little Yiddisha Queen"
Edgar Selden (W) & Melville J. Gideon (M)

There, with the light turned low, On such fine trips we go, We are both con - tent,____

We sim - ply close our eyes, Tra - vel to Par - a - dise, It don't cost a cent.____

Illustration 17
No. 7, from a set of eleven illustrated song
slides, which corresponds
to the start of the refrain for "Shine on
Harvest Moon" (1908).

Illustration 18
Cover and chorus of "The Yiddisha Rag"
(1909).

Ex. 7-31

"The Yiddisha Rag" (1909)
Joseph H. McKeon, Harry M. Piano & W. Raymond Walker

Yid-dish-a, Yid-dish-a Rag, Oh, oh that Yid-dish-a Rag, ___

Wig-gle and jig-gle when you feel that strain, ___ Ev-'ry-one hol-lers: "Please play it a-gain." ___

"Hatikvah"

First there came Top-lit-zky dan-cing with his Rif-ky, They did the Ka-zat-sky, Oh my!

That is a dan-dy rag, That is the can-dy rag, That is the Yid-dish-a Rag.

finally from Hollywood, Victor Young's classic "Stella by Starlight"(from the movie *The Uninvited*):

All three songs date from the 1940s. In earlier years the flatted 6th makes rare appearances. In 1937, an Academy Award-nominated song by Robert Wright and Chet Forrest (W) and Edward Ward (M) was mouthed by Joan Crawford in the movie *Mannequin*: "Always and Always/I'll go on ador-*ing*" [flatted 6th]. Also from the forties, there is Rodgers and Hammerstein's ardent ballad from *Oklahoma*, "Out of my dreams and into the hush of evening sha-*dows*" [flatted 6th]. Otherwise, the interval is an anomaly in the American sound, with the inevitable exceptions of Berlin and Gershwin. Berlin makes poignant use of it in a 1924 ballad that alternates minor and major submediants. A single flatted 6th at the end of a 1930 Gershwin standard lends an ache to a song that would otherwise have less longing:

Later examples can be heard in Frank Loesser's "Inchworm," from the movie *Hans Christian Andersen* (1952): "Two and two *are* four . . .," and in the Eliot Daniel (M)-Harold Adamson (W) 1953 theme for the television comedy series *I Love Lucy*: "Lucy kisses like no one can/She's my missus and I'm her *man*."

A major scale—let's say, starting on D—with a lowered sixth step (in the key of D, the pitch of B becomes B-flat) produces a mixed mode, major in the lower tetrachord and minor in the upper one. This is a characteristic orientalism straight out of the Jewish melodic tradition. Furthermore, to compound the mixture, if the second step (E or E-flat) is omitted, we cannot tell if we are in the major or minor mode until we cross over into the upper tetrachord:

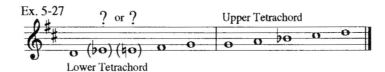

"Yascha Michaeloffsky's Melody," an obscure Berlin tune from 1928, exploits these ambiguities, first using B-flat and then B-natural, resulting in a hybrid Jewish-American tune. In the bridge section the flatted supertonic (i.e., E-flat) appears, but only in the upper octave:

The Jewishness of "Yascha Michaeloffsky's Melody" would be complete if Berlin had put the supertonic E-flat in the lower octave, D-E-flat-F-sharp-G-A-B-flat-C-sharp(or C-natural?)-D. But Berlin meant the tune to be ambiguous, preferring to keep Yascha's sources a veiled mystery. A strange tune, indeed, and quite unlike anything else on the American scene.

NOTES

1. See James Fuld, *The Book of World-Famous Music*, p. 417.

2. A line in "The Wonder of You," a Tin Pan Alley tune of 1945 by Duke Ellington and Johnny Hodges with words by Don George, similarly avers: "I've whistled Ochy Chornia/Spent June in California." (Not to be confused with the 1958 "Wonder of You" by Baker Knight.)

3. With a score by Werner R. Heymann, a refugee from Nazi Germany, *The Shop Around the Corner* was recycled twice as a musical film *In the Good Old Summertime* (1949) and then as *You've Got Mail* (1998). In 1963 it appeared on Broadway as *She Loves Me,* the confectionary musical comedy.

4. See Abraham Idelsohn, *The Jewish Song Book*, pp. 200 and 298 for the gypsy motive, and pp. 158 and 162 for samples of the cadence.

5. See Eric Werner, *The Sacred Bridge*, p. 419.

6. Yale Strom in the film *Carpati: 50 Miles, 50 Years*, as reported in the *Jewish Week*, 17 May 1996.

7. Spanish words and music by Consuelo Velazquez, English version by Sunny Skylar, 1943. "Besame Mucho" was a particular favorite of my Yiddish-speaking mother.

8. There is a fascinating precursor of this melody in "Jungle Rose" from black musical theater. See Chapter 12.

9. A more recent example of the gypsy motive filled to the core can be heard in the 1991 song "Apple Pie (Recipe)," on the album *This Is a Recording of Pop Art Songs by Bob Dorough*, Laissez-Faire Records CD05.

10. Heard in the Cary Grant-Deborah Kerr movie *The Grass Is Always Greener*.

11. Max Wilk, *They're Playing Our Song*, p. 118.

12. Milton Babbitt, interview with the author, Juilliard School of Music, 14 September 1989.

CHAPTER 6

"Yingish" Songs

"Oy, such a much is the touch that lingers in his Yiddisha fingers."
IRVING BERLIN, "The Yiddisha Professor"(1912)

One of the glorious mysteries of music is how motives modify their appearance like chameleons, depending on their environs. Recall the song "My One and Only" (see Ex. 2-5), shorten its third and fourth bars (Ex.6-1a), and out wiggles a tune from the show *Gypsy* (Ex.6-1b). Or go back to the first bar of "My One and Only" (Ex.6-1c), lengthen it a bit, and the opening of the promissory prayer of Yom Kippur emerges (Ex.6-1d)—

—from the Broadway stage to the synagogue stage (or *bimah*) on the Day of Atonement, the holiest day in the Jewish calendar, when the Book of Life is to be shut. Ex. 6-2a, from a Tin Pan Alley song, has music by Lew Brown—born Bronstein in Odessa, Russia, a nephew of Leon Trotsky, cofounder with Lenin of Bolshevik communism[1]—with words by Maurie Abrams, also Russian born. Abrams married singing actress Belle Baker, who had literally worked her way uptown to Broadway from downtown sweatshops. Having made good in vaudeville, her photograph is on the cover of "I'll Open the Door," which no doubt means she plugged it.

The lyrics recount a conversation between Cohen and Levy. When Cohen discloses how he will be firm with St. Peter upon his demise, Levy asks where he got

such an "immense idea." Cohen replies it came from an experience he had with his wife when she "shut him out of the house." But more fascinating to us is to see how a Jewish character expresses the Christian view of the afterlife in the musical language of *Kol nidrei*.[2]

The background organ score for D. W. Griffith's silent film masterpiece *Intolerance* (1916) anachronistically incorporates the sixteenth-century *Kol nidrei* into Bible scenes, including the New Testament's Marriage at Cana. (At Jewish weddings, however, *Kol nidrei* sometimes was played for the entrance of the groom to underscore the gravity of the new husband's responsibilities.) Equally anomalous is its role in the soundtrack of *Cast a Giant Shadow,* a 1966 film about Mickey Marcus, who died in Israel's 1948 War of Independence, when it would have made more sense if the film had been about the 1973 Yom Kippur War. Elsewhere in Hollywood biblical epics, Yul Brynner with a head of hair and Gina Lollobrigida wearing a fright wig portray *Solomon and Sheba* (1959), a film in which a chant attributed to the Russian Cantor Osias Abrass (1820-1884) for the memorial prayer *El malei rachamim* (God Full of Mercy) is intoned by the high priests during a mourning scene. Such incongruities can be explained by the prevalence of cantor-performers on the Jewish vaudeville circuit of the early1900s where *Kol nidrei, El malei rachamim, Eli Eli,* and other Ashkenazic chants were staple tearjerkers.

The bouncy beat of "I'll Open the Door" belies the old canard that only sad tunes are in minor, "apparently a German invention. Semitic, Latin, and Slavic nations do not share this notion."[3] And it is crucial to my proposition that Jewish seed idioms did fertilize American pop songs. Before the impact of East European Jewry was felt, camp-meeting songs, white spirituals of Appalachia and other modal ballads (e.g., "When Johnny Comes Marching Home") came from the British Isles or were meant to evoke the exotic orient. It could be argued that Little Egypt's hootchy-kootchy dance (Ex. 6-3a), from the runway at the Chicago Exposition of 1893, is traceable to a Yiddish folk song (Ex. 6-3b):

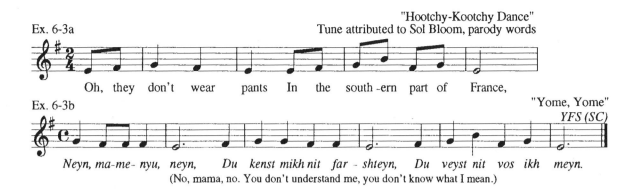

Ex. 6-3a

"Hootchy-Kootchy Dance"
Tune attributed to Sol Bloom, parody words

Oh, they don't wear pants In the south-ern part of France,

Ex. 6-3b

"Yome, Yome"
YFS (SC)

Neyn, ma-me-nyu, neyn, Du kenst mikh nit far-shteyn, Du veyst nit vos ikh meyn.
(No, mama, no. You don't understand me, you don't know what I mean.)

Sol Bloom, a songwriter and publisher from Chicago, and later a congressman from New York, claimed to be the author of the "Hootchy-Kootchy" dance tune when he was press agent for the Exposition. Although there are parallels in an earlier French song, the connection to Bloom is the stronger one, and that in turn could have been fed by Yiddish song sources.[4] James Thornton took Bloom's tune to parody the Chicago goings-on in a white-bread Yankee way: "I will sing you a song/And it won't be very long/'Bout a maiden sweet/And she never would do wrong." But Irving Berlin's take on it is more rye bread than white. His "In My Harem" (1913) ends with this same bromide on the words: "And the dance they do/Would make you wish that you were/In a Harem with Abie Cohen." As late as 1962, Berlin was still playing the same tune in "Song for a Belly Dancer," from *Mr. President*. Movie composer Roger Edens repeated it in an interpolated song—performed by Virginia O'Brien—for the film version of Cole Porter's *DuBarry Was a Lady* (1943): "No matter how you slice it, boys, it's still Salome." Elsewhere in filmology, Joan Crawford, playing the part of a "carny" girl, does a wiggle or two to the same tune in *Flamingo Road* (1949).

Novelties–Minor Verse/Major Chorus

It would be a Sisyphean labor to pore over all the popular songs written and sold for profit between 1890 and 1910 at the New York Public Library or the Library of Congress. But it is safe to assert that very few are in minor. In fact, not one song by Stephen Foster is in minor! Such a statistical finding could constitute much of the proof needed to stake out Jewish claims. On the other hand, I have had the pleasure of uncovering close to four hundred unknown songs (complete or lyrics alone) which I dub by the portmanteau word "Yingish."[5]

The first appearance in print of the better-known blend word "Yinglish" may have been in Jan Bart and William Gunther's collection of songs *The Yinglish Song Book* of 1964, which included the notice: "YINGLISH is registered in the U. S. Patent Office and is used by permission." If the Yinglish label were as well known as Spanglish, I would leave it alone. Otherwise, I feel it is not the most felicitous coinage since the letter "l" tilts it in favor of English rather than giving equal status to the two languages. For me a better choice is "Yingish" (no "l"), which blends the two prefix pairs of Yi-ddish and Eng-lish, along with the -ish suffix they share in common. More important, Yingish is evocative of the Yiddish word *yingele* (little one or youthful one), and indeed, the mostly humorous results of Yingish are filled with irreverent, youthful spirit.

Yingish songs date, predominately, from the 1910s through the 1920s and were written primarily as specialty material for revues and vaudeville headliners. Often these consisted of Jewish-Irish (i.e., Roman-Catholic) misalliances. Why Irish and not other nationalities? Italians were too close for comfort (Mediterranean origins, minor-key songs, swarthy complexions); Germans, too connected to the Yiddish language; little direct experience between Jews and the French, Scandanavians, etc. The Irish were the happy medium, no language complication and they afforded the opportunity to counterpoise priest and rabbi—

"Moysha Machree" (Kendis, 1916)
"My Yiddisha Colleen" (Madden & Edwards, 1911)
"When They Merge Mazeltoff with the Wearing of the Green"
        (Grossman, Silverstein & Handman, 1930)
"Yiddisha Luck and Irisha Love" (Bryan &Fischer, 1911)
"Abie Sings an Irish Song" (Berlin, 1913)

—and, inevitably, from the long-running (1922 to 1927) play of the same name and filmed both in 1928 and 1946, at least nine versions of "Abie's Irish Rose," even "Abie's Irish Nose." Variations on the Irish-Jewish juxtaposition included the 1926 "The Cohens and the Kellys Are Best Friends," based on the 1925 drama by Aaron Hoffman (and a series of films between 1930 and 1933), and "Kosher Kitty Kelly," a musical of 1925 that was filmed in 1926.[6] Abie also figured in another subcategory, viz., the "Name Song":

"Abie Springer Was a Tenor Singer" (Hertzberg, ca. 1910)
"Get a Girl with Lots of Money, Abie" (Bryan, Jansen & Meyer, 1908)
"Abie, Stop Saying Maybe" (Swerling, Johnson & Holland, 1924)

On the distaff side, Becky songs ran Abie a close second. The Becky lyrics, more or less streamed forth something like:

Becky wants her Jakie/But Jakie's on the make,
He wants his Sadie, married lady/Who wants her
Abie, Yiddish baby/But Abie's after Rose,
A girl with many beaux/And . . . So on and on it goes.

Another female song had a multilayered nuance unknown to both the movie-going public and its authors. The spoof "Since Sarah Saw Theda Bara," by Alex Gerber (W) & Harry Jentes (M),[7] has Sarah Cohn learning how to seduce suitors "by the score" by aping her screen idol, whose name was Arab in reverse. The notorious sloe-eyed vamp Theda Bara—forced to rhyme with Sarah and with "holy terror"— was born Theodesia Goodman (1885-1955) in Cincinnati to a Polish immigrant Jew. Thus both the Jewish star (hidden) and neophyte (overt) are marked by questionable probity. But such typecasting was minuscule compared to other images perpetuated by filmdom. The ongoing interchange between Broadway properties and Hollywood conversions was often de-Judaized, and puns on names such as

Levi could prompt levity. Among name titles shared by movies and Yingish songs there were:

	Film	Song
Tough Guy Levi	1912	"I'm a Yiddish Cowboy (Tough Guy Levi),"1908
Busy Izzy	1915	March (hooked-nosed Jew on cover), 1903
Rachel	1910	From the musical *Flo Flo*, 1904
Business Is Business	1915	"Business Is Business, Rosey Cohen," 1911
Second-Hand Rose	1922	From *Ziegfeld Follies of 1921*[8]

Cartoonist Milt Gross's uncouth dialect sketches of "Nize Baby" spawned an unpublished ditty by Jeanette Rosenson in 1926; but it became a catchphrase that motivated an independent tune about a buyer and a model by Ballard MacDonald (W) and James Hanley (M) for the *Ziegfeld Revue of 1926*. Harry Hershfield's "Abie the Agent," a comic strip predicated on Yiddish accents, was the source for unpublished song material by Eugene Platzman. Author Montague Glass's "Potash and Perlmutter" dialect routines (1910) between two Jewish salesmen were adapted for stage (1913) and screen (1923, 1924), and triggered the "Potash and Perlmutter Wedding Song," a 1914 waltz by Richard Malchien.

Current events and trends comprised another subgrouping. "There Never Was a White Hope Whose Christian Name Was Cohen" (Lee & Schwartz, 1912) was written before the days of Jewish boxing champ Barney Ross, but four years after Jack Johnson became the first black world heavyweight king. Then there was "Yiddisher Aviator Man" (Fischer & Gerber, 1915), who, in a subsequent real-life situation, was no laughing matter. Millionaire Charles Levine, on the heels of another Charles L. (i.e., Lindbergh), also flew the Atlantic in 1927, one month after "Lucky Lindy's" historic solo flight to Paris, a deed which inspired a rash of celebratory songs such as "Levine, Levine, der yid mit zayn mashin" (Levine, the Jew with His Machine, Gus Goldstein, 1927), "Levine, der groyser held" (Levine, the Great Hero) and "Mister Chamberlain and Mister Levine" (Harry Pease, Irving Mills & Edward G. Nelson, 1927).

The most winning tribute to Charles Levine has to be "Levine! With His Flying Machine" by Sam Coslow (M) & Saul Bernie (W), with additional words in Yiddish by Joseph Tanzman (1927). Coslow's tune, in a snappy, bright tempo, is irresistible.[9] More outlandish was the unpublished 1927 Yiddish song, registered in the Library of Congress and entitled "Levine der groyser man" (Levine the Great Man), words by Charles Tobias, music by one Harry Herschele. *Herschele* is Yiddish for "Little deer," often used as the anglicized version of Harry; and Harry Herschele was the pseudonym of the yet-to-be Hollywood-giant composer Harry Warren! His pen name, then, was "Harry Little Harry"; but it did not help launch his Levine song, an undistinguished effort from the otherwise powerhouse Warren legacy.[10]

In another Yingish number: "At the Yiddish Cabaret" (Gilbert & Muir, 1915), one could do "The Yiddisha Turkey Rag" (McKoen, Piano & Walker, 1909), the "Yiddisha Turkey Trot" (Fields & Carroll, 1912), and the "Yiddisha Charleston"

(Rose & Fischer, 1926). And regard the following generations: John Long's story *Madame Butterfly* begat David Belasco's play, begat Giacomo Puccini's opera, begat the pop song "Poor Butterfly" by Golden & Hubbell, 1916, which begat "My Yiddisha Butterfly" by Dubin & Burke, 1917.

Less attractive were such stereotypes as "Mosha From Nova Scotia" (Gilbert & Franklin, 1915) and "When Mose with His Nose Leads the Band" (Drislane, Fitzgibbon & Morse, 1906)— pejorative trash. Such meretricious oddballs rightly fall into a category known as "Hebe" songs, equal in ignominy to the "coon"-song category that degrades African Americans. Jews and Blacks may have led the parade of scapegoats, but they were not the only groups to be singled out. Orientals (more politely, Asians), Germans, Italians, etc. also were candidates for abuse. Gus Edwards (M) and Edward Madden (W) satirized Italian opera in "Rosa Rigoletto," wherein opera singer Luisa Tetrazzini, later immortalized in the dish turkey tetrazzini, gets the full treatment. Tenor Enrico Caruso also got a drubbing from the same authors in "My Cousin Carus'" (1909). Madden with Anatol Friedland then fashioned "My Sister Tetrazzin'" (1909); and to tie it all up, there was "When My Sist' Tetrazin' Met My Cousin Carus'"—Madden again with Lou A. Hirsch and Melville Gideon in 1910—sprinkled with quotes from Mascagni and Leoncavallo.

Dorothy Shapiro Jardon and Edward Madden were one of at least three other husband-wife songwriting teams.[11] Jardon, who as a singer recorded several Hebrew warhorses ("Eli, Eli" and "Rachem" among them) teamed up with her husband Edward Madden, a non-Jew, to come up with "Under the Hebrew Moon" in 1909:

> Verse: Oi! Such a sickness in the heart/Oi! Such a foolishness to start,
> I fell in love with Becky Cohen/Mit a heart just like a stone,
> Gave her all I own/All day sighing, all day crying:
> Becky! Becky!/Make it quick and come get thick
> Mit Jakey, Jakey!/Tonight it's a mazeltof June night,
> By the Yiddisher moonlight/ Won't you come and spoon right?

> Refrain: Under the Hebrew Moon/That's where I love to spoon,
> Holding mit hands when the hands is pining,
> Watching a cloud mit a silv'ry lining,
> Yiddisher birds in June/Sing that kasatzka tune,
> There'll be gold in the dawn/When the silver is gone,
> From the light of the Hebrew moon.

> Verse: Why should I bother mit a girl/That's like an imitation pearl?
> When I make love on bended knees
> She just answers with a sneeze,/"You're a piece of cheese."
> Head is aching, heart is breaking/Lovesick! Lovesick!/She won't flirt, my little turtle
> Dovechick! Dovechick!/Wooing, when she's always pooh, poohing,
> That's no billing and cooing/When there's nothing doing.

To be sure, this is not exactly deathless verse, but Madden did deliver two huge "moon" hits, "By the Light of the Silvery Moon" (1909), music by Gus Edwards, and "Moonlight Bay" (1912), music by Percy Wenrich. Madden must have also fancied himself a serious poet. Here are excerpts from his poem "The Jew" (1927):

> He's smart, it's admitted, as smart as can be,/And wins in his dealings with both you and me,
> And so would we too, if we, like the Jew,/Had learned through severe persecution

To study the methods and moods of the man/We deal with, while fearing he'll plot and he'll plan
To beat us before the bargain is o'er/With ne'er a chance of retribution.
But can you find anyone on this earth/More willing to give ev'ry cent that he's worth,
When charity calls for want that appals,/And poverty cries out its pleading?
You'll find that's true, though banned as a Jew,/As a friend you'll be damned glad to claim him![12]

It is clear Madden was more successful writing about the moon.

Generally, the music of Yingish songs has charm, vitality, and a kind of sophistication missing in songs from the same era from the Yiddish theater, where songwriters were less schooled and their songs not held in high regard by critics. "While the Yiddish theater usually found its richest materials in the Jewish past, the American Jewish entertainers were more at ease with their immediate moment: courting in broken English, poking fun at accents. . . ."[13] Yingish songs, however, were for the most part not written for Jewish audiences. Their verses are usually in minor with choruses in major. While this format had been old-hat for European composers, it was little known to America until new-hat songs about Jews rode in on waves of immigration.

Contrary to all expectations, the format appears to be nonexistent in Yiddish theater music, where the bulk of songs are exclusively in minor. Joseph Rumshinsky occasionally wrote songs entirely in major (see "Watch Your Step,"Ex. 4-12b and "Mayn goldele,"Ex. 2-14a); but these were exceptions, never the rule. Even more anomalous are the few Yiddish songs with a major verse and a minor chorus: e.g., Goldfaden's "Mirele's geburtstog" (Mirele's Birthday), Ilya Trilling's "Du shaynst vi di zun" (You Shine Like the Sun), and Louis Gilrod's "A malke oyf pesach" (A Queen for Passover). But the Yingish model of minor verse and major chorus is nowhere to be found.

It had appeared here and there in (1) conventional Broadway operettas: Victor Herbert's "A Good Cigar is a Good Smoke" and "The Isle of Our Dreams"; in (2) Tin Pan Alley Native-American clichés: "Tammany, a Navajo Indian Song" by Bryan & Edwards and "Big Indian Chief," by J. Rosamond Johnson, an African American; and (3) plantation songs[14] by other black songwriters: Ben Harney 's "Mister Johnson" (forbidden games versus the law) and Alex Rogers's "I'm a Jonah Man" (hard times).[15]

But the minor-major scheme is not characteristic or typical of operetta or Tin Pan Alley or plantation songs. Out of one hundred and sixty examined "coon" songs, only twenty-three have a verse in minor and the chorus in major. (Those which start in minor, but quickly modulate to major while still in the verse, were not included in the survey.) One of them—"Eli Green's Cake-Walk" by Sadie Koninsky—is particularly fascinating since it is a rare ragtime piece written by a Jewish woman, and because the music (both verse and chorus) is a precursor of an early Yingish song by Irving Berlin.[16]

In the Limelight–"Yiddle, On Your Fiddle, Play Some Ragtime"

In the Yingish genre the verse usually stays in minor until the last instant and this makes it unique. For while this verse portrayed the Jew in traditional garb, the chorus in major showed him off in American cloth. Toward the end, however, a brief reversion to minor was a reminder of the greenhorn not yet fully comfortable in his new wardrobe. An amiable song of 1909 by Irving Berlin, "Yiddle, On Your Fiddle, Play Some Ragtime," may well be the first Yingish tune to be promoted with a set of illustrated song slides. Edward Van Altena, of the Scott and Altena firm of slide makers, New York City, sent the following account to John W. Ripley, song slide conservator, about what happened at this photography session:

When Irving Berlin's publisher, Ted Snyder, ordered song slides for Berlin's "Yiddle, On Your Fiddle, Play Some Ragtime" he told Van [Altena] that Berlin had ideas for the scenario which, as it developed, were not approved by Scott and Altena. Berlin insisted that photography of the dance scenes be shot in the ballroom of a hotel that was popular with the Jewish community for receptions, etc. The use of calcium lighting (limelight) was prohibited in public places, due to fire hazard, and the photos had to be illuminated with flash powder. Berlin was told, when he insisted on furnishing friends as models in the dance scenes, that only three couples were needed. He brought in six couples, however, and he participated as a member of one of them. Following the first (and only) photo taken of the dancers, the room filled with smoke from the flash powder. Immediately all of Berlin's friends rushed up to Van and demanded: "Give us our three dollars." Van explained that the $3.00 fee was for a series of 14 scenes, but the dancer-models insisted: "Izzy said three dollars a picture."

When the models became hostile, Van and his partner Jack Scott, packed up and left, telling Berlin that under no circumstances would they complete the shooting at the hotel nor would they do this with Berlin's uncouth friends as models. Van and Jack got into their auto, and, after a few blocks, Jack began scratching his head, removed his derby to discover it wasn't his, but one infested with head lice.

At the risk of losing Ted Snyder's valued patronage, Van issued an ultimatum: the slides would be photographed in the Scott and Altena Studio with professional models or not at all. Apparently, they were given the go-ahead, and used a gentile male-model for Yiddle the violinist, who built up his nose with putty. [See Illustration 13] Van was supposed to have smashed the 4X4 glass plate negative of the scene in the hotel ballroom, but it can still be viewed in several other composites for other song scenarios, with Berlin's image cropped off. He was, according to Van, on the left hand end of the line of dancers.[17]

To set up the Yiddish ambience, the introduction of the song is made out of a two quotations. The first is from "Der rebe hot geheysn freylekh zayn," which Berlin was to use again in a more pointed way sixteen years later in the song "Don't Send Me Back to Petrograd." Then in the vamp section, foreshadowing the music of the verse, there is more than a hint of "Hatikvah."

Ex. 6-4   "Yiddle, On Your Fiddle, Play Some Ragtime"
                                                                                Irving Berlin

As alluded to in Edward Van Altena's narrative, the hotel scene (Illustration 14a, Ex. 6-5), where Berlin's ambitious plan was thwarted, appeared in at least two later song-slide sets. One of them was Charles K. Harris's waltz of 1912 "That Swaying Harmony," which recycled the image with some color changes (Illustration 14b, Ex. 6-6). More significant, however, was a set of composites made for "The Band Played On," a hardy perennial of American popular song literature. The band song was originally written in 1895, some nine years before "Yiddle, On Your Fiddle," but lyric changes indicate it is a later edition, as can be seen in Illustration 15a, Ex. 6-7. Note the wallpaper pattern in the background, and how the lady with the fan who appeared on the left now shows up on the right side. Casey would waltz with his strawberry blonde, but he did so in the same room where Yiddle first played his fiddle (Illustration 15b, Ex. 6-8). Early twentieth-century subliminal advertising? One author regrets that there are no period recordings of Berlin's tune "to help clarify the contemporary meaning of the song."[18] On the contrary, there was such a recording made in England, in January 1912 with Albert Whelan, known as "The Australian Entertainer."[19]

In later years Berlin, in seeming self-denial about his Jewish origins, disavowed his dozen or so early Jewish novelty songs. In a letter to Groucho Marx, dated April 23, 1956, Berlin said:

Frankly, there are some songs I would be tempted to pay you not to do. For instance, "Cohen Owes Me $97" would not be taken in the same spirit it was when I wrote it for Belle Baker . . . many years ago.[20]

Marx attributed another ditty to Berlin. Entitled "The Toronto Song," it concerned Mister Klein's relatives, the Wolf family, of whom Klein is driven to declare: "It's going to be a cold, cold winta/And I can't keep the wolves from the door."[21] No doubt Berlin's house cleaning would have deleted musicless lyrics discovered in Berlin's papers at the Library of Congress, including another "winta" item, "Yiddisha Eskimo" (date unknown), with the priceless couplet: "Living in a house of snow without a steeple, I'm one of God's frozen people." Still other titles among these papers are the 1909 "My Father Was an Indian" ("Just because my Christian name is Jake/That don't say I should believe in Christian Science"), "Yiddisha Ball" (Rebecca Klein marries Abie Rosenstein), and "Yiddisha Wedding" of 1913, whose participants involve the ubiquitous "Yiddle Upon the Fiddle."[22]

Illustrated song slides, an inspiration of Jewish publishers, were the humble beginnings of what ultimately became Music Television (MTV). Edward B. Marks, along with his partner Joseph Stern, originally a necktie salesman, wrote and published the 1894 tearjerker entitled "The Little Lost Child." Marks, a notions salesman, had the notion to market the song with colored lantern slides. In his memoirs he stated: "The slides for the song were my own idea," and that a stage electrician from Brooklyn, George H. Thomas, did "most of the work." John W. Ripley says the idea originated in 1892 with Thomas, who then teamed up with Marks and Stern.[23] Sigmund Spaeth has indirectly suggested that William Fox (born Fuchs?), who later became the founder of 20th Century-Fox, was also involved.

Charles K. Harris also laid claim to the distinction. "A Rabbi's Daughter," his 1899 weeper about an unfortunate interfaith courtship was hyped on the sheet-music cover as "The World's Greatest Song," while the *New York Clipper* of 10 February 1900 advertised it as

the only song of its kind ever written. This beautiful, sentimental song is creating a furor wherever sung. The novelty of the season. Twenty-two magnificent colored slides now ready, posed under the personal direction of the author, Harris. These slides will surprise you.

In the preparation of slide sets, prewritten scenarios determined which of one or more lyric lines of the latest song hit were to be photographed, the models posing against a black curtain. The glass negatives, when developed, were superimposed on other background negatives making special-effect composites, which were then color tinted by hand. These slides were a form of live song promotion requiring a pianist (known as the "professor," denoting a musician who could read music or a self-conferred title), a projectionist, and a vocalist. Sometimes the last would be a "stooge"— planted in cabarets, vaudeville emporia, or a storefront nickelodeon— who would attempt to whip up "spontaneous" audience participation in between one-reelers. Often these stooges were boys pirated from Lower East Side synagogue choirs. George Jessel, Al Jolson, and even Fanny Brice began their careers as stooges. To place some of his songs, Harry Von Tilzer hired Irving Berlin to be a stooge at Tony Pastor's restaurant.[24] All this took place during the era when feature-length films were not common and when any kind of film was regarded as low culture.

With the help of stooges and that of word slides, immigrants were both entertained and educated, a kind of early Berlitz School for learning English. Young mothers with nursing babies would spend entire afternoons hearing songs repeated enough times for them to understand and learn to sing the English words. By World War I, nickelodeons had been replaced by movie palaces and slides were a thing of the past.

Most Yingish songs are in a comic pejorative mode. There are, however, a few that show sensitivity without sentimentality. One such rarity is "My Little Yiddisha Queen," a 1909 number by Edgar Selden (W) & Melville J. Gideon (M). Its idomatic language and period slides stamp it as a genuine article.

Verse: Esther from Hester Street, she is the girl so sweet, and I love her so.
There, in her father's flat she lets me hang my hat, ev'ry time I go.
When me and Esther meet over on Hester Street, all the neighbors smile,
They give a nod and wink, we don't care what they think, It ain't worth our while.

Refrain: My Little Yiddisha Queen,
When you're my bride, on the East Side we will reside.
I've got a feelin' for you, so don't be mean.
When I am your boy, Oi! oi! such a joy!
My Little Yiddisha Queen.

Verse: Esther's a lovely name, so I am not to blame, if I am her beau.
She likes me pretty well, I know, for I can tell, when she calls me "Moe."

[Lyric continued in Ex. 6-9] (see Illustration 16)

Ex. 6-9

"My Little Yiddisha Queen"
Edgar Selden (W) & Melville J. Gideon (M)

There, with the light turned low, On such fine trips we go, We are both con - tent,___
We sim - ply close our eyes, Tra - vel to Par - a - dise, It don't cost a cent. ___

Audience participation events became more sophisticated for movie house patrons in the 1930s. Two-reelers by then had been replaced by double features and in between the two there was new filler material such as the sing-along. A crooner on screen now replaced the singing stooge. Through animation, the viewer could follow Paramount's bouncing-ball Screen Song Series. Other fillers combined cartoons and sing-alongs, featuring characters such as Betty Boop, whose singing voice could be the likes of Ethel Merman.[25]

Some thirty-one musical shorts made by Paramount between 1929 and 1941 included "Office Blues" in which Ginger Rogers sings: "I am cynical/He's rabbinical." In the late 1940s, the RCM company introduced, into taverns and other establishments, a contraption called Soundies. Youngsters such as Peggy Lee, Frank Sinatra, Nat King Cole, and Fats Waller were some of the recording artists for this visual jukebox which was geared to project twenty-one minutes worth of seven songs. The three-minute film shorts were originally released in reverse image so that they could be blown up onto a mirror and then viewed correctly. The initials of the company were derived from the founders, James Roosevelt, the President's son, and songwriters Sam Coslow and Irving Mills.[26] Coslow and Mills must have considered it a coup to get Roosevelt's name on their letterhead. By now, however, active audience participation had turned into passive audience viewing. It was only a matter of time before this was reduced even further to individual viewing by the advent of MTV in the 1980s. Thus did the quaint gaslight era of the "Little Lost Child" evolve into the glitz era of Prince and Michael Jackson.

Unlike songs of other ethnic groups, particularly the Irish variety, not one of these Yingish songs became a standard. As years went by, the gradual disappearance of verses swept away all Jewish connotations; but earlier on, the Yingish model of minor verse linked to major chorus did become a paradigm for many famous songs such as "Get Happy" (its exhortation to "sinners" evokes cantorial melismas, see Chapter 12), "Hallelujah," "Crazy Rhythm," "California, Here I Come," "Bye-Bye Blackbird," "Charleston," "Sweet Georgia Brown," "I'm Looking over a Four-Leaf Clover," "Stout-Hearted Men" and a slew of Gershwin songs, including "That Sweet and Low-Down," "Clap Yo' Hands," "I Got Rhythm," and "Swanee" (see Chapter 8). All have minor-key verses, followed by refrains in the major. Infinitely fewer in the American mainstream are those songs with both a minor verse and a minor chorus such as "Forty-Second Street," "You and the Night and the Music," and "Brother, Can You Spare a Dime?" Even more uncommon is major verse linked to minor chorus. One such rarity is "Here Lies Love," a Leo Robin-Ralph Rainger movie song from *The Big Broadcast* (1932), sung by Bing Crosby. Another, as if to prove my contention in reverse, is Irving Berlin's "Russian Lullaby." Here the major verse places the Jewish immigrant mother in America, while the nostalgic chorus in minor reveals her to be homesick.

* * *

Other Yingish songs were more blatant in their quotations from Jewish signature tunes, especially when the context had nothing to do with the tune's source.

Ex. 6-10

"Yonkle, the Cowboy Jew"
Will Harris (W) & Harry Robinson (M)

khosn kale mazl tov

Ev'-ry time _ I see some In - dians, I just kill _ a few, So I've changed my name from Fin-kle-stein____ To Yon - kle, the Cow - boy Jew.____

"Yonkle, the Cowboy Jew" (1917) by importing the connubial tune "Khosn kale mazl tov" into a nonwedding context, was one such embarrassment. Sometimes this particular quotation was used more appropriately with salubrious results. In "Casey's Wedding Night" (Vincent Bryan and Gus Edwards, 1901), Cohen's Hebrew band is hired to play at an Irish wedding and is sharply berated for playing the Hebrew wedding march. As we saw earlier, however, in "Rebecca" (Ex. 3-20), the march signals a forthcoming Jewish marriage. In yet another song, the marriage has already taken place. "Khosn kale mazl tov" inspired Nora Bayes (née Dora Goldberg)[27] and her husband Jack Norworth to transmogrify George M. Cohan, an Irish-American figurehead, into Boris Thomashefsky, the matinee idol of Second Avenue.[28]

From the "Khosn kale" tune, on the words "Georgie Cohan makes me sad,"[29] presto-chango into its related variant, "Who do you suppose went and married my sister?" That kind of musical development is the earmark of a bonafide songwriter, not a hack.

"Moon Shine"

At about the same time—between 1908 and 1910—Bayes and Norworth paid their respects to their friend Boris Thomashefsky, they wrote a love song for a Ziegfeld Follies edition that commences with the same musical tribute as "Who Do

You Suppose." Although it holds the copyright date of 1908, its success could well have prompted the publication of what may have been the earlier novelty song.[30] (The year a work is copyrighted is not necessarily the year of composition; and when a song becomes popular, other earlier songs in a writer's catalog take on greater commercial interest for publishers.) "Shine on Harvest Moon," a beloved gem of Americana, was born of the marriage that began with the Yiddish wedding signature tune, three times removed:

And from this blossoms the assimilated third generation of (see Illustration 17):

NOTES

1. A letter to the editor in the *New York Times* states that Lenin's maternal grandfather, Israel Blank, was a Jew. The letter writer also says that Jewish genealogical records from czarist Russia were at last being made available. Larry Horwitz, 5 August 1992.

2. Louis B. Mayer, in an attempt to show Jeanette MacDonald the kind of passion he wanted from her singing, purportedly got down on his knees and sang "Kol nidrei" through his tears. Reported by producer Samuel Mark on the PBS-TV documentary *MGM: When the Lion Roars*, 1992.

3. Abraham Idelsohn, *HOM*, vol. X, p. xviii, English edition.

4. See James Fuld, *The Book of World-Famous Music*, p. 276.

5. See Appendix B for an extensive list of "Yingish" song titles.

6. Later, more-substantial stage shows on Jewish themes that became musical films include *The Jazz Singer, Funny Girl, Fiddler on the Roof, Cabaret*, and *Yentl*.

7. Jentes is mistakenly identified as African American in Hoberman and Shandler, *Entertaining America*, p. 277. The name Jentes could be of Jewish origin, a derivative of Yentes or Yentis.

8. See Patricia Erens, *The Jew in American Cinema*. She is meticulous, but she erroneously claims that Ziegfeld was Jewish. According to Ziegfeld's daughter, Patricia, he was not (neither was Bertolt Brecht, another mistake by Erens).

9. Sam Coslow wrote, among other hits, "Cocktails for Two" and "My Old Flame." Inexplicably, Mark Slobin did not refer to the sheet music when he examined this "Levine" song in his book *Tenement Songs*, relying solely on a recording. Despite his errors, the analysis of the lyrics—the minority perspective versus the dominant viewpoint—is right on the money (pp. 199-202). For the music, see Mlotek, *New Pearls of Yiddish Song*, p. 221.

10. Apparently "Levine der groyser man" was published in English as "Levine" by Shapiro, Bernstein Co., 1927.

11. Jewish husband-wife teams included Nora Bayes and Jack Norworth² (portrayed by Ann Sheridan and Dennis Morgan in the 1944 film *Shine on Harvest Moon*), Gus Kahn and Grace LeBoy (Danny Thomas and Doris Day in the 1952 film *I'll See You in My Dreams*), as well as Belle Baker and Maurice Abrahams (one of her husbands; impresario

Lew Leslie was the other). In the 1941 movie *Lady Be Good*, Ann Sothern and Robert Young playing the roles of Dixie Donegan and Edward Crane, are a fictitious Gentile songwriting team who supposedly write Gershwin tunes. Today there is the real-life partnership of Alan and Marilyn Bergman.

12. Edward Madden, *The Fiddler at the Wedding: A Collection of 50 Famous Poems and Recitations* (New York: Frank Harding, 1927).

13. Irving Howe, *World of Our Fathers*, p. 562.

14. Pejorative lyrics from the late nineteenth century about African Americans were variously known as coon, race, yaller, plantation, and nigger songs. In the late twentieth century "gangsta" rap lyrics were equally offensive.

15. "I'm a Jonah Man" was revived in the 1980 Broadway revue *Tintypes*.

16. The name Eli Green could be black or Jewish; but the lyrics by Dave Reed, Jr., are predictably tawdry. Since the piano was typically a woman's instrument of the era, female ragtime composers were not uncommon.

17. John W. Ripley, letter to the author, ca. 1975.

18. Charles Hamm, *Irving Berlin: Songs from the Melting Pot*, p. 41.

19. There may be only one recording in Yiddish of Berlin songs, a 1912 pressing of "Di regtime fidl" and "Ale menshn tien dos" (Everybody's Doin' It Now). Reported by Henry Sapoznik, *The Forward*, 27 July 1990.

20. Groucho Marx, *The Groucho Letters*, p. 210. According to Robert Kimball, Berlin was embarrassed by these ethnic songs. Quoted by Anthony Tommasini in "An Archeologist on a Musical Dig," *New York Times*, 28 April 2002.

21. Recorded on A&M Records (SP3515) by Groucho Marx and Marvin Hamlisch, Carnegie Hall, 1972. Hilda Schneider, late secretary to Berlin, said "The Toronto Song" was not a Berlin song. Phone conversation with the author, July 1992.

22. Robert Kimball and Linda Emmet, *The Complete Lyrics of Irving Berlin*, pp. 83 and 218.

23. Edward Marks, *They All Sang: From Tony Pastor to Rudy Vallée*, p. 17. John Ripley, "Romance and Joy, Tears and Heartache, and All for a Nickel," *Smithsonian* (March 1982): 76-82. See also Sigmund Spaeth, *Read 'em and Weep*, p. 148.

24. Philip Furia, with Graham Wood, *Irving Berlin: A Life in Song*, p. 16.

25. Roy Hemming, *The Melody Lingers On: The Great Songwriters and the Movie Musicals*, p. 201.

26. Herb Graff, New York Sheet Music Society meeting, 14 October 1989.

27. Morrie Ryskind wrote the lyrics to a song for Nora Bayes called "One Dumb Goy." See Deena Rosenberg, *Fascinating Rhythm*, p. 203.

28. Grandfather of conductor Michael Tilson Thomas, Thomashefsky made two bids for triumph on Broadway: the first in 1922, an English-language production of Sholem Asch's play *God of Vengeance* and then in 1931 with *The Singing Rabbi*—book by Boris and his brother Harry—lasting four performances. The latter show also represented Joseph Rumshinsky's one Broadway offering on which he collaborated with Tin Pan Alley lyricist L. Wolfe Gilbert. Years later Thomashefsky's persona was emulated by movie star Robert Preston in a show that closed out of town in Boston, Bob Merrill's *The Prince of Grand Street* (1978), with the name changed to Rashumshy— perhaps in tribute to Rumshinsky. (A 2003 reconstruction done in concert by the Jewish Repertory Theater of NYC indicated that the show would have been better off if it had been written by Rumshinsky.) Jacob Adler, another idol of the Yiddish theater, was loosely portrayed by Theodore Bikel in *Café Crown* (1964), surviving only three performances.

Other Yiddish theater stars had better luck: Luther Adler (*Johnny Johnson*), Joseph Buloff (*Oklahoma*), David Opatoshu (*Silk Stockings*), Paul Muni (*At the Grand*, 1958, closed out of New York, but resuscitated as *Grand Hotel*, 1989), Molly Picon (*Milk and Honey* and several major films, including the movie version of *Fiddler on the Roof*), Menasha Skulnik (*The Zulu and the Zayde*), and Zvee Scooler (*Fiddler on the Roof*, both stage and movie, as well as other films). Not one of the major Yiddish theater composers ever achieved success in their English-language shows: Abe Ellstein (*Birdie*, 1933; *Marianne*, 1944; *Great to Be Alive!*, 1950; *Rebecca, The Rabbi's Daughter*, 1979); Alex Olshanetsky (*Try It, You'll Like It*, 1973, mostly in Yiddish); Sholom Secunda (*Bagels and Yox*, 1951, *The Kosher Widow*, 1959; *Bei Mir Bistu Shoen*, 1961).

29. For the sake of the record, the etymological root of Cohan is Celtic: O'Caomhan became Keohane which begat Cohan. It was sometimes assumed that Cohan was Jewish, especially because of his partnership with brother-in-law producer Sam Harris. The stage name of Cohan's first wife was Ethel Levey (neé Ethelia Fowler), whose stepfather, Sol Levey, was Jewish. See John McCabe, *George M. Cohan: The Man Who Owned Broadway*.

30. A sheet music edition in my collection gives the copyright date as 1918. New York: Jerome H. Remick and Co., undoubtedly a printer's error.

Song Sheets International
Proudly Presents The Story of

(Abner Silver & Alex Gerber, 1920)

—Babylon, Long Island, that is.

She dreams of becoming an actress one day. Her parents plead with her:

(Norman & Young, 1910)

But to no avail. Against their wishes,

(Irving Berlin, 1912)

117

The star of that show is Genevieve Malone,
famous for playing the part of Lena,
who's the Queen of

(Con Conrad & J. Russel Robinson, 1920)

Ginny's leading man, Izzy,
plays the part of Ali Cohn
and Becky falls for him
like a ton of bagels. But you know,

(Gus Kahn & Grace Le Boy, 1910)

Heart-broken, Becky leaves for Far Rockaway
places, and becomes an international celebrity.
In triumph,

(Bert Kalmar & Harry Ruby, 1921)

—where she chewed on Turkish tobecca, a star!
How the crowds flock to see her.
Becky is back in the belly
—oops!, the "Ballet."

(Blanche Merrill & Leo Edwards, 1922)

Izzy sees her with new eyes,
and now it's Ginny of Palestinny's
turn to fight for his affections.
She confronts her rival
—and Ginny wins him back!

(Lew Brown, Bud Green & Murray Sturm, 1924)

But not to worry. Becky
gets over that heel Izzy,
and falls head over heels for Jakey.

(James Brockman, 1910)

All ends happily,

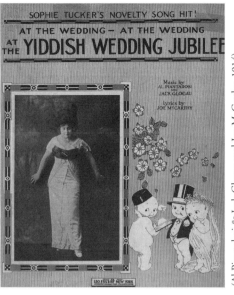

(Al Piantadosi & Jack Glogau and Joe McCarthy, 1914)

But a nagging question remains
as we bid good night to Jakey and
Becky snuggling between the
sheet music covers.
Will he have to go off to war, saying:

(Fred Fischer, 1910)

Or will he run off to Hawaii, boasting:

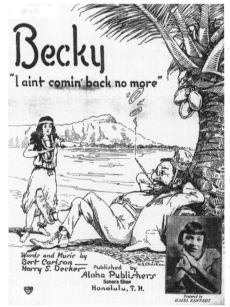

(Bert Carlson & Harry S. Decker, 1925)

PART II
Sacred Roots

CHAPTER 7

The Mood of Modes

Many a melody once chanted by the Levites in the Holy Temple is now in exile among the unlearned common people.

RABBI ISAAC of Kalev

The definition of modes in Jewish music is ambiguous. In an attempt to codify a vast repertoire of synagogue chants, late nineteenth-century cantor-theorists, notably the Viennese Josef Singer (1841-1911), the Russian Pinchos [Phineas] Minkowski (1859-1924), and the Lithuanian Aaron Friedman (1855-1936) endeavored to systematize the melodic structure of such music with varying success. This was followed in the 1920s by the more notable efforts of A. Z. Idelsohn, in midcentury by Eric Werner in various studies,[1] and since 1950, by such scholars as Max Wohlberg (1907 1996), Baruch J. Cohon (b. 1926), and Hanoch Avenary (1908-1994).[2] Particularly intriguing are Cohon's and Avenary's insights that a mode (or *shtayger,* in Yiddish) is based on an embroidery of varying note patterns or melody types within a given scale. In this sense, traditional Jewish modes may be regarded as being closer to the Near Eastern practices of the Arabic *maqām* or the Hindu ragas than they are to church modes. The latter have become popularly identified with the white keys on the piano—e.g., the octave span from "D to D" is the dorian mode and "E to E" is the phrygian mode—while the former signifies the linking of recurring melodic shapes in a mosaic fashion. Ragas and synagogue chants can be likened to necklaces, wherein beaded fragments of motives or phrases are strung together to form a tune. Segments either function as opening statements (known as *incipits*), connective passages (*linkages*), or as resting places or conclusions (*cadences*).

The *Adonai malakh* Mode

The introductory portion of the Friday evening liturgy known as *Kabalat shabat* (Welcoming the Sabbath) is concluded by the recitation of Psalm 93; but, at the same time, its messianic fervor introduces the main body of the service, *T'filat arvit* (Evening Prayers). The first of three primary modes—and the one with the greatest impact on popular American songwriting—is known by the music that usually individualizes the words of Psalm 93, *Adonai malakh* (God Is King), notable for its forthright character and especially apt for chants of praise:

Ex. 7-1a   Psalm 93, vs. 1   *HOM,* vol. VIII, no. 32

Opening motives   Intermediate motives

A - do - nai ma - lakh   gei - ut___ la - veish,   la - veish A - do - nai   oz   hit - a - zar;
(The Lord reigns, He is clothed in majesty; The Lord is clothed, He has girded Himself with strength)

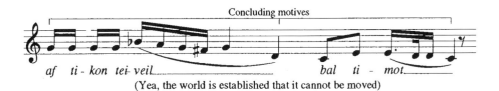

af ti - kon tei- veil_____ bal ti - mot._____
(Yea, the world is established that it cannot be moved)

Ex. 7-1b

Psalm 93, vs. 1

Opening motives

Intermediate motives

Katchkol, no. 10

A - do-nai ma-lakh_ gei-ut la veish,___ la-veish A-do-nai oz hit-a-zar;

Concluding motives

af ti - kon tei- veil _____ bal _____ ti - mot. _____

Opening, intermediate, and concluding motives amalgamate into larger melodies, as in this rendition of verses from Psalm 95:

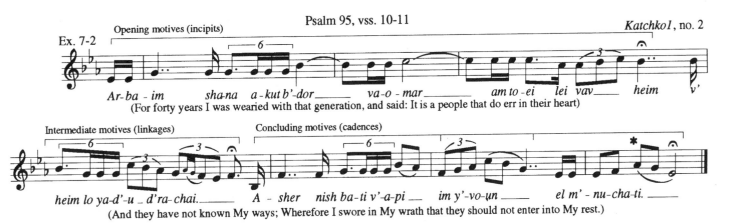

Psalm 95, vss. 10-11

Katchkol, no. 2

Ex. 7-2

Opening motives (incipits)

Ar-ba - im sha-na a-kut b'-dor_____ va-o - mar_____ am to -ei lei vav____ heim v'
(For forty years I was wearied with that generation, and said: It is a people that do err in their heart)

Intermediate motives (linkages)   Concluding motives (cadences)

heim lo ya-d'-u _ d'ra-chai._____ A - sher nish ba-ti v'-a-pi __ im y'-vo-un _____ el m' - nu-cha-ti. _____
(And they have not known My ways; Wherefore I swore in My wrath that they should not enter into My rest.)

Although the separate segment bits are reducible to a scale that resembles the mixolydian mode of the church (i.e., a major scale with a lowered 7th step), it would be a mistake to equate synagogue modes with theoretical scales. Baruch Cohon, differentiating between "scale" and "mode" says: "The American popular song 'Temptation' and the Yiddish 'Eli, Eli'[3] are basically in the same scale, but hardly in the same mode."

Characteristic phrases of *Adonai malakh* (henceforth *AM*) were incorporated directly from their synagogue origins into various Yiddish folk songs and from there into American pop songs. In *The Jazz Singer,* Al Jolson playing the cantor's son Jakie Rabinowitz (literally, "son of a rabbi") defies his screen father (Warner Oland) with the riposte: "My songs mean as much to my audience as yours do to your congregation." A similar conflict was known to occur among African-American congregations in the 1930s and 1940s. If a gospel singer dared to venture into commercial territories, he or she was chastised for being too "worldly." Thomas A. Dorsey, the founding father of gospel music, also struggled with his angel, writing Saturday night music—a double-entendre song called "Tight Like That"—in 1928 and Sunday hymns like "Precious Lord, Take My hand" in 1929.

Jolson qua Jolson did record "Chazn oyf shabes" (Cantor on the Sabbath), a

Yiddish song in the *AM* mode performed by him in the 1931 Broadway show *Wonder Boy*. Jolson rerecorded it for inclusion in the biopic *The Jolson Story*, with actor Larry Parks learning the Yiddish well enough to lip-synch to the soundtrack; but the scene was deemed "too ethnic" and was cut from the film:

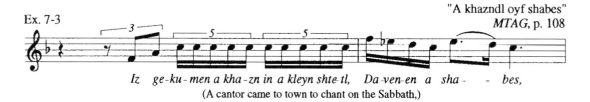

Ex. 7-3

"A khazndl oyf shabes"
MTAG, p. 108

Iz ge-ku-men a kha-zn in a kleyn shte-tl, Da-ven-en a sha- - bes,
(A cantor came to town to chant on the Sabbath,)

Whether or not by design, the curve of a well-traveled tune expands the second motive of the opening *AM* phrase into a kind of cranking-up device, as in "on your mark, get set, go." According to an expert researcher, a Romanian song was the mother lode for the many spin-offs in various languages.[4] In Yiddish, it was known as *Nokh a bisl* (A Bit More), a vulgar text that morphed into a Bulgar wedding dance, "Tentzl far di mekhetonem" (Dance for Relatives-by-Marriage, Ex.7- 4):

Ex. 7-4

"Nokh a bisl" (Freylekh)
Kammen Dance Folio No. 1, p. 12 (words added)

Nokh a bi-sl, nokh a bi-sl, kh'vil nokh, Nokh a bi-sl, nokh a bi-sl,

kh'darf nokh.

(A little more, I want more. A bit more, I must have more.)

It then shifted into a Hasidic tune *Ikh kum yetst fun mayn tsadik* (I've Just Returned from My Guru), with the words—alluding to a *piyyut* about the exalted High Priest of the ancient temple— devoted to a homey wonder-working *rebe* who radiates the holy spirit:[5]

Ex. 7-5: Conclusion

"Ikh kum yetst fun mayn tsadik"
YFS(SC), p. 79

Oy vey, oy vey ta - te! Ash-rei a - yin vos hot es tsu-ge - zeyn! Dos is dokh far unz kha-si-dim a
(Oh my, oh my Father! Blessed is the eye that has seen all this! This is a sight for us Hasidim alone.)

leyn, Tzu zeyn dem re-bns fray-e mi-ne, Neh- neh zayn fon der hay-li-ge sh'khi-no. Ir a-pi-kor-sim, ir kent es nit far-shteyn.
(To see the Rabbi's happy countenance, partaking of the holy spirit. You heretics, you cannot understand.)

In America, Louis Gilrod adapted the tune for the Yiddish theater as *A malke auf paissach* (A Queen for Passover), oddly subtitled "An Easter Song;"[6] and in 1934, it was transformed into "Koyft a paper" (Buy a Paper), for a Yiddish radio program, *The Newsboy*:

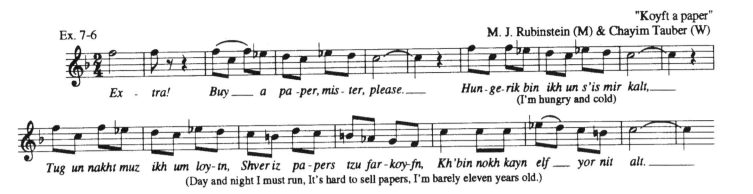

Ex. 7-6
"Koyft a paper"
M. J. Rubinstein (M) & Chayim Tauber (W)

Ex - tra! Buy __ a pa-per, mis-ter, please. __ Hun-ge-rik bin ikh un s'is mir kalt, __
(I'm hungry and cold)

Tug un nakht muz ikh um loy-tn, Shver iz pa-pers tzu far-koy-fn, Kh'bin nokh kayn elf __ yor nit alt. __
(Day and night I must run, It's hard to sell papers, I'm barely eleven years old.)

Inevitably, the tune was freshly minted for Tin Pan Alley by Con Conrad (b. Konrad Dobert) and J. Russel Robinson (b. Rosenberg[7]) who concocted the novelty song "Palesteena" (Ex. 7-7a), introduced in the Broadway revue *The Midnight Rounders of 1920*. The end result was a parody about a parody, from one on Hasidism to one about a lumpen female posing as a femme fatale (Ex. 7-7b):

Ex. 7-7a
"Palesteena"
J. Russel Robinson (W,M) & Con Conrad (W)

Le - na is the Queen O' Pal - es - tee - na, Just be-cause they like her con cer - ti - na,

Ex. 7-7b

She was fat, but she got lean-er, Push-ing on her con-cer-ti-na, Down old Pal-es-tee-na Way. __

Eddie Cantor's November 1920 recording of "Palesteena" (Emerson78 10292) included a quote from "Khosn kale mazl tov." One month later, the Original Dixieland Jazz Band recording, with Robinson at the piano, interpolated "Der rebe hot geheysn freylekh zayn" (Victor78 18717), a rendition which can be heard in the 1980 Woody Allen movie *Stardust Memories* backing up dialogue about Jews.[8] "Palesteena" was a favorite of Leonard Bernstein's; and in his musical *On the Town* there is a Coney Island carnival barker advertising the wares of hootchy-kootchy dancers that sounds something like it. For the studio cast album, you can actually hear Bernstein sing (!) the role of the pitchman—well, in a mixed *AM* mode. He is credited on the album as Randel Stirboneen, an anagram of his name:

Ex. 7-8
"Rajah Bimmy"
Betty Comden, Adolph Green & Leonard Bernstein

Ra - jah Bim - my's ha - rum sca - rum, where you

see the pret - ty girl who picks up the han' -ker - chief with her teeth. __

Walter Doyle's "Egyptian Ella" of 1931 concerned another *zaftig* (buxom) temptress "who doesn't care a fig about dates," and recorded by the likes of Benny

Goodman and Fats Waller as members of Ted Lewis's band, with "Hatikvah" quoted at the end (on Columbia 2428-D). These putative Far Eastern belly dancers, progeny of the dancer "Little Egypt," (see Chapter 6), would seem to indicate that the distinctiveness of *AM* is incapable of being acculturated. But Gershwin was able to accomplish as much in a song he wrote for *George White's Scandals of 1922* (Ex. 7-9a). Later on, he took advantage of the same musical motive in the finale of *Porgy and Bess* (1935), this time with a stroke of religiosity (Ex. 7-9b):

In "Mikitka," an unconventional Ukrainian-Jewish folk song, a sanctimonious Jew believing heaven to be a Jewish country club, doubts that Mikitka, a gentile peasant, has any chance of ever being admitted into the heavenly land. It ends: "The angel of death will come and ask 'What's your name?,' when you are lying in the grave, and you won't know what to answer." Too bad, because, at least musically speaking, Mikitka could have been one of the candidates climbing Gershwin's stairway, accompanying Porgy on his way to the Elysian fields:

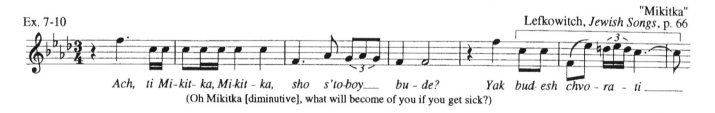

Harold Arlen utilized similar symbolism in a movie song that actor Eddie Bracken lip-synched to the voice of Bing Crosby:

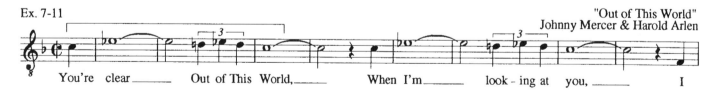

Why do all these musical portions employ the same motive for parallel euphemisms of spirituality: Gershwin's "Paradise" and "Heav'ly Lan'," Arlen's "Out of This World," and Mikitka's destiny in the hereafter? A possible answer is that they all are somehow associated with the *AM* mode, a formula assigned to expressions of exultation. Such revelations should not be thought of as being in the mixolydian mode. Rather it is the turn of expression that stamps it as characteristic, making it Jewish in spirit if not in intent. Paul Simon's "Quiet," from his 2000 album *You're the One*, would be one such example, whereas a celebrated Richard Rodgers melody, which duplicates the incipit of the *AM* mode, does not convey the same message. An ascending tonic major triad in E-flat-Major becomes a dominant V₇ to A-flat-Major, and the last note begins a new phrase:

* * *

In 1929 Harold Arlen, then a rehearsal pianist for Vincent Youmans's show *Great Day*, improvised a dance tune that eventually became "Get Happy," his first important song, and one very much under the spell of an earlier Youmans tune, "Hallelujah," from the show *Hit the Deck*:

Very much like "Get Happy," but not quite. For Arlen's literally is from *AM*, down to the cadence of "chase all your cares away" (see Ex. 7-2 at the asterisk). What is more, where the bridge section in Youmans's song uses C-flat (Ex.7-14a), Arlen adheres to the prayer mode with C-natural (Ex. 7-14b):

That last comparison may be subtle, but apparently it can make a difference between a Jewish and non-Jewish songwriter.[9] The deviation of even one little half-step is crucial to preserving the integrity of the mode:

*   *   *

There remains one striking feature of the *AM* mode which impregnated popular song writing, particularly in its symbiotic relationship to African-American blues. The "blue" note on the 7th step is the same in both traditions; but the blue 3rd step in the synagogue mode, unlike the blues, only occurs in the upper octave, never in the lower one:

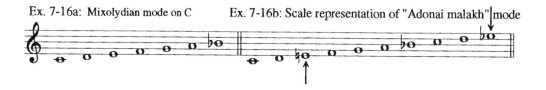

Typical usages in synagogue psalm recitatives are:

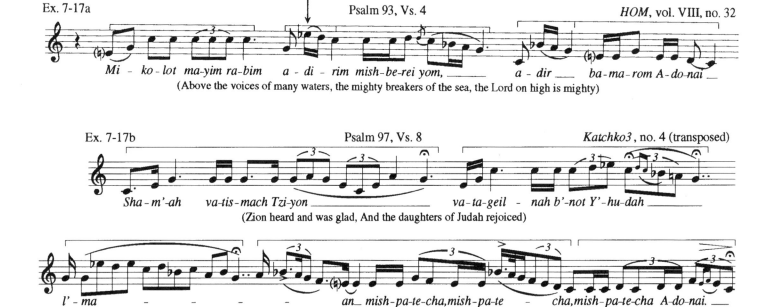

Here is how a setting of the Sabbath *V'shomru* prayer in the *AM* mode links up with Spencer Williams's classic "Basin Street Blues" (Exx. 7-18a and 7-18b).

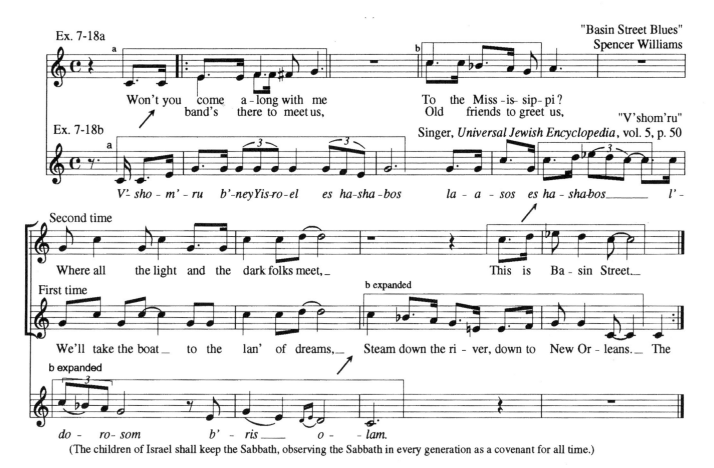

Ex. 7-18a

"Basin Street Blues"
Spencer Williams

Won't you   come   a-long with me   To   the Miss-is-sip-pi?
band's   there to meet us,   Old   friends to greet us,

Ex. 7-18b

"V'shom'ru"
Singer, *Universal Jewish Encyclopedia*, vol. 5, p. 50

V'-sho-m'-ru b'-neyYis-ro-el es ha-sha-bos   la-a-sos es ha-sha-bos____ l'-

Second time

Where all   the light and the   dark folks meet,_   This is   Ba-sin Street._

First time

b expanded

We'll take the boat_   to the   lan' of dreams,_   Steam down the ri-ver, down to   New Or-leans._ The

b expanded

do-ro-som   b'-ris____ o--lam.

(The children of Israel shall keep the Sabbath, observing the Sabbath in every generation as a covenant for all time.)

Although both traditions share a rhythmic (nonmetrical) freedom and continuing variational patterns, there is, nonetheless, that one important difference of octave placement between African-American and Jewish blues. In the first case, blueish-ness is established by quarter-tones, lying midway between one half step and the next. The third note of the scale is neither major nor minor, but a bent intonation. On the piano, it can be approximated by sounding adjacent black and white notes: The parallel for this in the singing voice would be to rapidly alternate a minor and

Ex. 7-19

a major 3rd (more accurately, a raised 2nd and major 3rd) as in Berlin's "Alexander's Ragtime Band" ("Come on an' hear," repeated) or W.C. Handy's "St. Louis Blues" ("Got de St. Louis Blues, jes blue as ah can be").[10] This kind of undu-lation is not found in traditional cantorial music. But the bluesy air of a minor 3rd in the upper octave and major 3rd in the lower octave is typical of the *AM* mode. Absorbed into American lungs, one clear example is, once again, by the team of Harold Arlen and Ted Koehler:

Ex. 7-20

"When the Sun Comes Out"
Ted Koehler & Harold Arlen

When the Sun   Comes   Out,____   and that rain stops beat-in' on my win-dow pane,____ When the

Sun Comes Out,_____ there'll be blue-birds 'round my door sing-in' like they did be-fore

Bernstein's torch song "Ain't Got No Tears Left" begins on a lower major 3rd, shoots up to the minor, but comes back down to waver in typical blues fashion. The pattern also spills over into music by non-Jews, as in this example by Harry Warren, first heard in the movie *Orchestra Wives* (1942), and in more recent times in *Rain Man* (1988), *Pleasantville* (1998), and *The Other Sister* (1999), as well as in a television car commercial:

"At Last"
Mack Gordon & Harry Warren
Ex. 7-21

At Last_____ my love_ has come a-long,_____ My lone-ly days are

o - ver_____ and life_ is like a song._

The last phrase of Joe Raposo's* theme song from a celebrated television children's show can also relate to the *AM* mode: "Can you tell me how to get/How to get to Sesame Street?" A song performed by Tony Martin in the MGM film *The Big Store*, exploits the upper minor 3rd and lower major 3rd cross-relation in a melody that leans toward the *AM* mode. "This turns out to be a piece with melting pot ideals subtly skewed toward . . . cultural pluralism; the ethnic groups are allowed to sing their traditional tunes before fusing in the Crucible":[11]

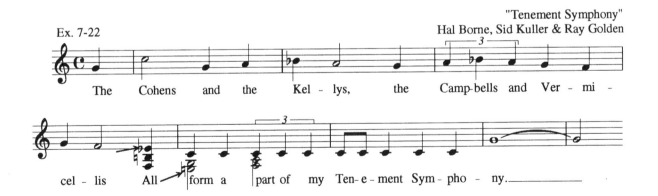

"Tenement Symphony"
Hal Borne, Sid Kuller & Ray Golden
Ex. 7-22

The Cohens and the Kel-lys, the Camp-bells and Ver-mi -

cel-lis All form a part of my Ten-e-ment Sym-pho-ny._____

The refrain ends: "It's my Tenement Symphony in four flats." (Get it?)

The same commonplace cross-relation can be found in Porgy's theme in *Porgy and Bess* (Ex. 7-23a). But try to reverse the order by putting the major 3rd on top and the minor 3rd on bottom (Ex. 7-23b), and the ear is less accommodating:

Ex. 7-23a: Porgy's theme, original version   Ex. 7-23b: Porgy's theme, reversed major-minor

The *Magein avot* Mode

The natural minor mode—also known as aeolian, A to A on the white piano keys—has *Magein avot* (Shield of our fathers, henceforth *MA*) as its synagogue counterpart. Named after a Sabbath evening prayer, the text of *MA* is an abridgement of the immediately preceding *Amidah* (standing) prayers, originally designed to accommodate latecomers who had to walk long distances to get to synagogue. Like the *AM* mode, the prayer concludes a section of the service. However, it is harder to pinpoint melody types within *MA* than it is for its sister (brother?) modes. Unlike *AM*, there are no "blue" notes in *MA* to give it distinction. In general, the melodic thrust of *MA* is an ascending line up to the fifth step where it tends to plateau. Also characteristic of the mode is a routine switch to the relative major and a quick return to the original minor. Used for expressions of comfort or gratitude, *MA* can be recognized in an alternate Yiddish rendition of "Chazn oyf shabes"—shown in an earlier version in the *AM* mode (Ex. 7-3)—and also in a harmonized setting of the Hebrew "Vay'chulu," a prayer which introduces the *MA* in the service order (Exs. 7-24a and 7-24b).

Ex. 7-24a

"A khazn oyf shabes"
YFS (SC), p. 68

Es iz ge - kum - en a - mol in a klyen shet-el, a kha-zn oyf sha-bes,__ a kha-zn oyf sha-bes,__ Es iz ge-
(Once, in a small town, there came a cantor on the Sabbath)

Ex. 7-24b

goes to relative major

"Vay'chulu," *The Brandeis Service*
Setting by Max Helfman

Va-y' - vo - rech e-lo-him   es   yom ha-sh'-vi-i   va-ya-ka - desh o - so   Ki   vo   sho-

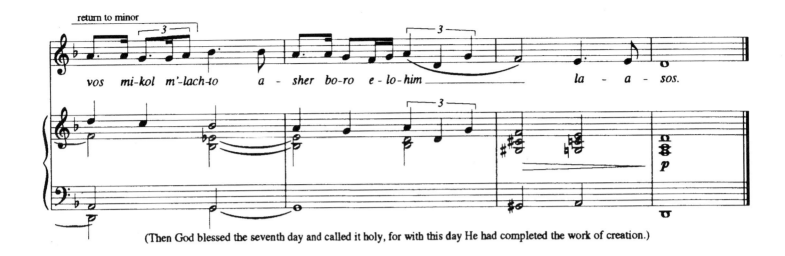

vos mi-kol m'-lach-to   a - sher bo-ro e - lo - him _____ la - a - sos.

(Then God blessed the seventh day and called it holy, for with this day He had completed the work of creation.)

The verses of many Yingish songs also begin in minor with the *MA* pattern of pivoting on the 5th step, making a detour to the sunny relative major, and then a return to the darker minor key before they reach the refrain, where major now rules and minor becomes subservient. (Cole Porter often also teases us with recurrent shifts from minor to major, but unlike Jewish melodies in *MA*, his minorish songs usually end up in major.) A prototype example is "Marry a Yiddisher Boy" (Ex. 7-25a). Another one by Irving Berlin is more adventuresome since its direction is to the relative minor (same destination, but not as bright). These two examples are followed by a selection of opening bars from verses to other whimsical ethnic novelties out of the same mold, all of them going back and forth to the relative major (not shown).

"Marry a Yiddisher Boy" (1911)
Seymour Brown (W) & George Botsford (M)

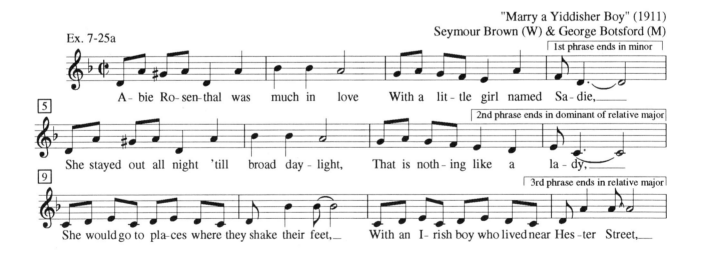

Ex. 7-25a

1st phrase ends in minor

A - bie Ro-sen-thal was   much in   love   With a lit-tle girl named Sa-die,_____

2nd phrase ends in dominant of relative major

She stayed out all night 'till   broad day-light,   That is noth-ing like a   la-dy,_____

3rd phrase ends in relative major

She would go to pla-ces where they shake their feet,_   With an I-rish boy who lived near Hes-ter Street,_

"Jake! Jake! The Yiddisher Ball-Player" (1913)
Blanche Merrill (W) & Irving Berlin (M)

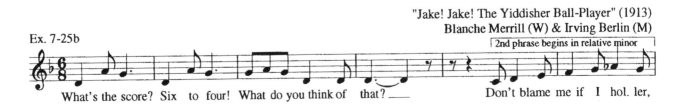

Ex. 7-25b

2nd phrase begins in relative minor

What's the score? Six to four! What do you think of   that?_   Don't blame me if I hol. ler,

Ex. 7-25c

"Abie, Dot's Not a Business for You" (1909)
Frank Davis (W) & Jacques Hertzberg (M)

A - bie Spring - er was a ten-or sing - er in a con - cert hall

Ex. 7-25d

"At the Yiddisher Ball" (1912)
Joe McCarthy (W) & Harry Piani (M)

In our neigh-bor-hood we have what you call Once a year a so-cia-ble hall,

Ex. 7-25e

"At the Yiddish Wedding Jubilee" (1914)
Joe McCarthy, Jack Golgau & Al Piantadosi

You should have been with me to the wed-ding last night, Co-hen had a drink, Then he near-ly looked for fight,

Ex. 7-25f

"Gootmon Is a Hootmon Now" (1916)
Sam Lewis/Joe Young (W) & Bert Grant (M)

Mau - ras Goot - mon sailed a - cross the o - cean, a no - tion,

Ex. 7-25g

"Moshe from Nova Scotia" (1915)
L. Wolfe Gilbert (W) & Malvin M. Franklin (M)

Way up north al - most in A-las - ka, There lives Mo - ses Cohen,

Ex. 7-25h

"There's a Little Bit of Irish in Sadie Cohn" (1916)
Afred Bryan (W) & Jack Stern (M)

Sa - die Cohn was a lit - tle Jew-ish girl Who came to this coun-try right from Russ-ian Po-land,—

An unexpected curio that belongs to this genre is by Indiana born and bred Hoagy Carmichael.* His 1925 "Jew-Boy Blues" about a deserted wife left "rocking the cradle" is gauche and musically unremarkable; but the verse does begin with an ascending 5th and the refrain alludes to "Hatikvah" in a major mode. The title hook also raises the question of attitude, whether or not the song is symptomatic of a negative mind-set concerning Jews, not unheard of in the Hoosier Bible Belt. However, such speculation is more than compensated for by "Baltimore Oriole," a remarkable 1942 Carmichael melody that imparts tender Jewish nuances in *MA* disguise. Although it bears a similarity to the white spiritual "Wayfaring Stranger," an early sketch with the handwritten title of "Kantor Song," surely must mean

that Carmichael was having another try at trying to capture a "Jewish" sound —considerably more successful than the clumsy "Jew-Boy Blues" . . . Indeed . . . the melody weds a strongly cantorial flavor with a sensibility drawn from the blues."[12]

Note how triplets are used to convey the sense of prayer chant in the song especially when viewed alongside two comparable samples from the Reform Jewish liturgy:

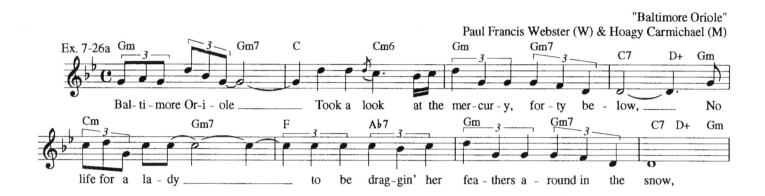

Ex. 7-26a

"Baltimore Oriole"
Paul Francis Webster (W) & Hoagy Carmichael (M)

Bal- ti-more Or-i - ole _____ Took a look at the mer-cur-y, for-ty be - low, _____ No

life for a la - dy _____ to be drag-gin' her fea - thers a - round in the snow,

Ex. 7-26b

"Let Us Adore," Julius Chajes

Let Us A- dore _____ the e-ver liv-ing God, _____ And ren-der praise un-to Him __ who spread out the

hea -vens _ and es-tab-lished the earth, Whose great -ness _ is re-vealed in the hea-vens a - bove,

Ex. 7-26c

"God Supreme," Joseph Achron
Union Hymnal, 3rd ed., no. 93

God Su - preme! To Thee _ we pray, Let our lips be taught _ to say Whe- ther good or

ill _ may flow, Hea-ven-ly Fa - ther, be _ it so, Hea-ven-ly Fa - ther, be _ it so.

The *MA* pattern weaves its way into songs about the Jewish experience: of immigration, a 1927 Tin Pan Alley curio by Jules Kerwin Stein (later known as Jule Styne); of the holocaust, Franz Waxman's theme for a Jewish concentration camp victim in the 1944 film *Mr. Skeffington*; and of the founding of the State of Israel, Ernest Gold's title song for the 1960 movie *Exodus*.[13] An Israeli song from the 1948 War of Independence foreshadows the more famous *Exodus* theme (Ex. 7-27d):

Ex. 7-27a

"Russian Doll" (1927)
Sonny Miller (W) & Jules Kerwin Stein (M)

My Russ - ian Doll, my lone -ly Russ- ian Doll, I'm com -ing back to Russ - ia for you,

Ex. 7-27b — Theme from *Mrs. Skeffington* (1944) / Franz Waxman

Ex. 7-27c — "The *Exodus* Song" (1960) / Pat Boone (W) & Ernest Gold (M)

This land is mine, God gave this land to me, This brave and an-cient land to me.

Ex. 7-27d — "L'moledet-imah" (To the Motherland) / Z. Winchell (W) & Moshe Bik (M)

Sha - lom, sha-lom ni - tzad__ ka-di-ma. Lik-rat ha-krav__ ha-a-cha-ron,
(Peace, peace, let us go forward. March forth, meet the next battle,)

But the *MA* motif also can function in non-Jewish contexts, as in the English folk song "Scarborough Fair," popularized in 1967 by Simon and Garfunkel, and in movies with no Jewish imagery such as a 1948 Arlen-Robin tune from *Casbah* (Ex. 7-28a), the 1959 title song from *Green Mansions*, music by Bronislau Kaper—based on themes of Heitor Villa-Lobos, no less—and words by Paul Francis Webster, and a 1967 Bacharach-David chart buster from *Casino Royale* (Ex. 7-28b).[14]

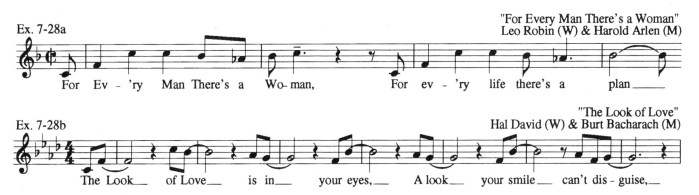

Ex. 7-28a — "For Every Man There's a Woman" / Leo Robin (W) & Harold Arlen (M)

For Ev - 'ry Man There's a Wo-man, For ev - 'ry life there's a plan____

Ex. 7-28b — "The Look of Love" / Hal David (W) & Burt Bacharach (M)

The Look__ of Love__ is in__ your eyes,__ A look__ your smile__ can't dis - guise,__

Although reminiscent of a section from Rimsky-Korsakov's *Scheherazade*, Neal Hefti's* pervasive *The Odd Couple* movie and television theme also alludes to *MA*:

Ex. 7-29 — Theme for *The Odd Couple* / Neal Hefti

Before we leave *MA*, another minor mode should be introduced, although in Chapter 12 the impact of this format on American music will be tackled in its particulars. For now, suffice it to say that it is called the Ukrainian Dorian mode. A recitative by Cantor Adolph Katchko from the *musaf* (additional) Sabbath service acts as a clear illustration. But the relationship of this chant to the verse of a 1960 pop ballad is baffling. Written by Bertolt Kaempfert,* Herbert Rehbein, and Milton Gabler, the chorus of "Sweet Maria" is congruent with the sound of

Kaempfert's famous song "Strangers in the Night," but its likeness to the chant is a puzzlement.[15] There are more similarities than anomalies:

Ex. 7-30a

"Mimkomo"
Katchko3, no. 126

Mim - ko - mo Hu yi-fen___ ' b' - ra-cha-mim v'-go - chon___ am_____
(From His place may He turn in mercy and favor the people)

Ex. 7-30b: Verse

"Sweet Maria"
Herbert Rehbein & Milt Gabler (W), Bert Kaempfert (M)

Count each day when I go, Then be - fore you know,

Time will fly be - fore your eyes and you will ne - ver re - al - ize I'm gone.___

"*Hatikvah*" (The Hope)

The melody for what eventually became "Hatikvah"—formally declared the Zionist anthem in 1933, but as yet to be officially sanctioned as the anthem of the State of Israel—is also related to *MA*: the first section is in minor, the second goes to the relative major and quickly gets back to the minor. Sung at the Sixth World Zionist Congress in 1903, it did not take long for the melody to filter down into popular consciousness. As early as 1909 it is quoted in a Yingish tune written by Messrs. Joseph H. McKeon, Harry M. Piano,[16] and W. Raymond Walker, and "respectfully dedicated to Miss Sophie Tucker," later less a Miss and more a red-hot Mama.[17] (see Illustration 18)

Ex. 7-31

"The Yiddisha Rag" (1909)
Joseph H. McKeon, Harry M. Piano & W. Raymond Walker

Yid-dish-a, Yid - dish -a Rag, Oh, oh that Yid - dish -a Rag, ___

Wig-gle and jig - gle when you feel that strain, ___ Ev-'ry-one hol - lers: "Please play it a - gain." ___

"Hatikvah"

First there came Top-lit - zky dan -cing with his Rif - ky, They did the Ka-zat - sky, Oh my!

That is a dan - dy rag, That is the can - dy rag, That is the Yid-dish - a Rag.

There, hidden in the middle of Ex. 7-31, is the opening strain of "Hatikvah." It has been musicologically authenticated that tunes resembling "Hatikvah" wandered like the Jews all over Europe—from Bohemia's Moldau, as immortalized by Bedrich Smetana in *Má Vlast* (My Country, 1874), to folk songs on the Iberian Peninsula.[18] It is not that Smetana influenced the melody of "Hatikvah" (or vice versa), but that an underlying melodic curve that was pervasive and persuasive was found to be irresistibly appealing to many nationalities. The Jews were particularly attracted to this musical magnet in a host of songs ranging from the secular to the sacred:[19]

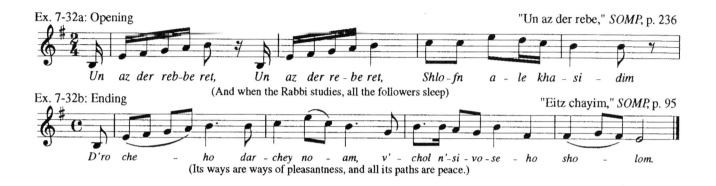

Ex. 7-32a: Opening · "Un az der rebe," *SOMP*, p. 236

Un az der reb-be ret, Un az der re - be ret, Shlo-fn a - le kha - si - dim
(And when the Rabbi studies, all the followers sleep)

Ex. 7-32b: Ending · "Eitz chayim," *SOMP*, p. 95

D'ro che — ho dar - chey no - am, v' - chol n'-si - vo - se - ho sho - lom.
(Its ways are ways of pleasantness, and all its paths are peace.)

Inevitably the pilgrim arrived on American shores. Berlin quotes from it in the introductory vamp to "Yiddle on Your Fiddle." But after the stock market crash of 1929, "Hope," became the symbol of depression when its first phrase was fleshed out with chromatic additions and its four bars were doubled to eight:

Ex. 7-33 · "Brother, Can You Spare a Dime?" E. Y. Harburg (W) & Jay Gorney (M)

Once I built a to - wer to the sun, __ Brick and ri - vet and lime,

"Hatikvah"

Kol __ od ba - lei - vav p' - ni - - - ma

Once I built a tow- er, Now it's done, __ Bro - ther, Can You Spare a Dime? __

ne - fesh Y'- hu - di ho - mi - - ya.
(As long as within the inmost heart a Jewish spirit still sings)

Isadore Hochberg, better known as E. Y. Harburg, wrote the words to this ten-cent threnody, music by Jay Gorney, born in Bialystok,[20] White Russia, 1896. In 1983 Mr. Gorney informed me that his mother sang words to the wistful melody of "Brother Can You Spare a Dime?" (a lullaby perhaps?); but, alas, he could not recall the words.[21] A Yiddish pastoral song that comes from the same general musical family as the dime-song suggests what it may have been like:

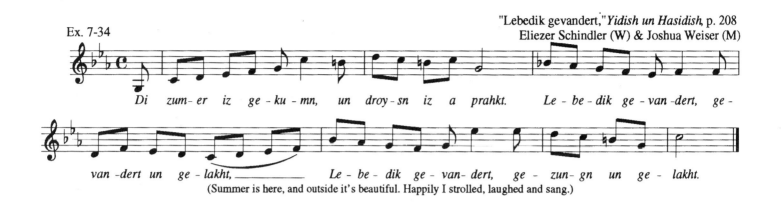

Ex. 7-34

"Lebedik gevandert," *Yidish un Hasidish*, p. 208
Eliezer Schindler (W) & Joshua Weiser (M)

Di zum-er iz ge-ku-mn, un droy-sn iz a prahkt. Le-be-dik ge-van-dert, ge-

van-dert un ge-lakht, _____ Le-be-dik ge-van-dert, ge-zun-gn un ge-lakht.
(Summer is here, and outside it's beautiful. Happily I strolled, laughed and sang.)

"Eli, Eli" (My God, My God)

For all our Jewish friends, in honor of the Passover holiday, here is "Hilly, Hilly."
LAWRENCE WELK on his television show, 1960s

Thus far we have witnessed the Americanization of "Khosn kale mazl tov" and "Hatikvah." But they were not the only *kinder* looking for a *garten*. Adoption papers were taken out for another drifter. Or, as expressed in a song lyric, "Ain't you heard the latest noise/Written by two Jewish boys?" The two boys in question were songwriters Fred Fisher (M) and Billy Rose (W),[22] and the "noise" was "Yiddisha Charleston," which concludes:

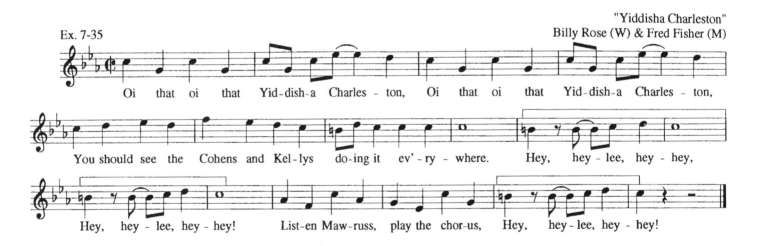

Ex. 7-35

"Yiddisha Charleston"
Billy Rose (W) & Fred Fisher (M)

Oi that oi that Yid-dish-a Charles-ton, Oi that oi that Yid-dish-a Charles-ton,

You should see the Cohens and Kel-lys do-ing it ev'-ry-where. Hey, hey-lee, hey-hey,

Hey, hey-lee, hey-hey! List-en Maw-russ, play the chor-us, Hey, hey-lee, hey-hey!

The latter phrase is fractured Aramaic and comes from the best known Yiddish song of its day, "Eli, Eli" (various spellings). Although Yingish songs were often peppered with quotes, this signature tune was rarely parodied since it was considered to be sacred stuff, but there are differing accounts about its actual origins. Both credit Jacob Koppel Sandler as composer and Sophie Karp as performer. Either it was from playwright Moishe Halevi Hurwitz's melodrama of 1896, *Brochoch: The Jewish King of Poland,* for which Sandler also wrote words, or it was from Hurwitz's operetta *Rouchel* (Rachel), with words by Boris Thomashefsky. In the first version, the heroine was a martyr to be crucified for her faith while hanging on a cross, and in the second she was to be stoned to death:[23]

"Eili, Eili"
Jacob Koppel Sandler

Ex. 7-36

Ei - li, Ei - - li, lo - mo a - zav - to - ni ?

Ei - li, Ei - - li, lo - mo a - zav - to - ni ?

(My God, my God, why hast Thou forsaken me?)

The translation from the Yiddish continues, "In fire and flames they burned us/Everywhere they shamed and mocked us/But no one could turn us away from You. . . ." Written originally for a female character, it became a theme song on the variety stage for Belle Baker, and was appropriated, among many others, by Boris Thomashefsky, Al Jolson, and Cantor Yossele Rosenblatt.[24]

African Americans were especially drawn to its highly charged drama of racial despair and delivered it in the original language. Ethel Waters, George Dewey Washington, and Jules Bledsoe (who was the first performer to sing "Ol' Man River") gave it their all on the vaudeville circuit. Eloise Uggins did the same on Broadway in the 1931 *Rhapsody in Black.* Will Marion Cook led the thirty-five member Clef Club orchestra in "Eli, Eli" at a 1925 concert with Georgette Harvey, vocalist, and Fletcher Henderson at the piano. Stride pianist Willie "The Lion" Smith knew it well enough to correct the diction of a Gentile performer who sang it with the Duke Ellington Band. The 1955 touring cast of *Porgy and Bess* performed it at a reception in Israel.[25] Vibraphonist Lionel Hampton recorded it (MGM Records); pop singer Johnny Mathis proffers a rendition on the album *Good Night Dear Lord* (Columbia label).[26] Why were blacks so drawn to this tearjerker? In the words of Ethel Waters, " 'Eili, Eili' moved me deeply . . . it tells the tragic history of the Jews . . . so similar to that of my own people . . . Jewish people crowded the theater to hear it: 'The schwarze sings "Eili, Eili!" The schwarze!'"[27]

One crucial matter is left out of this account, one that goes beyond its curiosity value. The opening words of "Eli, Eli" come from Psalm 22, and they are the utterance of Jesus on the cross. Indeed, as mentioned earlier, the original plot of the Yiddish melodrama called for the heroine (actress Sophie Karp) to sing it while being crucified! Although this religious arietta begins in Aramaic, with a central component of Christianity, the song continues in Yiddish and concludes in Hebrew with the affirmation of the monotheistic creed, *Sh'ma Yisrael.* Sadly and all too understandably, Sandler's lament was not forgotten in the Nazi slaughter camps.[28]

One further twist, "Eli, Eli" gets conflated elsewhere in theater song literature with the bathic themes of the despairing "Jewish mama" and the "Negro mammy." Sophie Tucker had helped turn the "humble east side tenement" of "My Yiddishe Momme" into a banality, and Al Jolson specialized in his blackface rendition of "My Mammy." The two matriarchal archetypes get fused in "My Yiddisha Mammy," a Yinglish oddity written for the 1922 revue *Make It Snappy.* The lyrics of the verse paint a picture of a stereotypical romantic southland in contrast to the refrain which heaves and sighs about a Bronx tenement. The music, however, shows no such differentiation; in fact, it incorporates no less than four signature quotations that culminate in "Eli, Eli":

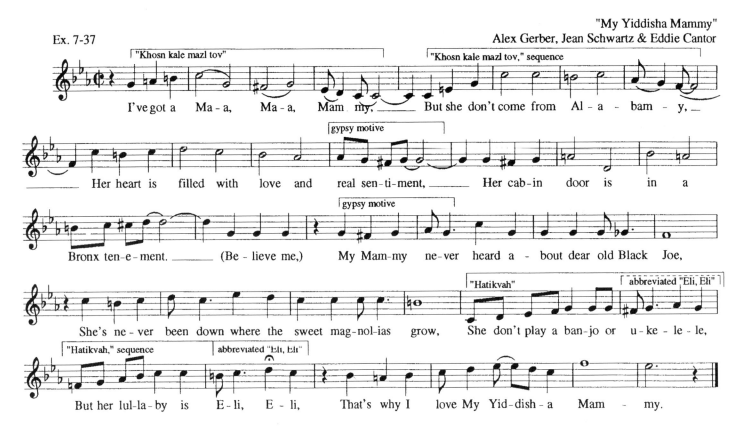

Burton Lane says he heard Judy Garland sing "Eli, Eli" at age eleven for her audition at MGM.[29] It was so far-reaching that as late as the 1930s dance bands recorded it under Harry James, Tommy Dorsey, and Fred Waring, as did popular vocalists Perry Como and Patti Page; Como in full-blown Yiddish and Page in an English version: "Father, Father" (adapted by Edward R. White and Mack Wolfson, 1953). Billy Rose's Charleston to the contrary, another English adaptation: "Peace and Love for All" (by Leo Corday and Leon Carr, 1941) shows the gravity with which this hoary melody was regarded: "No more stars shine on high/Dark is the sun in the sky."[30]

One adoption deserves rescue from oblivion. "That Eili, Eili Melody" by Leo Woods (W) and Archie Gottler (M) has a sensitive and lovely appeal:

The *Ahava raba* Mode–The *Freygish* Factor

The melody of "Eli, Eli" is appropriately enough couched in the synagogue mode most people, Jew and Gentile alike, believe to be the genuine article in Jewish music. Named after the Sabbath prayer *Ahava raba* (With infinite love), it is rarely chanted to that text—if at all—apparently because it is too long a text to be intoned. Like *Adonai malakh*, *Ahava raba* (henceforth *AR*) likewise functions as a delineation between the end of the Sabbath morning service introductory psalms and the call to worship, coming directly before the declaration of the *Sh'ma* creed. As a general rule, *AR* is "applied to texts with sad . . . content, confessions of sin, penance and lamentations over national calamities . . . .Whenever the precentor in moving the congregation to tears, such an ability was considered the highest art."[31]

AR is also known more affectionately in Yiddish circles as the *freygish* mode for its superficial resemblance to the Roman church phrygian mode (the white-note scale on the piano going from E to E). Although both modes share a half step between their first steps, the resemblance abruptly ends right there. The next step in *AR* is an intervallic leap of one and a half steps (i.e., an augmented 2nd), its identifying earmark. Very unchurchlike (the next step in the phrygian mode is only one whole step), but very Arabic sounding and, therefore, rather mosquelike.[32]

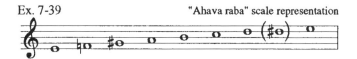

Ex. 7-39   "Ahava raba" scale representation

In Jewish music, *AR* is legion, used and abused in everything from cantorial wailing, as in "Eli, Eli," to joyous whoop-de-dos as in the evergreen "Hava Nagila," the hora which has been adapted into pop song literature at least five times.[33] But *AR*'s integration into American music is negligible, although its augmented 2nd intervallic feature has had surprising appeal for non-Jewish songwriters (see Chapter 11). Unsurprisingly, "Tradition," the opening number of *Fiddler on the Roof*, has sections in *AR*, explicitly in its harmonic scheme. Accompanied by the plain C Major and D-flat Major triads, the stage community stomps its way into Broadway history in an unambiguous *AR* mode.

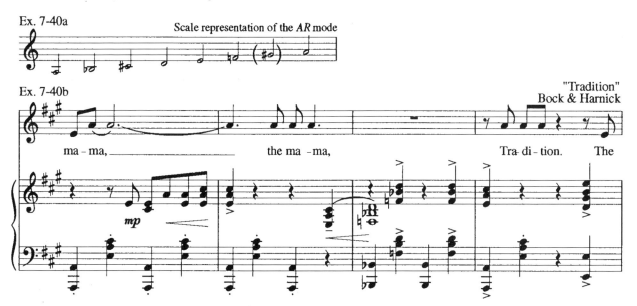

Ex. 7-40a   Scale representation of the *AR* mode

Ex. 7-40b   "Tradition"
Bock & Harnick

ma - ma,   the ma - ma,   Tra - di - tion.   The

Beyond ethnic contexts, there is an analogous accompaniment in "Luck Be a Lady" from Frank Loesser's *Guys and Dolls*. This lady is chaperoned by an *AR* escort, a thumping ostinato that alternates between a D-flat-Major triad and a D-Major triad. Unlike the triads in "Tradition," however, these are embellished with added 6ths, as if to mute any specific cultural reference. And yet, Sky Masterson—the character who sings the song in the show—makes a plea to Lady Luck immediately before the refrain begins: "You might refuse to stay/And so the best that I can do is pray":

NOTES

1. Abraham Idelsohn in *Jewish Music in Its Historical Development*, HOM, 10 vols., etc. Eric Werner in *A Voice Still Heard, In the Choir Loft*, etc.

2. Max Wohlberg in "The Music of the Synagogue as a Source of the Yiddish Folk Song," Baruch Joseph Cohon in "The Structure of the Synagogue Prayer Chant," Hanoch Avenary in *Encounters of East and West in Music*. Other significant theorists include Leib Glantz (1898-1964) and Joseph Yasser (1893-1982).

3. The "E" in "Eli, Eli" is pronounced as in the word "hey," not as in "eve."

4. Dr. Martin Schwartz of the Near Eastern Studies Department of UCLA, Berkeley, deduced that the ur-melody was *Colea 'n Gradinița* (Nearby in the Little Garden) by Narcisi Ludovic Daus, recorded by S. Bernardo in Bucharest before World War I. Among other Yiddish derivatives was the risqué "Tate ziser" (Sweet Daddy) recorded by Aaron Lebedeff.

5. The *piyyut (poetic passage)*, from the Yom Kippur *Avoda* (Service) section, yearns for the good old days: "Happy the eye that witnessed the splendor of the Temple . . . the singing of sweet songs." For the music, see

Idelsohn, *HOM*, vol. X, nos. 194 and 230.

6. Was this dubbed an Easter song because Christ's Last Supper was a Passover seder? Or, in jest, could it be that the Editor left off the letter "n" at the end of Easter? See *KJTS*, vol. 1, no. 14, p. 40.

7. According to Brooks Kerr, stride pianist, phone conversation with the author, July 1999.

8. "Palesteena" was also recorded in 1920 by the Vincent Lopez orchestra (Columbia A-3349) and in 1938 by Bob Crosby's Bobcats (Decca F6874).

9. Youmans was keenly aware of his position as the only "real American" among the Jewish writers of the 1920s starting to make their mark on Broadway. See Steven Suskin, *Show Tunes*, p. 146.

10. Handy's inspiration for "St. Louis Blues" was partially based on a chant he heard in church as intoned by a preacher.

11. Sarah Blacher Cohen, ed., *From Hester Street to Hollywood*, p. 34.

12. Sudhalter, Richard, *Stardust Melody*, p. 240. Music and lyric sheets are located in the Hoagy Carmichael Collection of Indiana University. A recording of "Jew-Boy Blues"

(a.k.a. "Jewish Boy Blues" and "Papa's Gone Bye Bye Blues") is on L'Art Vocal Records, vol. 18: 1927-1942. "Baltimore Oriole" can be heard in varying degrees of realization on the soundtracks for the films *To Have and Have Not* and *The Ghost Catchers* (both 1944) and *Stork Club* (1945).

13. Stephen J. Whitfield says the lyric should have read "This land is *ours*/God gave this land to *us*," *In Search of American Jewish Culture*, p. 229. In this day and age, the affirmation rings true for more than one affected plurality.

14. Cutting-edge Jewish composer John Zorn went so far as to release a 1997 album on his Tzadik label of Bacharach songs collectively entitled *Great Jewish Music*.

15. "Without You," the English version of the Mexican song "Tres Palabras" by Osvaldo Farre, begins with the same phrase.

16. A nom-de-plume for Al Piantadosi? The late William Simon, former editor of *Reader's Digest Songbooks*, believed Harry M. Piano to be a pseudonym for Irving Berlin. Conversation with the author.

17. In a peculiar turnabout, "Yiddisha Rag," an American-Jewish tune, was then acclimated into the Yiddish language in a Jewish-American adaptation as "Yidishe, Yidishe fish/Dem tam fun di Yidishe fish ... (Yiddish fish/The taste of the Yiddish fish...), Fred Somkin, "Zion's Harp by the East River," p. 194.

18. Idelsohn, *Jewish Music*, pp. 221-225.

19. For other melodies that belong to the "Hatikvah" family, see no. 138 from the *Union Hymnal*, 1943 edition or the *Union Haggadah* of 1923, p. 65.

20. Bialystok, from whence cometh the bread roll known as the bialy. It also serves as the name of a lead role in Mel Brooks's movie and Broadway musical comedy *The Producers*. In the same show, a gay character named De Bris could be read disparagingly as "debris" or with hubris after the Yiddish word for circumcision (*bris*).

21. Jay Gorney, interview with author, December 1983. See also Harold Meyerson and Ernie Harburg, *Who Put the Rainbow in the Wizard of Oz?*, p. 50. Another Gorney-Harburg song flecked with hues of Jewishness is their bluesy "What Wouldn't I Do for That Man?"

22. My first cousins, the Wernicks, children of my Aunt Celia, were first cousins to Billy Rose on their father's side. Rose's parents lived with the Wernicks for years, and Billy grew up in Park Ridge, New Jersey, in a house my Uncle Willie sold to the Roses. In later years, Rose was a noted philanthropist for Jewish causes (he produced the Moss Hart-Kurt Weill pageant *We Will Never Die* in 1943), but when he was climbing his way up, he was not generous toward his Jewish relatives. This is consistent with other general reports about this scrappy man of varied talents, famous for his small size and gigantic ego.

23. The first account is given in the foreword to "Eili, Eili," the sheet music edition of 1919, Maurice Richmond Music Co., publisher. For the second account, see Rosenfeld, *Bright Star of Exile*, p. 273. Peretz Sandler, another Yiddish theater composer, occasionally has been confused with Jacob Koppel Sandler.

24. Yossele Rosenblatt was the off-screen singing voice (in "Kol nidrei" and "Yahrzeit") of the cantor-father on the 1927 soundtrack for *The Jazz Singer* acted by Swedish-born Warner Oland, later famous as Charlie Chan. It may have been deemed unseemly for Rosenblatt to be seen on screen; but such decorum did not apply in 2000 when Cantor Raphael Frieder, singing fragments of "Kol nidrei," appeared in the film *Keeping the Faith*.

25. Ethel Waters and George Dewey Washington in *His Eye Is on the Sparrow*, p. 178; Jules Bledsoe in Melnick, *A Right to Sing the Blues*, p. 259; Will Marion Cook in *The Music of Fletcher Henderson*, p. 45; Willie "The Lion" Smith in *Music on My Mind*, p. 173; the cast of *Porgy and Bess* in Alpert, *The Life and Times of Porgy and Bess*, p. 202.

26. On this Columbia Legacy CD (CK6489), Mathis also performs "Kol nidrei" and "Where Can I Go?," from the Yiddish "Vi ahin zol ich geyn?".

27. Waters, *His Eye Is on the Sparrow*, p. 178. Waters was pleased to be labeled as "the Ebony Nora Bayes" (see Gary Giddins, *Riding on a Blue Note*, p. 6), perhaps a misleading appellation since, according to Brooks Kerr, Bayes was the daughter of a black mother and a Jewish father.

28. See Yale Strom, *The Book of Klezmer*, p. 279.

29. Burton Lane, interview on radio station (WKCR-FM, New York City), 12 February 1988.

30. "Eli, Eli": Harry James (1941), reissued on Classics Label, CD 1052; Tommy Dorsey, arr. by Axel Stordahl, trumpet solo by Ziggy Elman, on Victor; Fred Waring and His Pennsylvanians, as "Father, Why Hast Thou Forsaken Me?" on Decca; Patti Page on RCA-Victor (Flip side: "Kol Nidrei," with the Mitchell Ayers Orchestra and chorus under the direction of Ray Charles); Lionel

Hampton on MGM 1139, 78 rpm.

31. *HOM*, vol. VII, p. xx of English edition.

32. In the wake of the World Trade Center catastrophe of 11 September 2001, it was reported that a performing group known as the Afro-Semitic Experience received complaints about music they were playing in the *AR* mode as being "inappropriate" because of its Arabic sound. *The Jewish Week*, 28 September 2001, p. 20. See also n. 63, Chapter 12.

33. The music for "Hava Nagila" is based on a Hasidic tune of Bukovinian origin, attributed to Rabbi Abraham J. Friedman (1820-1883). The words were by Cantor Moshe Nathanson (1899-1981). Its pop song adap-tations include "Now" (Jule Styne, Comden and Green, 1963, not to be confused with the 1951 adaptation by Tom Glazer and Lou Singer, "Now! Now! Now!"), "Sing, Everyone, Sing!" (Stanley Lionel, 1949), "Dance, Everyone, Dance!" (Sid Danoff, 1958), and "This Night Is for Rejoicing" (David Taxe, 1960). The identification of the tune as the apotheosis of Jewish music is perpetuated in movies where it is usually used for incongruous comic effect: *The Duchess and the Dirtwater Fox* (1976), *Monty Python's The Life of Brian* (1979), the remake of *The Jazz Singer* (1980), *History of the World, Part I* (1981), *Monty Python's The Meaning of Life* (1983), *Joe Versus the Volcano* (1990), and *Snatch* (2001).

CHAPTER 8

Bits and Pieces

Instead of the burdens of the chosen people there were now the exhilarations of a choosing one.

TED SOLOTAROFF, "American-Jewish Writers: On Edge Once More," *New York Times*, 18 December 1988

A melody's opening, like first impressions of people, is often the most memorable part of a tune. The motive that introduces the main theme of the background score to the 1960 film *The Apartment* (Ex. 8-1a) is a case in point. But this same motive can also be found inside a tune. For example, in a famous Stephen Sondheim song of 1973, it appears at the end of the first full phrase (Ex. 8-1b). Similarly, David Baker finishes a phrase in an obscure song from an equally unknown 1961 show, *Smiling, the Boy Fell Dead* (Ex. 8-1c):

By now it should be apparent that much of Jewish folk, theater and traditional synagogue song is also tailored by stitching such scraps and shreds of melody together. The chanter (*Ba'al Tefila* or Prayer Leader) has a stockpile of inherited motives, bits and pieces from which he threads his melodies. But these are not random choices. Experience dictates which musical fragments work best with each other, a tried and true repository of melodic snatches from which whole cloth melodies are woven. In a nonreligious context, one sample of a linkage that gets recycled in different environments is the melodic unfolding of the notes that make up the dominant 7th chord. We find this in bridge sections as divergent as Irving Berlin's "The Song Is Ended" from Tin Pan Alley, a 1934 song from the Yiddish film *Mamele* (Mommy), and a song from Broadway, in *The Pajama Game* of 1954:

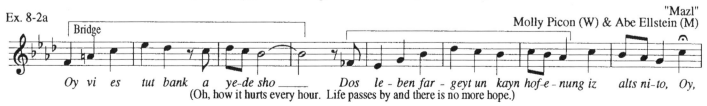

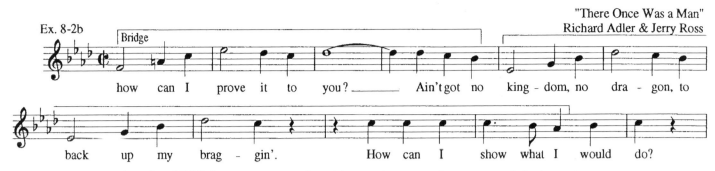

Another Yiddish mama song of 1954 uses the same dominant 7th linkage (Ex. 8-3a), echoed in a tango from *The Pajama Game* (Ex. 8-3b):

When Berlin starts off a ballad from the show *Call Me Madam* with this same broken chord as an incipit, it sounds as if he is beginning in midsection. It is, in its way, a daring choice, starting as it does with the dominant 7th of E Minor and concluding in the distant key of C Major.

A more common linkage from Yiddish songs undergoes an odd conversion when it gets transported into American surroundings. The primary feature of this connective phrase is a kind of yodel on the 7th step with a raised half tone on the 4th step. Jewish prototypes can be ascertained first in a folk song about a female, and then in a Yiddish theater song, also about a young woman:[1]

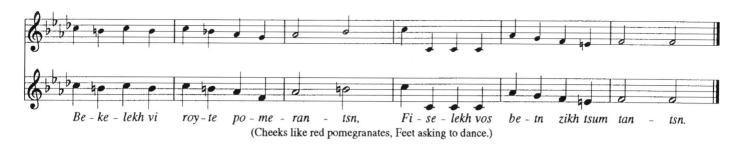

Be - ke - lekh vi roy-te po - me - ran - tsn, Fi - se - lekh vos be - tn zikh tsum tan - tsn.
(Cheeks like red pomegranates, Feet asking to dance.)

"Di grine kuzine" (The Green Female Cousin), based on an older dance tune, was a huge success on the Yiddish variety circuit and underwent several adaptations. However, there is little evidence that its characteristic linkage (see *"Sheyn vi gold"* in Ex. 8-5b) made a successful transplant because it—like the interval of the augmented 2nd—would have made the music sound "too Jewish." Curiously, later printed song-sheet versions smoothed out the Jewishness of the original—at least as compared to the recording by its composer—by removing the so-called Ukrainian raised 4th step. Even the best of the adaptations—"My Little Cousin" by Happy Lewis, Sam Braverman, and Cy Coben—does not make a comfortable adjustment, though it was recorded by the likes of song stylist Mildred Bailey and by Peggy Lee and Benny Goodman. This fox-trot could not hold a candle to the pithy irony of the original Yiddish as it bitterly traced the disintegration of the rosy-cheeked maiden to a sallow woman, old before her time: "Years have past, my cousin became a mess/Now when I meet her and I ask her how she is, she answers: 'To hell with Columbus's land!'"

A song from the Broadway show *On a Clear Day You Can See Forever* by Burton Lane and Alan Jay Lerner uses another form of the dominant chord, this time in the minor mode. Originally written for a musical set in Israel, to be produced by David Merrick and directed by Joshua Logan, Lane confirmed the tune's Jewish origins:

Years earlier when I was working on *Finian's Rainbow* I had an idea of doing a musical based on Israel becoming an independent state, but I couldn't get Yip [E. Y. Harburg] interested in it. Anyway, I loved this Israeli story [by Alfred Palca], but when Logan started to rewrite the script he destroyed everything that had attracted me.[2]

Ex. 8-6

"Melinda"
Alan Jay Lerner & Burton Lane

This is a dream, Me - lin - da, ____ Just a mir - age, so they say, ____
This whole af - fair, they all de - clare, Was dream'd each step of the way. ____

When the same phrase is lifted out of the minor mode and placed into a major tonality, its presence is much more conspicuous on Broadway. In a sense, it thereby becomes more assimilable—only half-Jewish. In fact, the following contrivance, all examples (save one) taken from the musical stage, can trace a male-female relationship from the initial exciting encounter all the way to the disheartening estrangement.[3]

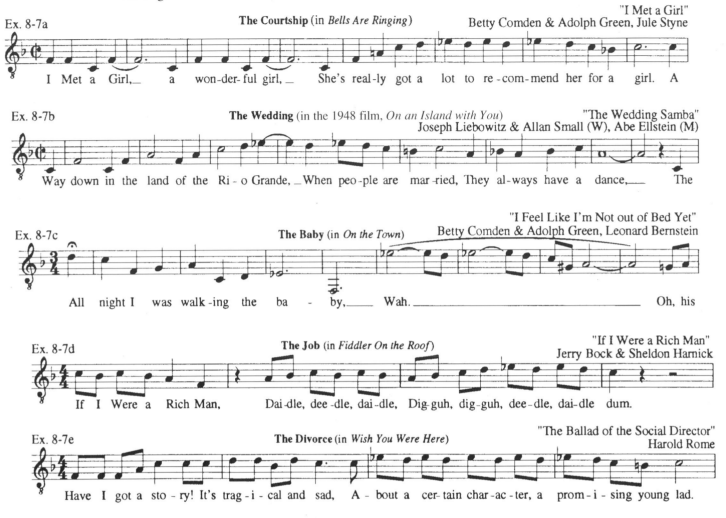

Popular music, like folk songs or synagogue tunes, almost by definition has to be constructed of short, reappearing motives. Obviously, it is these "shorties" that permit tunes to be more easily retained and more commercially viable—as well as valuable. Like the course of true love, as viewed in Exx. 8-7, the sequence of notes in Ex. 8-8 span the gamut from hope to despair. And if there is any question this survey has nothing to do with Jewish music, see Ex. 8-8f.

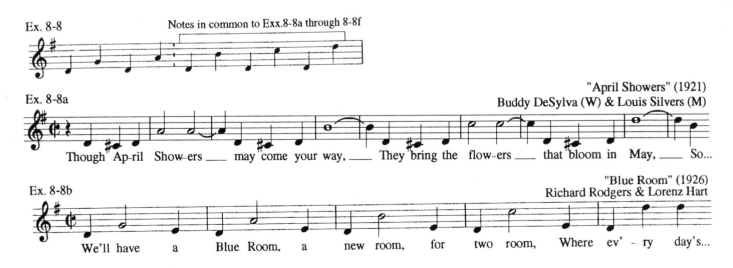

Ex. 8-8c
"Makin' Whoopee" (1928)
Gus Kahn (W) & Walter Donaldson (M)

An-o - ther bride, _____ an - o - ther June, _____ an - o - ther sun...

Ex. 8-8d
"Am I Blue?" (1929)
Grant Clarke (W) & Harry Akst (M)

Am I Blue? _____ Am I Blue? _____ Ain't these tears __ tell-ing you __

Ex. 8-8e
"The Glory of Love" (1936)
Billy Hill

You've got to laugh a lit - tle, cry a lit - tle, And let your poor heart break...

Ex. 8-8f
"Kedusha Response"
Salomon Sulzer

Ka - dosh, ka - dosh, ka - dosh, A - do - noy ts' - vo - os
(Holy, holy, holy Lord God of Hosts)

Jumping Jehosaphat, how did that last example get in there? I leave it to you; but do keep in mind that this sequence was not unknown even to the likes of J. S. Bach as can be ascertained by listening to his keyboard Invention No. 11.

The Impact of the Synagogue

How shall we sing the Lord's song in a foreign land? Psalm 137, Verse 4

Even if songwriters appear to be copycats, they are under no obligation to follow guidelines like a cantor. Songwriters are free to invent completely; but some Jewish composers, nevertheless, cannot entirely escape their heritage. A conspicuous suspect is British composer Lionel Bart and his 1960 musical *Oliver!* Even though it did not originate on American shores, *Oliver!* had nearly eight hundred performances on Broadway and spawned several standards, including a couple trolled by the lovable villain Fagin, who is portrayed both as a literary and as a musical stereotype. One of his folksy minor songs, "Reviewing the Situation" (Ex.8-9a), plausibly, has its roots in a Hebrew chant. Called *Havdalah* (Separation), it comes from the ceremony that bids a bittersweet farewell to the Sabbath (Ex. 8-9b).

Ex. 8-9a
"Reviewing the Situation"
Lionel Bart

I'm Re - view-ing _____ the Sit-u - a - tion, _____ I must quick-ly look up ev - 'ry-one I know, _____ Ti - tled

peo-ple _____ with a sta - tion, _____ Who can help me make a real im-press-ive show. _____ I will

Ex. 8-9b

"Hamavdil"
HOM, vol. IX, no. 210

Ha - mav - dil   bein   ko - desh l' - chol   cha - to - sei - nu   hu __ yim - chol,   Zar

ei - nu v' - chas pei - nu   yar - be cha - chol   v' - cha - ko - cha - vim   ba - loi - loh __

(May He who separates the holy from the profane, pardon our trangressions, multiply us as the sand and as the stars of night)

Other embodiments of the same parallel phrase constructions (broken tonic and dominant chords) are to be found in two "mazl" songs, one already examined as Ex. 8-2a, the other in the 1947 Tin Pan Alley novelty "Mahzel" by Artie Wayne and Jack Beekman:

> You've gotta have a little Mahzel/'Cause Mahzel means "Good Luck,"
> And with a little Mahzel, You'll always have a buck.

However, in a whole other context, the Jewish source goes unnoticed. "Comes Love" (Ex. 8-10), first introduced in *Yokel Boy*, a modest 1939 Broadway musical, starred the very non-Jewish actors Judy Canova and Buddy [Christian Rudolf] Ebsen and was subsequently made into a screen vehicle for the equally nonethnic Joan [Madonna] Davis and Eddie Foy, Jr. [Edwin Fitzgerald].

Ex. 8-10

"Comes Love"
Sam H. Stept, Charles Tobias & Lew Brown

Comes a   rain - storm,   Put   your rub - bers on   your feet,   Comes a   snow - storm,   You can

get   a lit - tle heat,   Comes Love, _____   noth - ing can   be   done. _____   Comes a

The title of a 1932 song: "Lawd, You Made the Night Too Long" obviously suggests some kind of prayer. Victor Young,* the composer, was born in the United States, but received his elementary music education in Poland where he could have been exposed to Jewish music.[4] His "Lawd" song (Ex. 8-11a), a synthesis of blues and Hebraic chant style, was milked dry in performance by Sophie Tucker and Ethel Waters and was recorded in a striking cantor style by Louis Armstrong; but it had an afterlife in a whole other context. Comedian Milton Berle was friendly with a tailor who had a show-business clientele. Berle writes, "When Sam announced he was getting married, a bunch of us decided to throw him a stag dinner at the McAlpin Hotel."[5] For this 1940 occasion, Berle and Fred Whitehouse concocted a parody of the "Lawd" number that was made into a hit by Joe E. Lewis, and was later recorded by Barbra Streisand (Ex. 8-11b). Menasha Skulnik, the Woody Allen of the Yiddish stage, then recorded a macaronic Yiddish response to the "Sam" lyrics, but to a new tune written by Robert Duke Leonard:

Ex. 8-11a: Verse

"Lawd, You Made the Night Too Long"
Sam M. Lewis (W) & Victor Young (M)

Night am creep - in' ____ slow-ly creep - in' ____ down the lane, Stars are

peep - in' ____ and I'm weep - in' ____ once a - gain. I'm not

Ex. 8-11b: Verse

"Sam, You Made the Pants Too Long"
Milton Berle & Fred Whitehouse (W)

Trou - sers drag - ging, slow - ly drag - ging thru the street, Yes! I'm

walk - ing, ____ but I'm walk - ing ____ with-out feet. I'm not

The verse to Sam's complaint suggests the synagogal *lern steiger* (study mode) chanted by a bearded *melamed* (teacher) as he interprets Talmud in a singsong manner for his hair sidelocked students struggling with the niceties of Jewish law.[6] Visualize him thrusting his thumb up or down to drive home a point in this bittersweet tutorial (based on a text from Talmud tractate *Berakhoth*) with modal patterns emphasizing intervals of the 3rd:

Ex. 8-12

"Omar Rabi Elozor"
Alter, *The Sabbath Service*, p. 10

O - mar ____ Ra - bi El - o - zor, ____ o - mar ____ Ra - bi Cha - ni - no: ____ Tal - mi -

dei cha - cho - mim, ____ tal - mi - dei cha - cho - mim ____ mar-bim sho - lom, ____ sho - lom bo-o - lom. O -

mar ____ Ra - bi E - lo - zor, ____ o - mar ____ Ra - bi Cha-ni - noh: ____ Tal-mi -

dei cha-cho-mim ____ mar-bim sho - lom, ____ mar-bim sho - lom, ____ sho - lom bo - o - lom.

(Rabbi Eleazar said in the name of Rabbi Hanina: "Scholars increase peace throughout the world.")

The music to Young's "Lawd" song also reverberates Jewishly in a classroom setting. A wrenching Yiddish poem by Avrom Reisen poignantly portrays a struggling Yeshiva student in Poland.[7] Its obvious basis in Talmudic chant is evoked by Gershwin in *Porgy and Bess*. As mentioned earlier, before he had decided on the DuBose Heyward play, Gershwin had entertained the notion of musicalizing Solomon Ansky's Yiddish drama *The Dybbuk*, a play with scenes of Hasidic students struggling with their studies. Although hindsight is rarely fruitful, we may catch a glimmer of what might have been in the Act I wake scene where the melancholy air of the Yiddish song adumbrates Serena's threnody, even down to the opening homophones of "Mai" and "My" (Exx. 8-13a and 8-13b).

Ex. 8-13a

"Mayko mashmelon" (based on Talmudic chant)
POYS, p. 116

May-ko mash-me-lon der re-gn, Vos-zhe lozt er mir tsu he-rn? Zay-ne
sht-vl iz tse-ri-sn, Uhn es vert in gas a blo-te, Bald vet

tro-pns oyf di shoy-bn kayk-len zikh vi tri-be tre-rn, Un di
oykh der vin-ter ku-men, Kh'hob keyn va-re-me ka-po-te. May-ko-

(What is the meaning of the rain? What does it say to me? Its drops roll down the windowpane like sad tears.
And my boots are torn and there's mud in the street. Soon the winter will be here and I don't have a warm coat.)

Ex. 8-13b: continuation

"Mayko mashmelon"

mash-me-lon dos likh-tl? Vos zhe lozt es mir tsu he-rn? S'ka-pet un es trift ir khey-lev, Un s'vet

(What is the meaning of the candle? What does it say to me? Its tallow drips,...)

"My Man's Gone Now"
Ira & George Gershwin

My Man's Gone Now, Ain't no use a - listen-in' For his ti - red foot-steps

bald fun ir nisht ve - rn, A - zoy tsank ikh do in klay - zl,

(...and soon will be no more. This is how I flicker here in the house of study)

climb-in' up __ de stairs, ____

The verse to the Gershwin-Irving Caesar 1919 hit "Swanee" yearns for a kind of Promised Land.[8] Did Gershwin subconsciously recall a synagogue tune that asks God to "renew our days as of old?" (Ex. 8-14). This is the verse for the song that launched Gershwin's career, but its milestone rendition by Al Jolson sent mixed signals. Is this the Swanee or the Jordan River? Black, Jewish or a hybrid? The boundaries between the American southland and the Holy Land begin to blend, and popular American music became all the richer:

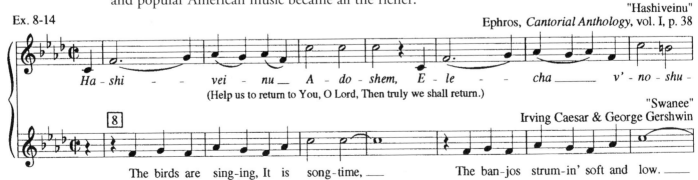

Ex. 8-14

"Hashiveinu"
Ephros, *Cantorial Anthology*, vol. I, p. 38

Ha - shi - vei - nu __ A - do - shem, E - le - cha ____ v' - no - shu -

(Help us to return to You, O Lord, Then truly we shall return.)

"Swanee"
Irving Caesar & George Gershwin

The birds are sing-ing, It is song-time, ___ The ban-jos strum-in' soft and low. ___

Even more provocative is hearing Betty Grable* sing a torch song that could be mistaken for a cantor's sob story. Written by the Italian-born (presumably Roman-Catholic) James Monaco (M) and Mack Gordon (W), it comes from the 1944 film *Pin-Up Girl* and begins with a trumpet wail by Charlie Spivak[2] and his orchestra that begs for a Hebrew prayer text:

NOTES

1. A point of clarification regarding Ex. 8-5a: *kashrut* (dietary law) in the East European tradition prescribes that dairy products are not to be eaten until six hours after meat consumption. German custom cuts the waiting time in half, while one hour is sufficient in Scandinavia. A recording of "Di mama kokht varenikes" may be found on Laser Light 1585: *Yiddish Songs*, Orchestra of the Yiddish Theater of Bucharest, Chajim Schwartmann, conductor.

2. Burton Lane at the April 1988, New York Sheet Music Society meeting.

3. Check out Rodgers and Hart's "Johnny One Note" for the same sequence.

4. Victor Young did record an album of *Four Horah Dances* as arranged by Leonard Bernstein, Darius Milhaud, David Diamond,

and Ernst Toch. In addition to gold-plated movie hits, he wrote novelties such as "She Wasn't Just a Tartar's Daughter."

5. Milton Berle with Haskel Franklin, *Milton Berle: An Autobiography*, p. 149.

6. The Talmud is a compendium of Jewish law, folklore, and ethics.

7. There are considerable differences between one version of *Mayko mashmelon*—found in *HOM*, vol. X, no. 109—and the version given here (Ex. 8-13a), which is from the Schack-Cohen collection. A very similar tune, with another text: *Ver mir zaynen*, may be found in the Platon Brounoff collection.

8. Irving Caesar quoted in *Jewish Week*, 27 December 1996.

CHAPTER 9

Sons of Cantors

A cantor sings in a public and hyper-emotional way. . . . It's not much of a leap to go from there to Ethel Merman.

MAURY YESTON, *Show Music*, Spring 1997

Although a few Russian fathers in their homeland were sanguine about musical careers for their sons—Jascha Heifetz's father, for one—many were not. Nevertheless, in much the same way that repressive conditions plus talent could engender impressive results within Russia, so conflict between an intransigent father and a transcendent son could become an energizing force outside of the motherland. In the annals of popular culture, the cantor-father and his rebellious pop-singer son are the classic pairing. Film expert J. Hoberman provides a meticulous chronology of *The Jazz Singer*, a mighty stream that began with Yiddish novels by Sholem Aleichem, gushed forth with stories, plays, and films in both Yiddish and English, peaked in the 1927 Al Jolson interpretation, followed by radio and television tributaries,[1] and more or less flowed out to sea with Neil Diamond's 1980 movie.[2] In spite of or because of papa, the battle lines set up with both sons and daughters paid off handsomely when East European Jews came to America. For a brief while, fiction writer Anzia Yezierska (b. in Pinsk, Russia, 1885, died in New York City, 1970) rebelled against her father when she "went Hollywood."

Of course, a parent's resistance to an offspring's musical ambitions was not exclusive to Jews. Tyne Daly, star of *Gypsy* (1989 revival), said: "To be refused by one's father is always very, very good for encouraging ambition." The same observation could be made about the opposition of musician-father Salvatore Liberace to his son's choice of pop pieces over classic repertoire.[3] Hoagy Carmichael's father hoped he would become a lawyer; and, in fact, he briefly did practice law, after a fashion. *Gypsy*, at least in show business history, is an example of the stage mother (specifically, Rose Hovick) who exchanges places with the stern patriarchal figure. It is the smother-mother who now becomes the domineering family influence, and the father is meek or indifferent. In some instances, the child gains the upper hand by denying parental demands and, therefore, deprives the parent of *nakhes* (pleasure, satisfaction).

However, an examination of real-life relationships between cantor-fathers and sons reveals *The Jazz Singer* model to be mostly a myth. Obviously, a parent who makes a livelihood from music must serve as a role model. Since cantors often refine improvisations into written compositions, it is no revelation that their progeny would harbor ambitions as songwriters. Jacques Offenbach and Harold Arlen were encouraged by their cantor-fathers; and, even though for reasons of financial security, Kurt Weill's father would have preferred if his son had pursued a career in medicine, he never stood in the way. *The Jazz Singer* parable to the contrary, none of these bonds were tainted by conflicts of sacred traditions vs. secular innovations. The same can be said for the heirs of Jewish songwriter-fathers, even at times pairs of brothers, who became songwriters or performers.[4]

Kurt Weill

1921 . . . seeks part-time employment as synagogue organist; plays piano in a *Bierkeller* cabaret.
DAVID DREW in *Kurt Weill Handbook*, p. 56

Ironically, the first synagogue piece to be written in an overtly American popular style was by a German émigré. In 1935, Kurt Weill, a victim of Nazi oppression, came to the United States, where he settled. The premiere of his score for the massive pageant about Jewish peoplehood, *The Eternal Road*, took place in New York City two years later.[5] Among various traditional synagogue melodies (*Kaddish* and *Kol nidrei*) used in this extravaganza was the *Mi-sinai* tune *Eli tsiyon* (God of Zion). Although the Hebrew appellation implies ancient origins, as if handed down from the heights by Moses,[6] these tunes actually originated in southwestern Germany. Weill, the son of Albert Weill (1867-1953), cantor of the synagogue in the north German town of Dessau, was familiar with these melodies from his childhood. As a young adult, Kurt also coached a synagogue choir in Berlin.

In nineteenth-century Germany, the reckless, improvisatory nature of hazanic recitatives was tamed by the cantor-composers Salomon Sulzer and Louis Lewandowski. While there is a curious, albeit distant, affinity between the free-wheeling nature of cantorial music and that of melodies in mainstream twentieth-century music—both reveling in irregular meters and in scales other than major and minor—the Sulzer-Lewandowski duumvirate forced rhythmic irregularities into metric straitjackets, and introduced alien chromaticism into older modes to make them conform to the standard secular practices of the day. This is the received, sanitized tradition of Albert Weill, who wrote in the sturdy four-square style of Lewandowski.

Did Kurt Weill adapt this manner for his one venture into synagogue music? Basically no. His setting of the *Kiddush* prayer (sanctification over wine), which is dedicated to the memory of his father, is a fascinating amalgam of Germanic stolidity, American blues, and Broadway pop harmony. It was commissioned by Cantor David Putterman of Park Avenue Synagogue, New York City, in 1946. To the extent that Weill's setting utilizes *nusach* (prayer patterns), it does so in a distinctive Weillian way. The composer's choice of the *Adonai malakh* (*AM*) mode is particularly efficacious for the text; but as a venturesome composer and not a slavish imitator, he exhibits variants of the mode. Note Weill's take on the well-known cadential formula of "good evening friends," used by Gershwin in *Rhapsody in Blue*, Darius Milhaud in *Creation of the World*, and a host of others—and not always as a cadence. For instance, the verse of Jerome Kern's "Can't Help Lovin' Dat Man" opens with a whiff of it (Ex.9-1b):

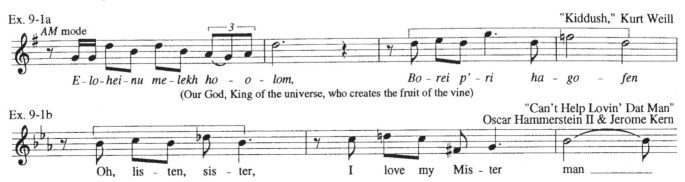

Ex. 9-1a   "Kiddush," Kurt Weill

AM mode

E - lo - hei - nu me - lekh ho - o - lom,   Bo - rei p' - ri   ha - go - fen
(Our God, King of the universe, who creates the fruit of the vine)

Ex. 9-1b   "Can't Help Lovin' Dat Man"
Oscar Hammerstein II & Jerome Kern

Oh, lis - ten, sis - ter,   I   love my Mis - ter   man _____

Further on in Weill's *Kiddush* there is another variant of a traditional formula, this one as heard in the blessing prior to the reading of Torah. In fact, it is something like Gershwin's gloss on the Torah blessing as used in his Bible song: "It Ain't Necessarily So" (see Chapter 13). Was this a conscious reference? Weill did attend rehearsals of *Porgy and Bess* before its premiere in 1935 and was deeply moved. The blessing variant, as worked out by Weill, is an allusion to Genesis, the biblical account of the creation of the Sabbath day. Furthermore, the word *v'reishis* (the end of Ex. 9- 2), is accompanied by a descending scale in a harmonized reference to the *Ahava raba (AR)* mode.

As a commemoration of the work of creation, it is a solemn moment. Hence the mode of *AR* (C-D-flat-E-natural). However, the mood is fleeting and, in fact, two bars later it is transformed into a whole-tone scale, completely vacating its Jewish overtones. So much for Weill's allegiance to Jewish practice.

Weill's opening to "Kiddush" is an old-fashioned American blues formula:

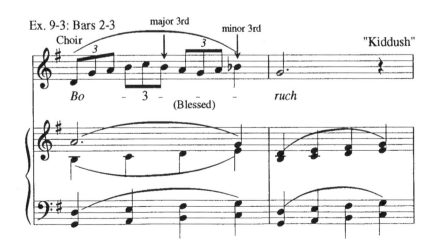

That alternation of a major 3rd closely followed by a minor 3rd is not to be found in traditional synagogue music. Furthermore, the accompaniment is a standard parallelism found in pop music, although it is also suggestive of Germanic chorale writing. Elsewhere, we find a keyboard figuration that spilled over into a musical theater work by Weill:

Ex. 9-4: Bars 135-139

Mi-kol ho-a-mim v'-sha-bas kod-sh'-cho b'-a-ha-vo uv-ro-tson hin-chal to — — nu____
(Above all the peoples and Thy holy Sabbath, In love and favor you have given us an inheritance)

"Kiddush" was completed in March 1946 (the end date in Weill's hand is Purim, 1946). For most of that year, Weill was writing the operatic musical *Street Scene*. It is not surprising, then, to learn that part of the accompaniment to a bluesy *Street Scene* song bears a close similitude to the "Kiddush" accompaniment:

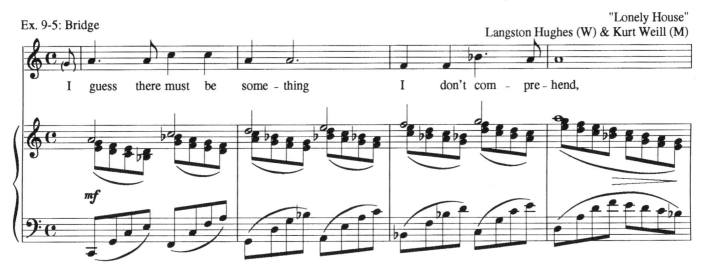

Ex. 9-5: Bridge

"Lonely House"
Langston Hughes (W) & Kurt Weill (M)

I guess there must be some-thing I don't com - pre-hend,

Which came first: the Jewish chicken or the Broadway egg? It should be noted that it is a Jewish character, Sam Kaplan, who sings the song. Evidently, Weill not only was a crossover composer from concert hall to stage, but also from choir loft to stage. Whatever its provenance, as the first synagogue piece to use a popular American idiom, his "Kiddush" is historically important. It must have been a disorienting experience at first hearing, especially at the august Park Avenue Synagogue's seventy-fifth anniversary service on 10 May 1946. But as one music critic has pointed out, Weill's so-called split personality was "an ambivalence that unites rather than divides his work."[7] Similarly, as mentioned earlier, German (i.e., western) Jews have notoriously been ambivalent about their coreligionists in the east.

A close associate of Weill felt that he was "totally outside Jewishness and religiousness."[8] German Jews generally thought of themselves as Germans first, Jews second; Russian Jews were always reminded by others (including their German brethren) they were Jews first and second. Germans preferred to designate themselves with the more genteel (if not gentile) label of "Israelites"or as persons of the "Hebrew persuasion." At a conference in 1983, Weill was quoted by Henry Marx as having said: "The most American composer is Irving Berlin, a Russian Jew, and I am a German Jew. That's the difference."[9] But this is feigned flattery since the implication is that the accomplishment of the Russian Jew is less distinguished than that of the German one. Compare east to west:

German (Western)	*Russian* (Eastern)
Hamlisch/Kern/Loesser	Gershwin/Gould/Lane
Loewe/Rodgers	Arlen/Berlin/Bernstein
Sondheim/Weill	Blitzstein/Rome/Ross/Styne

Representing:

Elite	Proletariat
"Kultur"	Folk
Urbanism	Ruralism
Assimilation	Ethnicity
High Art	Low Art

There are exceptions. Bernstein, Blitzstein, Gershwin, Gould, as well as Weill, all combined so-called high and low art in their output. All this may help to explain a puzzling passage from the instrumental suite Weill extracted from his *Die Dreigroschenoper* (The Threepenny Opera). This concert spin-off introduces an extensive section in the "Kanonensong" that does not appear in the opera itself. Normally suites are abridgements and do not include new additions of any consequence. This expansion is virtually a parody of a *freylekh*, the generic Jewish wedding dance:

Ex. 9-6   From *Little Threepenny Music* for Wind Ensemble
Maestoso (♩ = 84)   Kurt Weill

As if to confirm this hypothesis, the "Kanonensong" appears immediately before the wedding scene. Why wasn't it part of the stage version? I have a theory: Weill (if not Brecht) had a hidden subtext which associated the underclass (ultimately victorious) with East European Jewry. The Act II Finale of *The Threepenny Opera*, for example, is reminiscent of Yiddish bundist anthems. The pre-Nazi atmosphere when the work was first produced would only have helped to fan the flames of such infra dig sentiments. By placing the passage into an instrumental suite, it was possible to camouflage my suggested subtext. The Nazis soon banned the opera, anyway. Woody Allen uses this same music as the main theme for the background score to *Shadows and Fog*, a Kafkaesque film in which he plays the part of Max Kleinman (small man).

Weill expert David Drew has shown how the concluding refrain in

"Seeräuberjenny" (popularly known as "Pirate Jenny," from *The Threepenny Opera*) can be traced to the opening phrase of Soviet composer Lev Kniepper's famous "Meadowlands (Calvary of the Steppes)," and from there, even further back to one of the *Ofrah Lieder* Weill wrote, in German translation, on poetry of Hebrew poet Yehudah Halevi. Drew observes: "At the unconscious level where his mature imagination is always most deeply stirred, Weill has returned to his origins, to his home, and his earliest creative experience."[10]

Jacques Offenbach

He used to refer to himself as "O de Cologne."
JAMES FULD, *The Book of World-Famous Music*, p. 104

A predecessor of Albert Weill was Isaac Judah Eberst, a native of Offenbach-Am-Main, Germany, who, after he moved to the city of Cologne, worked as an itinerant performer. Eventually, however, he became a distinguished cantor-composer. His musical son Jakob, born in Cologne, enrolled at the conservatoire in Paris, where he also joined a synagogue choir.[11] The son, of course, was Jacques Offenbach who, according to Eric Werner in *A Voice Still Heard,* borrowed "trivial synagogue ditties and ennobled [them] in his operettas" (p. 238). Contrarily, Gdal Saleski disparaged Offenbach for melodies that "were open mockeries and burlesques of traditional synagogical chant."[12] Werner does not give examples of these in his book, but elsewhere he showed how Offenbach refashioned a Germanic setting of the "Reader's Kaddish" (Ex. 9-7a), that might have been chanted by his father, into a tune for one of his operettas: *Bataclan* (Ex. 9-7b):[13]

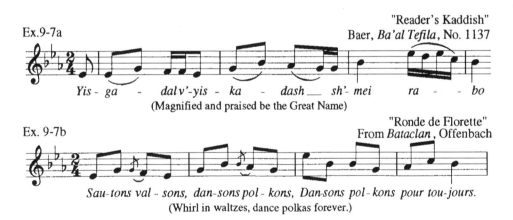

Ex.9-7a

"Reader's Kaddish"
Baer, *Ba'al Tefila*, No. 1137

Yis - ga - dal v'-yis - ka - dash __ sh'- mei ra - - bo
(Magnified and praised be the Great Name)

Ex. 9-7b

"Ronde de Florette"
From *Bataclan*, Offenbach

Sau - tons val - sons, dan-sons pol - kons, Dan-sons pol - kons pour tou-jours.
(Whirl in waltzes, dance polkas forever.)

Although Offenbach had paved the way for acceptance of Jews in the theater, thumbing his nose at high society and politics,[14] one can hardly imagine a Jew spoofing the Russian Czar at the same time Offenbach was conquering stages from Vienna to New York. However, a Yiddish version of his operetta *Bluebeard*, first performed in New York in 1868, was presented in 1882. More weighty is the indebtedness of the United States to Offenbach for a march tune from his 1859 operetta *Geneviève de Brabant* which surprisingly became the basis for the U.S. Marine Hymn. There are differing accounts about the word origins of the "Marine Hymn," fewer about the tune. None of them point out John Philip Sousa's possible role in its genesis. Sousa, named head of the U.S. Marine Band in 1880 (the

year Offenbach died), was concertmaster in Offenbach's orchestra a few years earlier when Offenbach toured the United States.[15]

"Les deux hommes d'armes" (Two Soldiers)
From *Geneviève de Brabant*, Offenbach

Ex. 9-8

Pro-te-ger le re-pos de vil - les, Cour-ir aux sus mau - vais gar - çons.   Ne par-ler
qu'a des im-be - cil - es, En voir de tou - tes les fa - - -

çons.   Un peu de calme a - pres vous char - me
(Protecting the peace of the villages, chasing the bad boys, speaking only with imbeciles. Seeing all sorts, a little calm afterwards charms you.)

* * *

Another link from the old world to the new that should be noted is Rubin
Goldmark, a teacher of both Gershwin and Copland. Goldmark was a nephew of
composer Karl Goldmark (1830-1915), who in turn was the son of a Hungarian
cantor. The first music lessons of *enfant terrible* composer Leo Ornstein (1892-
2002, making him the oldest composer ever) were with his Russian cantor-father.
One of famed Hollywood composer Alfred Newman's grandfathers was a cantor;
and two other songwriter offspring of old-world cantors were Al Hoffman (of
"Mairzy Doats" fame) and Louis Herscher, son of Cantor Eliss Herscher.

Irving Berlin

IRVING BERLIN, "Come along and listen to the Yiddisha Professor, Mister Abie Cohen," 1912

From 1910 to 1915, the character of Abie Cohen appears in no less than five Irving
Berlin songs, almost one a year. Abie was a generic name for East European Jews
and, as we have seen in Chapter 6, Berlin was hardly the only songwriter to feature
the name in Yingish songs. Berlin's own name change obviously was a sensitive and
crucial matter. On November 16, 1911—the same year that "Alexander's Ragtime
Band" was first heard 'round the world—Isadore Baline's name was officially
changed to Irving Berlin in a petition from the New York County Clerk archives
that stated:

Musical compositions composed by your petitioner have been uniformly successful and
have earned vast sums of money. The name has become exceedingly valuable and the
name Irving Berlin on a musical composition tends to increase the sales thereof.

The document goes on to declare "Your petitioner's Christian name is Irving."
That, in a nutshell, encapsulates the life and times of the Jewish composer of
"White Christmas" and "Easter Parade."[16] To quote novelist Philip Roth in
Operation Shylock, Berlin "de-Christs" Easter and Christmas by turning the one
"into a fashion show" and the other "into a holiday about snow." By today's crite-

ria, the "Christian name" of Irving (or Irwin) has reverted to being "too Jewish." Perhaps Berlin himself contributed to this metamorphosis in his pursuit of the American dream, a quest that in some ways may have backfired on him. Was he too zealous a patriot, too preoccupied with reinventing himself while being over-protective of his humble beginnings and Jewish origins?

Like the Weill family tree, Berlin's was studded with cantors and rabbis. His great-grandfather, grandfather, and father, Moses Baline (1846-1901) all officiated at synagogue services. Irving was thirteen years old when his father died. (A 1901 photo in a Berlin biography is captioned as a possible Bar Mitzvah portrait.[17]) If Moses Baline had lived longer, perhaps Irving would have continued the family tradition. In any case, he did sing in a synagogue with his father during high holy days: "I suppose it was singing in *shul* with my father that gave me my musical background. It was in my blood."[18] But in short order, the sectarian high holy days were replaced by the secular high holy days of the Fourth of July and Memorial Day. It was the American civil religion with its "dogmas" of freedom and brotherhood "from sea to shining sea" that made it possible for a Jew to be the musical voice of a Protestant Christian nation. And yet—one does detect an echo from a well-known Rosh Hashanah tune by Louis Lewandowski in Berlin's song "The Piccolino," from the 1935 film *Top Hat*.[19]

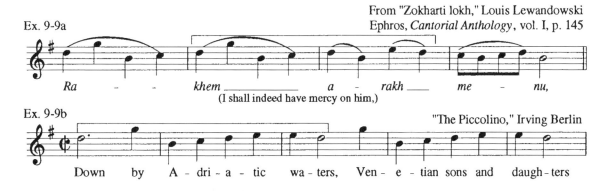

And a hint of Berlin's famous paean to show business might be traced to *Di fir kashes* (The Four Questions), a rubric assigned to the youngest child at family Passover seders. Surely Berlin must have sung this as a youngster. Notice how both pieces of music emphasize repeated tonic and dominant tones.

The love duet from Gershwin's *Porgy and Bess* similarly contains a passage suggestive of "The Four Questions" chant and echoes an intonation of young Hasids perusing their holy books:

Ex. 9-10c   "Bess, You Is My Woman Now," George & Ira Gershwin

Morn - in' time an' eve - nin' time an' sum - mer time an' win - ter time.

The Lower East Side of New York City was a cauldron of ethnicities which Berlin early on portrayed in numerous songs about blacks and the common folk of Irish, Italian, German, French, Russian, Asian, and Spanish ancestry. Late in life, Berlin was quoted as being embarrassed by these ethnic songs, especially the Jewish ones, and repudiated them.[20] Despite his discomfiture, what is particularly noteworthy about many of the individuals who inhabit Berlin's unsophisticated Yingish songs is that they are all adroit Jewish musicians with phenomenal skills, performers who can totally enrapture their listeners. The aforementioned Abie Cohen is a Svengalilike bandleader in "That Kazzatsky Dance" (1910) with the power to put people into a trance; piano virtuoso Abie Cohen in "The Yiddisha Professor" (1912) is able to drive fans into a frenzy about his "first class Yiddisha tone." As seen earlier, the unnamed fiddler (who could be Abie again) in "Yiddle on Your Fiddle, Play Some Ragtime" (1909) has the capacity to make Sadie feel "two years young." In addition to all this, Abie has energy to burn as a sexual athlete. In 1913's "In My Harem"—in which Berlin quotes both Grieg's "March of the Dwarfs" from the *Lyric Suite* and Sol Bloom's Hoochy Koochy dance—Abie surpasses King Solomon himself.

The least appealing characters in Berlin's early gallery of Yiddish characters are those who are stereotypical money-grubbers: Benny Bloom in "Yiddisha Eyes" (1910) and old man Rosenthal in "Cohen Owes Me Ninety-Seven Dollars" (1915). By pretending to be on his death bed, Rosenthal dupes Cohen (is he Abie, once more?) to force him to pay up accounts—a scheme worthy of the plot of Puccini's comic opera *Gianni Schicchi*.

Women receive less attention in these early songs. Nevertheless, the Abie Cohen of 1911's "Yiddisha Nightingale" is smitten by Minnie Rosenstein's singing voice which both outclasses opera star Luisa Tetrazinni and makes him a strongman (with a quote from the Mendelssohn Wedding March[21]). Berlin also took advantage of the scandal that erupted when Richard Strauss's opera *Salome* (based on Oscar Wilde's play) opened at the Metropolitan Opera in 1907. It so outraged sensibilities that the Met was forced to drop it for twenty-seven years. Newspapers had a field day with this, and soon Salome's notoriety became a standing joke. In "Sadie Salome" of 1909, Edgar Leslie's lyric tells of the eponymous female who "left her happy home" to become a "sad disgrace" as a racy dancer.[22] On the other hand, Becky Rosenstein as a high-stepping "Yiddisha chicken" in "Becky's Got a Job in a Musical Show" (1912) is the pride and joy of her family.

Besides Edgar Leslie, the few lyricists who collaborated with Berlin early on included Ted Koehler—who later worked so successfully with Harold Arlen—and Blanche Merrill. Together she and Berlin came up with "Jake! Jake! The Yiddisher Ball-Player" of 1912, and it is a winner; for despite the fact that Jake is a "regular fake," Berlin depicts him with Jewish musical overtones.

As he became more skilled, Berlin was drawn to the plight of Russian Jewry in the 1920s. Clearly, the rueful tune of his "Russian Lullaby" is rooted in the environs of "Hatikvah," the Jewish anthem of hope,[23] echoed by Berlin's lyric: "Somewhere there may be a land that's free for you and me." Although we are cautioned to "Look Out for That Bolsheviki Man" (1929), a shady figure "full of 'bull' just like his name," the composer in "Yascha Michaeloffsky's Melody" (1928) turns out to be a thinly veiled self-portrait of the songwriter, with one exception—a telling passage which says "with all his wealth and fame . . . [Yasha] hasn't changed his name"; but also it continues: "no one [else can] write[s] such music." (Once again Berlin quotes from Edvard Grieg, this time a snippet of "In the Hall of the Mountain King" from the incidental music to *Peer Gynt*.) One begins to wonder if Berlin, as the so-called untutored musician, may not be part of the myths he helped to perpetuate.

The aforementioned petition for change of name gave Berlin's place of birth as way out west in Tabulsk, Siberia.[24] Other sources state that he was born in Temun (or Temum), Siberia. However, as Berlin biographer Laurence Bergreen rightly points out, not only is this doubtful—since that would have placed the Baline family outside the Pale of Settlement in the east—but there is no such town as Temun. The Map Division of the New York Public Library confirms there is no place called Tabulsk, either. In fact, when Berlin applied for American citizenship, only four years later in 1915, the birthplace was given as Mohilev, near Minsk. Now, under the obligation of oath, the jig was up. Was Berlin trying to cover his traces as if he were a cryptofugitive? Can we attach any personal significance to the song "Don't Send Me Back to Petrograd" from the *Music Box Revue of 1924*, a song that pertains to that year's National Origins Act?[25] The singer pleads, "Now that I'm over here, they won't let me stay, . . . Please don't send me away." As he had done once before in "Yiddle on Your Fiddle, Play Some Ragtime," Berlin paraphrases a Yiddish song by Abraham Goldfaden (Ex. 9-11, bar 4).[26]

Ex. 9-11
"Don't Send Me Back to Petrograd," Irving Berlin
Moderato

Don't Send Me Back, __ I don't want to go back __ to Pet - ro - grad! __

Near the end of the song there is even a quatrain based on the gypsy motive:

Ex. 9-12: Bars 24-28
gypsy motive
"Don't Send Me Back to Petrograd," Irving Berlin

I'll prom-ise to work the best I can, __ I'll e - ven wash sheets for the Klu-Klux-Klan, __ Oh!-

At the very end, Berlin puts the Goldfaden quote into a major tonality. That and an extract from "The Star-Spangled Banner" indicate the greenhorn will get to stay in America.[27]

The reference to Goldfaden is deliberate, unlike "Blue Skies" where, as noted in Chapter 2, it is not. Such a subliminal allusion can also be found in another song by Goldfaden. "Flaker fayerl" (Flickering Flame, from the operetta *Shulamis*) was later transformed by Yiddish poet Mordecai Rivesman into a peppy song about Purim, the holiday that celebrates the heroism of Queen Esther (Ex.9-13a). Could magician Berlin have put that into his memory high hat and pulled out a strutter for Fred Astaire in the 1948 movie *Easter Parade*? (Ex. 9-13b):

Ex. 9-13a

"Haynt iz Purim," Mordecai Rivesman (W)
based on Abraham Goldfaden (M)
TOJFS, p. 160

Haynt iz Pur - im, bri - der, Es iz der yom - tev groys.
Lo - mir zin - gen li - der, Un geyn fun hoyz tsu hoyz.
(Today is Purim, brothers, It is the great holiday. Let us sing songs and go from house to house.)

Ex. 9-13b

"Steppin' Out with My Baby," Irving Berlin

Step-pin' Out__ With My Ba - by, Can't go wrong__ 'Cause I'm in right,__
It's for sure,__ Not for may - be, That I'm all dressed up to-night.__
(Haynt iz Pur - im, bri-der, Es iz der yom - tev groys.)

Not only do the first seven notes correspond—the difference, of course, is in Berlin's syncopated rhythms—but the B-section of the Purim song (Ex. 9-14a) echos in the bridge section of Berlin's "Puttin' on the Ritz"(Ex. 9-14b):[28]

Ex. 9-14a: B section

"Haynt iz Purim"

Lakh, Mord-khe- le, lakh, A yom-tev-l makh, Kinds kin-der ge-den-ken dem nes,_____ Zingt
bri- der-lakh zingt, Tanst frey-lakh un shpringt, Dem tay - er - n tog nit gar - gest.
(Laugh Mordecai, laugh, make a holiday. Children's children will recall the miracle.
Sing, brothers, sing, dance a freylakh and jump. Do not forget this precious day)

Ex. 9-14b: Bridge

"Puttin' on the Ritz," Irving Berlin

Stroll- ing up the a - ven - ue so hap - py,_____ All dressed up just
original lyrics (That's where each and ev' - ry Lu - lu - Belle goes,_____ Ev' - ry Thurs-day

Conclusion

like an Eng- lish chap - pie,__ ve - ry snap - py, Put - tin' on the Ritz._____
eve - ning with her swell beaus,__ rub - bing el - bows,)

Compare the third phrase of Berlin's "How Deep Is the Ocean?" to the opening
of a Hasidic song of faith, "A Dudele" (A Thou Song):

The descending melodic unfolding of the minor triads in Exx. 9-15a and b might
be deemed ordinary or coincidental; but as previously noted with regard to the
downward minor scale pattern of Exx. 4-20a and b, where else are such broken
minor chords—especially in a kind of davening mode—to be found in pop song
literature? The devices may be simple, but their frequency is rare. One way to
explain the cognates between the phrases in "A Dudele" and in "How Deep Is the
Ocean?" is that both rise out of the same wellspring of ethnicity. Berlin did not
consciously imitate a Hasidic tune. Nor, to reverse the chronological order, was the
opening phrase of a Yiddish World War II song a deliberate quotation from
Berlin's "Ocean" tune. The authors of both songs subconsciously drew upon the
wellsprings of their cultural heritage:[29]

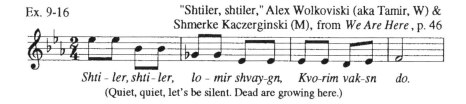

Growing up in a Yiddish-speaking household, Berlin lived in the midst of the
Yiddish theater district. We know he attended this theater as an adult. It is plausible that as a child he saw Yiddish shows, the entertainment outlet of the day.
Heredity, environment, personal disposition all entered into the development of
his psyche. Berlin undoubtedly would have vehemently denied all this. His discomfort with Jewishness is made evident when in 1959, after making three
attempts to complete a lyric called "Israel," he confided to a colleague: "I've grown
quite cold on it." As well he should have, with such platitudes as "The skies above
burn bright/With the Star of David" and "Today's the day we sing and pray/And
thank God that at last we're here."[30]

And yet, long after he achieved fame and fortune, the only other time Berlin
chose to set words that were not his own, they came from the pen of the Jewish
poet Emma Lazarus and were inscribed on the Statue of Liberty, the uplifting 1949
anthem, "Give Me Your Tired, Your Poor." He had to have remembered what it
was like in the old days, and took the text very much to heart.

Harold Arlen

The Cantor . . . delighted the congregation . . . by weaving such melodies as "Over the Rainbow" and "Come Rain or Come Shine" into the services.

EDWARD JABLONSKI, *Happy with the Blues*, p. 37

Russian Jews, with justifiable reason, could be anti-Gentile in their folk songs. Part of a Ukrainian polka, "Near the Woodland a Girl Is Ploughing," was turned by shtetl Jews into an observation of Cossack drunkards:

(A gentile goes into a tavern and drinks a full glass of wine. Oh! a gentile is a drunkard, drunk is a gentile. Drink he must because he's a gentile.)

Paradoxically, the Jew who sang that (albeit covertly) was unaware that when he partook of sacramental wine in the synagogue, his drinking was portrayed in similar musical goblets. From the Yiddish into the Hebrew (or the other way around):

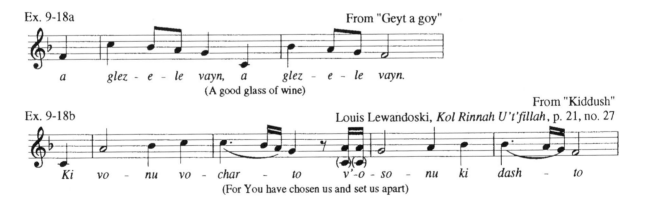

Perhaps that's a "long shot" since this *Kiddush* prayer over wine is in a setting by Louis Lewandowski, a composer educated in Germany, but born in Poznan, Poland. Although east did meet west in big city synagogues, we cannot be certain that cantors sang such citified chants in country villages. However, we can be sure that Hyman Arluck[31]—better known as Harold Arlen—did know that *Kiddush* since both his grandfather Moses Arluck (Erlich) and his father, Samuel (1890?-1953), were cantors. Harold sang in his father's synagogue choir, Pine Street Synagogue in Buffalo, New York (later Samuel took up residency in Syracuse, New York, at Temple Adath Yeshurun). Note the similarity to Irving Berlin: both Berlin's and Arlen's grandfathers and fathers were cantors, both grandfathers were named Moses and both boys sang in their fathers' choirs. From father to son, a 1932 Arlen song evokes Lewandowski's *Kiddush* setting:

Ex. 9-19a
"Paper Moon"
E. Y. Harburg, Billy Rose (W) & Harold Arlen (M)

Say, it's on-ly a pa-per moon,___ Sail-ing o-ver a card-board sea,___

Ex. 9-19b
From "Kiddush" (modified)
Louis Lewandowski

Ki vo-nu vo-char - to v'-o-so - nu ki dash - - to

Far fetched, you say? (Or as they say in pidgin Yiddish, *farfetsht?*) But isn't "Paper Moon" a kind of secular prayer with its allusions to heaven and faith: "But it wouldn't be make believe, If you believed in me"? An observer once said, after hearing Arlen sing "Paper Moon": "It was as if he were praying."[32] Arlen did feel that inspiration was a divine gift; nor was "Paper Moon" an isolated nexus with Hebrew liturgy. *Shir hashirim* (The Song of Songs), as chanted during Passover, echoes in a classic Arlen song, both of them about love:

Ex. 9-20a
"The Song of Songs," Georgian-Russian Jewish tradition
Saminsky, *Sechs Lieder aus dem Russichen Orient*

Shir ha-shir-im a-sher li-shlo-mo,___ yi-sha-kei-ni min-shi-kot pi-u___

ki___ to - vim do-de-kha mi___ ya - - - - in

(The Song of Songs by Solomon: Kiss me with the kisses of your mouth, for your love is sweeter than wine)

Ex. 9-20b
"Come Rain or Come Shine"
Johnny Mercer & Harold Arlen

I'm gon-na love you Like no-bod-y's loved you, Come Rain or Come Shine.___

High as a moun-tain, And deep as a ri-ver, Come Rain or Come Shine.___

With words by the incomparable Johnny Mercer, this 1946 song plainly is a progenitor of Billy Joel's 1975 "New York State of Mind." A secondary phrase of "Come Rain or Come Shine" could have come straight out of a Jewish folk song about a supplicant's plea to an all-powerful Rabbi for assistance through prayer in "A Letter to the Liady Rabbi."[33] Nothing goes to waste.

Ex. 9-21a: Bars 9-12
"Come Rain or Come Shine"

I guess when you met me It was just one of those things,

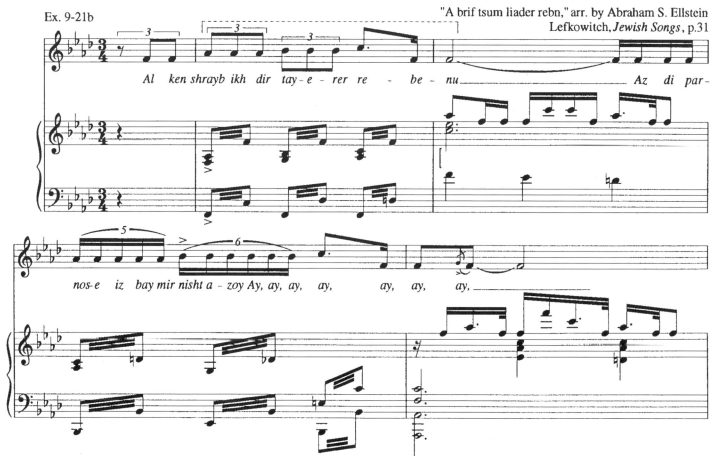

Ex. 9-21b

"A brif tsum liader rebn," arr. by Abraham S. Ellstein
Lefkowitch, *Jewish Songs*, p.31

Al ken shrayb ikh dir tay-e-rer re-be-nu____ Az di par-

nos-e iz bay mir nisht a-zoy Ay, ay, ay, ay, ay, ay, ay,

("A Letter to the Liady Rabbi": Therefore, I write to you dear Rabbi. My livelihood is not so great)

By itself, a tenuous thread to the Arlen song. But the same phrase, in the verse to another Mercer-Arlen song, is something else again as it introduces the sermon that exclaims: "You've got to Accent-chu-ate the Positive/Eli-my-nate the negative/Latch onto the affirmative/Don't mess with Mister-in-Between." Combine the rumbling chords of the Arlen-Mercer verse (Ex. 9-22) to the Yiddish folk song, and the tenuous thread becomes a thick rope, especially in a 1935 arrangement by Abraham Ellstein, as seen in Ex. 9-21b.[34]

Ex. 9-22: Verse

"Ac-cent-chu-ate the Positive"
Johhny Mercer & Harold Arlen

Ga-ther 'round me,____ ev-'ry-bo-dy,____ Ga-ther 'round me____ while I

preach some,____ Feel a ser-mon____ co-min' on me.____

It could be that Arlen never heard "A Letter to the Liady Rabbi" in its original form, but, instead, as a Catskill Mountains parody by Jacob Jacobs, *Jeckele, shik mir a tcheckele* (Jackie, send me a check). The words, which parallel those of Ex. 9-21b, follow:

> *Itst mayn tayerer man vil ikh dir erklern (Ay, ay)*
> *Ikh hob do a "rum" men ken dershtikt vern, (Ay, ay)*
> *Ikh hof fun dir dos zelbe tsu hern (Ay, ay)*

> Now, my dear husband, I want to tell you I have a room here that you could choke from,
> I hope to hear the same from you.[35]

Parodies of one Yiddish song transferred to another are not uncommon.[36] Caricatures of Tin Pan Alley tunes in fractured Yiddish by bandleader Mickey Katz had a vogue; and Seymour Rockoff redefined Gershwin's "Let's Call the Whole Thing Off" as "Let's Call the Holy Rov," and Berlin's "Puttin' on the Ritz" as "Sitting in the Shvitz." Very unconventional, however, is a Yiddish gloss on mainstream world literature. One important exception is the Jewish interpretation of a poem by the towering German writer Johann Wolfgang von Goethe, "a literary text [from the novel *Wilhelm Meister*] as familiar to German speakers as, say, Shakespeare's 'To be or not to be' from *Hamlet* is to Anglophones."[37]

> *Kennst du das Land, wo die Zitronen blühn,*
> *In dunkeln Laub die Gold-orangen glühn,*
> *Ein sanfter Wind vom blauen Himmel weht,*
> *Die myrtle still und hoch der Lorbeer steht?*
> *Kennst du es wohl? Dahin! Dahin!*
> *Möcht'ich mit dir, o mein Geliebter, ziehn.*
> *Kennst du das Haus? Auf Säulen ruht sein Dach, . . .*

> Do you know the land where the lemon trees bloom,
> Among dark leaves where gold oranges glow,
> Where a soft wind floats from the blue heaven,
> Where the myrtle stands still and the laurel grows high?
> Do you really know it?—There! there!
> Would I go with you, my beloved.
> Do you know the house? Its roof rests on columns, . . .

At least sixteen composers, ranging from Beethoven to Tchaikovsky, were inspired to set this poem from the *Mignon Lieder*. Goethe's yearning for a better world also appealed to the Yiddish poet Simon S. Frug, who converted it into a Hasidic Jewish vision of the afterlife. Ruth Rubin considers Frug's version to be "gentle banter . . . which satirized the Chasidic vision of Zion as a Garden of Eden where goats nibble at St. John's-Bread and roast ducklings fly about in the air." Since many Hasidic sects are in principle anti-Zionist, she suggests that the song may be a variant on another text which starts: "Do you know of the land where our Saint, the Messiah, will come riding on his white horse?"[38] Frug's words follow:

> *Tsi kent ir den dos land vu esrogn blien?*
> *Vu tsign esn bokser azoy vi groz, groz, groz.*
> *Gebrotene katshkelekh un indikes flien,*
> *Un tsumkim vayn trinkt men on a mos, mos, mos?*
> *Un mit lulovim, un mit lulovim, tut men dekher dekn,*
> *Un di rozhinkes un di mandlen vaksn oyf yedn shtekn.*

Oy ahin, ahin, ahin, oy, rebenyu gevald,
Voltn mir avek, avek, avek, oy, take bald!

Do you know the land where citrons bloom, where goats feed on thistles like grass?
Where roast duck and geese fly about, and raisin wine flows in the glass.
With branches of green palm trees all the roofs are covered,
And raisins and almonds grow on every bush.
Oh there, there, Oh Rabbi, help. There is where I would go right away.

From Goethe's *Zitronen* and *Dach* (lemon trees, roof) to Frug's *esrogn* and *dekher* (citrons—a sweet lemon-colored fruit—and roofs), there is a plausible jump to E. Y. Harburg's "lemondrops" and "chimney tops" in his and Arlen's "Over the Rainbow." Could Harburg have known the Yiddish song? Did it linger in his subconscious to inspire the words that transport us to the Land of Oz? Arlen's emphasis on the 3rd and 5th steps of the key is also stressed in the Yiddish song (composer unknown), but beyond that, there are no other resemblances. However, Arlen's visionary ideal did inspire Leonard Bernstein's quest for paradise in *Candide*:

Sammy Fain

. . . how much Fain is imbedded in our subconscious. *Show Music* magazine, Fall 1999

Harold Arlen inherited an appealing singing voice, attractive enough to launch a singing career. So did Sammy Fain, a cousin of vaudevillians Willie and Eugene Howard, and the son of Cantor Abraham Feinberg. (The same could not be said for Kurt Weill or Irving Berlin, although Berlin parlayed his thin, piping sound to marketing advantage.) Like Berlin and Arlen, Fain sang as a youth in his father's synagogue choir, South Fallsburg, New York. His great standard "I'll Be Seeing

You," written with Irving Kahal for the 1938 Broadway revue *Right This Way*, went on to become the title of a nonmusical 1944 movie. In the Danny Thomas version of *The Jazz Singer* (1953), Fain adapted a melody "based on a theme of Thomas"— Ambroise, that is, not Danny—whose *Raymond Overture* serves as provender for "Hush-a-bye." Of French origin, the theme is quickly acclimated to becoming a Yiddish-sounding lullaby. (An arrangement for piano and violin by A. Teres, a publisher of Jewish music, was available as early as 1909.) Another movie title song, this time by Fain and Paul Francis Webster (W) and made popular by Johnny Mathis in 1958, echoes an Israeli ballad of 1948:

Ex. 9-24a

"Kalaniyot"
Nathan Alterman (W) & Moshe Wilensky (M)

Ka-la-ni-yot, _____ ka-la-ni-yot, _____ ka-la-ni-yot a-da-ma-mot ad-mo-ni-yot, _____
(A young girl gathering anemones)

Ex. 9-24b

"A Certain Smile"
Paul Francis Webster (W) & Sammy Fain (M)

A Certain Smile, _____ a cer-tain face, _____ Can lead an un-sus-pec-ting heart on a mer-ry chase, _____

Could Fain have known the Israeli tune? Quite possibly, and it is of no consequence, except to note that Shoshana Damari, the popular Yemenite singer whose signature tune was "Kalaniyot," toured the United States from 1948 to 1958.[39] With the exception of a few novelty songs, not much else of Jewish content is to be found in Fain's work. He does quote "Di grine kuzine" in the patter section of "Valeska (My Russian Rose)," written in 1925 with Irving Kahal and Irving Mills: "And in the land where herrings grow/We'll build a bungalow." An unpublished "A Refugee's Lullaby" of 1947 by Fain and Jack Yellen is registered at the Library of Congress. The same year, the same team also wrote "The Jews Have Got Their Irish Up," a tribute to stalwart Zionists about to establish the State of Israel. It makes clever use of "Eli, Eli"[40]:

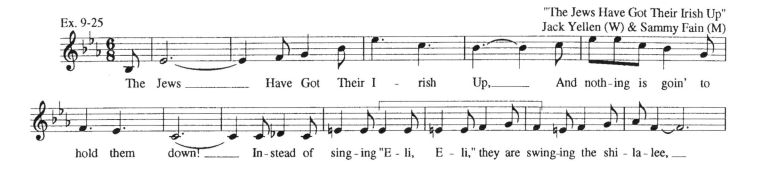

Ex. 9-25

"The Jews Have Got Their Irish Up"
Jack Yellen (W) & Sammy Fain (M)

The Jews _____ Have Got Their I-rish Up, _____ And noth-ing is goin' to

hold them down! _____ In-stead of sing-ing "E-li, E-li," they are swing-ing the shi-la-lee, _____

Cantors' Sons as Performers

Even though Al Jolson is credited as author-collaborator of several standards: "California, Here I Come," "Avalon," and "Me and My Shadow," there is room for doubt since this son of a cantor was notorious for getting a cut of the royalty pie if his name was going to guarantee sales. Jolson boasted that the starring role in the movie version of *The Jazz Singer* was rightfully his, and not that of George Jessel who had originated it on stage, on the claim that the story was a mirror of his life history. But this was true only in a few details.[41]

Comedian George Burns and the brother-team of Willie and Eugene Howard were also sons of cantors. Much of their freewheeling style, forged on the streets of New York's Lower East Side along with many other budding entertainers, traded more on Yiddish vulgarisms than on any spillover from the synagogue, although a defense could be posited that the comic routines of Burns and Allen went off into hair-splitting tangents that relate in form, if not content, to Talmudic discourse.[42]

Brooklyn-born Steve Lawrence, the star of the musical *What Makes Sammy Run?* (1964) was born Stephen Liebowitz, the son of Cantor Max Liebowitz, and as a child he sang in synagogue choirs. Lawrence recorded "Where Can I Go?," from the Yiddish theater song "Vi ahin zol ikh geyn?" by O. Strock (W) & S. Korn-Tuer (M). The best-known song from the "Sammy" score by Ervin Drake² recalls a traditional march tune, sung processional style around the synagogue, prior to the Torah's being undressed and read aloud:

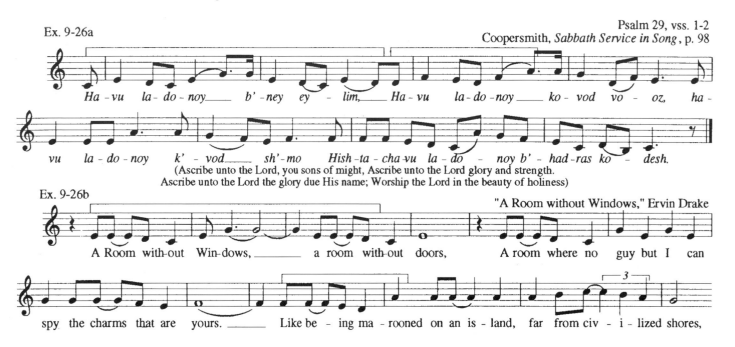

Ex. 9-26a

Psalm 29, vss. 1-2
Coopersmith, *Sabbath Service in Song*, p. 98

Ha – vu la – do – noy____ b' – ney ey – lim,____ Ha – vu la – do – noy____ ko – vod vo – oz, ha –
vu la – do – noy k' – vod____ sh' – mo Hish – ta – cha – vu la – do – noy b' – had – ras ko – desh.
(Ascribe unto the Lord, you sons of might, Ascribe unto the Lord glory and strength.
Ascribe unto the Lord the glory due His name; Worship the Lord in the beauty of holiness)

Ex. 9-26b

"A Room without Windows," Ervin Drake

A Room with – out Win – dows, _____ a room with – out doors, A room where no guy but I can
spy the charms that are yours. _____ Like be – ing ma – rooned on an is – land, far from civ – i – lized shores,

Although crooner Eddie Fisher was not from a cantor's background, he vouched that "my greatest influence remained the music of the temple and the cantorial style. My favorites were David Kusevitzky, [Ben-Zion] Kopov-Kagan, and Yosele Rosenblatt."[43] Fisher was a discovery of Eddie Cantor's, as was Bobby Breen (b. Michele Borsuk), a child star in Toronto synagogues and in movies. Opera singers Neil Shicoff and Evelyn Lear are the offspring of cantors also.

Let us assume that the majority of Jewish songwriters and show people from Yiddish speaking families of the first half of the twentieth century had no religious training or were nonpracticing Jews. Nonetheless, they must have been exposed to musical liturgy via the ceremonial motives that permeate Yiddish folk and theater songs. Blended into original tunes were pilfered marches and waltzes from German and French operettas; but it was the cantorial recitative performed by the likes of Sigmund Mogulesco and Boris Thomashefsky, who had been trained singers from synagogue choirs, that permeated early Yiddish theater. Perhaps it is this doctrinal element, more than anything else, that distinguishes Yiddish theater music from other ethnic musical theater in the United States (Swedish, German, Italian, etc.) with the possible exception of gospel music and the role it has played in African-American theater. Is Viennese operetta infused with Lutheran chorale tunes? Do Spanish zarzuelas provide moments of Catholic plainchant?

"Love Thy Neighbor" (Ex.9-27c), a song by two Jewish immigrants, Polish-born Mack Gordon and English-born Harry Revel and crooned by Bing Crosby in the 1934 movie *We're Not Dressing*, begins with a motive that parallels a motive from the final blessing over the *Haftarah* (additional) reading of the Torah portion (Ex. 9-27b), as chanted by Bar Mitzvah candidates. The same musical cell is intoned by the leader of the service (Ex. 9-27a) to call the Bar Mitzvah hopeful up to the reading desk so that he can demonstrate his prowess and readiness to join the community, a thrilling moment in a youngster's life. The correlation of the words "Love Thy Neighbor" to these four notes reminds us of a biblical passage which either songwriter might have been trained to chant as a Bar Mitzvah candidate: "Thou shalt love thy neighbor as thyself" (*Leviticus* 19:18). What is more, the fragment appeared again, in a different 1934 song by the same authors, sung by Lanny Ross in the film *College Rhythm*. This time, it adds a lower neighbor tone, and instead of being an incipit, it demarcates a half-cadence (Ex. 9-27d):

Other popular songwriters obviously went through the rigors of preparing their Bar Mitzvah portion, among them Jerry Herman and the Sherman Brothers.[44] Art Garfunkel sang in a synagogue choir, also a source of inspiration for Paul Simon. Sheldon Harnick attended Hebrew School four days a week, attended weekly orthodox services, and admired his Rabbi enough to consider going into the rabbinate himself. But he became disillusioned by another Rabbi "of the old school, quick with the ruler on the knuckles," who replaced his role model.[45]

Still others were more conscientious. Sophie Tucker, reminiscing about Jack Yellen, composer of "Ain't She Sweet?," "Happy Days Are Here Again" and Tucker's signature tune, "My Yiddishe Momme," said: "He's a student . . . of the history of our Jewish people, and . . . one of the most devoutly religious persons I've ever known."[46] Marvin Hamlisch, who faithfully attended services at a Reform congregation in New York City, once played the organ for services and managed to sneak in a worshipful version of one of his pop songs as a silent meditation.[47] Aaron Copland became a Bar Mitzvah, and although some of his early works have a parochial slant, they are small-sized and not well-known. Minimalist Steve Reich, on the other hand, is Sabbath observant and large works of his delve into Jewish themes.

While none of this is a guarantee of genuine inward commitment—and it is mostly irrelevant—it does indicate that some fledgling composers at least set foot inside a synagogue. Musically gifted adolescents cannot have been oblivious to such exposure, whether in their own preparations for the Bar Mitzvah ceremony or to the sounds of a cantor.

On the other hand, masters of rock 'n' roll, Jerry Lieber and Mike Stoller, would not agree. They dismiss as "hogwash" any suggestion that "songwriters enriched rock 'n' roll with a Jewish sensibility."[48] Theirs were different or more compelling experiences. As teenagers, they were both drawn toward African-American sounds—Lieber as a delivery boy in Baltimore black neighborhoods and Stoller as a camper at an interracial, leftist-leaning summer camp.[49] Cultural exposure in one's youth, perhaps even more than religious indoctrination, must in general terms inform later artistic expression. There is a curious footnote to all this.[†]

As I have endeavored to demonstrate throughout this book, latent snatches of song incubating in the subconscious later take wing in the creative process.

[†] Alfred Goldman, a biographer of Elvis Aaron Presley, relates that when Presley was eighteen, his family moved to a two-family house in Memphis. The top floor was occupied by the family of Rabbi Alfred Fruchter, of Temple Beth El Emeth, who played cantorial recordings of Shlomo Kussevitzky (sic, Goldman probably means Moshe Koussevitzky) and Moyshe Oysher. The biographer concludes, "in all the digging around for the roots of the Presley sound, no one has ever considered the possibility he was influenced by Jewish cantorial singing." (Albert Goldman, *Elvis*, p. 112). A columnist in mid-1992 went so far as to claim Presley was a Jew! Apparently his maternal grandmother, Lucy Mansell, was Jewish, and the memorial stone on his mother's grave had a Star of David added to it by Elvis (John Heilpern, "Elvis Lives-But Did You Know He's Jewish?" *New York Observer* 27 (July -3 August 1992). In fact, a documentary film called *Schmelvis* (2002, Toronto Jewish Film Festival) explores the issues in detail. I leave it to others to investigate these ramifications, except to note that among the songwriters who wrote for Presley there were many Jews: Sid Tepper, Aaron Schroeder, Martin Kalmanoff, George Weiss, Doc Pomus, Mort Shuman, Alex Gottlieb, and the teams of Ira Kosloff-Maurice Mysels, Fred Wise-Ben Weisman, and, most prominently, Jerry Lieber-Mike Stoller.

NOTES

1. See Hoberman, *Entertaining America: Jews, Movies and Broadcasting*, pp. 84-92. Hoberman's time line includes a 1974 reference to unfulfilled plans to produce a black stage version of *The Jazz Singer*. However, he fails to mention *Broken Strings*, an all-black musical film of 1940 starring Clarence Muse, wherein the cantor's role is replaced by another Jewish model: a classical violinist and teacher whose swing-loving son refuses to follow his father's example of a musical career. *Broken Violin,* incidentally, is the title of a 1916 Yiddish operetta by Thomashefsky and Rumshinsky.

2. Neil Diamond has spoken of the effect his father's practice of lip-synching Yiddish recordings had on his own sense of melody. He goes on to say: "So many . . . songwriters . . . have come from that same place. . . . The religious music was what [they] based their songs on." (*New York Times* Sunday Magazine, 22 July 2001.) A 1935 Yiddish song, "Chazonim oyf probe" (Cantors in Audition), has the job go to a cantor who sings a liturgical text to a bit of the Gus Kahn/Walter Donaldson 1925 song "Yes Sir, That's My Baby." The conclusion? "That's what the public wants!" With music by Sholom Secunda, the words are credited to "Sholom Ben Avrohom," that is, Sholom, son of Abraham, a pseudonym since Secunda's father was so named.

3. Re Daly: *Playbill* 89 (no. 11, November 1989). Re Liberace: Darden Ashbury Pyron, *Liberace, An American Boy.*

4. These brother pairs include Gus and Leo Edwards, Harry and Albert Von Tilzer, George and Ira Gershwin, Mack and Hal David, Richard M. and Robert B. Sherman, Frank and Arthur Loesser (a writer on music), Leonard and Burton Bernstein (an author), Harry, Henry, and Charles Tobias, et al. Others have become three-generation dynasties: the Hollywood Newman clan headed by Alfred, the Broadway Rodgers lineage, and the offspring of Fred Fisher. There also is widespread fraternal representation in the dance-band/jazz field: Benny and Harry Goodman, and non-Jews: Jimmy and Tommy Dorsey, Nat King and Freddy Cole, Fletcher and Horace Henderson, Erroll and Linton Garner, Wynton and Bradford Marsalis, et al. With the exception of the Dorseys, who enjoyed equal fame, the latter names in these sets of pairs are outshone by the former.

5. Weill later raided this score for two other Jewish pageants on which he collaborated with Ben Hecht: *We Will Never Die* (1943) and *A Flag Is Born* (1946).

6. One presumes that the ragtag tribe of Israelites must have been literate. Who else was going to read the Ten Commandment carvings on those tablets?

7. Edward Rothstein, "Kurt Weill's Deadly Sin," *The New Republic*, 23 November 1987, p. 25.

8. "Recollections by Maurice Abravanel," *Kurt Weill Newsletter* 5 (no. 1, spring 1987: 8

9. Henry Marx, "The Americanization of Weill and Lenya," paper presented at the Kurt Weill Conference, Yale University, 4 November 1983.

10. David Drew, "How Was Weill's Success Achieved," *Kurt Weill Newsletter* 4 (no. 2, fall 1986).

11. "Offenbach," *The New Grove Dictionary of Music and Musicians*, vol. 13, p. 510.

12. Gdal Saleski, *Famous Musicians of a Wandering Race*, p. 51.

13. As demonstrated at a concert in the *Musica Hebraica* series at Hebrew Union College, New York (directed by Jack Gottlieb), 15 May 1977.

14. Earlier, Giacomo Meyerbeer had opened doors for Jews to Gentile society via his operas.

15. "The Greek Marine Hymn," a song from *The Happiest Girl in the World*, based on Offenbach melodies with lyrics by E. Y. Harburg, is an obvious homage to the "Marine Hymn," beginning with the words: "From the shores of Macedonia," a gloss on "From the halls of Montezuma."

16. Mel Tormé and Robert Wells's "Christmas Song" (1946) and Johnny Marks's "Rudolph the Red-Nosed Reindeer" (1949) are other perennial Yuletide favorites by Jewish songwriters; and whereas cowboy Gene Autry* popularized "Rudolf," radio comedian Eddie Cantor made a hit out of "Santa Claus Is Coming to Town" (1934) by J. Fred Coots* and Haven Gillespie.* Is Betty Comden being serious when she says: ". . . Christmas at our house was just like Christmas in any other normal Jewish-American home."? Betty Comden, *Off Stage*, p. 231.

17. Philip Furia, *Irving Berlin: A Life in Song*, p. 9.

18. Laurence Bergreen, *As Thousands Cheer*, p. 12.

19. A 1914 film, *Song of Solomon*, is purport-

ed to be about Berlin. See Patricia Erens, *The Jew in American Cinema*, p. 68.

20. According to Robert Kimball. See n. 20, Chapter 6.

21. Berlin's 1909 "That Mezmerizing Mendelssohn Tune" is a gloss on Mendelssohn's "Spring Song."

22. "Sadie Salome" established the career of Fanny Brice. Berlin also wrote "Yiddisha Eskimo" for Fanny Brice, left incomplete. See Chapter 6.

23. This was not the first time Berlin made use of "Hatikvah." See Chapter 7.

24. Michael Freedland, *Irving Berlin*, p. 14.

25. The National Origins Act (a.k.a. the Johnson-Reed Act) of 1924 effectively barred East Europeans from immigrating to the U.S. during World War II and therefore contributed to the horrors of the Holocaust. The Act was repealed in 1965.

26. See the Dimitri Tiomkin epigram at the top of Chapter 2.

27. The citation of the "Star-Spangled Banner" is most interesting since it did not officially become the American national anthem until 1931.

28. In *Idiot's Delight* (1939), Clark Gable sings "That's where each and every Lulu Belle goes/Every Thursday evening with her swell beaus"(the original 1929 version of "Puttin' on the Ritz"). Why Thursday? A likely explanation is that Thursday was the traditional day off for domestic servants; but another explanation might spring from the Yiddish expression: *ale montik un donershtik* (every Monday and Thursday), traditional market days or, in other words, the days for going out in public. In *Young Frankenstein* (1974), Gene Wilder sings the revised couplet as "Strolling up the Avenue so happy/All dressed up just like an English chappie."

29. See Mlotek, *We Are Here: Songs of the Holocaust*, p. 47.

30. Robert Kimball and Linda Emmet, *The Complete Lyrics of Irving Berlin*, p. 466.

31. Arlen's "Rhythmic Moments: A Modern Piano Solo," was published by Robbins Music Corp. in 1928 under the name Harold Arluck, as were other early piano pieces: "Minor Gaff," "Buffalo Rhythm," and "Rhythmic Moments"(1926-1928).

32. Edward Jablonski, *Happy with the Blues*, p. 74.

33. Rabbi Shneur Zalman of Liady (1747-1813) was the founder of the Chabad

Lubavitch sect of Hasidism which still thrives today in the Crown Heights neighborhood of Brooklyn.

34. Henry Lefkowitch, *Jewish Songs, Folk and Modern*.

35. *KJTS,* vol. 2, no. 15, p. 38.

36. Another example is Isadore Lillian's parody of "Chazn oyf shabes" as "Three Hotel Keepers," recorded by the Yiddish theater star Jennie Goldstein on Deluxe Records #1109, 78 rpm.

37. Richard Buell, "Demonstrating What Makes German Art Songs Great," *Boston Globe*, 29 March 1999.

38. See Ruth Rubin, *Voices of a People*, pp. 380 and 396.

39. The second musical phrase of "Kalaniyot" is also prominent in "Guess Who I Saw Today" by Murray Grand and Elisse Boyd (from *New Faces of 1952*).

40. I am grateful to Frank Fain, Sammy's son, for sharing information with me. Phone conversation, 16 June 1999. A cousin of Sammy Fain is Andy Statman, a well-known contemporary klezmer clarinetist.

41. For one thing, Jolson was a cantor's son whereas Jessel's father was a playwright. See also Sarah Blacher Cohen, ed., *From Hester Street to Hollywood*, p. 38.

42. George Burns, as an adolescent, formed an all-Jewish singing group, the Pee Wee Quartett. Willie Howard recorded "Tyrone Shapiro, The Bronx Caballero," a takeoff on Vincent Youmans's "Carioca."

43. Eddie Fisher, *Eddie: My Life, My Loves*, p. 142.

44. Source received from Broadcast Music, Inc. Richard Rodgers also became Bar Mitzvah, which had negligible effect on his work; but so did Leonard Bernstein, who reveled in his Jewishness.

45. Tim Boxer, *The Jewish Week*, 13 April 1990, p. 28.

46. It is farcical to observe that "My Yiddishe Momme" begins with the same six-note motive (plus one) that opens Wagner's "Ride of the Valkyries" from *Die Walküre*! Tucker originally recorded it in both Yiddish and English on 20 June 1928, Columbia 4962. Her statement about Yellen's devotion to religious practice is rather disingenuous since he married a non-Jew. See Sophie Tucker, *Some of These Days*, p. 165.

47. See *The Way I Was*, p. 50. Hamlisch's congregation was Mount Neboh in New

York City, then located a few doors away from my apartment building, later abandoned to be torn down and replaced by a high-rise. During the transition, its cornerstone was defiled by a painted swastika, an obscenity which I took upon myself to expunge with whitewash late one night.

48. Letters to the Editor, *New York Times*, Arts and Leisure, 9 September 2001.

49. Camp Wochika in New Jersey was run by Jewish union groups. *New York Times*, 29 December 1996 and *The Jewish Week*, 24 August 2001.

CHAPTER 10

Symbols of Faith in the Music of Leonard Bernstein

Mi alone is only me. But *mi* with *sol*, Me with soul. . . . Means a song is beginning to grow, Take wing, and rise up singing From me and my soul *Kadosh! Kadosh! Kadosh!*

From BERNSTEIN's *Mass*

Career decisions in music may have been blessed by some fathers—and apparently that was the case with cantor-fathers—but relationships between other *pere-fils* pairs were considerably more strained when such determinations came to the fore. As previously noted, this was not unique to Jewish fathers. Throughout musical history there has been paternal encouragement (viz., the Mozarts) as well as discouragement (viz., the Glucks). George Chadwick (1854-1931), a composer who grew up in Leonard Bernstein's hometown of Lawrence, Massachusetts, actually was disowned by his father for his musical aspirations. One suspects that such an aversion to a life in music was "manly" opposition to what was then perceived to be "unmanly" ambition in American society. In the case of Russian-Jewish fathers from a shtetl background, having had little contact with city life, they viewed musicians with disdain. Inside their tightly knit communities, klezmer musicians played lowly roles in a highly structured socioeconomic system. Since such performers functioned as if they were vagabonds, a shtetl father understandably was not thrilled if his son decided to become a musician. He saw no security in such aspirations, and would have preferred his offspring to concentrate on "scholarly" studies.

On American shores that attitude continued. Tunesmiths like Arthur Schwartz, Harold Arlen, Sammy Cahn, Mack David, and his brother Hal had a formidable time convincing their fathers they did not wish to be lawyers or doctors. Irving Berlin and Eddie Cantor, before they could get married to their respective brides, had to endure the wrath of their future fathers-in-law; and when Al Jolson blackened his face, his relatives thought he had done the same to his reputation. Martin Charnin's father, in fact, was a singer who sang at the Metropolitan Opera; but he found Broadway musicals so distasteful that he would have nothing more to do with Ezio Pinza when Pinza, late in his career, starred in *South Pacific*. When Charnin's son landed a role in the original production of *West Side Story* (as Big Deal, one of the Jets) he told his father he was "going downtown to look for a job in . . . advertising." Finally the show was leaving New York for out-of-town previews, and Charnin had to tell his father the truth. Apparently it was acceptable when papa was informed that all the authors were Jewish.[1] Leonard Bernstein, one of those four, put it this way:

When I was a boy, and announced I wanted to be a musician, my father screamed in horror because to him "musician" was a word like "beggar," a person who came around to weddings scraping on his fiddle and begging a few kopeks. My father didn't know that there was a highly intellectual world of music.

Neither, for that matter, did the *klezmorim* know about it; and given the lowly status of Jewish musicians in East Europe, such reaction was not untypical.[2] After Bernstein had become successful, Sam Bernstein was asked how he could have ever opposed his son's career. His immortal reply: "How did I know he was going to be Leonard Bernstein?"[3]

Bernstein's earliest memory of music, dating from about 1926, was in his father's temple, Mishkan Tefila (Dwelling of Prayer) in Roxbury, Massachusetts, a sanctuary where, to quote him from a 1989 interview: "I felt something stir within me, as though I were subconsciously aware of music as my raison d'etre." Elsewhere he says. "We had a fabulous Cantor . . . then the organ would start and the choir would begin . . . and I began to get crazed . . .".[4] One would be hard-pressed to find another composer in history who is as widely known for having written so many large compositions on Jewish themes as Bernstein, due in no small measure to the energizing conflict between him and his father.[5]

This need for Jewish expression carried over into some of his nonspecific Jewish works. As I have shown elsewhere, his Symphony No. 2: *The Age of Anxiety* and his theater piece *Mass* have significant Jewish content.[6] Although his symphonic works were sparked by the interaction between his American conditioning and his Jewish heritage, motives of synagogue music crept into his Broadway musical scores, vividly demonstrating how Judaism as religious indoctrination—as opposed to Jewishness as cultural conditioning—can consciously, or not, suffuse musical creativity.

The most obvious borrowings by Bernstein is his usage of shofar calls. The blowing of the ram's horn on the holy days of Rosh Hashanah and Yom Kippur is decreed by the Bible: "In the seventh month, on the first day of the month, you shall observe complete rest, a sacred occasion commemorated with loud blasts" (*Leviticus* 23:24) and "You shall observe it as a day when the horn is sounded" (*Numbers* 29:1). The rabbinic tradition evolved a set of musical patterns (Ex. 10-1a) for these commands: *tekiah* (blast), a held tone; *shevarim* (breaks), detached tones; *teruah* (noise) and *tekiah gedolah* (the big blast).

In Bernstein's *Candide*, trumpeters are instructed to play "like a shofar" (Ex. 10-1a). Elsewhere in *Candide*, a battle scene is announced by a fanfare blast of *tekiah gedolah,* the very same configuration that opens the *Overture to Candide* (Ex. 10-1b), probably Bernstein's most performed concert work:

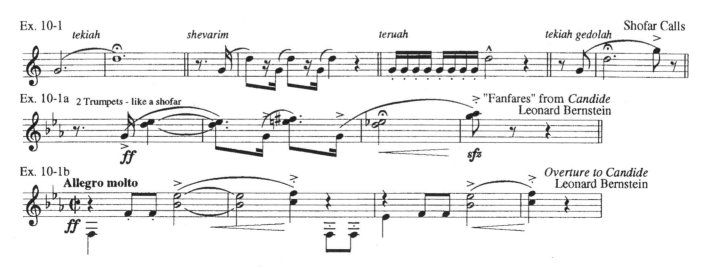

Ex. 10-1

All four shofar patterns abound in the aleatoric first movement of the *Concerto for Orchestra (Jubilee Games)*. Throughout, the players are instructed to select notes of their own choice within given rhythmic boundaries. The last three bars are precisely labeled in the score as an "LB signature," in which only the last three notes are intended to be performed as written. This is proof positive for those who always suspected that the whistles alerting the gangs in *West Side Story* are based on shofar calls. There is no doubt that two of Bernstein's most acclaimed shows begin[7] with a Jewish call to worship (Ex.10-1c and 10-2b):

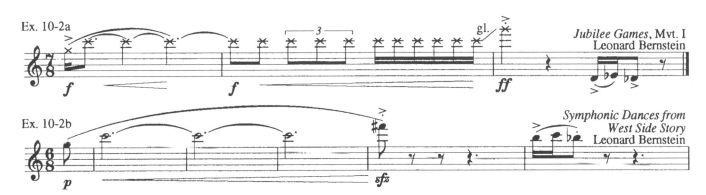

"Maria," the eponymous song of the heroine in *West Side Story*, suggests that when it comes to matters religioso, even ostensible Catholics have a tinge of Judaism in their souls. In German, the word for major is *dur* (hard) and for minor it is *moll* (soft). Perhaps that is why Bernstein goes from major, on the words "Maria, say it *loud* and there's music playing," to minor on the words, "Say it *soft* and it's almost like praying." Or is it even more symbolic than that? Mandy Patinkin's singing style, very much shaped by cantorial models, helps to explain why, out of the innumerable songs he could have selected—such as Richard Rodgers's "Maria" from *The Sound of Music*—he chose to record Bernstein's "Maria" in Yiddish translation.[8] The original pencil copy of the song deposited at the Library of Congress shows the first draft of the lyric to be: "Maria, when I say it, there's music playing/Like the music in church when they're praying." But the music indicates that Tony, Maria's smitten one, not only went to confession, but also was *shomer shabos* (Sabbath observant):

"Somewhere," also from *West Side Story,* is one of several Bernstein expressions of the Utopian ideal (or, to put it in Jewish terms, the yearning for Zion), songs such as "Never Land" from *Peter Pan* and, as illustrated in Chapter 9, "Eldorado" from *Candide*, with its nuances of Arlen's "Over the Rainbow." The third movement of the "Kaddish" Symphony paints the same landscape.

Two songs from *On the Town* sound as if they could have come straight out of the *Adonai malakh* mode. One is in the opening strain of "Some Other Time." The other, "Ya Got Me," has the minor 3rd in the upper octave (on the word "love") and the major 3rd in the lower octave (at **C**), typical of the *AM* mode (see Chapter 7). Using the sheet music version, the breakdown of "Ya Got Me" may be evaluated for its *nusach* content, where **A**, **B**, and **C** demarcate phrases:

Ex. 10-4

"Ya Got Me" (from *On the Town*)
Betty Comden & Adolph Green (W), Leonard Bernstein (M)

Throughout Bernstein's concert works there is a persistent opening and/or closing musical motive that is associated with matters of faith: a descending interval of a 4th followed by a falling whole or half-step (see Kurt Weill's approach in Exx. 5-4a and b). In *Symphony No. 1: Jeremiah* (1942, dedicated to Bernstein's father), the motive represents God's voice through His prophet.

Ex. 10-5a

Jeremiah, Mvt. I
Leonard Bernstein

Ex. 10-5b

Jeremiah, Mvt. III
Leonard Bernstein

An observant Jew would recognize this motive as coming from the Rosh Hashanah liturgy, heard for the first time as part of the prayer section called the *Amidah*, a compilation of fixed benedictions recited at all services with varying interpolations, and which comprises the second most important set of Jewish prayers after the monotheistic creed of *Sh'ma Yisrael*:

Ex. 10-6

"Misod chachomim" (Rosh Hashanah liturgy)
Katchko2, p. 16

In the Epilogue to *The Age of Anxiety*, Bernstein's second symphony (1949), the motive's prominence is extended by an additional descending 4th (Ex. 10-7a). With the Finale of *Kaddish, Symphony No. 3* (1963), the symbolism of the motive becomes God's image as created in man, and begins to be launched from the pitch of F ("F" for Faith?, Ex. 10-7b); and inescapably, it continues in *Chichester Psalms* (1965) at both the beginning and the end (Exx. 10-7c and d):

In the last choral section of *Mass* (1971), as much a Jewishly inspired work as a Catholic one—for one thing, it is a "Theater Piece," not a worship service—the motive is partially inverted into:

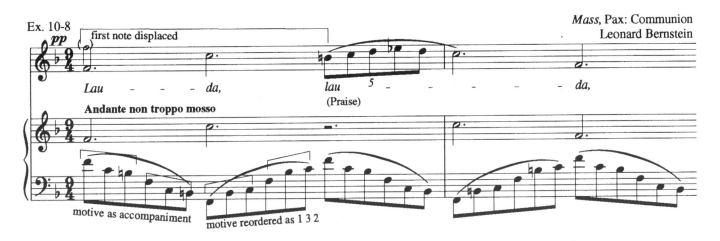

In 1974, the motive's retrograde form is assimilated into the twelve-tone row used for the blessing: "Praised Are You, O Lord," from both the first and last movements of *Dybbuk* (Ex. 10-9a), from which arises the theme of the second section of the ballet (Ex. 10-9b):

Ex. 10-9a: Opening tone row

Dybbuk
Leonard Bernstein

(Blessed are You O Lord)

Ex. 10-9b

Dybbuk, Mvt. II
Leonard Bernstein

Although this faith motive is mostly associated with Bernstein's concert music, it appears, albeit in retrograde form, in his show music, specifically in *On the Town*, where it outlines the motto of "New York, New York" (Ex. 10-10). The same phenomenon occurs when the descending motive from the "Epilogue" to *The Age of Anxiety* (Ex. 10-7a) is played backwards:

Ex. 10-10

"New York, New York"
Comden & Green, Bernstein

"Tonight," from *West Side Story*, also can be said to open with the faith motive, but this time extended from a descending 4th to a 6th, the same pitch relationships that open "To What You Said" in Bernstein's *Songfest*, both beginning with "To":

Ex. 10-11a

"Tonight" (from *West Side Story*)
Stephen Sondheim & Leonard Bernstein

Ex. 10-11b

"To What You Said" (from *Songfest*)
Leonard Bernstein

Why this motive clings to Bernstein's musical expression of faith is a matter of conjecture. But perhaps it can be interpreted as a by-product from his youth of his father's indoctrination. The motive not only permeates the liturgy of High Holy Day music, where it is fraught with ritual and doctrinal significance, but it is endemic to the Three Festivals of Sukkot, Passover and Shavuot, where it is used as a final cadence. (See also Exs. 5-4a and b and Ex. 5-14.) During these holidays, for example, the final benediction is chanted as:

Ex. 10-12

"Three-fold Benediction"
Traditional

cadence

Ya - eir A-do-nai pa - nav ei-le-cha v'-ya - seim l'-cha _____ sho - lom _____
(May the Lord lift up His countenance upon you and give you peace)

Even if one were only a "holiday Jew," such a faith motive heard repeatedly in a musical service is bound to seep into and take hold of the impressionable mind of a growing musician. All this results in an inevitable question: did Bernstein create any of these musical symbols purposely and would he have admitted to them? The answer is ambiguous. His own words on the matter might be those taken from the Preface to his printed score for *The Age of Anxiety*: "I trust the unconscious implicitly, finding it a sure source of wisdom and the dictator of the condign in artistic matters." On the other hand, a look at the music uncovers an explicit use of the motive in a liturgical context; but against all expectation, it is from a Christian "Alleluia."[9] Go figure!

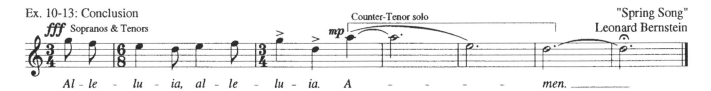

Ex. 10-13: Conclusion

Counter-Tenor solo

"Spring Song"
Leonard Bernstein

fff Sopranos & Tenors   *mp*

Al - le - lu - ia, al - le - lu - ia. A - - - - men. _____

Finally, if this faith motive was good enough for a Jewish boy from Lawrence, Massachusetts, to place into a Christian Mass, then it is also was good enough for an Episcopalian lad from Peru, Indiana, to profit therefrom in his self-described "Jewish" tunes:

Ex. 10-14

"Were Thine That Special Face," from *Kiss Me Kate*
Cole Porter

Were Thine That Spe-cial Face, _____ The face which fills my dream-ing, _____ Were

NOTES

1. Tim Boxer, *The Jewish Week*, p. 48, 6 April 1990.

2. Serge Koussevitzky, who was Bernstein's musical father, came from a family of klezmers, but kept it quiet.

3. "Leonard Bernstein: An Exclusive Interview," *ASCAP Today* 6 (no. 1, July 1972): 9. Samuel Bernstein is quoted somewhat differently elsewhere: "How was I to know that he was Leonard Bernstein?" "A Dialogue: Rabbi William Berkowitz and Leonard Bernstein, In Observance of the Tenth Anniversary of Maestro Bernstein's Yahrzeit," *The National Jewish Post & Opinion* 67 (no. 37, 23 May 2001): 10. See, also, Yale Strom, *The Book of Klezmer*, p. 133.

4. Humphrey Burton, *Leonard Bernstein*, pp. 8-9.

5. For orchestra: *Jeremiah: Symphony No. 1, Kaddish: Symphony No.2, Chichester Psalms, Dybbuk, Halil, Concerto for Orchestra (Jubilee Games), Opening Prayer*. It is not generally known that Randall Thompson, Bernstein's mentor and orchestration teacher at the

Curtis Institute, wrote songs and did the orchestrations for the off-Broadway 1926 edition of *The Grand Street Follies*.

6. For *Age of Anxiety*, see Jack Gottlieb's "Symbols of Faith in the Music of Leonard Bernstein," *Musical Quarterly* LXVI (April 1980): 287-295. For *Mass*, see Jack Gottlieb's "A Jewish Mass or a Catholic Mitzvah?," *Journal of Synagogue Music* III (December 1971): 3-7.

7. Actually, it is *Symphonic Dances from West Side Story*, rather than the show, that begins with the shofar motive.

8. Mandy Patinkin, *Mamaloshen*. Nonesuch Records CD-79459-2, 1998.

9. The music for *The Lark* originally was part of the incidental music to a play about Joan of Arc, most of which was later reconstituted as a *Missa Brevis*.

CHAPTER 11

Porter's Trunk

He had discovered the secret of writing hits. As I breathlessly awaited the magic formula, he leaned over and confided, 'I'll write Jewish tunes.'

RICHARD RODGERS quoting Cole Porter in *Musical Stages,* p. 88

American-Jewish composers of popular music have infrequently used the indigenous augmented 2nd interval of the *Ahava raba* mode—fleetingly, if at all—as if they want to get away from its ghettolike connotations. It is simply too much of an eastern wail within their western walls.[1] Non-Jews, however, have had no compunctions about using augmented 2nds out in the open, hinting at the *AR* mode. Nacio Herb Brown—born in New Mexico—used them in a torch song for Bing Crosby[2] in torment over temptress Fifi D'Orsay (Ex. 11-1a) in the 1933 film *Going Hollywood* (later heard as party music in 1952's enduring movie musical *Singin' in the Rain*) and in a swirling fandango (Ex. 11-1b) from the 1948 Kathryn Grayson movie *The Kissing Bandit,* where the augmented interval is concealed in the harmony:

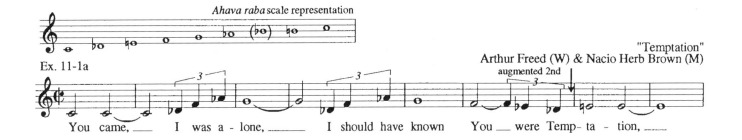

But Cole Porter does something that can be construed more as a Jewish put-down than as a sultry Latin enticement (Ex. 11-2). With the last stretched out tribute to a sugar daddy (starting bar 6), we are back in *Eli, Eli* (N.B. My Father, My *Dad*) territory:

Was Porter taking a swipe at the unsavory rich-Jew-with-mistress caricature? In his "Why Should I Care?" he likewise seems to be saying that a well-heeled provider can be counted on by his lady fair since his big bucks are also augmented by 2nds. Contrast Porter's tune to an old Jewish waltz tune:

At the behest of Fanny Brice, Porter wrote a little-known ballad, "Hot-House Rose" (1926), which tells the bitter tale of a Jewish sweatshop (or hothouse) girl who laments "I'm Hot-House Rose from God knows where/The kind that grows without fresh air." Brice never sang it; and although it contains no augmented 2nd, it uncharacteristically utilizes the pentatonic scale. But he also wrote about another female who does get to enjoy the great outdoors. In "Love for Sale," Porter portrays a streetwalker who builds up her trade, so to speak, with augmented steps (Ex. 11-4a). But did he have to end with the augmented 2nd between the words "I" and "o-pen"? There are other choices (Ex. 11-4b). And what is one to make of the stereotype impression of small Jewish businessmen implied by the words "I open shop"?

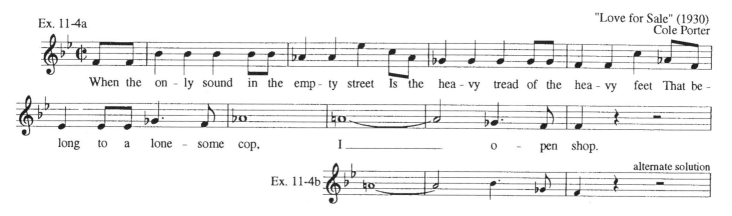

In all fairness, the Jewish baggage that Porter carried with him was not always decorated with prejudicial decals. His 1929 supplication to the Almighty (Ex. 11-5b), while in the melodic minor mode, has an *AR* mode underpinning in the harmony which could qualify it for honorable mention on a synagogue *bima*.[3] Comparison with "Miserlou," a melody of 1934 (Ex. 11-5a), shows the affinity; and though "Miserlou" was of *rembetika* (so-called Greek blues) origin, it was so smoothly adapted into Spanish (by José G. Pina), Yiddish (by Chaim Tauber), and Hebrew, that few were the wiser. In fact, Velvel Pasternak reports the process of how the Bratislav Hasidic sect came to regard it is as a "holy nigun":[4]

Or take the climactic parts of the Hasidic tune "A Dudele" (A Thou Song, Ex. 11-6a) and Porter's "Begin the Beguine" (Ex. 11-6b). Chop them up together and out comes a kind of "Cole" slaw:

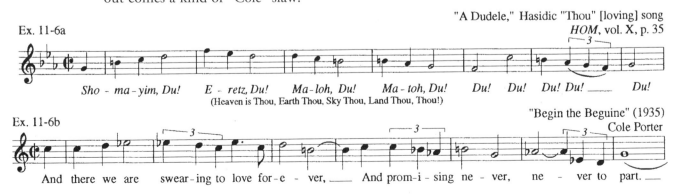

Cole Porter did cultivate the image of being a playboy. He traveled in high society circles, and perhaps his attraction to things Jewish was a kind of musical slumming, like the swells of Café Society who used to frequent Harlem night spots.[5] But it had to be more than mere tourism. Was Porter revealing envy or admiration for the sheer number of his Jewish colleagues, while, at the same time, reveling in how he could do better than they?

Undoubtedly, it was the distinctive Schubertian alternation of minor and major modes in many Porter tunes that brought a Jewish-sounding association to them. Ira B. Arnstein was an inept songwriter whose one claim to fame were his notorious crackpot suits of plagiarism against many composers, including Cole Porter. Among the songs Porter had allegedly plagiarized were five by Arnstein based on Jewish themes:

Porter	*Arnstein*
"Begin the Beguine"	"The Lord Is My Shepherd"
"I Love You"	"La Priere"
"You'd Be So Nice To Come Home To"	"Sadness Overwhelms My Soul"
"Don't Fence Me In"	"A Modern Messiah"
"My Heart Belongs to Daddy"	"A Mother's Prayer"

An examination of Arnstein's "A Mother's Prayer" (words by L. Wolfe Gilbert) makes clear that this was one "mother" who did not have a prayer in heaven to justify the charge. Porter was accused by Arnstein of having "stooges follow and live in the same apartment with me." Not surprisingly, Porter categorically denied all of this. It turned out, however, that in a few scattered spots, there were some fleeting similarities between the plaintiff's and the defendant's work. But, apparently, all these were based on remnants of scattered melody, not enough to justify an inference of improper appropriation.[6] Later on, Arnstein wanted to bring up a case against the authors and publisher of "Chattanooga Choo Choo." He showed an earlier copyrighted song of his to Milton Rettenberg, a New York lawyer, who felt he clearly had a case![7] But, by that time, no one wanted to represent a client who had cried wolf once too often.

If nothing else, the saga of Ira Arnstein provides an insight into the Jewish quotient of Porter's music, even though recognized for the wrong reasons. There is a link between Porter's "You'd Be So Nice to Come Home To" (Ex. 11-7c) and Mark Warshavsky's widely popular "Oyfn pripetshik" (In the Fireplace, Ex. 11-7a). Like Goldfaden's "Der rebe hot geheysn freylekh zayn" earlier in the century (see Ex. 2-10a), "Oyfn pripetshik" has been so identified with Yiddish culture that it has been used as background material in Hollywood films ranging from the Gershwin pseudobiopic *Rhapsody in Blue* (underscored for the death of Gershwin's father as played by Morris Carnovsky) to the Dustin Hoffman vehicle *Billy Bathgate,* to the close of the offbeat comedy *Next Stop, Greenwich Village* as well as the poignant scene of the little-girl-in-the-red-coat in Steven Spielberg's *Schindler's List.* Porter also uses the image of the fireplace, and its first seven notes glow with the flame of the *pripetshik.* An even closer Yiddish analogue to the wistful World War II ballad can be heard in a song from the 1920s (Ex.11-7b). Porter conjures up a Russian-Jewish world to such an extent that Gregory Ratoff, the Russian-born movie producer-director, on first hearing "You'd Be So Nice to Come Home To," thought it came from the Caucasus:[8]

The theme song for Molly Picon, the Yiddish theater star, comes from *Yankele*, a musical of 1923 written by her husband Jacob Kalich, et al. It is atypically in major (Ex. 11-8b). In 1940, Porter, while on a boat trip to the South Seas, wrote a tune called "So Long, Samoa." (Five years earlier he had written "Begin the Beguine" on another trip to Samoa.) This subsequently was transformed into "Farewell, Amanda" for the 1949 Tracy-Hepburn film *Adam's Rib* (Ex. 11-8c). While it would be presumptuous to declare that Porter was aware of "Yankele," his "Farewell, Amanda (Samoa)" resembles less the South Seas and more the Russian Steppes since its head-motive elicits the main theme to the finale of Tchaikovsky's Fifth Symphony; and in "Yankele," even more so:

Porter's "Ca, C'est l'Amour" (from the 1957 film *Les Girls*) hints at another Warshavsky song: "80 er un 70 zi" (He Is 80, She Is 70). The Jewish-sounding "I Love Paris" more accurately mirrors the turn-of-the-twentieth-century French music hall of *Can Can*, the show from which it comes; but it also is suggestive of Rumshinsky's great theater song "Sheyn vi di levone" (Beautiful as the Moon). "Just One of Those Things" begins with the gypsy motive, although one would never hear it that way. "So in Love," an A^1-B-A^2 song, parallels the *Magein avot* mode by going from F-minor (in section A^1) to the relative major of A-flat in the bridge portion, returning again to F-minor in section A^2. But before it ends in A-flat major, there is a detour, in the last eight bars, to the gypsy motive.

A lesser-known torch song, "Goodbye, Little Dream, Goodbye," from Porter's 1936 musical *Red, Hot and Blue* is echoed in a Yiddish theater song of 1938 (Exx. 11-9a and b). When he heard Porter play "Goodbye, Little Dream," movie producer Sam Katz remarked, "it's—why it's Jewish."[9]

Richard Rodgers, Yip Harburg, and others have stated in print that Porter, in his constant shifting from minor to major keys, consciously wrote Jewish melodies. Rodgers included "Night and Day," "Begin the Beguine," and "Love for Sale" among these. Porter once told Sammy Cahn how envious he was that Cahn had come from the Lower East Side of New York. Charles Schwartz, a biographer of Porter, feels that implicit in Porter's "Jewish formula were undercurrents of anti-Semitism . . . nor did he have much to do with Jews socially."[10] It is fascinating and extraordinary that someone whose background was upper-class Episcopalian could have had in his music such a strong Jewish component. And if this giant had it, American music has it. But was Cole Porter anti- or philo-Semitic? A bit of both, I believe.

NOTES

1. While the word "ghetto" is generally conceded to derive from the name of a Venetian foundry, Franz Liszt in his egregious writings about the musical interaction between Jewish and Rom folk music, offers the intriguing notion that it is based on the Hebrew word *ghet*, for divorce or separation. See Franz Liszt, *The Gipsy in Music*, p. 36.

2. Crosby's contribution to the American songbook cannot be overestimated. Even though the only recording he made with specific Jewish content was "And the Angels Sing," other titles he popularized imparted a more subtle Jewish slant. In addition to "Temptation," there are "Brother Can You Spare a Dime?," "Love Thy Neighbor," and "Lawd, You Made the Nights Too Long." Crosby credited Al Jolson as a primary influence; and other Jews he counted among his close associates were Jack Kapp, his recording maven, Harry Barris, songwriter and co-performer, Barney Dean, his general factotum, and Irving Berlin. See Gary Giddins, *A Pocketful of Dreams*.

3. *Bima* is Hebrew for "platform." Leonard Bernstein's brass piece *Fanfare for Bima* has been mistaken as a call to worship. However, it is a summons to an animal; Bima was the name of Serge Koussevitzky's cocker spaniel.

4. Velvel Pasternak, *Beyond Hava Nagila*, p. 133 ff.

5. Café Society was a term coined in 1919 by gossip columnist Cholly Knickerbocker, pseudonym of Ghighi Cassini, brother of Oleg. See Kirk Douglas, *The Ragman's Son*, p. 159.

6. See *Copyright Decisions*, 1944-1946, pp. 11ff.

7. Phone conversation with Milton Rettenberg, Esq., 1984.

8. Quoted by lyricist Edward Eliscu at a New York Sheet Music Society meeting, September 1984. The song was written for the film *Something to Shout About*.

9. George Eells, *Cole Porter*, p. 155.

10. Richard Rodgers, *Musical Stages*, p. 88; E. Y. Harburg in Rosenberg and Goldstein, *Creators and Disturbers*, p. 148. See also Max Wilk, *They're Playing Our Song*, p. 186 and Charles Schwartz, Cole Porter, p. 118. Sammy Cahn on *Les Davis Show*, radio station WNEW, "Irving Berlin's 100th Birthday," 11 May 1988. Producer Cy Feuer, *I Got the Show Right Here* (Simon & Schuster, 2003), p. 161.

Affinities Between Jewish Americans and African Americans

Jews have stolen the Negroes' thunder . . . Tin Pan Alley has become a commercialized Wailing Wall.
CONSTANT LAMBERT in *Music Ho!: A Study of Music in Decline*, p. 212

Jews [were] responsible for perverting "authentic" African American music.
JEFFREY MELNICK in *A Right to Sing the Blues: African Americans, Jews, and American Popular Song*, p. 151

Debunking Canards

Sixty-five years separate the first epigraph above (1934) from the second one (1999), but there is a big difference in how these accusations are presented. Constant Lambert is rightly condemned, even by Jeffrey Melnick, as an arrant anti-Semite; and he remained unrepentant as late as 1948—post war, post Holocaust—when he declared in the preface to the third edition of his infamous book:

I am content to leave it as such, making no attempt to soften out the more controversial passages which may read surprisingly enough today when there seems to be a general view that all forms of culture are on the right side and should therefore be praised.

In other words, he was not about to change a word in his invective against Jews. Melnick, however, is too cagey to be charged with bigotry. By using voices like Lambert's to convey his message, he circumvents such an indictment. The excerpt from his book quoted above is preceded by a passage from the writings of African-American[1] essayist Alain Locke:

The very musicians who know the folk-ways of Negro music are the very ones who are in commercial slavery to the Shylocks of Tin Pan Alley (in artistic bondage to the ready cash of our dance-halls and the vaudeville stage).[2]

But it is not altogether clear if Melnick's remark is his own or a gloss on Locke's contentions since the entire book comes across as a study (an exposé?) of how Jews capitalized on blacks, made money off them, and took credit for their work.

Louis Armstrong would not have agreed with this assessment. From his oral history comes the statement, "If it wasn't for the nice Jewish people, we would have starved many a time. I will love the Jewish people all of my life." Armstrong's account of his childhood refutes an earlier story that "People thought my first horn was given to me at a colored waif's home for boys [reformatory-cum-orphanage], but it wasn't." Armstrong was taken under the wing of the Karnoffskys, a New Orleans Jewish family which "inadvertently became one of the earliest and most important incubators of American jazz." He earned pennies helping the two

Karnoffsky sons as they made their rounds as junk dealers. To gain the notice of customers, young Louis taught himself how to play simple tunes on a crude ten-cent tin horn. The Karnoffskys were most encouraging and soon advanced a loan on his salary for him to procure a five-dollar cornet from a pawn shop. After having dinner with the family, before the nighttime junkets on the wagon, Louis joined in as Mrs. Karnoffsky sang a baby to sleep with "Russian Lullaby." (Armstrong's memory is in error here. It could not have been Berlin's 1927 song of the same title—which Armstrong recorded three times: 1949, 1950, and 1953—despite the fact that lyrics of the Berlin verse are quoted in his testimony.) In the most extraordinary statement of all, he declared, "when I reached the age of eleven [1912], I began to realize it was the Jewish family who instilled in me singing from the heart."[3]

Reprehensible as they are, at least Constant Lambert's remarks—along with similar commentaries by miscreants Daniel Gregory Mason, Henry Ford,[4] and others—can be judged in the context of their fermenting times, an era when Americans were striving, especially through the popular arts, to find themselves. But how to account for Melnick's position at the end of the century? Can it be justified as a symptom of the cultural revisionist movements of recent decades? Paul Berman reminds us of Freud's postulation that "racial intolerance finds stronger expression, strange to say, in regard to small differences than to fundamental ones." Resentments smolder when similarities, rather than precise identities, are perceived by the injured party. In terms of music, this means that if a piece seems *like* another, it is prima facie incriminating evidence.[5]

The 1990s were marked by ever-increasing divisiveness between African Americans and Jews, erupting into the brazen rhetoric of demagogues Leonard Jeffries, Louis Farrakhan, and his exlieutenant Khalid Abdul Muhammad.[6] This may have colored the thinking of serious scholars—to say nothing of negative images about Jews in lyrics by Michael Jackson and the rap group, Public Enemy.[7] Even Melnick admits that "any chronicle of Jews making money out of African Americans . . . flirts uncomfortably with conventional anti-Semitic stereotypes . . ." (p. 41). But on the same page, note his intimation of Jewish conspiracy theory: "The Jewish presence in American popular music has to be *plotted* [always my emphasis] along a minstrel continuum. . . ." Elsewhere we are surfeited with implied allegations of the Jewish cabal: "Jews and their friends" (p. 61), "Jews and their fans" (p. 62); and other more direct contentions: "a loose network of Jewish business people and . . . the support Jews . . . could offer one another" (p. 38); "the Jewish takeover of popular music" (p. 69). Melnick tars with a wide brush as he accuses "parvenu" Jews of forcing blacks into "pariah" status. Thunderbolts hurled at Berlin and at Gershwin impugning everything from their literary and musical writings to their sexuality, singe all "upstart" Jews in the business.[8]

Exploitation

These pejorative declarations are put into the mouths of others or the author manages to speak out of both sides of his own mouth. But a comparison of the 752 pages of Melnick's original doctoral thesis, on which the book is based, to his 277-

page book reveals a less unsavory perspective on his part. In the dissertation he has the luxury to elaborate and soften the harder edges of his premise; but even there he makes outrageous statements such as "Jews had come to function as modern-day slaveholders" (p. 603). Such sweeping accusations cannot be justified and must not go unchallenged. Indeed, I am grateful to him for helping me to gauge more precisely Jewish contributions to American popular music within the crucible of Negritude. In this connection, a distinction must be made between white and black Jews. With the exceptions of Willie "The Lion" Smith, Sammy Davis, Jr., and Nell Carter (the latter two, converts to Judaism) no other African American mentioned in this chapter can be regarded as being Jewish (although Langston Hughes had Jewish ancestry).

Since there are no musical examples, Melnick's purported cases of Jewish larceny or encroachment upon African-American sources must be taken on faith, much of it supported by anecdotal evidence or buttressed by lengthy digressions into novels, which are fictive by definition.[9] In this respect, he follows the creed of "new" musicologists who believe "that music can be read for sexual or ideological meanings," and one does not have to talk *about* music per se as much as talk *through* music in the quest for cultural identity.[10]

Yet even his anecdotes must be viewed with suspicion since he does not always tell both sides of a troubling issue. Take, for example, his evaluation of Irving Berlin's "Alexander's Ragtime Band" as an instance of how "Jews capitalized on their ability to convey both . . . 'blackness' and distance themselves from actual African Americans" (p. 43). To nail this down, Melnick refers to a 1991 essay about Scott Joplin by ragtime authority Edward Berlin which "showed convincingly that . . . Joplin believed Irving Berlin [no relation] stole 'Alexander's Ragtime Band' from a theme he had been working on for his opera *Treemonisha*" (p. 56).

But the allegations of theft might be looked at as having worked in reverse. Elsewhere, Edward Berlin has suggested it is possible Joplin may himself have toyed with Jewish song material, specifically in his 1914 "Magnetic Rag," the last piano piece he was to see in print.[11] In the second strain, Joplin atypically goes into minor:

"Magnetic Rag," Scott Joplin

Ex. 12-1

Match this up against Mordecai Gebirtig's song "Avreml der marvikher" (Avreml the Pickpocket):

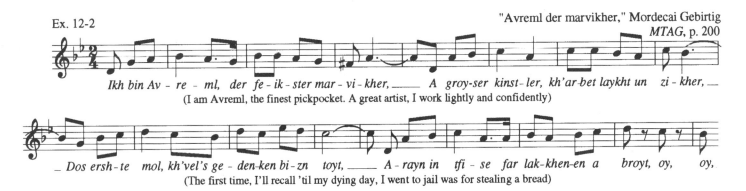

Ex. 12-2

"Avreml der marvikher," Mordecai Gebirtig
MTAG, p. 200

Ikh bin Av - re - ml, der fe - ik - ster mar - vi - kher, ___ A groy-ser kinst- ler, kh'ar-bet laykht un zi - kher, ___
(I am Avreml, the finest pickpocket. A great artist, I work lightly and confidently)

___ Dos ersh - te mol, kh'vel's ge - den - ken bi - zn toyt, ___ A - rayn in tfi - se far lak-khen-en a broyt, oy, oy,
(The first time, I'll recall 'til my dying day, I went to jail was for stealing a bread)

Gebirtig (1877-1942) was a contemporary of Joplin (1868-1917). Joplin had been living in New York City since 1907, and while it is improbable that he heard this song directly, "Magnetic Rag" is so unconventional in his output, it does indicate he might have been introduced to something like the material of the song from a teacher or a student. Joplin's first significant music teacher, Julius Weiss, with whom he maintained a lifelong correspondence, was Jewish. A student of Joplin's, a middle-class German Jew named Martin Niederhofer, studied "Magnetic Rag" with the composer in 1916, and was quoted as saying: "Isn't it strange that a colored fellow wrote such Jewish music in this rag?"[12] To contend that Joplin *believed* Berlin stole his thunder does not make it so any more than do the coincidences between the Yiddish song and Joplin's rag prove plunder.

James Weldon Johnson, the prominent Negro writer who was favorably disposed to Jews, is quoted extensively by Melnick, but selectively. Johnson is making a comparison when he states: "There are few things more ludicrous to an American than the efforts of European music hall artist to sing a jazz song. . . ."[13] But Melnick does not include this sentence, and instead leaps ahead to: "those who have mastered these rhythms most completely are Jewish Americans." Therefore, according to Melnick, Johnson: "with a wink for those in the know, hints at the countless African American ragtime musicians who had yet to publish—either because of their lack of technical training or *their lack of access to the appropriate outlets*" (p. 141). How are we to interpret: "Given the lack of access to the copyrighting process or the sheet music industry which plagues many African-American artists," and on whose shoulders are we to place blame? Here's a hint: Gershwin's *Rhapsody in Blue* is cited (unclearly) as one of the culprits as to why "the artistic project drafted in Johnson's work became the special province of *Jews*" (p. 162; please note how one Jew's work is made to hold all Jews responsible). A remarkable statement made in 1937 about *Rhapsody in Blue* by Johnson's brother, J(ohn) Rosamond, is probably closer to the genuine feelings of both Johnson brothers:

The writer is among many others who consider that it [i.e., the *Rhapsody*] is the greatest one-hundred-percent exposition of Negro American idioms and characteristics, and that it is a firm stepping-stone in the right direction of a modern American school of music. It is gratifying to be able to quote from Mr. Gershwin's dedication [he means a handwritten inscription]: "For Mr. Handy [i.e., W.C. Handy] whose early blue songs are the forefathers of this work. George Gershwin, August 30, 1926."

He goes on to praise the recently premiered *Porgy and Bess*.[14]

Were black composers at the mercy of white (for which read, Jewish) publishers? Black composer Will Marion Cook, eager to get a production of his 1898 show *Clorindy*, approached publisher Isidore Witmark, and said: "I will give you the publication rights and all the royalties accruing." Witmark replied: "I will do my best to get you a production, and publish the score, but I will not accept your royalties. You shall enjoy these yourself." (During the course of negotiations, Witmark meets Paul Laurence Dunbar, Cook's lyricist, whom Witmark describes as "one of the finest of men, white or black.") When *Clorindy* became a success, Cook now not only desired his first royalty check, but expected it to be "commensurate with the success of the play." Witmark refused, reminding him of the prior agreement and that it would take time to recoup the investment.[15] He then melodramatically showed the door to Cook: "You can't publish another number with this house as long as you live."[16]

But if Cook suffered from this dismissal, how then is one to estimate Cook and Dunbar's subsequent and most famous accomplishment—the first all-black Broadway show: *In Dahomey* (1902-1905)? And thereafter, until 1924, how are we to measure Cook's success as the composer of *Abyssinia, Bandanna Land, The Cannibal King, Darkydom, In the Jungles, Jes Lak White Folks, Negro Nuances, The Policy Players*, and *The Sons of Ham*?[17]

These titles, among others, may also refute Barry Singer's contention (quoted by Melnick on p. 36) that "1907-1920 were drought years for African Americans on Broadway." Author Allen Wohl, on the other hand, numbers only the years 1910-1917 as a "term of exile" when blacks "abandoned Broadway for advantages elsewhere . . . throughout the United States, an extended roadshow tryout to allow [black theater] to develop without white audiences and artists who had so often determined its course."[18] In other words, both black writers and performers had to buy into the conventions and stereotypes expected of them from white audiences in order to be successful.

The well-known black team of Sissle and Blake found Witmark to be a "prestigious and ethical firm . . . never reluctant, as some were, to produce and encourage the work of Negro artists."[19] But whatever the reality of the Cook-Witmark dispute may have been, at least Witmark paid out royalties. According to Edward Berlin, Gotham-Attucks, an early Tin Pan Alley music company devoted solely to the publication of songs by black writers, paid their songwriters nothing. Clarence Williams, another leading black publisher, credited Armand Piron as the writer of "I Wish That I Could Shimmy Like My Sister Kate," when Louis Armstrong claimed it was his.[20] In the 1920s and early 1930s, Fats Waller did not bother to copyright any of his material, "preferring rather to sell his compositions outright to a publisher for immediate cash, or perform them himself without troubling to see to their eventual publication."[21] Willie "The Lion" Smith says that royalties were an unknown quantity in the early days of jazz musicians.[22] Duke Ellington tells of a writer who sold his song outright, and when the song became a hit "blew his top, completely forgetting the fact that he had sold this same blues who knows how many times?"[23]

Certainly, as businessmen interested in making a profit, publishers were (and are) not social workers and, therefore, not altruistic to their composers. But why single out blacks as the only victims? Indeed, publishers of Yiddish theater music further downtown could be equal opportunity discriminators, and if they swindled blacks, they also could do the same to their own stable of writers. Sholom Secunda sold "Bay mir bistu shein" to the J. & J. [twins Jacob/Jack and Joseph] Kammen Music Co. for a pittance of $30, divided 50-50 with his lyricist, losing out on a major cash cow.[24] Actress-writer Molly Picon relates: "I wrote over 20 [songs]— which were used in the shows I did on Second Ave.—some were published & have my name on as writer—but that was all I ever received."[25] Composer Abe Ellstein, who wrote music for Picon's songs in the renowned 1936 film *Yidl Mitn Fidl*, signed a work-for-hire agreement with Joseph Green, the producer, with the understanding that Green owned the material as used in the film, but that Ellstein would retain the copyrights. Evidently, however, he had unknowingly agreed to forfeit the copyrights also. Sixty years later, the National Center for Jewish Film, which now controls Green's films, was sued by Ellstein's estate to recover these copyrights, but the court settled in favor of the Center (in 1996).[26]

Blackface

Nothing seemed more absurd than to see a colored man making himself ridiculous in order to portray himself.

GEORGE WALKER, quoted in Henry Sampson, *Blacks in Blackface*, p. 328

There is no denying that the practice of blackface was a shameful chapter in American theatrical history, and that it was widely practiced, more out of practicality than of racist insensibility, by Jewish entertainers Eddie Cantor, Sophie Tucker, Fanny Brice and, especially, Al Jolson. They all get raked over the coals by Melnick for their songs of "Mammy in the land of Dixie."[27] (He omits Lou Holtz, George Jessel, Belle Baker and Molly Picon from his rogue's gallery.) But why do they get singled out over all the others who were not Jewish?

Then, irony of ironies, blacks themselves were forced to imitate whites imitating blacks by donning blackface. Since it was the only way they could appear in front of an audience and prove their worthiness, they had to cover up their real skin color. This ugly tradition began with the Irish-dominated minstrel shows of the antebellum mid-1800s,[28] before Jews were an American presence, and continued well into the 1930s. Although some light-skinned performers passed as Creoles or Filipinos, vaudevillians burnt-corked themselves not so much to make them darker as to hide them from audiences who were not ready to accept them qua blacks in the theater. Flournoy E. Miller, Irvin C. Miller, S. H. Dudley, Billy King, Gallie DeGaston, Ethel Waters, and the teams of Bert Williams and George Walker and Bob Cole and Billy Johnson were all victims of this deception. As late as 1943, Lena Horne, in the movie version of *Cabin in the Sky*, had to wear a darkening makeup called "Light Egyptian" in order to have her match the skin color of Eddie "Rochester" Anderson. She writes, "I looked as if I were a white person trying to do a part in blackface." But, worse, the makeup department used this blend "on white actresses they wanted to play Negro or mulatto parts, which meant even less work for the Negro actors."[29] She was referring to Hedy Lamarr as Tondelayo in *White Cargo* and Ava Gardner as Julie in *Show Boat*, who were shaded to make them look more like a sultry Lena Horne![30]

In hindsight, blackface was not forgivable and no doubt was a highly questionable custom in its day. While some Jewish entertainers relate in their memoirs that they derived comfort from being so camouflaged, others positively hated it, but felt compelled to do it in order to get employment. "In blackface, they were no longer the immigrant . . . the ritual mask of the powerless gave them, the underdogs, sacred strength in this strange and dangerous New World."[31] Nonetheless, blackface was a template inherited, not created, by Jews; and the fact that the above-cited performers were better at their game than others has much to do with the canard that Jews were culpable in making forays onto black culture. Jazz critic Gary Giddins writes, "Economically and socially, minstrelsy is . . . unjust; aesthetically, it is the key with which some . . . white performers unlocked the doors to their personalities."[32] This is not to say, however, that Jews were not capable of deplorable wrongdoing.

Cab Calloway encountered bigotry among Jews, but he writes: "There's bad in every group. You can't blame the whole group for what one or two do; that's a shitty way to treat people."[33] In an interview, Miles Davis, expressing dissatisfaction with Columbia Records, said: "They don't do anything for you unless you're white or Jewish."[34] (This perception did not prevent him from recording Johnny Carisi's chart for "Israel," based on Al Jolson and Benee Russell's 1948 paraphrase of "Khosn kale mazl tov"). While Lena Horne faults "Jewish merchants . . . in Harlem and the . . . slave-market tactics of Bronx housewives," she also maintains a flip-side position—along with song stylists Billie Holiday, Pearl Bailey, and Ella Fitzgerald—in paying tribute to various Jewish producers, personal managers, and impresarios who guided their careers: Lew Leslie, mastermind of the *Blackbird* musical revues; Frank Schiffman, owner of Harlem's Lafayette and then Apollo Theaters; Moe Gale (b. Galowski), proprietor of the Savoy Ballroom; Norman Granz, known for his Jazz at the Philharmonic concerts; Barney Josephson, Max Gordon, and Herbert Jacoby, who ran, respectively, the New York City-based nightclubs: Café Society, Village Vanguard and Blue Angel.[35] Chanteuse Josephine Baker, who was particularly empathic to injustices against Jews, had a famous battle over civil rights issues at the Stork Club, run by Sherman Billingsley, a non-Jew, who in turn harbored adverse opinions of Jews.

In the instrumental jazz field, Benny Goodman broke down the color barrier. He not only employed black arrangers, Fletcher and Horace Henderson and Benny Carter, but also featured black soloists Teddy Wilson, Lionel Hampton, and others. Elsewhere, away from New York, jazz artists had less contact with Jewish bandleaders or entrepreneurs.[36] Pianist Willie "The Lion" Smith, a New Yorker, asserts that "the people with whom I have had the least trouble in life have been the Jews."[37] Regrettably, Melnick's trenchant analysis of Smith in his dissertation—a section of thirty-one pages arrestingly entitled "A Black Man in Jewface"—is not reproduced in his book. If it had been, his condemnation of Jews in blackface would have had some degree of balance since he discloses how Smith traded on his self-imposed Jewishness for self-promotion.

It should be noted that some songs for Jews who performed in blackface were written by black teams: Henry Creamer & J. Layton Turner and by Joe Jordan & Will Marion Cook.[38] More surprising is the disclosure that black vaudevillians were known to caricature Jewish stereotypes. Edward Berlin, in researching the *Indianapolis Freeman,* the first black-owned newspaper "to carry an entertainment page on a continuing basis," has uncovered items about the following African-American thespians: (1) Harry L. Gillam, "the Acrobatic Hebrew . . . a Hebrew by profession only and not by race as many people in the audience thought" (1/21/1899); (2) D. Ireland Thomas, "one of the few colored jew impersonators . . . with the Meloroy-Chandler Minstrels" (9/2/1899); (3) John Moore, a "colored character artist . . . impersonator of Italian, Jew, Indian, Chinese, Blackface and Mexican" (3/23/1912); (4) Jack Denton, "the hunchback Jew" (12/2/1912); and (5) J. B. Verdun, "Jewish impersonator" (3/1/1913).

Not only did Jewish blackface performers come into their own *after* non-Jews and blacks had set the precedent, their glory days were essentially over *before* the even more famous movie stars who appeared in blackface. It is true these were one-time affairs, and not a regular routine as with the stage entertainers; but this convention was more than balanced by the much wider audiences reached by movies.

In today's cultural climate, it is startling to see Judy Garland and Mickey Rooney in blackface for the finale of *Babes on Broadway* (1942). The producers had to insert a prior scene showing them blacking up because preview audiences did not realize who they were! Then there were blackface Marion Davies spouting "massa" and "is you" in *Going Hollywood* (1934); Bing Crosby (with Marjorie Reynolds) in *Holiday Inn* (1942) and in *Dixie* (1943) as Daniel Decatur Emmett; George Murphy joining Eddie Cantor in *Show Business* (1944); Fred Astaire blacking up in *Swingtime* (1936) as Bill Bojangles Robinson; and Jose Ferrer smearing on fireplace ashes in "Jazz a Doo," a phony Jolson bit in the Sigmund Romberg biopic, *Deep in My Heart* (1954). Martha Raye's scene with Louis Armstrong in *Artists and Models* (1937, performing Arlen and Koehler's "Public Melody Number One") became a cause célèbre for its candid sexuality between a black man and a white woman posing as a black. Irene Dunne put on burnt cork for the movie version of *Show Boat* (1936), as she did on Broadway, for "Gallavantin' Around." Even Edgar Bergen's dummy Charlie McCarthy got into the act in *You Can't Cheat an Honest Man* (1939). Most unnerving is to witness Joan Crawford in her first color film, *Torch Song* (1953), dubbing the Dietz and Schwartz number "Two-Faced Woman" to a track previously laid down, but not used, by India Adams for Cyd Charisse in another film, *The Band Wagon.* Surrounded by a full cast of stage folk in blackface, Crawford lip-synchs the lines "Some day I'll wake up and find out what's wrong with my dual makeup." Ha!

Topsy and Eva, a 1924 Broadway musical, was played in blackface by the Duncan Sisters, Rosetta and Vivian.[39] Italian actress Tess Gardella originated the blackface role of Queenie in *Show Boat* (1927) so successfully that her stage image became the model for Aunt Jemima. The radio team of Charles Correll and Freeman (incongruous name in this context) Gosden did the white Negro voices of *Amos 'n' Andy,* and then appeared in blackface in a 1930 movie entitled *Check and Double-Check* (one of the *Amos 'n' Andy* expressions). Marlin Hurt, a white man, was the voice of Beulah on the *Fibber McGee and Molly* radio of the 1940s.

None of these entertainers was Jewish.

Author Mark Slobin makes astute observations about how "attenuated, ventriloquized ways . . . of blackface have lived on" in background jazz scores of midtwentieth-century movies—where the term *black and white* applies both to the cast roster and to film stock—and also how "the use of 'spaceface' [is an aspect of] sci-fi vehicles."[40]

Pastiche

Like "eclectic" and "macaronics," the word "pastiche," when applied to pieces of music, more often than not has negative connotations. At one extreme, this label is pasted on composers to disparage their inability to be "original." At the other end, they are applied to imitations (and therefore alleged limitations) in the style of, or borrowings from, already existing sources. Ronald Sanders may be more generous in his use of the term when he considers pastiche to be "a gift of peoples who live in culturally ambivalent situations"—a description equally applicable to Jews and blacks. Still, one is left with the impression that this "old American-Jewish specialty" is thought of as more a weakness than a strength.[41]

In religious circles, the proselytizing Salvation Army during its heyday, was known to set hymn texts to popular songs. "Rock-a My Soul in the Bosom of Abraham," the Negro spiritual, is a version (in 4/4 time) of "The Irish Washerwoman" reel (in 6/8 time).[42] The Hasids (i.e., pious ones), insular factions of East European orthodoxy, were also known to commandeer melodies from their surroundings and convert them into tunes called *nigunim* (wordless tunes), a process they believed was an act of sanctification and salvation. Into this mix went French marches—from Napoleonic armies, tramping through Russia—Slavic dances, Russian ballads, Ukrainian shepherd songs, waltzes, Polish drinking songs, and even the tunes of their persecutors, the Cossacks. The custom was encouraged in order to "elevate, purify, and sanctify" the imports;[43] and, in fact, Hasidic *rebes* felt it "was a greater virtue than creating an original melody."[44] Such freeloading was rarely literal. If nothing else, the fact that Yiddish or Hebrew prosody underlay Gentile languages did necessitate changes in rhythms. While this could result in a macaronic jumble, it also contributed to the evolution of a more fertile song literature than would have otherwise blossomed. Even today, Sephardic cantors in Mediterranean countries are expected to incorporate new commercial Arabic tunes into worship music.[45]

As previously noted, Irving Berlin's early songs were all over the map in an international melange of dialects. But Melnick singles out only the "coon" song as racialization at work. Citing the line "mine choc'late baby," from Berlin's "Yiddle, On Your Fiddle, Play Some Ragtime," Melnick claims that it "contributed to the success of Jewish musicians in subsuming blackness into . . . ethnic cut-and-paste jobs" (p. 77). If he had bothered to examine the music, he would have found no ragtime syncopation, but, instead, a quote from a Yiddish tune. (See my Chapter 6.) Philip Furia observes that Sadie, the girl in the song, who calls Yiddle "mine choc'late baby" is actually complimenting him—"perhaps because he had mastered black music."[46]

As if to reciprocate the dubious favor, some black composers indulged in formulaic Jewish mockery. Chris Smith, of Smith and Bowman vaudeville fame, and best known for writing "Ballin' the Jack," produced "Oi, Yoi, Yoi, Yoi (A Hebrew Love Song)" in 1904 wherein the hook-nose Jew caricatured on the cover "was made of money/Because his name was Gold." Creamer and Turner, authors of "After You're Gone," came up with "Simon and Healy and Cohen (Skinners and Dealers in Hides)" in 1920: "With Simon in front and Cohen behind/What chance has poor Healy to pick up a dime?" Paul Reynolds and Clarence Williams provided "The Cohens and Kellys, They're in Scotland Now" in 1929, and in 1939, Spencer Williams, who wrote "I Ain't Got Nobody," is one of three writers credited for "Mazl Tov," based on the by then cliché-ridden "Khosn kale mazl tov."

As we have seen in the lives of Jerome Kern and Kurt Weill, West European Jews and their descendants often expressed patronizing tolerance for their less fortunate coreligionists in the east, at best, and at worst, contempt. "Yiddish is not German. Jews do not know German and Germans do not know Yiddish. That Yiddish was once a form of German is of no account since it did not remain German."[47] This discomfort is not unlike that felt between light-skinned blacks and their darker brothers and sisters. According to at least one evaluation, the song "Black and Blue" (by Andy Razaf, Fats Waller, and Harry Brooks) is not, as is commonly thought, about oppression of blacks by whites, but about a dark-skinned woman's grief at not being preferred by black men.[48]

Consequently, past histories of both blacks and Jews show them to be simultaneously insiders and outsiders,[49] a stance that sensitizes the more pluralistic-minded among them to different ethnic groups. Others—with ideological, religious or ethnic agendas—are more inbred, and therefore self-limiting in their musical expression. Shows by blacks, exclusively intended for black audiences in Harlem or regional theater, were based on themes of return to Africa, relationship to white society, fast-talking dandies, rent-party scenes, etc.[50] Similarly, Yiddish theater was based on bloodline themes: sacred versus secular strife, upward mobility ambitions, historical and biblical subjects, nostalgia for the shtetl, etc., all designed for Jewish audiences on Second Avenue and in regional theaters.

In between these uptown and downtown localities, Broadway beckoned to both groups where blacks continue to explore their own ethnocentric themes, but where Jews venture into other cultures, including the African-American, more often than their own. Before World War II, musicals tended to have American plots; but in the postwar era, first-generation composers hit their full stride and began to excel in musicals that had foreign settings with consequential kinds of subject matter: intergenerational conflicts, clash of cultures, and the like. Deena Rosenberg writes, "The contrast between their parents' insular past and their own wide-open present made them acute social observers."[51] In analyzing *Fiddler on the Roof*, Joseph Swain declares: "Of all ethnic sources, perhaps Jewish folk music is most apt to adaptation;"[52] but he does not address the extraordinary attraction of Jewish songwriters to a host of other ethnic idioms.

It should also be obvious that pastiche was not an attribute unique to Jews. Grand opera composers Verdi in *Aida* (about Ethiopians), Puccini in *Madame Butterfly*, et al., were eminent practitioners, even though their exoticisms remain firmly rooted in Italian opera. Early twentieth-century operettas, primarily by Gentiles,[53] were typically located in exotic locales: *Rio Rita* by Harry Tierney and

Joe McCarthy, *Eileen,* an Irish operetta by Victor Herbert, an Irish immigrant, etc. Cole Porter was nonpareil in writing "Russian" for *Leave It to Me* and *Silk Stockings,* "French" for *Can Can* and other works, as well as "Latin" for *Mexican Hayride.*

Showbiz Religion

The same year Abraham Lincoln promulgated the Emancipation Proclamation, in 1862, the Emancipation Act of Poland granted Polish Jews civic equality. Much of East European Jewish music is Slavic in nature, and, indeed, the very word "slave" derives from Slavic nations, subjugated peoples. African Americans, forced to abandon home and family, were also compelled to adopt alien customs and religious practices. Inevitably, the interbreeding between Christian and African rituals flowered into the enduring legacy of spirituals. Alain Locke, mentioned earlier for his denunciation of so-called Jewish exploiters on Tin Pan Alley, elsewhere observes that the Negro sorrow songs are "a tragic profundity of emotional experience, for which the only historical analogy is the spiritual experience of the Jews and the only analogue, the Psalms."[54] While many spirituals draw upon Old Testament stories and characters–e.g., Moses, Joshua, Ezekiel, Jacob, David, and Daniel— there is, curiously enough, no such equivalent in sacred Jewish music.[55] In point of fact, "Go Down Moses" is borrowed for Passover seders.

Instead, Jewish songwriters transmute these themes into show-biz spirituals. Among them are Arlen's "Get Happy" (*Nine-Fifteen Revue*) and "Accent-chu-ate the Positive" (*Here Come the Waves,* film), Berlin's "Shaking the Blues Away" (*Ziegfeld Follies of 1927*), Kern's "Ol' Man River" and "Mis'ry's Comin' 'Round" (*Show Boat*), Gershwin's "Clap Yo' Hands" (*Oh, Kay!*), Loesser's "Sit Down, You're Rocking the Boat"[56] (*Guys and Dolls*), Harburg and Lane's "The Great Come and Get It Day" (*Finian's Rainbow*), "Rhythm River" (Cotton Club revue song) and "Stay on the Right Side, Sister" (*Love Me or Leave Me,* a Doris Day film) both by Rube Bloom and Ted Koehler, Fain and Harburg's "Jump Little Chillun" (*Flahooley*), "All God's Chillun Got Rhythm" by Gus Kahn, Walter Jurmann and Bronislau Kaper (*A Day at the Races,* the film comedy in which the Marx Brothers blacken up in order to hide from the sheriff), Schwartz and Fields's "(If the Devil Answers) Hang Up!" (*By the Beautiful Sea*), Jack Lawrence and Stan Freeman's "Faith" (*I Had a Ball*), Sondheim's "Miracle Song" (*Anyone Can Whistle*), etc. Although the convention has been prominent among Jewish songwriters, such faux preachments were not limited to them alone. Billie Holiday wrote "God Bless the Child," but in tandem with Arthur Herzog, Jr. In addition to Youmans's "Hallelujah," there was his "Great Day," along with Porter's contributions, the rousing "Blow, Gabriel, Blow"(*Anything Goes*) and "Climb up the Mountain" (*Out of This World*).[57]

While Negro spirituals often express the trials and tribulations of the "Hebrew Chillun"—the Nation of Islam preaches that the Hebrew tribes of the Bible, including the enslaved people of Egypt, were black—Gospel songs concentrate more on the proximity of Jesus Christ. One tends to be narrative, the other is charismatic. Something like the Gospel tradition of slow, rapturous melody leading to exuberant bodily movement is also found in the songs of Hasidim in which words are frequently considered to be an impediment. They are replaced by carrier syllables—such as "yai-di-dai-di" or repetitions of *Du*, meaning "Thou"—making for a kind of elated Jewish scat. Like a fingerprint, a particular Hasidic sect can be identified by its choice of these neologisms. One group's "oy-yoy" would be another's "bim-bom." Indirectly, these vocalizations are a substitute for instruments, generally banned in synagogue worship. The quasi-instrumental sounds, coupled with dance rhythms, open the way for Hasids to achieve *dveykus* (union) with the divine. Gradual steps of elevation lead to this euphoria; and so these dances can last as long as thirty minutes, a custom that continues to this day in various Hasidic sects.[58] (A social psychologist might detect a hint of sublimated sexuality hereby released in an acceptable manner.) The Hasid strives to become the embodiment of words from Psalm 35: "*Kol atzmotai*: all my bones shall exult in the Lord." Like the Negro in a camp-meeting style of jubilation, the Hasid at a *farbrengn* (gathering) also has the assurance of heavenly feasting in the afterlife.[59]

Sometimes the showbiz spirituals are begun by individual black performers which then get taken over by white characters. One critic wryly describes them as being enacted "with an air of 'I can be dignified, but I can display Negro abandon.'"[60] But Jewish writers also reverse that formula, with whites playing a minor role, in an array of shows about Blacks that feature group prayers, expressed as lusty ring shouts, jubilees and gospel hymns or in angst-ridden blues, spirituals and funeral dirges. Some of them do so on a grand scale: *Amen Corner, Cabin in the Sky, Carmen Jones, Golden Boy, Hallelujah, Baby!, House of Flowers, Jamaica, Little Ham, Lost in the Stars, Porgy and Bess, Purlie, Raisin*, and *St. Louis Woman*. Elsewhere, blacks appear only in scenes: *A Broadway Musical, Bloomer Girl, The First, Mister Wonderful, Gone with the Wind, Grind, Look to the Lilies, Regina, Saratoga*, and *1600 Pennsylvania Avenue*.[61]

When we contrast this statistic to synagogue backdrops or religious motifs in the many shows by Jews on Jewish subjects (sometimes described as "Jewsicals"), the pickings are very lean, almost nonexistent. Cantors have participated in pageants targeted to the in-group: extravaganzas such as the Chicago-based *The Romance of a People* of 1933 (with music based on Abraham Idelsohn's research), Kurt Weill's *The Eternal Road* of 1937 and its subsequent spin-offs of the 1940s, as well as the Madison Square Garden spectacles devised by Max Helfman and his collaborators in the1950s. But for the wider non-Jewish audiences, a cantor is prominent only in *The Jazz Singer*, in its variegated versions, and much less so in the 1971 MGM film *Sunday, Bloody Sunday* (Cantor Henry Danziger) and in the 2000 film *Keeping the Faith* (see Chapter 7, n. 24). On the stage, there are scattered cantorial and Hasidic idioms in *Fiddler on the Roof*, and a synagogue scene occurs in the unfamiliar *The Prince of Grand Street*. Bar mitzvahs take place, respectively, in a hospital room (*Falsettos*), a penthouse (*I Can Get It for You Wholesale*), or in a rabbi's office (*Bar Mitzvah Boy*), but never in a synagogue, although Jerome Robbins's unrealized autobiographical *The Poppa Piece* was to include such a setting.

Why the imbalance? For one thing, first-generation Jews are still strangers in a foreign land and have a deep ancestral memory. Their shaky status is continually being assaulted, so observant Jews—only one generation away from pogroms—are not about to share their religious practices with the larger community (assuming the community wishes to participate); and even nonobservant Jews sustain somewhere in their psyches a vestige of the Third Commandment—not to take the name of the Lord in vain. Richard Rodgers once observed that in the theater, "Jews are for off-stage, not on."

Another more obvious fact, but necessary to mention: God-fearing blacks on stage do not sing in Hebrew. "If intelligibility is compromised in the interest of ethnic authenticity, communication breaks down and so does the drama."[62] By serving up Christianity, the American national religion, in a familiar, but spiced-up recipe, theatergoers are titillated, but still made comfortable. Behind the footlights, sins owned up to in public are more easily expiated than in a private confessional booth.

Although there are explicit shared musical idioms between a Jewish boy and his family's black maid in *Carolyn, or Change,* or between *The Zulu and the Zayde,* the male-bonding protagonists of Harold Rome's musical, and in spite of the amiable affiliation forged by black comedian Geoffrey Cambridge and Yiddish comedienne Molly Picon in *How to Be a Jewish Mother,* less explicit are the Jewish and black musical elements that cross-pollinate each other in diverse musicals about African Americans. The bottom line here is that blacks are generally perceived to be more theatrically viable—and, therefore, have greater commercial appeal—than parochial Jews. Jewish and African-American writers may have at times joined forces in creating some of these shows and related projects,[63] but as far I know, no African American has written a musical on a Jewish theme. On the other hand, there have been extraordinary collaborations of Jewish and black writers: black lyricists and book writers such as Paul Francis Webster (who worked with Jewish composers Sammy Fain, Johnny Mandel, and Dimitri Tiomkin), Walter Bishop (with Jule Styne), Countée Cullen (with Harold Arlen), and Langston Hughes (with Kurt Weill); and black composers with Jewish wordsmiths: Duke Ellington (with lyricists Marshall Barer, Herbert Martin, Mitchell Parish, Irving Mills, and John LaTouche), Cab Calloway (with Mills), and James Mundy (with LaTouche).

Beyond black religious traditions, Jews have also dipped into nonblack Christian subjects, most prominently in *Godspell* (Stephen Schwartz and John-Michael Tebelak*) on the strength of which, Schwartz was invited to collaborate on Leonard Bernstein's theater piece *Mass.* In Richard Rodgers's operetta-style collaborations with Oscar Hammerstein II, nuns "Climb Every Mountain" (*The Sound of Music)*[64] and appeals are made to Buddha (*The King and I*). In Bernstein's operetta *Candide,* both bishop and rabbi get their comeuppance. In musical comedy, Salvation Army evangelists plead with sinners to "Follow the Fold" (Loesser's *Guys and Dolls*).

The Ukrainian Dorian Mode

Some observers have heard affinities between the emotive art of the black preacher and that of the Jewish cantor, as well as between dirges played by Dixieland bands at New Orleans funeral marches and memorial rituals of the synagogue. Indeed, there are times when the lines between African and Jewish Americana begin to blur. At the end of Part I of this book the metamorphosis of "Khosn kale mazl tov" into

"Shine on Harvest Moon" was delineated. The common ground this tune shares with African-American music is via the Ukrainian Dorian (henceforth *UD*) mode—so named for its idiosyncratic presence in East European folk songs—represented by a minor scale with raised 4th step and variable raised and lowered 6th and 7th steps:

Ex. 12-3

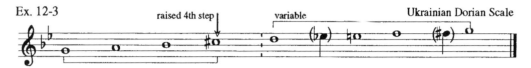

The spiritual "Father Abraham" is in this mode:

Ex. 12-4

Many Hebrew benedictions also invoke the name of Father Abraham, along with Isaac and Jacob. A standard rubric, it opens, for example, the prayer of *Mi sheberach* (May He Who blessed):[65]

Ex. 12-5

But the *UD* mode does not always travel in such high-toned circles. The musical language of a cantor can also be good enough for the dregs of society. In the Yiddish underground, for instance, a con man wavers between his devotion to his lady and to his profession, but it is obvious he will never keep his promise to reform:

Ex. 12-6

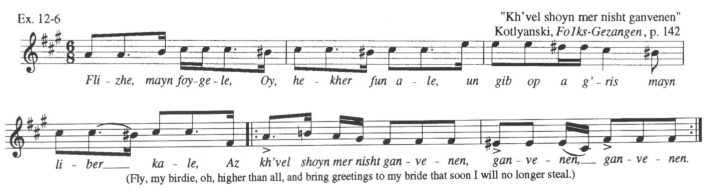

Or a Negro chain-gang song makes an appeal for relief in an unadorned *UD* mode:

Ex. 12-7

"Water Boy"
(Chain gang origin?)

Wa - ter Boy, __ Where are you hi - din'? If you don't a come Gwine tell a your Mam — my __

There is an even more specific link between African-American and Jewish *UD* traditions. The opening musical phrase of "Water Boy" can be heard at the end of a lampoon made at the expense of a Hasid's unwavering devotion to his *rebe*. Such mockery was the stock-in-trade of *maskils* (proponents of the nineteenth-century Jewish enlightenment called *Haskalah*):

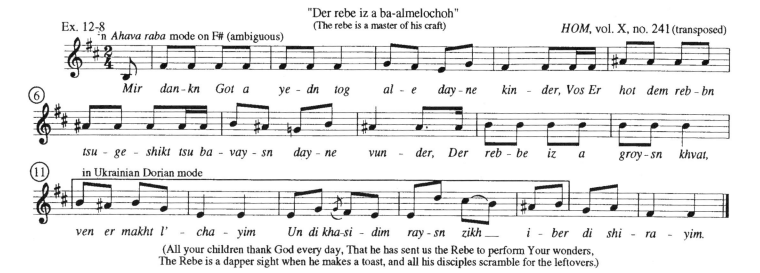

Ex. 12-8

"Der rebe iz a ba-almelochoh"
(The rebe is a master of his craft)

HOM, vol. X, no. 241 (transposed)

'n *Ahava raba* mode on F# (ambiguous)

⑥ Mir dan-kn Got a ye-dn tog al-e day-ne kin-der, Vos Er hot dem reb-bn

tsu-ge-shikt tsu ba-vay-sn day-ne vun-der, Der reb-be iz a groy-sn khvat,

⑪ in Ukrainian Dorian mode

ven er makht l'-cha-yim Un di kha-si-dim ray-sn zikh __ i-ber di shi-ra-yim.

(All your children thank God every day, That he has sent us the Rebe to perform Your wonders,
The Rebe is a dapper sight when he makes a toast, and all his disciples scramble for the leftovers.)

In *The Tune Detective*, a Paramount Pictures short of the early 1930s, Sigmund Spaeth describes the similarities among "Water Boy," *Marche Slav*, and a minstrel show song about a hop-head[66] (Ex. 12-9) —all three pieces, please note, are about forms of slavery.

Ex. 12-9

"Willie the Weeper"
Spaeth, *Read 'Em and Weep*, p. 104

mixed *UD* & minor modes

Did you e - ver hear tell a - bout Wil- lie the Weep - er, __ Wil- lie the Weep - er, yes, the

chim-ney_ sweep-er, __ Had the dope ha - bit __ and had it bad. __ Lis-ten and I'll tell you 'bout the dream he had. __

In his comparative survey, Spaeth also includes "St. James Infirmary," a white classic folk song often performed by Louis Armstrong, Cab Calloway, and others. But there is not a raised 4th step anywhere in it to be found—close, but no Ukrainian cigar.[67] Spaeth goes on to include two pop songs of 1931 by African-American composers: "Minnie the Moocher" by Calloway (written in collaboration with Irving Mills and Clarence Gaskill) and "I'll Be Glad When You're Dead, You

Rascal You" by Sam Theard (used as source music in the 1932 RKO film *What Price Hollywood?*).

At the urging of Mills, Calloway had been persuaded to come up with an original theme song to replace "St. James Infirmary,"[68] which he did by fashioning his "Minnie the Moocher" along the same lines as "St. James Infirmary." In fact, he says, "the melody is close in some sections." He then used the ideas of "Willie the Weeper" for the lyrics of the Moocher song (also about a drug addict).[69] But neither Minnie nor St. James use the raised 4th, while Theard's blues song does (Exx. 12-10 and 12-11):

Spaeth might have added the spiritual "Never Said a Mumbalin' Word" to his list; and if the film short had been made after 1935, he could have tossed in Irving Berlin's "Let Yourself Go" (from the movie *Follow the Fleet*), a snappy tune in the *UD* mode:

Match this against the opening formation of a 1943 pop song by Billy Austin and Louis Jordan, an African-American team:

Ex. 12-13

"Is You Is, or Is You Ain't"
Billy Austin & Louis Jordan

Is You Is, or   Is   You Ain't ma ba — by?__   The   way you're act - ting   late - ly   makes me doubt,__

Again, no raised 4th step and, therefore, not Jewishly inflected. Similarly, in "It Don't Mean a Thing If It Ain't Got That Swing," Duke Ellington sticks only to the lowered 5th step. However, both the raised 4th (C-sharp in Ex.12-14) and lowered 5th (D-flat equals C-sharp when spelled enharmonically) are ubiquitous in *Porgy and Bess*:

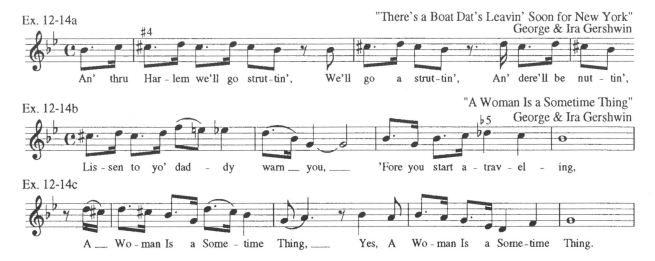

Ex. 12-14a

"There's a Boat Dat's Leavin' Soon for New York"
George & Ira Gershwin

An' thru Har - lem we'll go strut-tin',   We'll   go a strut-tin',   An' dere'll be nut - tin',

Ex. 12-14b

"A Woman Is a Sometime Thing"
George & Ira Gershwin

Lis - sen to yo' dad — dy warn__ you,__   'Fore you start a - trav - el — ing,

Ex. 12-14c

A __ Wo - man Is   a Some - time Thing, ___   Yes, A Wo - man Is a Some - time Thing.

Elsewhere, is Louis Armstrong simulating African-American or Jewish-American styles in the song "Shadrach, Meshach, and Abednego" (from the movie *The Strip*) or in "Remember Who You Are and What You Represent" on the cast recording of *The Real Ambassadors* (1961)? The same question comes up regarding a 1943 novelty song by Walter Kent (M) and Bob Russell (W). Compare it to a wedding dance by Max Helfman, from his Yiddish oratorio of 1948 based on the battle of the Warsaw ghetto, *Di naye hagode* (The New Hagadah):[70]

Ex. 12-15a

"Wedding Dance" from *Di naye hagode*
Max Helfman

Ex. 12-15b

"Who Dat Up Dere?"
Walter Kent & Bob Russell

Who Dat Up Dere?__   Who dat down there? __   Who Dat Up Dere?__   Who dat ___ down there?__

Kurt Weill merges the raised 4th (Jewish) and lowered 5th (African-American) steps in his "The Saga of Jenny" (from *Lady in the Dark*, 1941). Exhibiting the same kind of playfulness as the *Porgy and Bess* numbers, this time we are one generation removed. No longer is it a matter of connecting African-American and Jewish sounds; now we can consider the alternative that Jewish sound materials go

directly into popular music, bypassing considerations or evidence of any African-
American correlation:

Ex. 12-16a

"The Saga of Jenny"
Ira Gershwin & Kurt Weill

Jen - ny made her mind up when she was three,__ She, her-self, was going to trim the Christ-mas tree,__

And five bars thereafter:

Ex. 12-16b

Poor Jen - ny! Bright as a pen-ny! Her e - qual would be hard to find.

A song by Roger Edens and Comden and Green from the 1949 film *Take Me
out to the Ballgame* follows Jenny's example. The verse is based on the alternation
of the raised 4th and 5th steps, and the opening strain of its chorus echoes that of
"Jenny." Performed by Frank Sinatra and Betty Garrett, this baby has come a long
way from "Khosn kale mazl tov."

"It's Fate, Baby"
Betty Comden & Adolph Green (W), Roger Edens (M)

Ex. 12- 17a: Verse

It's time you made your mind up not to stall with me, Start play-ing ball with me;

Ex. 12- 17b: Refrain

It's Fate, Ba-by, It's Fate,__ And it's knock-ing at our door,__ It's Fate, Ba-by, And that's__

* * *

Through his association with Irving Mills, Cab Calloway was introduced to
Jewish prayer style. In 1939 he recorded "Utt-da-zay, The Tailor's Song," an adaptation by Mills and Samuel "Buck" Ram of the Yiddish folk song "Ot azoy neyt a
shnayder," "This Is How a Tailor Sews."[71] In the recorded version, Calloway finds
an uncanny kinship between the coloratura style of *hazanut* (cantoring) and his
individualized "hi-dee-ho" riffs—as a satirical poke at Hebrew?— embellishments
not found on the sheet music:

Ex. 12-18

Approximate transcription from recording of "Utt-da-zay"
Cab Calloway improvisation

slide

A- di wah-di da - di -doo- wah day,   Tee-dle oo-dle rah-de wah-de-way,   Are you hip to the jive that I'm laying on you?
                                        (N. B. "Are you hip to the jive" is the title of a whole other song by Buck Ram.)

This ostensible improvisation must have had particular resonance for Calloway
since he uses something like it elsewhere, in his famous renditions of "Minnie the

Moocher" and "St. James Infirmary" as well as in "Nain, Nain" (No, No), a 1941 song he wrote in collaboration with Buck Ram, and in "The Ghost of Smokey Joe," a 1939 Cotton Club specialty number by Rube Bloom (M) and Ted Koehler (W), where the ululation is used to produce a spooky effect. Beyond its novelty display, the choice of impersonating a cantor in songs that had nothing do with sacred matters presupposes that Calloway must have felt a connection between his free-flowing style and the bravura idiom displayed by certain peacock cantors who were more absorbed in surface effects than by inner spirituality. Calloway's "eccentricities of dress [i.e., zoot suit] extended into his vocal style, which carried echoes of the blues, class sentimentality and cantorial religiosity."[72]

Both the "star" cantor and the scat singer were stimulated by an adoring, undiscriminating public dazzled by the pyrotechnics. The artistry of an Ella Fitzgerald or a Mel Tormé, when they were hot and jamming, may have displayed a virtuosity for its own sake, but their vocal acrobatics never pretended to be brandished as a manifestation of religious conviction. On the other hand, Louis Armstrong (in an overheard conversation with Cab Calloway about the origins of scat) said that "he got it from the Jews 'rockin,' [by which] he meant davening . . . But Louis never talked about this in public, because he feared people would assume he was making fun of Jews praying, which wasn't his intention at all."[73] In "Chimes at the Meeting," a novelty number recorded in 1935 by Willie Bryant and Band (with Benny Carter on trumpet, Ben Webster on sax, et al.), the comic proceedings are interrupted with a welcome to "Brother Goldberg, oy, oy, oy," a signal to burst into "Khosn kale mazl tov," which is followed by a roulade of "oys" mixed in with scat (on Victor 24847).

Calloway was not the only African American to record "Utt-da-zay;" Leo Watson also laid it down on the Decca label in 1939.[74] Calloway's discography also lists other Jewish-related curios from 1939-1940: "A Bee Gezindt" by Henry Nemo and "Who's Yehoodi?" by Bill Seckler (W) and Matt Dennis (M); and in 1958, "Tzotskele" (a pet name), also known as "My Darling," that contains a smattering of Yiddish mixed in with Borscht Belt humor that may have been hilarious for Jewish audiences in the Catskills in the fifties, but now would be considered politically unacceptable.[75]

Other African Americans who recorded or performed Jewish material include Paul Robeson singing "Chant of Levi Isaac" and "Hassidic Chant: Kaddish" (both arranged by Joel Engel) and "Vi azoi lebt der kaiser?" (How Does the Kaiser Live?); piano-stylist Hazel Scott, who went to town with "Ich vil zikh shpiln" (I Want to Play for You) by Adolf King; and The Ravens, who recorded Artie Wayne's "Mahzel (Means Good Luck)."[76]

In the late thirties, pianist Bulee ("Slim") Gaillard, in jive lingo of his own invention, tossed off a menu of Jewish foodstuffs: "Matzoh Balls"(1939), a hilarious beguine heard in the film version of *Hellzapoppin* (Universal, 1941), "Drei Six Cents," extolling pickled herring that costs thirty cents (*draysik* in Yiddish is the number 30) and "Dunkin' Bagel." Among his other spoofs there was "Mishugana Mambo" and a spin-off of "*Bay mir bist du sheyn*" written with Bud Green?, called "Vol Vist Du Gaily Star?" (1938, recorded also by Jimmy Dorsey's band). Is this last title nonsensical or is there a coded message? *Voyl bistu* is Yiddish for "you are good/worthy." Look closely at the words Gaily and Gaillard. Could he be saying of himself, "you're a worthy star, Gaillard"? Or is his jumbled language rooted in the soil of glossolalia (speaking in tongues), common to black Pentecostals?[77]

Gaillard recorded "BMBDS" itself, as did Ella Fitzgerald and pianists Wilson Garland and Willie "The Lion" Smith. According to Dan Morgenstern, Smith also performed "I Found a New Baby" in Yiddish; and Smith himself claims to have taught a Yiddish song to Duke Ellington, designed to entice customers to fork over fatter tips. There is a recording of Smith singing this particular song, "Nokh a bisl," in which he only approximates the tune and the Yiddish (*nokh* is pronounced as knock).[78]

Lionel Hampton recorded "Shalom, Shalom," a version of "Artza Alinu" on the vibes; and after a trip to Israel that obviously moved him, he made a recording that had him singing "Hava Nagila" in Hebrew (with some shaky enunciation), the Israeli songs "B'arvot Hanegev/Song of the Negev," and "The Wine Song," as well as "Exodus" (not the famous Ernest Gold melody, but a ballad by Fershka and Discant.)[79] Sammy Davis, Jr., recalling his impassioned performance of the more renowned "Exodus" song in Israel, remarked, "I don't know where my music came from. I sang like a cantor in a temple." Blues singer Alberta Hunter, who emulated Sophie Tucker, learned to sing "Ikh hob dikh tsufil lib"(I Love You Much Too Much) in Yiddish on a trip to Jerusalem.[80] Eddie Harris, the tenor saxophonist, launched his career with a recording of "Exodus." Trumpeter Charlie Shavers could blow a mean *freylekh*, "better than Ziggy," in the estimation of Dan Morgenstern. Don Byron, the clarinetist who grew up in a Jewish neighborhood listening to Jewish variety radio music, is a well-known klezmer exponent. Similarly, Herb Jeffries, the movie cowboy known as the Bronze Buckaroo, learned Yiddish in his childhood days.

Ethel Waters and other black singers sang "Eli, Eli" (see Chapter 7). Irving Berlin also wrote two classic songs for Waters in *As Thousands Cheer*: "Harlem on My Mind" and "Suppertime." The latter, a lament about the travails of a lynch-mob victim's wife, is dismissed by Jeffrey Melnick as a "muted protest"; but Philip Furia describes it as a "quiet outrage . . . a lyrical marvel of understatement" in which the mother pleads: "How can I be thankful when they [her fatherless children] start to thank the Lord, Lord?"[81]

Such sorry ordeals in American history were inevitable themes for African-American composers as well, ranging from Wynton Marsalis's concert hall oratorio *Blood on the Fields* to Broadway's *Bring in 'da Noise, Bring in 'da Funk*. By the same token, Jason Robert Brown, a Jewish-American composer, provided the score for the 1998 musical *Parade,* about the lynching of a Jew, Leo Frank. The African-American composer William Grant Still also wrote the choral work *And They Lynched Him on a Tree.* Encouraged by his second wife, pianist Verna Arvey—who was of Russian-Jewish stock—W. G. Still wrote a work for synagogue use, which may still be the only such piece by an African American. Written in 1946 on commission from the Park Avenue Synagogue of New York City, Still made a brave attempt to compose a setting in English of Psalm 29 (clumsily titled *Mizmor LeDovid, The Voice of the Lord*) in the *Ahava raba* mode. He might have been better off if he had tried the *Adonai malakh* mode instead, since the affinity between that mode and the blues would have been more familiar to him.

Perhaps the best-known antilynching reproach is to be heard in "Strange Fruit"

(1940), a Billie Holiday specialty number written by Lewis Allan,[82] although Holiday claimed otherwise in her autobiography. (She credits Sonny White and Danny Mendelsohn with helping her to complete the music,[83] but Allan was the sole writer.) In a private recording made at the New York apartment of a clarinetist friend, Tony Scott, Holiday is heard coaxing a baby to make sounds into a microphone so that she can present it as a gift to the parents, the Bill Duftys. In her efforts to elicit a response from the child, she starts to sing various standards, with Scott providing rudimentary piano support. Out of the blue, she abruptly deviates from doing "Some of These Days" and goes into a complete run through of "My Yiddishe Momme." Something about this domestic scene must have stirred a deep craving in her, and what is especially touching is how the baby starts to gurgle during Holiday's obviously heartfelt rendition. Doo-wop singer Jackie Wilson also recorded "My Yiddishe Momme" with cantorial flair (on the Brunswick label, 1961).

Harry Belafonte made "Hava Nagila" so famous in a recording that eight thousand Japanese fans sang it along with him at a concert.[84] Jule Styne and Comden and Green wrote "Now,"an adaptation of "Hava Nagila," for Lena Horne to premiere at a Carnegie Hall concert during the Civil Rights movement of the 1960s. Horne, who had previously learned other Hebrew songs for benefits, recalled, "It became a cause célèbre when the networks refused to allow the recording I made of it to be played."[85] Here was an event operating on several simultaneous levels: a recognizable Hebrew song of celebration is altered by Jewish writers to be sung in English by a well-known African-American artist for political action on behalf of blacks, "We want more than just a promise/Say goodbye to Uncle Thomas."

Jungle Fever, Blues, and Jews

In Chapter 5, the 1926 Picon-Rumshinsky song "Vu iz mayn zivig" was cited as a representation of the gypsy motive at work. Three years before, an African-American team had written a number for the musical *Go-Go* where the same gypsy idea appeared:

Ex. 12-19

"Jungle Rose"
Jo Trent (W) & Ford Dabney (M)

Ar-rayed in all her jun-gle splen-dor, ___ The pea-cocks stared a - mazed in won-der, ___

There is no copyright date on the printed sheet music of Rumshinsky's song. Perhaps he had heard the earlier Harlem show and recalled it; but this is as believable as Frank Sinatra and his collaborators being acquainted with the Dabney or the Rumshinsky melodies since they also are precursors of "I'm a Fool to Love You" (see Ex. 4-15a).

Just as Creamer and Layton wrote for whites, Dorothy Fields and Jimmy McHugh,* a white team, wrote for blacks, first at Harlem's famous Cotton Club in 1927, and then one year later on Broadway. Compare their pseudojungle tune written for and notoriously executed by Adelaide Hall in *Blackbirds of 1928* to a

Hasidic jingle—probably dating from the early twentieth century, and note how two improbable cultures intersect:[86]

"Dundai"
Nathanson, *Maginoth Shireynu*, p. 13

Ex. 12-20a

E - retz Yis-ra - el b' - li to - rah, Hi k' - guf___ b' - li n' - sha - mah.

Dun - dai, dun- dai, dun-dai, dun - dai dai, Dun - dai dun- dai, dun-dai, dun - dai, dai.
(The land of Israel without Torah is like a soul without a body. Dundai.)

"Diga-Diga-Doo"
Dorothy Fields (W) & Jimmy McHugh (M)

Ex. 12- 20b

Zu - lu man is feel - ing blue, Hear his heart beat a lit - tle tat - too,

Di - ga - Di- ga -Doo, Di - ga doo - doo. Di - ga - Di - ga -Doo, Di - ga Doo.

As "Diga-Diga-Doo" continues, even the sense of the words begins to converge with "Dundai." Both are about the need to belong, to a homeland in the first case and to a spouse in the other: "I'm so very diga-diga-doo by nature/If you don't say diga-diga-doo to your mate/You're gonna lose a papa."

According to Cab Calloway, Dorothy Fields "wasn't funky enough" to maintain a writing career at the Cotton Club. She and McHugh were followed by Ted Koehler and Harold Arlen, a team who, in contrast, "could carry a Negro revue," and who wrote "double-entendre nasty songs, hurly-burly bump and grind mixed with high-class swinging jazz."[87] Arlen was declared by singer-actress Ethel Waters to be "the Negro-ist white man she had ever known."[88] E.Y. Harburg defined Arlen's hallmark as a "synthesis of Negro rhythms and Hebraic melodies. They make a terrific combination, a fresh chemical reaction. George Gershwin did this too, in his own brilliant way. Gershwin and Arlen created a new sound in American theater music by combining black and Jewish elements."[89]

A paradigm of the Arlen style is his and Mercer's classic "Blues in the Night," a film song which contains a variety of Jewish inflections in its extended A-B-C-A form. Written in the key of B-flat-Major, the lower 3rd step is D-natural, the upper 3rd is D-flat, maintained by Arlen throughout the A section (the first twelve bars of the melody). It begins with repetitions in the style of Jewish cranking-up songs (see Ex. 7-4):

The lower D-flat does function in the harmony, at which point Arlen recalls the opening of the benediction chanted prior to the biblical reading from *Prophets* (*Haftarah*):

When spelled enharmonically as C-sharp, D-flat shows up once in the A sections, as a lower neighbor to D-natural, in the black-blues manner, and is conjoined to a typical *AM* fragment:

The A section of the "Blues" concludes with a phrase that has the upper flat 3rd in the melody and the lower major 3rd in the harmony (refer to Ex. 7-18b for full Hebrew example):

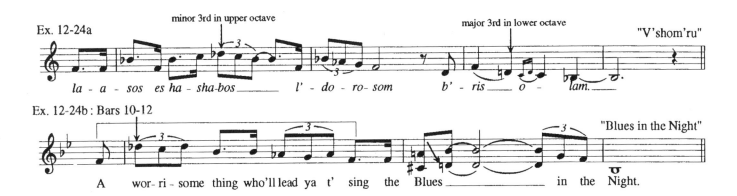

The B section begins in blues style with alternating major and minor modes in a two-bar phrase, "Now the rain's a-fallin'/Hear the train a-callin,' whooee." This is followed by a parenthetical "My mama done tol' me," a layout reminiscent of call (i.e., solo) and response (i.e., group) formats used by both Jews and African Americans in prayer settings. The parenthetical phrase might well be redrafted as "O Lord, please help me."[90] The four bars are then repeated in a variant form; and in the ninth bar of this B section, Arlen turns to the Ukrainian Dorian mode:

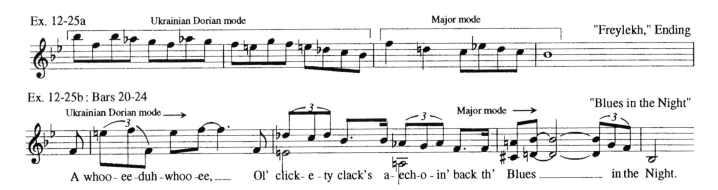

The C section of eighteen bars stays in minor until the very end when the D-flat, always in the upper octave, switches to D-natural. There is, finally, a touch of the "charming" flatted sixth in the harmony.

It is evident that Arlen delighted in his Jewishness, whether or not he was always aware of it.

Davenen—Jewish Prayer Style

Anyone who has ever witnessed a traditional Jewish service cannot help but be impressed by a congregation of worshipers wrapped in prayer shawls swaying their torsos as if conducted by an invisible baton from on high. It is a practice known as *davenen* (a word, among other possible derivations, drawn from the French *diviniser*), musically very much like the study mode. Add some harmony to the singsong davening of congregants, and you may observe their bodies "Go down and up/And back and forth,/It feels hypnotic, an exotic incantation"—a kind of lyric one could almost set to the melody of an equally mesmerizing Gershwin piano piece:

Ex. 12-27

Piano Prelude No. 2, George Gershwin

Jazz pianist Dick Hyman and others have pointed out that W. C. Handy's "Aunt Hagar's Blues" (note the Biblical name) was the source of this Gershwin Piano Prelude No. 2. The dronelike davening on top coupled with the substructure of blues harmonies is an authentic commingling of Jewish and African Americana. "Blues in Orbit," an instrumental piece in vivid davening style by Duke Ellington and Billy Strayhorn, compellingly clarifies this bond (on *Duke Ellington, The Private Collection*, vol. 6: Dance Dates, California, 1958, CD Saja/1989).

One of the earliest incidents of davening in broad stream popular arts was proffered by comedian Eddie Cantor. In a 1929 film, *Glorifying the American Girl*, Cantor repeats his stage shtik as Moe the Tailor, singing in a davening mode as he measures a curvaceous customer. Jule Styne, in *Funny Girl* (1964), wrote a "Poker Chant" for two lady card sharks:

Ex. 12-28

"Poker Chant" (from *Funny Girl*)
Bob Merrill (W) & Jule Styne (M)

Now *that* is davening!

Marc Blitzstein's "Gus and Sadie Love Song" (from *The Cradle Will Rock*) and his theater pieces, *Goloopchik* and *Idiots First*, demonstrate his Russian-Jewish roots. But Blitzstein's 1945 cabaret number "The New Suit" (a.k.a. "Zipper Fly")[91] is a particularly affecting example ostensibly vocalized by a shoeshine boy. The verse opens with a patois that might pass to the uninitiated for ersatz Hebrew and continues in a monotone *davenen* style. Blitzstein's refrain then begins and ends prayerfully:

Ex. 12-29 Refrain: Conclusion   "The New Suit (Zipper Fly)," Marc Blitzstein

Now I lay me down to sleep, I pray the Lord my soul to keep, __ And if be-fore __ I wake, I should die, __

rit.

Please lay me out __ in my won-der-ful suit, __ My un-speak-a-ble suit __ with the zip-per fly. _____

But not to worry. Our twelve-year-old has been studying hard; comes the big day of Bar Mitzvah, he gets his new suit. Proudly he faces the congregation and begins the time-honored blessing over the Torah—a consecration that was to be transmogrified by the smarmy character known as Sportin' Life in *Porgy and Bess* (a persona based on Cab Calloway):

Ex. 12-30   "It Ain't Necessarily So"
                                          George & Ira Gershwin

It Ain't Ne-ces-sar-i-ly So,   It Torah blessing

Bo-r'-chu es A-do-shem ha-m'-vo-rach,   Bo-ruch A-do-shem ha-m'-vo-rach l'-o-lam vo-

Ain't Ne-ces-sar-i-ly So,   De t'ings dat yo' li'-ble to

ed,   E-lo-kei-nu me-lech __ ho-o-lom, a-sher bo-char ba-nu _____ mi kol ho-a-

read in de Bi-ble, It Ain't Ne-ces-sar-i-ly So.

mim v'-no-san lo-nu es   to-ra-so,   Bo-ruch A-toh A-do-shem no-sein ha-to-roh. _____

(Praise the Lord, to whom our praise is due ... Blessed is the Lord, giver of the Torah.)

How could the Gershwins not resist making reference to the Bible via the Torah Blessing!

NOTES 1. Is this the end of the journey from "colored" (and other more offensive slurs) to "Negro" to "black" to "Afro-American"? Is the hyphen still acceptable in "African American" as an indication of joint experience? I use different terminology when it seems historically germane and—as in Latin American—no hyphen when used as a noun, but include a hyphen when used as an adjective, e.g., African-American music.

2. In maintaining his posture, Melnick does not bother to complete Locke's sentence. If downtown Jews are Shylocks, is *our* dance-halls" to be interpreted as uptown black ownership?

3. See Laurence Bergreen, *Louis Armstrong, An Extravagant Life*, in order of quotes: pp. 59, 41, 75, and 56, taken from a memoir written by Armstrong on 31 March 1969 while he was in Beth Israel Hospital, New York City, the same hospital where Joe Glaser, his Jewish manager, was dying. Glaser had a unsavory reputation, but Armstrong regarded him as a father figure. See also Gary Giddins, *Satchmo*, pp. 62-64, which spells the name of the family as Karmofsky; *The Louis Armstrong Companion* spells it with one "f." In the latter book, the Berlin lyrics are quoted, preceded by the sentence: "Russian lullaby song donated by Dr. Gary Zucker, M.D., Beth Israel Hospital." According to the Ken Burns PBS TV series *Jazz*, Armstrong wore a Star of David necklace all his life.

4. Henry Ford, pub., *The Dearborn Independent*, articles about "the Jewish song trust" and the corrupt goods of "Yiddish Tin Pan Alley." See MacDonald Smith Moore, *Yankee Blues*.

5. See Paul Berman, *Blacks and Jews*, p. 6.

6. Farrakhan studied violin with Elaine Skorodin Fohrman, a Russian-Jewish immigrant. See Florence H. Levinson*, Looking for Farrakhan* (Chicago: Ivan Dee, 1997), p. 186. Born Harold Moore, Jr., January 1948, Muhammad died in February 2001 of a brain hemorrhage. In his tirades against Jews, he quoted words from "Strange Fruit," oblivious to its authorship by a Jew. See David Margolick, *Strange Fruit*.

7. The rap group Public Enemy in "Swindler's Lust" (a word play on the movie *Schindler's List*) from *There's a Poison Going On* (Maste, 1999) uses coded anti-Semitic language to fault Jews for the destitution of underprivileged blacks. Michael Jackson in "They Don't Care About Us," from *HIStory-Past, Present, and Future* (Sony, 1995), spews

forth "Jew me/Sue me" and "Kick me/Kike me," soon changed, after howls of protest, to "Do me/Sue me" and "Kick me/Strike me." However, since 1999 Jackson has shown an interest in Judaism by attending Jewish services in New York City.

8. In an unfinished lyric, Leonard Bernstein sardonically has the Jews being blamed for everything from bad weather to the vagaries of the stock market. One of the quatrains goes:
    "If there's war tomorrow night/It's the Jews, it's the Jews.
    But if men refuse to fight/It's the Goddamn Jews, the Jews."
Ironically, the tune for this mocking verse, which only exists in sketch form, later was fleshed out by Bernstein to become a satiric number about the African-American experience, "Bright and Black," from the flawed musical *1600 Pennsylvania Avenue.*

9. Melnick cites Samuel Ornitz, *Haunch, Paunch and Jowl,* Jean Toomer, *Fern,* Gloria Naylor, *Bailey's Café*. Melnick also relies on the life story of "Mezz" Mezzrow [b. Milton Mesirow], a Jewish-born clarinetist who was a notorious drug pusher.

10. From Nicholas Cook, "Vital Signs: Musicology," *BBC Music Magazine*, May 1999, pp. 32-33. One of the rare times Melnick uses musical terminology, he bungles. He says "Summertime" and "Sometimes I Feel Like a Motherless Child" are organized around *major* thirds in *Ancestors and Relatives: The Uncanny Relationship of African Americans and Jews,* Ph.D. Dissertation, Harvard University,1994, p. 555.

11. Edward Berlin, letter to the author dated 11 March 1980.

12. Quoted by Edward Berlin, letter to the author. See also Edward Berlin, *King of Ragtime*, p. 230. Niederhofer's same question might be asked about the main theme of Dizzy Gillespie's piano solo "The Rain," which also resembles Mordecai Gebirtig's tune. Recorded by Bobby Timmins, *The Syncopation of Dizzy Gillespie*, Riverside Records.

13. James Weldon Johnson, *The Book of American Negro Spirituals*, p. 28.

14. J. Rosamond Johnson, *American Negro Spirituals*, p. 26.

15. Isidore Witmark and Isaac Goldberg, *From Ragtime to Swingtime*, pp. 196-197.

16. In his memoirs, Duke Ellington also points out that Will Marion Cook was famously argumentative, and "always caused a

furor." Melnick does not entertain the notion that Witmark's refusal to give in to Cook's demands may have been based on his being insulted by Cook.

17. Bernard Peterson, *Early Black American Playwrights and Dramatic Writers.*

18. Allen Wohl, *Black Musical Theater*, p. 50.

19. Al Rose, *Eubie Blake*, p. 62.

20. See Laurence Bergreen, *Louis Armstrong*, pp. 128-130.

21. Paul S. Machlin, *Stride: The Music of Fats Waller*, p. 3. Waller claimed that he had sold "I Can't Give You Anything But Love, Baby" (1928) and "On the Sunny Side of the Street" (1930) to Jimmy McHugh for peanuts, but only after the songs had become big hits in two of Lew Leslie's revues. He also charged Irving Berlin with plagiarism (song not cited). Like Armstrong's claim of authorship, none of these acts was ever proven. See Iain C. Williams, *Underneath a Harlem Moon*, p. 367.

22. Willie "The Lion" Smith, *Music on My Mind*, p. 162.

23. Duke Ellington, *Music Is My Mistress*, p. 73.

24. Secunda and Jacobs did get a cut of two cents per copy, respectively, from publishers Kammen and Harms in sales of the "Bei mir bistu sheyn" adaptation.

25. Molly Picon, letter to the author, 10 November 1982.

26. Patricia Nealon, "Court Solves Fight over Song Rights," *Boston Globe*, 29 October 1996.

27. Charles Hamm in *Irving Berlin* argues that the so-called plantation songs were substitute icons for the Jewish mother and the longing for the old homeland, p. 69.

28. Famous Irish minstrels included Dan Bryant, Dan Emmett, Joel Walker Sweeney, and E. P. Christy.

29. Lena Horne with Richard Schickel, *Lena*, p. 136.

30. John Kobal, *Gotta Sing, Gotta Dance*, p. 272.

31. Sarah Blacher Cohen, *From Hester Street to Hollywood*, p. 36. See also pp. 45ff.

32. Gary Giddins, *Riding on a Blue Note*, p. 17.

33. Cab Calloway, *Of Minnie the Moocher and Me*, p. 45.

34. Gary Carner, *The Miles Davis Companion*, p. 154.

35. Passim in Lena Horne with Richard Schickel, *Lena*; Pearl Bailey, *The Raw Pearl*; Billie Holiday with William Dufty, *Lady Sings the Blues*; Sid Colin, *Ella*. Both Lena Horne and Pearl Bailey married Jewish musicians, Lennie Hayton and Louis Bellson, respectively. Horne's daughter, Gail, married film director Sidney Lumet, who as a child actor performed in the Yiddish theater (he introduced Yablokoff's "Papirosn"). Harry Belafonte, Diana Ross, and Josephine Baker also married Jews. Despite the positive experiences of these and other artists, director Spike Lee demonized Jewish managers in his 1990 film *Mo' Better Blues*.

36. Louis Armstrong, *Satchmo: My Life in New Orleans*, notes: "In less than two hours, I would be broker than the Ten Commandments," p. 106.

37. Willie "The Lion" Smith, *Music on My Mind*, p. 17.

38. Fanny Brice made it into the *Ziegfeld Follies* through the efforts of Joe Jordan and Will Marion Cook. See Norman Katkov, *The Fabulous Fanny*, p 65.

39. I am grateful to songwriter-historian Barry Kleinbort for these references.

40. See Hoberman, *Entertaining America: Jews, Movies, and Broadcasting*, pp. 93-99.

41. See Ronald Sanders in Villers, *Next Year in Jerusalem*, pp. 202 and 214. For an essay entitled "The American Popular Song," it is curious that Sanders only discusses elite Broadway composers, but not a single Tin Pan Alley tunesmith.

42. Out of three examined melodies set to "Rock-a My Soul," from various sources, the one that resembles the Irish reel may be found in the collection *American Negro Spirituals*, edited by J. Rosamond Johnson.

43. Even "La Marseillaise" was converted to a *nigun*. Quoting Eric Werner in "Jews Around Richard and Cosima Wagner," *Musical Quarterly* (1985): 187: "The habit of singing tunes of their enemies was not restricted to East European Jews: the German Jews sang the *Natsionaldeutsche Hymnen* in their synagogues and the Sephardim of the Maghreb imitated the chants of the Arabs in their neighborhoods. This is, however, a common fact in cultures where a minority is dependent upon the tolerance of the majority."

44. Velvel Pasternak, "Chasidic Music," *Congress Bi-Weekly*, New York: American Jewish Congress, 14 January 1972.

45. Seroussi, et al. "Jewish Music," New Grove Dictionary of Music, 2nd ed., vol. 13, p. 72.

46. Philip Furia, *Irving Berlin: A Life in Song*, p. 36.

47. Y. L. Peretz, quoted in Emanuel S. Goldsmith, *Modern Yiddish Culture*, p. 231.

48. Sandra W. Jacobson, letter to the *New York Times*, 21 August 1991. Apparently, "Black and Blue" was originally performed this way. See also Mary Wilson, *Dreamgirl: My Life As a Supreme*, p. 42, and Laurence Bergreen, *Louis Armstrong: An Extravagant Life*, pp. 9 and 59.

49. The very word *Ivri* (Hebrew) denotes a stranger from the other side—that is, from the other side of the Euphrates.

50. John Graziano, "Black Musical Theater," in Floyd, ed., *Black Music and the Harlem Renaissance*, pp. 87, ff. It should be noted that a lively black presence was felt in the Tenderloin district (downtown Manhattan) early on before Harlem (uptown Manhattan), at first a Jewish locality, emerged as a black enclave.

51. Deena Rosenberg, *Fascinating Rhythm*, p. 19.

52. Joseph P. Swain, *The Broadway Musical*, p. 249.

53. Sigmund Romberg, however, was an exception.

54. Alain Locke, *The New Negro*, pp. 200 ff.

55. "Old Testament" is a term not recognized by discerning Jews.

56. A 1913 song by William Jerome and Grant Clark also named "Sit Down, You're Rocking the Boat," was about a sailor making advances on his lady fair.

57. Ancillary to these white spirituals are showbiz hymns, inspirational songs such as "You'll Never Walk Alone" (*Carousel*), "Look to the Rainbow" (*Finian's Rainbow),* "Tall Hope" (*Wildcat*), and "Somewhere" (*West Side Story*).

58. Muslim whirling dervishes also strive to achieve this ecstatic state as do certain Christian factions: Holy Rollers "speaking in tongues" and Shakers who "fall under the power."

59. In "spirituals" like "Shout All Over God's Heaven" or "Zu veystu dos land?" (Do You Know the Land?).

60. Margo Jefferson, "The Art of the Musical: Lessons from the Civil War," *New York Times*, 17 May 1999.

61. Contrary to expectation, the composer of *Cabin in the Sky*, composer Vernon Duke (b. Vladimir Dukelsky) was not Jewish, but John LaTouche, the lyricist, had a Jewish mother (see Gore Vidal, *Virgin Islands*, p. 25). Arlen and Harburg contributed to the movie version. The book for *A Broadway Musical* was written by a black, William F. Brown.

62. Joseph P. Swain, *The Broadway Musical*, p. 250.

63. In the mid-1990s, African-American composer Walter Robinson, created *Moses: A Gospel Concert* which claimed to "share what is . . . common" between blacks and Jews. David Chevan, a Jewish pianist, collaborated with Warren Byrd, an African-American bassist, on a 1998 recording "Avadim Hayinu (Once We Were Slaves)." "A Mixed Blessing,"album track on *Gershwin the Klezmer* (1999), interweaves cantorial and gospel chant.

64. Richard Rodgers, *Musical Stages*. Rodgers says that due to his lack of familiarity with liturgical music he had to do some research for the first time in his career, p. 301. Weighty issues do not figure in Rodgers's musical comedy work with Lorenz Hart, where the scores for a few foreign settings—the tongue-in-cheek Greeks of *By Jupiter* or *The Boys from Syracuse*—have no ethnic distinction.

65. When the Ukrainian Dorian scale functions in the synagogue, it is a mode known as the *Mi sheberach* (May He Who Blessed) or *Av horachamim* (Compassionate Father). Arab and Greek scholars give other names to the scale: *Hijaz* and *Aulos*, respectively.

66. For three different variants of "Willie the Weeper," see Sigmund Spaeth, *Read 'Em and Weep*, p. 104, Alan Lomax, *American Ballads and Folk Songs,* p. 184, and Elie Siegmeister and Olin Downes, *A Treasury of American Song*, which also has an alternate distaff version, "Cocaine Lil," p. 344.

67. Although there is a touch of the raised 4th step in another version of "St. James Infirmary," found in Siegmeister and Downes, *A Treasury of American Song*, p. 380.

68. It is likely that Irving Mills shares credit with Calloway more as publisher than as writer, a common practice in the business. Mills was also instrumental in developing the Duke Ellington band, writing the lyrics for many of Ellington's hit songs.

69. Cab Calloway, *Of Minnie the Moocher and Me*, p. 111. Calloway not only credits Mills for getting him into songwriting, but he also lauds Mills and Herman Stark for break-

ing down barriers for Negro musicians, p. 106.

70. Max Helfman may have borrowed a dance tune from Idelsohn, *HOM*, vol. X, no. 118.

71. Buck Ram?, who used various pseudonyms, also adapted ethnic songs of other nationalities and wrote hit songs for The Platters: "Great Pretender" and "Twilight Time," and for Bing Crosby: "I'll Be Home for Christmas."

72. Peter Gammond, *The Oxford Companion to Popular Music*, article on Calloway. One sterling example of his cantorial style can be observed in a Warner Bros. Melody Maker film short where Calloway bewails the fate of "Frisco Flo" who "kicks the gong" (i.e., is on drugs).

73. Bergreen, *Louis Armstrong: An Extravagant Life*, pp. 267 and 268. Armstrong's personal library of records had several 78 rpm Yiddish recordings, most significantly, Al Jolson's version of "The Cantor," a copy of which Armstrong kept with him during his extensive travels. Jolson's showmanship take on cantorial melismas may have provided fodder for—if not the father to—Armstrong's scat technique. Housed at the Louis Armstrong Archive at Queens College, Flushing, New York.

74. Betty Comden, *Off Stage*, cites a whole other "Utt-da-zay" song, used to effect an all-clear signal after terrorist attacks in Russian shtetls, p. 47. The Casman-Steinberg song "Yosl, Yosl" served a similar purpose, which was to alert victims of approaching Nazi overseers in the death camps. See *YIVO News*, no. 195, winter 2002, p. 23.

75. *The Chronological Cab Calloway*, Classics label: "Utt-da-zay"(1939) CD 595 (also Leo Watson on Decca 2750, 1939);"A Bee Gezindt" (1940), CD 595; "Nain, Nain" (1941), CD 682; "The Ghost of Smoky Joe" (1939), CD 595; "Who's Yehoodi?" (1940), CD 614 (also Jerry Colonna on Columbia 3704, 1940. Yehoodi.com is a swing music link, derived from Calloway's recording: "G-man Hoover's getting moody/Got his men on double duty/Trying to find out Who's Yehoodi!"); and "Tzotskele" (My Darling) (1958), Glendale GL5-9007, 1984.

76. Paul Robeson: "Kaddish, vi azoi lebt di kayser"and "Zog nit keynmol" on Monitor MP580; "Chant of Levi Isaac" on Vanguard VRS-9193. The Ravens: "Mahzel" on National, 9034-a.

77. *The Chronological Slim Gaillard*, Classics label: "Vol Vist Du Gaily Star?" (1937-1938), CD 705 (also Jimmy Dorsey on RCA-Victor 25849, 78rpm), "Matzoh Balls" (1939-1940), CD 724, "Dunkin' Bagel"(1945), CD 864, "Drei Six Cents" (1945), vol. 2, CD 911. "Mishugana Mambo" (1952) is on Verve 314 521651-2.

78. "Nokh a bisl" (A Bit More) on *The Memoirs of Willie "The Lion" Smith*, RCA-Victor LSP-6016, Side 3. "Bei mir bistu sheyn": (1) Willie "The Lion" Smith with Milt Herth Trio (1938) on Decca 1612, (2) Ella Fitzgerald (1937) on Decca 1596 and (3) Garland Wilson (1938) on Classics CD 808.

79. "Eli, Eli" and "Shalom, Shalom" on MGM 11039-78 rpm. "Hava Nagila," "Song of the Negev," "Exodus," and "The Wine Song" on *The Many Sides of Hamp*, Glad Records, GLP 1001.

80. Sammy Davis, Jr., *Why Me?*, p. 195. Alberta Hunter on a television interview with Dick Cavett, located at the African-American Music Collection at the University of Michigan. In the interview Hunter says that Harold Arlen filched the melody for "Stormy Weather" from black musician Lukie Johnson, an unsubstantiated claim.

81. Philip Furia, *Irving Berlin: A Life in Song*, p. 155.

82. Born Abel Meeropol (the town in the Yiddish play *The Dybbuk* is Meirpolya, Ukraine), Lewis Allan (pen name), a New York City schoolteacher, was devoted to left-wing causes. Early on, his two sons Lewis and Allan had tragically died, which no doubt persuaded him and his wife Anne to become foster parents of the two Rosenberg boys after the execution of their parents, Julius and Ethel. His plea for tolerance, *The House I Live In*—an Academy Award-winning short performed by Frank Sinatra—was another expression of his political leanings.

83. Billie Holiday with William Dufty, *Lady Sings the Blues*, p. 84. See also David Margolick, *Strange Fruit*.

84. See Stephen J. Whitfield, *In Search of American Jewish Culture*, p. 164. The recording is on *Harry Belafonte: Live in Concert at Carnegie Hall*, BMG Int. 07863-56002-2; originally on RCA LSO-6006, 1959.

85. Lena Horne with Richard Schickel, *Lena*, p. 289.

86. "Hot Voodoo," a song by Leo Robin and Ralph Rainger, from the Marlene Dietrich film *Blonde Venus* has the same anomalous combination.

87. Horne and Schickel, *Lena*, p. 93.

88. Jim Haskins, *The Cotton Club*, p. 77.

89. Harold Meyerson and Ernie Harburg, *Who Put the Rainbow in The Wizard of Oz?*, p. 176.

90. In the 1941 Warner Bros. movie (originally entitled *Hot Nocturne*), the song is introduced by blacks in a jail scene where this phrase is, in fact, done as a call and response. The movie—with a cast that included future directors Elia Kazan and Richard Whorf—is a hodgepodge of soap opera, jazz musical, and film noir. The plot alludes to white appropriation of black music, even though the music for "Blues in the Night" was written by whites.

91. Rights to Blitzstein's "The New Suit" were bought by nightclub comedian Jimmy Savo for a one-man act; but the song was never performed by him—possibly because of its Jewish idiom.

CHAPTER 13

Afterword–Society and Musical Politics

Popular songwriting was and always will be not merely an American art, but a Jewish one.
ROD GREENBERG, *Gershwin*, p. 195

Creativity often arises out of adversity; and, paradoxically, humor flourishes in times of struggle. Only during eras of comparative tranquility and affluence does the comic muse become less vital. Indeed, since the enormity of the September 11, 2001 events in the United States, there are signs that musical comedy has been making a comeback on the American stage. At the end of the twentieth century, the Broadway musical had become moribund; in fact, some critics had pronounced its last rites. Explanations abounded, ranging from economic realities to the yearning for less complicated times, from writers who once worked in collaboration with performers to performers who write their own material and sing no else's, from songs that once were melody-based to those that are now rhythm-driven. But following the turmoil spawned by the terrorist attacks of 9/11 and the ongoing quagmire of world events that has ensued, a yearning for diversion and relief was inevitable.

Although Americans in the twenty-first century are also "rhythm-driven," characteristically on the move—unsettled, they are caught between a nostalgia for the extended family or some kind of group identity and the increasing challenge of coping with a depersonalized society that encourages a splintering apart. This is quite the opposite of Jewish immigrants to America at the turn of the twentieth century who maintained a fierce loyalty to their birthplaces by banding together in *landsmanshaftn* (fellow countrymen associations), mutual-aid societies based on their East European communities, and by forming individual family cousin clubs that met on a regular basis.

It follows that pioneers like Ira Gershwin, E. Y. Harburg, and their peers were more mutually supportive than they were competitive. In Ira's words: "We're not highbrows, we're not lowbrows . . . we're Hebrows."[1] In a sense, they became the founders of new *landsmanshaftn* based on theater networking. Joseph Swain and Stephen J. Whitfield in their surveys of "New York operas" (i.e., musicals), remind us that the same names repeatedly turn up in all the collaborative theatrical disciplines. This may well be a legacy of the earlier boosterism, a collegiality that the roster of writers for the contemporary musical theater struggles to maintain. Among them, William Finn, Adam Guettel, Ricky Ian Gordon, Henry Krieger, Tony Kushner, Andrew Lippa, Alan Menken, David Yazbek, Maury Yeston, Mark Shaiman and Jason Robert Brown are Jewish.[2]

Succeeding generations, instead of persisting in a retreat away from their heritage, explore their ethnocultural roots, when, at least in theory, some sort of synthesis between old and new genres is achieved.[3] They reject the "melting pot" inheritance. Look at the success of klezmer music in the so-called new music scene;

but klezmer sounds are at the same time also being sampled by such groups as *Brave Old World* as only one component in an overlay of other musical genres including sounds from the Levantine, Central Asia, and sub-Saharan Africa.[4] Still, in the new millennium—and the fifth one-thousand-year period of recorded Jewish history—it is unclear where the dialectical process is taking American Jews.

More evident is a lot of fumbling and grumbling, all of it even messier than it was at the end of the nineteenth century when "European Jewry was coming apart at the seams."[5] The Reform and Conservative denominations of Judaism find themselves increasingly at odds with Orthodoxy as well as with each other. Name calling ricochets back and forth as the Reform movement wrestles with ways to return to more traditional practices. Historians argue that American Jews, formerly fearful that Holocaust studies "made God look bad," now are too preoccupied with the Holocaust and use it to downplay other atrocities. Survivor testimonies supersede the preservation and translation of vast amounts of Yiddish papers deteriorating in Lithuanian libraries. Offspring of Yiddish-speaking families go on tours of Eastern Europe in an oxymoronic attempt "to go back to places where they never have been." At the same time, the escalation of Hitler-worshipers, the reemergence of the infamous forgery *Protocols of the Elders of Zion* and terrorist outbreaks of anti-Semitism plague Jewry all over Europe and the United States. In fact, anti-Zionism has become a code word for anti-Semitism. The State of Israel is no longer regarded as being in a state of eternal grace. Black-Jewish relations are at an unsettling standstill. Stereotypes are making a comeback; witness the Broadway sensation of Mel Brooks's 2001 musical comedy version of his 1968 movie *The Producers* (avaricious Jews among other outsized stereotypes) or television's *The Sopranos* (menacing mafiosi). One American rabbi notes that the excesses of contemporary rites celebrating the onset of puberty are "too much bar and not enough mitzvah."[6] The Hegelian model may be faulty; Jewishness may well have reached a level of being postreligion and postethnicity.

Popular music is still regarded with disdain among certain factions of the intelligentsia. William Bolcom, an accomplished composer of both popular-song-based and concert hall works says "the schism between pop and serious, or vernacular and aristocratic (just as bad) music, is so deep that neither side benefits from the other. Both industries are distinct—one is for profit, the other resolutely 'nonprofit'—and their mutual dislike is always under the surface."[7] But signs are that the tide is changing. In the 1990s, a steady flow of analytical studies of Gershwin and other Golden Age popular songwriters were published by trade and university presses. Colleges nationwide and overseas with research centers began to offer survey courses in popular music and degrees in jazz studies. The Society for American Music (formerly the Sonneck Society), a university umbrella organization, regularly prints scholarly articles on popular music in its journal *American Music*.

At the same time, AM radio stations that used to feature Frank Sinatra and Ella Fitzgerald are on the wane, classical radio on FM radio is fading while a program on National Public Radio—*Schickele* [Peter] *Mix*—makes no distinction between popular and concert music. Crossover albums of opera singers recording classics of Broadway and Three Tenors giant concerts were all the rage in the midnineties, and conversely, pop singers began to offer operatic fare in public.[8] At times these ventures have a phony ring, and it is debatable as to which has the greater or lesser influence: serious music on popular music or the other way around. Orchestra Pops programs are still segregated from regular symphonic fare; but community outreach perform-ances by major orchestras often combine the two. However, it would be inane to expect orchestras to fully decompartmentalize and grant equal time to a popular music that was originally designed for venues other than the concert hall.

Following the lead of Andy Warhol in the visual arts, composer Michael Daugherty has used pop icons Superman, Jackie, Marilyn, and Elvis as subject mat-ter for symphonic works; and others—notably, Paul Schoenfield and Osvaldo Golijov—incorporate Jewish folk idioms in concert works that speak to a non-Jewish audience.[9] Does it matter if these works are "impure" hybrids? At least the ephemeral nature of the vernacular is given a fighting chance of survival in these new contexts. Eric Werner has described the process (following the lead of German folklorist Johann Gottfried von Herder) as one of "ascending culture" versus "descending culture" where "art music [sinks] down to street and hit songs."[10]

In the 1930s, Gershwin supposedly asked Stravinsky to give him composition lessons. When asked how much money he had made the previous year, Gershwin replied: "About $100,000. Why?" Stravinsky answered: "I should be asking you to teach me."[11] By any standard, Stravinsky is considered to be the greater composer. But Gershwin's output, in his territory, is as distinguished as Stravinsky's in his. If Gershwin had remained on Tin Pan Alley and had not aspired to the stage and con-cert hall, he would have been considered a member of the lower echelon. He aimed higher; and conversely, when Stravinsky aimed lower, writing for a less sophisti-cated audience—in, e.g., *Firebird* (1910) versus the esoteric *Symphonies of Wind Instruments* (1920)—he not only captured the larger audience, but also contributed a lasting staple of orchestral repertoire.

Gershwin's lead suggests that when commercial composers are encouraged to apply aesthetic values of higher art, and their listeners make the effort to under-stand the resulting complexities, popular music can become less a limited artistic expression and more a valued life-enhancing experience. In the past, pop tunes were expected to be soothing, unproblematical escapist or background entertain-ment designed to relieve the listener of pressing problems. The latter days of rock 'n' roll (and its evolution into rap) went overboard in the opposite direction, engag-ing the listener in political theater and excess. In between these extremes, popular songs can—within the confines of their prescribed territory—reflect the highest virtues of human thought and feeling.

It has always been fashionable for elitists to debunk the popular arts as compared to so-called "serious" works. Songs that make money are, ipso facto, artistically suspect. Poppycock! Shortly after his arrival in America, Kurt Weill put it bluntly: "I have never acknowledged the difference between 'serious' and 'light' music. There is only good music and bad music." Or in the words of Duke Ellington: "If it sounds good, it is good." Such proportions are the same in any creative endeavor. It is only in recent times that we have begun to recognize that songs which have always been part of our daily routine have become as enduring and as endearing as any German lieder.

This is due, in no small measure, to Jewish professionals who have raised a low art form to a high standard. Although some alarmists feel that non-Orthodox Jews are facing cultural extinction, let those who despair at the decline of *Yidishkayt* (Jewishness) take heart. Some of the insights offered in this book must offer hope that not all is lost. Yiddishisms, musical and otherwise, have been transmuted into

Americanisms. The melody may not always sound Jewish, but it's funny how often we croon one as if there were a *dybbuk* (attachment) crooning inside of us.

More optimistic observers feel that a distinctive American *nusach* has already replaced the venerable, but hoary, heritage of Europe, and now soft folk-rock idioms predominate. If this is to be regarded as genuine, it is not by means of eliminating the past, but through an evolving process, as demonstrated in this book. Follow, for example, the meanderings of a Yiddish song originally derived from an English nursery rhyme song: "Old King Cole" (Ex. 13-1a). Adapted by Moshe Nadir[12] in the 1920s and reshaped as "Az der Rebe Elimelekh" (Rabbi Elimelekh, Ex. 13-1b), recognition of its authorship by Nadir did not occur until after it had achieved folk-song status. Whereas King Cole had three fiddlers in his court, Nadir's poor Rebe could only afford two:

Ex. 13-1a

"Old King Cole"
HOM, vol. IX, p. XX

Old King Cole was a mer-ry old soul, and a mer-ry old soul was he   When he
called for his pipe, and he called for his bowl, and he called for his fid - lers __ three.

Ex. 13-1b

"Az der Rebe Elimelekh," Moshe Nadir
MTAG, p. 168

Az der Re-be E-li-me-lekh iz ge-vo-rn zey-er frey-lekh, Iz ge-vo-rn zey-er frey-lekh E-li - me - lekh, Hot er
(When Rabbi Elimelekh was feeling very merry,)
oys-ge-ton di tfi-ln Un hot on-ge-ton di bri-ln, Un ge - shikt nokh di fid - lers di tsvey.
(He removed his phylacteries and put on his spectacles, And sent for his two fiddlers.)

Nadir lived in the United States, where he may have been diverted by Tin Pan Alley tunes. The second phrase of his "Elimelekh" contrafact (which first appeared in print in 1922), duplicates that of the 1917 TPA novelty "I'll Open the Door" (see Chapter 6). Perhaps the provenance for the latter also was "Old King Cole" or it could be that all these phrasal identities—in the nursery strain, the Yiddish song, and the Tin Pan Alley tune—were created totally independent of each other. Hard to say:

Ex. 13-2a: from the Refrain

"I'll Open the Door and Close the Door"
Lew Brown & Maurice Abrahams

Un – til St. Pe - ter asks me what I want. _____

Ex. 13-2b

"Az der Rebe Elimelekh"

Iz ge -vo - rn zey - er frey - lekh E - li - me - lekh
(Elimelekh became very jolly)

What a curious mishmash of wonder rabbis and miracle saints! But they could have joined forces with and fulfilled the wishes of Simon and Garfunkel in their 1970 hit "El Condor Pasa."[13] Significantly, it is the secondary phrase of the Rebe tune that has now become the opening for the Spanish-Incan melody, one of the ongoing processes of popular songwriting.

Ex. 13-3

"El Condor Pasa"
Paul Simon (W) & Daniel Robles (M)

I'd ra-ther be a spar-row than a snail, Yes I would, if I could, I sure-ly would,___

But our Rebe has even more potent disciples in his concluding phrase (Ex. 13-1b). Like the "Kaddish Response" (see Ex. 3-14), the note pattern of the Rebe phrase has had musical analogues in various cultures. When Edith Piaf sings "Misericorde," the sequences that comprise this segment are heard as being indigenously French, or it sounds typically Greek in a popular ballad, "Ke Then Boro" (And I Can't Forget You) and also in "Htan 18 Noembph" (The Eighteenth of November), a song by Mikis Theodorakis from the film *Z*. In Mexico it dons mariachi garb in "Quien Será" by Pablo Beltran Ruiz, translated by Norman Gimbel as the 1954 song "Sway" (Ex. 13-4c). But when popularized in the United States by Dean Martin (Capitol Records), does "Sway" retain its Mexican origin and/or take on a coloration that might be defined as Jewish?[14]

Mordecai Gebirtig incorporated the same itinerant bars (as the Rebe tune and "I'll Open the Door") into his dance tune "Kum, Leybke, tantsn" (Come, Leybke, Dance, published in 1936):

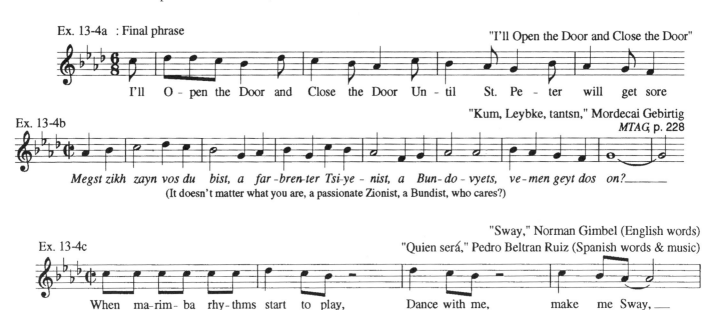

Ex. 13-4a : Final phrase

"I'll Open the Door and Close the Door"

I'll O- pen the Door and Close the Door Un- til St. Pe- ter will get sore

Ex. 13-4b

"Kum, Leybke, tantsn," Mordecai Gebirtig
MTAG, p. 228

Megst zikh zayn vos du bist, a far-bren-ter Tsi-ye - nist, a Bun-do - vyets, ve-men geyt dos on?___
(It doesn't matter what you are, a passionate Zionist, a Bundist, who cares?)

Ex. 13-4c

"Sway," Norman Gimbel (English words)
"Quien será," Pedro Beltran Ruiz (Spanish words & music)

When ma-rim- ba rhy-thms start to play, Dance with me, make me Sway, ___
Quien se - rá la que me quie - raa mi, Quien se - rá, Quien se - rá, ___
(Who will be the one who wants me for myself, Who will it be, Who will it be,)

Like the la - zy o - cean hugs the shore, Hold me close, Sway no more.___
Quien se - rá la que me de sua-mor, Quien se - rá, Quien se - rá?___
(Who will be the one to gives me her love, Who will it be, Who will it be?)

The Rebe's good deeds were spread by John Wayne in a song from the 1960 movie *The Alamo.* The melody, by Dimitri Tiomkin,[15] begins with a variant of the *Kol nidrei* formula. Regarding its concluding analogue to the Rebe song, the component motives have been juggled from a straightforward order of A, B, C, D, E to a rearrangement of motives B, D, A, C, E:

Well, if Tin Pan Alley and Hollywood were going to climb onto the Rebe's *tzitzis*—the fringed prayer undergarment worn by observant Jews—Broadway was not going to be left off the bandwagon. Ergo, in 1964:

In 1970, an Israeli song became popular in the United States as "Any Time of the Year" (English version by Robert Brittan), and guess who shows up in its final section:

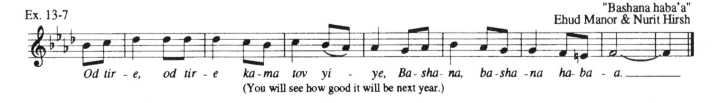

And then Lionel Ritchie, the African-American video star of the 1980s, shook hands with the ever faithful Rabbi Elimelekh in his Motown hit "Hello":

Ex. 13-8

"Hello"
Lionel Ritchie

'Cause you know just what to say,— And you know just what to do,— And I

want to tell___ you so much, I love you.

Funny, but that one *does* sound Jewish.

NOTES

1. This witticism comes from the Gershwin brothers' party song "Mischa, Yascha, Sascha, Toscha."

2. One questions if Brown's "My Shiksa Goddess" (from the musical *The Last Five Years*), when heard out of its theatrical context, might not be considered a self-hating portrait.

3. In 1997, on a best-selling CD collection of inspirational songs called *Higher Ground* (Sony) Barbra Streisand became the first popular artist of international stature to record a prayer in Hebrew, Max Janowski's setting of the Rosh Ha'shanah supplication: *Avinu Malkeinu* (Our Father, Our King).

4. What is one to make of the use of the Yiddish folk song "Tshiribim"—a nonsense word that conveys the same sense of frivolity as the Italian "Chiribiribin"—behind scenes of violence for the edgy 1999 film *Fight Club*? Now even wedding *badkhens* (emcees) are rapping in Yiddish.

5. James E. Young, reviewer of David Vital's *A People Apart: The Jews In Europe, 1789-1939* (Oxford University Press, 1999), *New York Times*, 7 November 1999.

6. Rabbi Marc Schneier, quoted in the *New York Times*, 21 April 1996.

7. William Bolcom in Thomas P. Lewis, ed., *An Anthology of Critical Opinion.*, p. 98

8. Pop stars Michael Bolton, Andrea Bocelli, Sarah Brightman, and Audra Macdonald have recorded arias. Aretha Franklin has sung Puccini in public.

9. Golijov, a Jew, has written a Spanish version of *The Passion According to St. Mark,* which incorporates a setting of the Kaddish prayer in Hebrew, while Thomas Beveridge, a Christian, has composed a *Yizkor Requiem* in Hebrew and Latin.

10. Eric Werner, *A Voice Still Heard*, p. 238.

11. Most likely this was a tall tale fabricated by Gershwin that has also been attributed to Ravel, Schoenberg and others. See Charles Schwartz, *Gershwin: His Life and Music*, p. 126.

12. Moshe Nadir is the pen name of Yitzhok Reiss (1885-1943). Another English folk tune, "Green Grow the Rushes-O," a cumulative song with Christian content, was adapted into "Ver ken zogn, "a Yiddish rendering of the Hebrew Passover text "Echod mi yode-a?" (Who Knows One?).

13. A Parisian composer, George Michberg, at first took credit for this "Incan" tune; but actually it was by Daniel A. Robles, a Peruvian march composer nicknamed the "John Philip Sousa" of South America. Michberg, an Argentinian Jew, brought Robles's song to Simon and Garfunkel's attention when he was part of The Incas, a group act that opened for them in one of their tours.

14. "Sway" has been recorded by a newer generation of middle-of-the-road singers: Peter Cincotti on Concord Jazz and by Michel Bublé on Reprise.

15. Dimitri Tiomkin racked up an impressive record of writing scores for westerns and rural settings. In addition to the *The Alamo*, he also scored *Rio Bravo, Red River, The Big Sky, Giant, High Noon,* and *Friendly Persuasion.*

Photo Gallery of Yiddish Songwriters and Poets

Top: Sholem Aleichem, Pesachke Burstyn, Nellie Casman
Middle: Abraham Ellstein 1 and 2, Mordecai Gebirtig
Bottom: Abraham Goldfaden, Max Helfman, Jacob Jacobs

Top: Pinchos Jassinowky, Jacob Kalich, Adolf King
Middle: Aaron Lebedeff, David Meyerowitz, Itsik Manger
Bottom: Moshe Nadir, Julius Nathanson, Alexander Olshanetsky 1 and 2

Top: Arnold Perlmutter, Molly Picon,
    Abraham Reisen
Middle: Joseph Rumshinsky 1, 2, and 3
Bottom: Jacob Koppel Sandler, Sholom Secunda 1 and 2, Abe Schwartz and daughter Sylvia

Top: Solomon Small, Joseph Tanzman, Boris Thomashefsky
Middle: Chaim Tauber, Ilia Trilling
Bottom: Mark Warshavsky, Herman Wohl, Herman Yablokoff 1 and 2

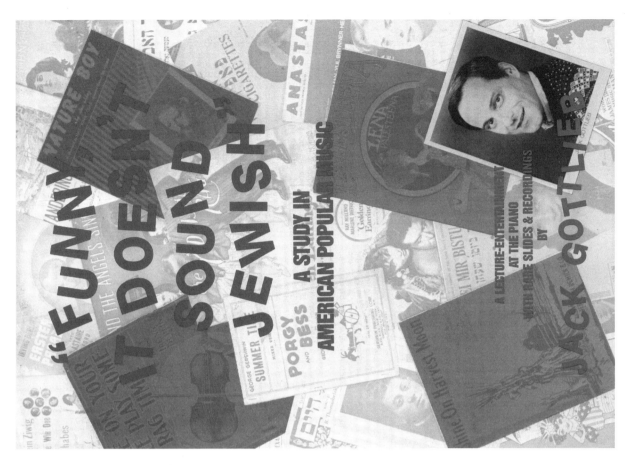

A promotional flyer for the author's original lecture.

Joseph Rumshinsky among his song sheets with words by Molly Picon and others.

Composers, Authors, and Performers

Composers (c) include songwriters and writers of larger forms. Authors (a) include lyricists, librettists, writers of books and musicologists. Performers (p) include cantors and show business personalities. Birth names are contained in brackets. NYC = New York City.

No data on more than sixty names mentioned in this book is accessible; but if only one detail is available, a name is listed. Due to conflicting sources, some names may have two birth or death dates.

	Birth		Death	
Abrams, Maurie [Maurice Abrahams] (a)	18-Mar-1883	Russia	13-Apr-1931	NYC
Abreu, Zequinha de [José Gomes de—] (c)	1880	São Paolo, Brazil	1935	São Paolo, Brazil
Achron, Joseph (c,p)	13-May-1886	Lozdzieje, nr. Suwalki, Poland	29-Apr-1943	Hollywood, CA
Adamson, Harold (a)	10-Dec-1906	Greenville, NJ	1980	
Adler, Richard (c,a)	3-Aug-1921	NYC		
Ager, Milton (c)	6-Oct-1893	Chicago, IL	6-May-1979	Los Angeles, CA
Ahbez, Eden [Alexander Aberle] (c)	15-Apr/May-	Brooklyn, NY 1908	4-Mar-1995	Sky Vallcy, CA
Ahlert, Fred E. (c)	19-Sep-1892	NYC	20-Oct-1952	NYC
Akst, Harry (c)	15-Aug-1894	NYC	31-Mar-1963	Hollywood, CA
Albert, Morris [Mauricio Alberto Kaiserman] (c)	7-Sept-1951	Brazil		
Aleichem, Sholem [Solomon Yakov Rabinowitsch] (a)	2-Mar-1859	Persyaslav, Ukraine	13-May-1916	Bronx, NY
Allan, Lewis [Abel Meeropol] (c,a)	1903	Bronx, NY	30-Oct-1986	Longmeadow, MA
Alstone, Alex [Siegfried Alex Stein] (c)	1903			
Alter, Israel (c,p)	1901	Lvov, Austro-Hungary	1979	NYC
Alter, Louis (c)	18-Jun-1902	Haverhill, MA	11-Mar-1980	NYC
Alterman, Nathan (a)	Aug-1910	Warsaw, Poland	1970	Tel Aviv, Israel
Arlen, Harold [Hyman Arluck] (c)	15-Feb-1905	Buffalo, NY	23-Apr-1986	NYC
Armstrong, (Daniel) Louis "Satchmo" (c,p)	4-Aug-1901	New Orleans, LA	6-Jul-1971	Corona, NY
Ashman, Howard (a)	3-May-1950	Baltimore, MD	14-Mar-1991	Los Angeles, CA
Astaire, Fred [Frederick Austerlitz] (c,p)	10-May-1899	Omaha, NE	22-Jun-1987	Los Angeles, CA
Austin, Billy (c?)	6-Mar-1896	Denver, CO	24-Jul-1964	Hollywood, CA
Babbitt, Milton Byron (c)	10-May-1916	Philadelphia, PA		
Bacharach, Burt F. (c)	12-May-1928	Kansas City, MO		
Baker, Belle [Bella Becker] (p)	26-Dec-1895/96	NYC	28-Apr-1957	Los Angeles, CA
Baker, David Keith (c)	6-Jun-1926	Portland, ME		
Bart, Lionel [Lionel Begleiter] (c,a)	1-Aug-1930	London, England	3-Apr-1998	London
Bayes, Nora [Leonora or Dora Goldberg] (c,p)	22-Feb-1880	Joliet, IL	29-Mar-1928	Brooklyn, NY
Berle, Milton [Milton Berlinger] (a,p)	12-Jul-1908	NYC	27-Mar-2002	Los Angeles, CA
Berlin, Irving [Yisroel, Israel/Isadore Baline](c,a,p)	11-May-1888	Mohilev, Russia	22-Sep-1989	NYC
Bernstein, Leonard [Lewis] (c,a,p)	25-Aug-1918	Lawrence, MA	14-Oct-1990	NYC
Bigelow, Frederick Ellsworth (c)	1873	MA	1929	
Bik [or Bick], Moshe (c)	26-Jan-1899	Dubossary, Bessarabia	1979	Haifa, Israel
Bikel, Theodore (p)	2-May-1924	Vienna, Austria		
Blake, Eubie [James Hubert —] (c,p)	7-Feb-1883	Baltimore, MD	12-Feb-1983	Brooklyn, NY
Blitzstein, Marc (c,a)	2-Mar-1905	Philadelphia, PA	22-Nov-1964	Port-de-France, Martinique
Bloom, Rube (c)	24-Apr-1902	NYC	30-Mar-1976	NYC

Bloom, Sol (c?)	9-Mar-1870	Pekin, IL	7-Mar-1949	Washington, DC
Bock, Jerry [Jerrold Lewis —] (c)	23-Nov-1928	New Haven, CT		
Boone, Pat [Charles Eugene —] (a,p)	1-Jun-1934	Jacksonville, FL		
Borge, Victor [Borge Rosenbaum] (p)	3-Jan-1909	Copenhagen, Denmark	23-Dec-2000	Greenwich, CT
Botsford, George L. (c)	1874	Sioux Falls, SD	11-Feb-1943/49	NYC
Bowman, Euday Louis (c)	9-Nov-1887	Fort Worth, TX	26-May-1949	NYC
Braham, David [Anthony Cannon] (c)	1838	London, England	11-Apr-1905	NYC
Braham, John [John Abraham] (c,p)	20-Mar-1774	London, England	17-Feb-1856	London
Braham, Sr., John J. (p)	1919	Brooklyn, NY	1947	
Brand, Oscar (c,a,p)	2-Feb-1920	Winnipeg, Manitoba, Canada		
Brecht, Bertolt [Eugen Berthold Friedrich—] (a)	10-Feb-1898	Augsberg, Bavaria	14-Aug-1956	East Berlin, Germany
Brent, Earl Karl (a)	27-Jun-1927	St. Louis, MO	8-Jul-1977	Brentwood, CA
Brice, Fanny [Fania Borach] (p)	29-Oct-1891	NYC	29-Jun-1951	Hollywood, CA
Brockman, James (c)	8-Dec-1888	NYC	22-May-1967	Santa Monica, CA
Brooks, Harry (c)	20-Sep-1895	Teaneck, NJ		
Brown, A. Seymour (c)	1885		1947	
Brown, Lew [Louis Brownstein] (a)	10-Dec-1893	Odessa, Ukraine	5-Feb-1958	NYC
Brown, Nacio Herb [Herb Brown Nacio] (c)	2-Feb-1896	Deming, NM	28-Sep-1964	San Francisco, CA
Bryan, Alfred (c)	15-Sep-1871	Brantford, ONT, Canada	1-Apr-1958	Gladstone, NJ
Burke, Joseph A. (a)	18-Mar-1884	Philadelphia, PA	9-Jun-1950	Upper Darby, PA
Caesar, Irving (Isidore) (a)	4-Jul-1895	NYC	17-Dec-1996	NYC
Cahan, Yehuda Leib (a)	15-Feb-1881	Vilna, Lithuania	3-Apr-1937	NYC
Cahn, Sammy [Samuel Cohen, a.k.a. Cohen/Kahn] (a)	6-Jun-1913	NYC	15-Jan-1993	NYC
Calloway, Cab [Cabell] (c,p)	25-Dec-1907	Rochester, NY	18-Nov-1994	Hockesin, DE
Campbell, James (a)		England		
Cantor, Eddie [Israel/Isidore Itzkowitz] (p)	31-Jan-1892	NYC	10-Oct-1964	Hollywood, CA
Carmichael, Hoagy [Howard Hoagland—] (c,a,p)	22-Nov-1899	Bloomington, IN	27-Dec-1981	Rancho Mirage, CA
Carr, Leon (c)	12-Jun-1910	Allentown, PA	27-Mar-1976	NYC
Carroll, Harry (c,p)	28-Nov-1892	Atlantic City, NJ	1962	Mt. Carmel, CA
Carter, Nell (p)	13-Sep-1948	Birmingham, AL	23-Jan-2003	Beverly Hills, CA
Casman, Nellie (c)	1896	Philadelphia, PA	1984	
Chajes, Julius (c,p)	21-Dec-1910	Lemberg (Lvov), Galicia	1985	Miami, FL
Chaplin, Saul [Saul Kaplan] (a)	19-Feb-1912	Brooklyn, NY	19-Nov-1997	Los Angeles, CA
Charig, Phil (c)	31-Aug-1902	NYC	21-Jul-1960	NYC
Charlap, "Moose" (a.k.a. Morris Mark) (c)	19-Dec-1928	Philadelphia, PA	8-Jul-1974	NYC
Charnin, Martin (a)	24-Nov-1934	NYC		
Clarke, Grant (a)	14-May-1891	Akron, OH	16-May-1931	CA
Coben, Cy (c)		Jersey City, NY		
Cohan, George M(ichael) (c,a,p)	3-Jul-1878	Providence, RI	5-Nov-1942	NYC
Cohen, Ethel Silberman (a)	1895		1990	
Cohon, Baruch Joseph (a,p)	28-Apr-1926	Chicago, IL		
Coleman, Cy [Seymour Kaufman] (c)	14-Jun-1929	Brooklyn, NY		
Collins, Will (a)	22-Oct-1893	NYC	14-May-1968	Ann Arbor, MI
Comden, Betty [Basra Cohen] (a)	3-May-1917	Brooklyn, NY		
Como, Perry [Pierino Como] (p)	18-May 1912	Canonsburg, PA	12-May-2001	Jupiter, FL
Connelly, Reginald (c,a)	1895	Buckhurst Hill, Essex, England	23-Sep-1963	Bournemouth, England
Conrad, Con [Conrad K. Dober] (c)	18-Jun-1891	NYC	28-Sep-1938	Van Nuys, CA
Cook, Will Marion (c)	27-Jan-1869	Washington, DC	19-Jul-1944	NYC
Coopersmith, Harry (c,a)	1902	Chicago, IL	1975	NYC
Corday, Leo (a)	31-Jan-1902			
Coslow, Sam (c,a)	27-Dec-1902	NYC	2-Apr-1982	NYC

Coward, Noël (c,a,p)	16-Dec-1899	Teddington, Middlesex, UK	29-Mar-1973	Jamaica, BWI
Creamer, Henry (a,p)	21-Jun-1878/79	Richmond, VA	14-Oct-1930	NYC
Crosby, Bing [Harry Lillis—] (p)	3-May-1903	Tacoma, WA	14-Oct-1977	nr. Madrid, Spain
Crumit, Frank (a,p)	26-Sep-1889	Jackson, OH	7-Sep-1943	Springfield, MA
Dabney, Ford T. (c)	15-Mar-1883	Washington, DC	21-Jun-1958	
Dale, Charles [Charles Marx] (p)	1881		1981	
Daniel, Eliot (c)	1908		6-Dec-1997	Los Angeles, CA
Danoff, Sidney (Sid) (c)	27-Jun-1920	Baltimore, MD		
David, Hal B. (a)	25-May-1921	Brooklyn, NY		
David, Mack (a)	5-Jul-1912	NYC	30-Dec-1993	Rancho Mirage, CA
Davis, Benny (c)	21-Aug-1885/95	NYC	20-Dec-1979	Miami, FL
Davis, Frank (c)	30-Jun-1894	Brooklyn, NY	9-Oct-1970	NYC
Davis, Gussie L. [Lord] (c)	3-Dec-1863	Dayton, OH	18-Oct-1899	Whitestone, NY
Davis, Miles Dewey (p)	25-May-1926	Alton, IL	28-Sep-1991	NYC
Davis, Jr., Sammy (p)	8-Dec-1925	NYC	16-May-1990	Los Angeles, CA
Dennis, Matt (c)	11-Feb-1914	Seattle, WA		
de Oliveira, Aloysio (c)	30-Dec-1914	Rio de Janeiro, Brasil		
DeSylva, B. G. "Buddy" [George Gard —] (a)	27-Jan-1895	NYC	11-Jul-1950	Los Angeles, CA
Deutsch, Emery (c)	10-Sep-1906/07	Budapest, Hungary	16-Apr-1997	Miami, FL
Diamond, Neil [Noah Leslie Kaminsky] (c,p)	24-Jan-1941	Brooklyn, NY		
Dietz, Howard (a)	8-Sep-1896	NYC	30-Jul-1983	NYC
Donaldson, Walter (c)	15-Feb-1893	Brooklyn, NY	15-Jul-1947	Santa Monica, CA
Dorough, Bob (c, a)	12-Dec-1923	Cherry Hill, Arkansas		
Dorsey, Thomas Andrew (c,p)	1-Jul-1899	Volla Rica, GA	13-Jan-1993	Chicago, IL
Doyle, Walter (c,a)	8-Jul-1899	Scranton, PA	3-Mar-19??	Millville, NJ
Drake, Ervin [Ervin Maurice Druckman] (c,a)	3-Apr-1919	NYC		
Dresser, Paul (c)	24-Apr-1857	Terre Haute, IN	30-Jan-1906	Brooklyn, NY
Dubin, Al (Albert) (a)	10-Jun-1891	Zurich, Switzerland	11-Feb-1945	NYC
Dunayevsky, Isaac Osipovitch (c)	30-Jan-1900	Lokhvitza, nr. Poltava, Ukraine	25-Jul-1955	Moscow, USSR
Dunbar, Paul Lawrence (a)	27-Jun-1872	Dayton, OH	9-Feb-1906	Dayton, OH
Dylan, Bob [Robert Allen Zimmerman] (c,a,p)	24-May-1941	Duluth, Minnesota		
Ebb, Fred (a)	8-Apr-1932	NYC		
Edens, Roger (c)	9-Nov-1905	Hillsboro, TX	13-Jul-1970	Los Angeles, CA
Edwards, Gus [Gustave Edward Simon] (c)	18-Aug-1879	Hohensaliza, Prussia	7-Nov-1945	Hollywood, CA
Edwards, Leo (c)	22-Feb-1886	Germany	12-Jul-1978	NYC
Eliscu, Edward (a)	2-Apr-1902	NYC	18-Jun-1988	NYC
Ellington, Edward Kennedy "Duke" (c,p)	29-Apr-1899	Washington, DC	24-May-1974	NYC
Ellstein, Abraham S. (c)	9-Jul-1907	NYC	22-Mar-1963	NYC
Elman, Ziggy [Harry Finkelman] (c,p)	26-May-1914	Philadelphia, PA	26-Jun-1968	Van Nuys, CA
Englander, Ludwig (c)	1859	Vienna, Austria	13-Sep-1914	Far Rockaway, NY
Ephros, Gershon (c,p)	1890	Serotsk, Poland	1978	
Evans, Raymond Bernard (c,a)	4-Feb-1915	Salamanca, NY		
Fain, Sammy [Samuel Feinberg] (c)	17-Jun-1902	NYC	6-Dec-1989	Los Angeles, CA
Feldman, Y. L. (c)		Russia		
Field, Arthur (p)	6-Aug-1888	Philadelphia, PA	29-Mar-1953	
Fields, Arthur B. (Buddy) (a)	24-Sep-1889	Vienna, Austria	4-Oct-1965	Detroit, MI
Fields, Dorothy (a)	15-Jul-1905	Allenhurst, NJ	28-Mar-1974	NYC
Fields, Irving (c)	4-Aug-1915	NYC	2001	
Fields, Joseph Albert Lew (a)	28-Feb-1885	NYC	3-Mar-1966	Beverly Hills, CA
Fisher, Doris (c,a)	2-May-1915	NYC	Los Angeles	23-Jan-2003
Fisher, Fred [Albert Von Breitenbach] (c)	30-Sep-1875	Cologne, Germany	14-Jan-1942	NYC
Fitzgerald, Ella (c,p)	25-Apr-1918	Newport News, VA	15-Jun-1966	Beverly Hills, CA

Name	Birth	Birthplace	Death	Death place
Forrest, "Chet" [George Forrest Chichester, Jr.] (a)	31-Jul-1915	Brooklyn, NY	10-Oct-1999	Miami, FL
Franklin, Malvin Maurice (c)	24-Aug-1889	Atlanta, GA		
Freed, Arthur [Arthur Grossman] (a)	9-Sep-1894	Charleston, SC	12-Apr-1973	Hollywood, CA
Frey, Hugo (c,a)	26-Aug-1873	Chicago, IL	13-Feb-1952	NYC
Friedland, Anatole (c)	21-Mar-1881	St. Petersburg, Russia	24-Jul-1938	Atlantic City, NJ
Friml, Charles Rudolf (c)	7-Dec-1879	Prague, Czechoslovakia	12-Nov-1972	Los Angeles, CA
Frug, Shimon Shmuel (a)	1860	Bobroy Kut, Ukraine	22-Sep-1916	Odessa, Ukraine
Gabler, Milton (a)	20-May-1911	Harlem, NYC	20-Jul-2001	NYC
Gaillard, "Slim" Bulee (c,p)	4-Jan-1916	Detroit, MI	2-Jun-1991	London, England
Gallop, Sammy (c)	1915	Duluth, MN	1971	Hollywood, CA
Gaskill, Clarence (c,a)	2 Feb 1892	Philadelphia, PA	29-Apr-1947/48	Ft. Hill, NY
Gasté, Louis Felix Morris (c)	1908			
Gebirtig, Mordecai (c,a)	4-May-1877	Cracow, Poland	Jan-1942	Cracow ghetto
Genaro, Pat (c?)	1922			
Gerber, Alex (c)	2-Jun-1895	NYC	10-Apr-1969	Mt. Vernon, NY
Gershwin, George [Jacob Gershowitz/Gershvin] (c,p)	26-Sep-1898	Brooklyn, NY	11-Jul-1937	Beverly Hills, CA
Gershwin, Ira [Isadore Gershovitz] (a)	6-Dec-1896	NYC	17-Aug-1983	Beverly, Hills, CA
Gideon, Melville Joseph (c)	1884	NYC	11-Nov-1933	
Gilbert, Herschel Burke (c)	20-Apr-1918	Milwaukee, WI		
Gilbert, L. Wolfe (c,a)	31-Aug-1886	Odessa, Ukraine	12-Jul-1970	Beverly Hills, CA
Gilrod, Louis (a)	10-Dec-1879	Roizana, Ukraine	10-Mar-1930	NYC
Gimbel, Norman (a)	16-Nov-1927	Brooklyn, NY		
Glan[t]zberg, Norbert (c)	1910			
Gold, Ernest [Ernst Goldner](c)	13-Jul-1921	Vienna, Austria	17-Mar-1999	Santa Monica, CA
Gold, Wally (Walter) (c)	15-May-1928	Brooklyn, NY		
Golden, John (a)	27-Jun-1874	NYC	17-Jun-1955	NYC
Goldfaden, Abraham [Avrom Goldinfodim] (c,a)	12-Jul-1840	Alkonstantin, Volhynia	9-Jan-1908	NYC
Goldfarb, Israel (c)	1879	Sieniawa, Galicia	1956	Brooklyn, NY
Goldstein, Gus (Gustave) (c,a)	1884	Jassy, Romania		
Goldstein, Jennie (p)	8-May-1895	NYC	9-Feb-1960	NYC
Goodhart, Al (c)	26-Jan-1905	NYC	30-Nov-1955	NYC
Goodman, Benny [Benjamin David —] (p)	30-May-1909	Chicago, IL	13-Jul-1986	NYC
Gordon, Mack [Morris Gitler] (c)	21-Jun-1904	Warsaw, Poland	1-Mar-1959	NYC
Gorney, Jay [Daniel Jason Gorney] (c)	12-Dec-1896	Bialystok, Russia	14-Jun-1990	NYC
Gottler, Archie (c)	14-May-1896	NYC	24-Jun-1959	CA
Gottlieb, Alex (c)	21-Dec-1906	Zhitomir, Russia		
Grant, Bert (c)	12-Jul-1878	NYC	10-May-1951	NYC
Green, Adolph (a)	2-Dec-1915	Bronx, NY	24-Oct-2002	NYC
Green, Bud (c)	1897	Austria		
Green, John (Johnny) (c)	10-Oct-1908	NYC	15-May-1989	Beverly Hills, CA
Greer, Jesse (c)	26-Aug-1896	NYC		
Grey, Clifford (a)	5-Jan-1887	Birmingham, England	25-Sep-1941	Ipswich, England
Grossman, Bernie (Bernard) (c)	21-Aug-1885	Baltimore, MD	2-Oct-1951	Hollywood, CA
Hague [Marcuse], Albert (c)	13-Oct-1920	Berlin, Germany	11-Dec-2001	Marina del Ray, CA
Hamlisch, Marvin F. (c)	2-Jun-1944	NYC		
Hammerstein II, Oscar (a)	12-Jul-1895	NYC	23-Aug-1960	Doylestown, PA
Hampton, Lionel (p)	20-Apr-1908	Louisville, KY	31-Aug-2002	NYC
Handman, Lou (c)	10-Sep-1894	NYC	9-Dec-1956	Flushing, NY
Handy, W. C. (William Christopher) (c)	16-Nov-1873	Florence, AL	28-Mar-1958	NYC
Hanley, James Frederick (c)	17-Feb-1892	Rensselaer, IN	8-Feb-1942	Douglaston, NY
Harbach, Otto [Otto Abels Hauerbach] (a)	1-Aug-1873	Salt Lake City, UT	24-Jan-1963	NYC
Harburg, Edgar "Yip" [Isadore Hochberg] (a)	8-Apr-1896	NYC	15-Mar-1981	Los Angeles, CA
Harney, Ben [Benjamin Robertson] (c,p)	1-Mar-1871	Middleboro, KY	1-Mar-1938	Philadelphia, PA
Harnick, Sheldon (a)	30-Apr-1924	Chicago, IL		

Name	Birth	Birthplace	Death	Death place
Harris, Charles K(assel) (c,a)	1-May-1867	Poughkeepsie, NY	22-Dec-1930	NYC
Harris, Will J. (c)	14-Mar-1900	NYC	14-Dec-1967	Chicago, IL
Harrison, George (c,p)	25-Feb-1943	Liverpool, England	30-Nov-2001	Los Angeles, CA
Hart, Lorenz Milton (a)	2-May-1895	NYC	22-Nov-1943	NYC
Hefti, Neal Paul (c,p)	29-Oct-1922	Hastings, NB		
Helfman, Max (c)	25-May-1901	Radsin, Poland	9-Aug-1963	Dallas, TX
Hellman, Lillian (a)	20-Jan-1905	New Orleans, LA	30-Jun-1984	Martha's Vineyard, MA
Henderson, Ray (c)	1-Dec-1896	Buffalo, NY	31-Dec-1970	Greenwich, CT
Herbert, Victor (c)	1-Feb-1859	Dublin, Ireland	26-May-1924	NYC
Herman, Bernard (c)	28-Jun-1911	NYC	24-Dec-1975	Los Angeles, CA
Herman, Jerry (Gerald) (c,a)	10-Jul-1933	NYC		
Herron, Joel S. (c)	17-Jan-1916	Chicago, IL		
Herscher, Louis (c)	19-Apr-1894	Philadelphia, PA	12-Mar-1974	Beverly Hills, CA
Hershfield, Harry (a)	13-Oct-1885	Cedar Rapids, IA	1974	
Herzog Jr., Arthur J. (c)	11-Sep-1883	Detroit, MI		
Heymann, Werner Richard (c)	14 Feb-1896	Königsberg, Prussia	30-Apr-1961	Munich, Germany
Heyward, DuBose (a)	31-Aug-1885	Charleston, SC	16-Jul-1940	Tryon, NC
Hill, Billy (William J.) (c)	14-Jul-1899	Boston, MA	24-Dec-1940	Boston
Hilliard, Bob W. (a)	28-Jan-1918	NYC	1-Feb-1971	Hollywood, CA
Hirsch, David (c)	1870	Chyrow, Galicia		Chicago
Hirsch, Louis Achille (c)	28-Nov-1887	NYC	13-May-1924	NYC
Hirs[c]h, Nurit (c)	13-Aug-1942	Tel Aviv, Israel		
Hoffman, Al (c)	25-Sep-1902	Dcrevno, nr. Minsk, Russia	21-Jul-1960	NYC
Holiday, Billie [Eleanora Fagan] (c,p)	7-Apr-1915	Baltimore, MD	17-Jul-1959	NYC
Howard, Eugene [? Levkowitz] (p)	1-Jul-1881	Russia?	1965	
Howard, Willie [Wilhelm Levkowitz] (p)	13-Apr-1886	Neustadt, Germany	12-Jan-1949	NYC
Hubbell, Raymond (c)	1-Jun-1879	Urbana, OH	13-Dec-1954	Miami, FL
Hughes, Langston (a)	1-Feb-1902	Joplin, MO	23-May-1967	NYC
Hunter, Alberta (c,p)	1-Apr-1895	Memphis, TN	17-Oct-1984	Roosevelt, NY
Hurwitz, Moshe (a)	27-Feb-1884	Stanislawov, East Galicia	4-Mar-1970	NYC
Idelsohn, Abraham Zvi (a)	13-Jul-1882	Pfilsburg, Latvia	14-Aug-1938	Johannesburg, South Africa
Ivanovici, Ion (Ivan/Jon) (c)	1845	Banat, Rumania	29-Sep-1902	Bucharest, Romania
Jacobs, Jacob [Yankev Yakubovich] (a)	1-Jan-1890	Risk, Hungary	14-Oct-1977	NYC
Jansen, Ben (Benjamin/Benny) (a)			14-May-1911	NYC
Jardon, Dorothy Shapiro (a,p)	1883		30-Sep-1966	Hollywood, CA
Jeffries, Herb [Umberto Alexandro Balantino] (p)	24-Sep-1911	Detroit, MI	13-Dec-1969	
Jentes, Harry (c,p)	28-Aug-1887	NYC	19-Jan-1958	NYC
Jerome, M. K. (c)	18-Jul-1893	NYC		
Jessel, George Albert (p)	3-Apr-1898	NYC	22?-May-1981	Los Angeles, CA
Jobim, Antonio Carlos (c,p)	1927	Rio de Janeiro, Brazil	8-Dec-1994	NYC
Johnson, Howard E. (c)	2-Jun-1887	Waterbury, CT	1-May-1941	NYC
Johnson, J. (John) Rosamond (c)	11-Aug-1873	Jacksonville, FL	11-Nov-1954	NYC
Johnson, James Weldon (a)	17-Jun-1871	Jacksonville, FL	26-Jun-1938	Wiscassette, ME
Jolson, Al [Asa Yoelson] (a,p)	26-May-1886	Shednick, Russia	23-Oct-1950	San Francisco, CA
Jones, Spike [Lindley Armstrong —] (p)	14-Dec-1911	Long Beach, CA	1-May-1965	Beverly Hills, CA
Joplin, Scott (c)	24-Nov-1868	Texarkana, TX	1-Apr-1917	NYC
Jordan, Joe (c)	11-Feb-1882	Cincinnati, OH	11-Sep-1971	Tacoma, WA
Jordan, Louis (c,p)	8-Jul-1908	Brinkley, AR	4-Feb-1975	Los Angeles, CA
Jurmann, Walter (c)	12-Oct-1903	Vienna, Austria	17-Jun-1971	Budapest, Hungary
Kaczerginski, Shmerke (a)	1908	Vilna, Lithuania	1954	Buenos Aires, Argentina
Kaempfert, Bert (Bertolt) (c)	16-Oct-1923	Hamburg, Germany	21-Jun-1980	Majorca, Spain
Kahal (pronounced "Kale"), Irving (a)	5-Mar-1903	Houtzdale, PA	7-Feb-1942	NYC
Kahn, Gus [Gustave K. Gerson] (a)	6-Nov-1886	Coblenz, Germany	8-Oct-1941	Beverly Hills, CA
Kalich, Jacob (a)	18-Nov-1891	Rimanov, Galicia	16-Mar-1975	Lake Mahopac, NY

Name	Born	Birthplace	Died	Death place
Kálmán, Emmerich (Imre) (c)	24-Oct-1882	Siófok, Hungary	30-Oct-1953	Paris, France
Kalmanoff, Martin (a.k.a. Marty Kenwood) (c)	24-May-1920	NYC		
Kalmar, Bert (a)	16-Feb-1884	NYC	18-Sep-1947	Los Angeles, CA
Kander, John Harold (c)	18-Mar-1927	Kansas City, MO		
Kaper, Bronislau/w) (c)	5-Feb-1902	Warsaw, Poland	26-Apr-1983	Beverly Hills, CA
Katcher, Robert (c)		Vienna, Austria?		
Katchko, Adolph (c,p)	1886	Varta, Kaliscz, Poland	16-Sep-1958	NYC
Katz, Mickey [Meyer, Myron —] (p)	15-Jun-1909	Cleveland, OH	30-Apr-1985	Los Angeles, CA
Kendis, James (c)	9-Mar-1883	St. Paul, MI	15-Nov-1946	Jamaica, NY
Kennedy, James (Jimmy) B. (a)	20-Jul-1902	England	6-Apr-1974	Somerset, England
Kent, Walter (c)	29-Nov-1911	NYC	2-Mar-1994	CA
Kern, Jerome David (c)	27-Jan-1885	NYC	11-Nov-1945	NYC
Klein, Lou (c)	11-Oct-1888	Albany, NY	7-Sep-1945	Hollywood, CA
Koehler, Ted (a)	14-Jul-1894	Washington, DC	17-Jan-1973	Santa Monica, CA
Koninsky, Sadie (c)	Aug-1879	Troy, NY	1952	
Kremer, Isa (p)	1887	Beltsy, Moldavia	7-Jul-1956	Cordova, Argentina
Kuller, Sid C. (c)	27-Oct-1910	NYC	16-Sep-1993	Sherman Oaks, CA
Kurtz, Manny (or Curtis) [Emanuel Kurtz] (c)	15-Nov-1911	Brooklyn, NY		
Kusevitzky, Moshe (p)	1899	Smorgon, Lithuania	1966	Brooklyn, NY
Lane, Burton [Burton Levy] (c)	2-Feb-1912	NYC	5-Jan-1997	NYC
Lateiner, Joseph (a)	25-Dec-1853	Iasi, Romania	23-Feb-1935	NYC
Latouche, John (a)	13-Nov-1917	Richmond, VA	7-Aug-1956	Calais, VT
Lawrence, Jack (c,a)	7-Apr-1912	Brooklyn, NY		
Lawrence, Steve [Sidney Liebowitz] (p)	8-Jul-1935	Brooklyn, NY		
Lebedeff (or Lebedov), Aaron (c,p)	1873	Homel, White Russia	8-Nov-1960	NYC
LeBoy, Grace [Grace Liebowitz] (a)	22-Sep-1890	Brooklyn, NY	23-May-1983	Los Angeles, CA
Lee, Irving [Blumenstock] (a)			12-Sep-1912	Denver, CO
Lee, Lester (c)	7-Nov-1905	NYC	19-Jun-1956	Los Angeles, CA
Lee, Peggy [Norma Doloris Egstrom] (c,a,p)	26-May-1920	Jamestown, ND	21-Jan-2002	Los Angeles, CA
Leigh, Mitch [Irwin Mitchnik] (c)	30-Jan-1928	Brooklyn, NY		
Leonard, [Duke] Robert (c,p)	23-Oct-1901	Utica, NY	19-Nov-1963	Miami Beach, FL
Lermontov, Mikhail (a)	3-Oct-1841	Russia		
Lerner, Alan Jay (a)	31-Aug-1918	NYC	14-Jun-1986	NYC
Leslie, Edgar (a)	31-Dec-1885	Stamford, CT	22-Jan-1976	NYC
Leslie, Lew [Lev Lessinsky]	1886	Orangeburg, NY		
Levinger, Elma Ehrlich? (a)	1887			
Lewandowski, Louis (c)	3-Apr-1821	Wreschen (Posen), Poland	3-Feb-1894	Berlin, Germany
Lewis, Al (c,a)	18-Apr-1901	NYC	4-Apr-1967	NYC
Lewis, Herbert (Happy)? (c)	1909		13-Jan-1982	Pampano Beach, FL
Lewis, Sam(uel) M. (a)	25-Oct-1885	NYC	22-Jan-1959	NYC
Lewis, Ted [Theodore Leopold Friedman] (c,p)	6-Jun-1890	Circleville, OH	25-Aug-1971	NYC
Lieber, Jerry (c,a)	25-Apr-1933	Baltimore, MD		
Lillian, Isadore (a)	7-Sep-1882	R'zeszow, Poland	26-Aug-1960	Yonkers, NY
Livingston, Jay Harold (c,a)	28-Mar-1915	McDonald, PA	17-Oct-2001	Los Angeles, CA
Loesser, Frank Henry (c,a)	29-Jun-1910	NYC	28-Jul-1969	NYC
Loewe, Frederic (a)	10-Jun-1901	Berlin, Germany	14-Feb-1988	Palm Springs, FL
Low, Leo (c)	1878	Volkovysk, Russia	6-Oct-1960	NYC
Lowenworth (Loewenwirth), Sam (c)			1954	
Luban, Francia (a)	1-Dec-1914	Kiev, Russia		
MacDonald, Ballard (a)	15-Oct-1882	Portland, OR	17-Nov-1935	Forest Hills, NY
Madden, Edward (a)	1878		1952	Hollywood, CA
Manger, Itsik (a)	28-May-1901	Czernowitz, Romania	Feb-1969	Tel Aviv, Israel
Manilow, Barry [Barry Alan Pincus] (c,p)	17-Jun-1946			

Manor, Ehud (a)	13-Jul-1941	Binyamina, Israel		
Marks, Edward Bennett (c)	1865		1934 (45?)	
Marks, Gerald (c)	13-Oct-1900	Saginaw, MI	27-Jan-1997	NYC
McCarthy, Joseph (a)	27-Sep-1885	Somerville, MA	18-Dec-1943	NYC
McHugh, Jimmy (c)	10-Jul-1894	Boston, MA	23-May-1969	Beverly Hills, CA
McKeon, Joseph H. (c,a)			15-May-1934	Brooklyn, NY
Menken, Alan (c)	22-Jul-1949	New Rochelle, NY		
Mercer, Johnny (John Herndon) (c,a)	18-Nov-1909	Savannah, GA	25-Jun-1976	Los Angeles, CA
Merrill, Blanche (a)	23-Jul-1895	Philadelphia, PA	5-Oct-1966	Jackson Heights, NY
Merrill, Bob [Henry Robert Merrill Lavan] (c,a)	17-May-1921	Atlantic City, NJ	7-Feb-1998	Culver City, CA
Meyer, George W (c)	1-Jan-1884	Boston, MA	28-Aug-59	NYC
Meyerowitz (Meyrovitz), David (c)	2-Apr-1867	Dvinsk, Latvia	1943	NYC
Miller, Sonny (c,a)			13-Sep-1969	London, England
Mills, Irving (a)	16-Jan-1894	NYC	20?-Apr-1985	Palm Springs, CA
Milner, Moses [Michael Melnikoff] (c)	1886	Rokitno, Russia	1952	Leningrad, USSR
Mogulesco, Sigmund [Zelig] (c,p)	16-Dec-1858	Bessarabia, Russia	1914	NYC
Monaco, James (c)	13-Jan-1885	Fornia, Italy	16-Oct-1945	Beverly Hills, CA
Morse, Theodore F. (c)	13-Apr-1873	Washington, DC	10-Nov-1953	White Plains, NY
Muir, Lewis F. (c)	1884	St. Louis, MO	19-Jan-1950	London, England
Mysels, Maurice (c?)	22-May-1921	Pittsburgh, PA		
Nadir, Moshe [Yitzhak Rayz] (a)	May-1885	Narayev, Ukraine	8-Jun-1943	NYC
Nelson, Edward G. (c)	18-Mar-1885		30-Mar-1969	Miami, FL
Nemo, Henry (c)	8-Jan-1914	NYC		
Newman, Alfred (c)	17-Mar-1900/1	New Haven, CT	17-Feb-1970	Hollywood, CA
Nicholls, Horatio [Lawrence Wright] (c)	15-Feb-1888	Leicester, England	9-May-1964	London
Noble, Ray (Stanley Raymond) (c,a)	17-Nov-1903	Brighton, England	3-Apr-1978	London
Norworth, Jack [John Knauff] (c)	5-Jan-1879	Philadelphia, PA	1-Sep-1959	NYC
Offenbach, Jacques (Jacob) (c)	20-Jun-1819	Cologne, Germany	5-Oct-1880	Paris, France
Olshanets[z]ky, Alexander (a.k.a. Alex Olshey) (c)	23-Oct-1892	Odessa, Ukraine	3-Jun-1946	NYC
Oysher, Moishe (c,p)	8-Mar-1906	Lipkany, Moldavia	27-Nov-1958	New Rochelle, NY
Papiernikov, Joseph (c)	22-Jan-1899	Warsaw, Poland	1930s	Tel Aviv, Israel
Parish, Mitchell [Hyman Peretz] (a)	10-Jul-1900	Lithuania (most sources list Shreveport, LA, others cite NYC)	31-Mar-1993	NYC
Patinkin, Mandy (Mandel Bruce) (p)	30-Nov-1952	Chicago, IL		
Pease, Harry (c)	6-Sep-1886	Mt. Vernon, NY	8-Nov-1945	NYC
Perlmutter, Arnold (c)	24-Dec-1859	Zolochev, Ukraine	1953	NYC?
Piaf, Edith [Edith Giovanna Gassion] (p)	19-Dec-1915	Paris, France	11-Oct-1963	Paris, France
Piano (Piani?), Harry (c)			4-Jan-1957	Mount Kisco, NY
Piantadosi, Al (c)	18-Jul-1884	NYC	8-Apr-1955	Encino, CA
Picon, Molly [Margaret Pyekoon] (a,p)	2-Feb-1898	NYC	6-Apr-1992	Lancaster, PA
Pokrass, Daniel (c)	17-Nov-1904	Kiev, Ukraine	16-Apr-1954	Moscow, Russia
Pokrass, Dimitri (c)	26-Oct-1899	Kiev, Ukraine		
Pomus, Doc [Jerome Solon Felder] (c)	27-Jun1925/26	Brooklyn, NY	14-Mar-1991	NYC
Porter, Cole Albert (c,a)	9-Jun-1891	Peru, IN	15-Oct-1964	Santa Monica, CA
Presley, Elvis Aron (p)	8-Jan-1935	Tupelo, MI	16-Aug-1977	Memphis, TN
Prev[w]in, André (c,p)	6-Apr-1929	Berlin, Germany		
Prima, Louis (c,p)	7-Dec-1910/11?	New Orleans, LA	24-Aug-1977/78	New Orleans, LA
Prince [Prince Rodgers Nelson] (c,p)	7-June 1958	Minneapolis, MN		
Prizant, Hyman (a)	ca. 1890	Kishniev, Moldavia		
Ram, Buck [Samuel —] (c)	21-Nov-1907	Chicago, IL	1-Jan-1991	Las Vegas, NV
Raposo, Joe (Joseph) (c)	8-Feb-1937	Fall River, MA	5-Feb-1989	Bronxville, NY
Raskin, Gene (Eugene) (a)	5-Sep-1909	NYC		
Raye, Don [Donald MaCrae Wilhoite, Jr.] (a)	16-Mar-1909	Washington, DC	Jan-1985	

Razaf, Andy [Andreamenentania Paul Razafinkeriefo] (a)	6-Dec-1895	Washington, DC	3-Feb-1973	Hollywood, CA
Reingold, Isaac (a)	1878	Russia?	1903	Chicago, IL
Reisen, Abraham (a)	10-Apr-1875	Koidenov, Russia	3-Mar-1953	NYC
Revel, Harry (c)	21-Dec-1905	London, England	3-Nov-1958	NYC
Ritchie, Lionel (c,p)	20-Jun-1950			
Rivesman, Mordecai [Max Semyonovich] (a)	1868	Vilna, Lithuania	9-May-1924	Leningrad, Russia
Roberts, Allan (c,a)	12-Mar-1905	Brooklyn, NY	14-Jan-1966	Hollywood, FL
Robin, Leo (a)	6-Apr-1895	Pittsburgh, PA	30-Dec-1984	Los Angeles, CA
Robinson, Harry (c)	26-Jun-1888	NYC	22-May-1954	
Robinson, J. Russell [b. Rosenberg?] (c)	8-Jul-1892	Indianapolis, IN	30-Sep-1963	Palmdale, CA
Robles Alomía, Daniel (c)	1871	Huánuco, Peru	1942	Lima, Peru
Rodgers, Mary (c)	11-Jan-1931	NYC		
Rodgers, Richard Charles (c,a)	28-Jun-1902	Averne, NY	30-Dec-1979	NYC
Rodriguez, Jose Luis [a.k.a. El Puma] (c,p)	14-Jan-1943	Caracas, Venezuela		
Rogan, James (Jimmy) Edward (a)	28-Oct-1908	Perth Amboy, NJ		
Romberg, Sigmund (c)	29-Jul-1887	Szeged, Nagy Kanizsa, Hungary	9-Nov-1951	NYC
Rome, Harold Jacob (c,a)	27-May-1908	Hartford, CT	26-Oct-1993	NYC
Rose, Billy [William Samuel Rosenberg] (a)	6-Sep-1899	NYC	10-Feb-1966	Jamaica, BWI
Rosenblatt, (Joseph) Yossele (p)	9-May-1882	Byela Tzerkov, Russia	19-Jun-1933	Jerusalem, Palestine
Rosenfeld, Munroe H. [F. Belasco, Eitteirer, et al.] (c,a)	22-Apr-1862	Richmond, Virgina	13-Dec-1918	NYC
Ross, Jerry [Jerold Rosenberg] (c)	9-Mar-1926	Bronx, NY	11-Nov-1955	NYC
Roubanis, Nicholas (c)		Greece		
Rozental, Zalman (a)	1892	Telenetch, Bessarabia (Moldavia)	1959	
Rubinstein, Max J. (?) (c)	1856		9-May-1922	Bronx, NY
Ruby, Harry [Harry Rubinstein] (c,a)	27-Jan-1895	NYC	23-Feb-1974	Los Angeles, CA
Rumshinsky (or Rumshisky), Joseph M. (c)	9-Apr-1881	Vilna, Lithuania	6-Feb-1956	Kew Gardens, NY
Russell, Bob [Sidney Keith] (c)	25-Apr-1915	Passaic, NJ	18-Feb-1970	Beverly Hills, CA
Russell, Henry (c)	24-Dec-1812	Sheerness, England	8-Dec-1900	London
Saminsky, Lazare (c)	8-Nov-1882	nr. Odessa, Russia	30-Jun-1959	Port Chester, NY
Sandler, Jacob Koppel (c)	1853	Bialotzerkov, Ukraine	23-Feb-1931	Brooklyn, NY
Savino, Domenico (D. Onivas) (c)	13-Jan-1882	Taranto, Italy		
Schindler, Eliezer (a)	28-Apr-1892	Titchin, Galicia	22-Sep-1957	Lakewood, NJ
Schoen, Vic (p)	26-Mar-1916	Brooklyn, NY	5-Jan-2000	Corona Del Mar, CA
Schonberger, John (c)	1-Oct-1892	Philadelphia, PA	1983	
Schonberger, Marvin (c)	1-Oct-1892	Philadelphia, PA		
Schroeder, Aaron Harold (c)	7-Sep-1926	Brooklyn, NY		
Schwartz, Abe (c)	1881	near Bucharest, Romania	1963	
Schwartz, Arthur (c)	25-Nov-1900	Brooklyn, NY	3-Sep-1984	Kintnersville, PA
Schwartz, Jean (c)	4-Nov-1878	Budapest, Hungary	30-Nov-1956	Sherman Oaks, CA
Schwartz, Phil (c)	1890		22-Jul-1964	Los Angeles, CA
Schwartz, Stephen Lawrence (c)	6-Mar-1948	NYC		
Scott, Clement (a)	6-Oct-1841	London, England	25-Jun-1904	London, England
Scott, Hazel (p)	11-Jun-1920	Port of Spain, Trinidad	2-Oct-1981	NYC
Seckler, Bill (c)	1905		3-Oct-1983	Woodland Hills, CA
Secunda, Sholom [Samuel —] (c)	23-Aug-1894	Aleksandria, Russia	13-Jun-1974	NYC
Shaw, Artie [Arthur Jacob Arshawsky] (c,p)	23-May-1910	NYC		
Sherman, Al (c)	7-Sep-1897	Kiev, Russia	15-Sep-1973	Los Angeles, CA
Sherman, Richard M. (c,a)	12-Jun-1928	NYC		
Sherman, Robert B. (c,a)	19-Dec-1925	NYC		
Shuman, Mort (c)	12-Nov-1936	NYC	3-Nov-1991	Paris, France

Silver, Abner (c)	28-Dec-1899	NYC	25-Nov-1966	NYC
Silvers, Louis (c)	6-Sep-1889	NYC	26-Mar-1954	Hollywood, CA
Silverstein, Dave (c?)	1897		6-Jul-1944	Staten Island, NY
Simon, Paul Frederick (c, p)	5-Nov-1941	Newark, NJ		
Sinatra, Frank (Francis Albert) (c, p)	12-Dec-1915	Hoboken, NJ	14-May-1998	Los Angels, CA
Sissle, Noble (a)	10-Jul-1889	Indianapolis, IN	17-Dec-1975	Tampa, FL
Skylar, "Sunny" [Selig Sidney Shaftcl] (a)	11-Oct-1913	Brooklyn, NY		
Small, Alan [Alexander Schriebman] (c)	7-May-1910	NYC		
Smith, Chris (c)	12-Oct-1879	Charleston, SC	4-Oct-1949	NYC
Smith, Joe [Joseph Sulzer] (c)	1884		1971	
Smith, Richard B. (a)	29-Sep-1901	Honesdale, PA	28-Sep-1935	NYC
Smith, Willie "The Lion" [William Henry Joseph Bonaparte Bertholoff—] (p)	23-Nov-1897	Goshen, NY	18-Apr-1973	NYC
Smulewitz, Shlomo [Solomon Small] (c)	13-Apr-1868	Pinsk, Poland/Russia	1-Jan-1943	NYC
Snyder, Ted (c)	15-Aug-1881	Freeport, IL	16-Jul-1965	Woodland Hills, CA
Sondheim, Stephen Joshua (c,a)	22-Mar-1930	NYC		
Spaeth, Sigmund (a)	10-Apr-1885	Philadelphia, PA	12-Nov-1965	NYC
Steinberg, Samuel (a)	1891	Sveksna, Lithuania	1-Jul-1938	NYC
Steiner, Max [Maximilian Raoul Steiner] (c)	10-May-1888	Vienna, Austria	28-Dec-1971	Beverly Hills, CA
Stept, Sam (Samuel) H. (c)	18-Sep-1897	Odessa, Ukraine	2-Dec-1964	Los Angeles, CA
Stern, Jack (c)	6-Mar-1896	NYC		
Stewart, Dorothy (c)	21-Mar-1897	Melbourne, Australia	18-Jun-1954	NYC
Still, William Grant (c)	11-May-1895	Woodville, MI	3-Dec-1978	Los Angeles, CA
Stoller, Michael Endore (c)	13-Mar-1933	NYC		
Stone, Jon	13-Apr-1931	New Haven, CT		
Stothart, Herbert (c)	11-Sep-1885	Milwaukee, WI	1-Feb-1949	Los Angeles, CA
Straus, Oscar (c)	6-Mar-1870	Vienna, Austria	11-Jan-1954	Ischl, Austria
Sturm, Murray (Maurice) (c)	12-Apr-1899			
Styne, Jule [Julius Kerwin Stein] (c,p)	31-Dec-1905	London, England	20-Sep-1994	NYC
Sulzer, Salomon (c)	30-Mar-1804	Hohenems, Voralberg, Austria	17-Jan-1890	Vienna, Austria
Swerling, Jo (Joseph) (a)	18-Apr-1893	Russia	23-Oct-1964	Los Angeles, CA
Tauber (or Towber), Chaim (a)	14-Jun-1901	Mohilev, Podolski, Ukraine	1972	NYC?
Tepper, Sid (c)	25-Jun-1918	NYC		
Theard, Sam (c)	10-Oct-1904	New Orleans, LA	7-Dec-1982	Los Angles, CA
Theodorakis, Mikis (c)	29-Jul-1925	Chios, Greece		
Thomashef[v]sky, Boris (Borukh) (c,a,p)	12-May-1868	Asitniatchka, near Kiev, Russia	9-Jul-1939	NYC
Thornton, James (c)	4-Dec-1861	Liverpool, England	27-Jul-18-1938	Astoria, NY
Timm, Wladimir A. (a)	1-Dec-1885	St. Petersburg, Russia	28-Aug-1958	Hendersonville, NC
Tiomkin, Dimitri (c)	10-May-1894	Poltava, Russia	11-Nov-1979	London, England
Tobias, Charles (c)	15-Aug-1898	NYC	7-Jul-1970	NYC
Tormé, Mel [Melvin Howard Torma] (c,p)	13-Sep-1925	Chicago, IL	5-Jun-1999	Los Angeles, CA
Trent, Jo (a)	22-May-1921	Chicago, IL	19-Nov-1954	Barcelona, Spain
Trilling, Ilia (c)	2-May-1895	Elberfeld, near Rhein, Germany	1947	
Tucker, Sophie [Sophie Kalish/Abuza] (p)	1-Jan-1884	Russia	9-Feb-1966	NYC
Tuvim, Abe (a)	10-May-1895	NYC	15-Jan-1958	NYC
Vallée, Rudy [Hubert Prior —] (p)	28-Jul-1901	Island Pond, VT	3-Jul-1986	Hollywood, CA
Van Alstyne, Egbert Anson (c)	5-Mar-1882	Chicago, IL	9-Jul-1951	Chicago, IL
Van Heusen, James [Edward Chester Babcock] (c)	26-Jan-1913	Syracuse, NY	7-Feb-1990	Rancho Mirage, CA
Vejvoda, Jaromir (c)	1898/1902	Prague, Czechoslovakia	1988	

Name	Birth date	Birth place	Death date	Death place
Velazquez, Consuelo Torres Orti (c)		Mexico City, Mexico		
Von Tilzer, Albert [Albert Gumbinsky/Gumm] (c)	29-Mar-1878	Indianapolis, IN	1-Oct-1956	Los Angeles, CA
Von Tilzer, Harry [Aaron Gumbinsky/Gumm] (c)	8-Jul-1872	Detroit, MI	10-Jan-1946	NYC
Walker, W. Raymond (c)	1883		1960	
Waller, "Fats" (Thomas) (c,p)	21-May-1904	Waverly , NY	15-Dec-1943	Kansas City, MO
Ward, Charles B. (c)	21-Aug-1865	London, England	21-Mar-1917	NYC
Ward, Edward (c)	2-Apr-1896	St. Louis, MO		
Warren, Harry [Salvatore Guarangna] (c)	24-Dec-1893	Brooklyn, NY	22-Sep-1981	Los Angeles, CA
Warshav[w]sky, Mark (c)	26-Nov-1840	Odessa, Ukraine	1907	Kiev, Ukraine
Washington, Ned (a)	15-Aug-1901	Scranton, PA	20-Dec-1976	Los Angeles, CA
Waxman, Franz [Wachsman] (c)	24 Dec 1906	Königshutte, Germany	24-Feb-1967	Los Angeles, CA
Wayne, Artie (c)	1914		14-Feb-1974	Nassau, Bahamas
Webster, Paul Francis (a)	20-Dec-1907	NYC	22-Mar-1984	Beverly Hills, CA
Weill, Kurt (c)	2-Mar-1900	Dessau, Germany	3-Apr-1950	NYC
Weinkranz, David (c)	Mar-1947	Israel		
Weisman, Ben (c)	16-Nov-1921	Providence, RI		
Weiss, George David (c,a)	9-Apr-1921	NYC		
Weisser [Pilderwasser], Joshua Samuel (c,p)	1888	Novaya Ushitsa, Ukraine	1952	
Wenrich, Percy (c)	23-Jan-1887	Joplin, MO	17-Mar-1952	NYC
Werner, Eric (a)	1-Aug-1901	Vienna, Austria	30-Jul-1988	NYC
White, Edward (Eddie) R. (c)	18-Jun-1919	NYC		
Whitehouse, Fred [Frederick E.] (a)	1924		8-Sep-1954 (?)	NYC
Whiting, Richard A. (c)	12-Nov-1891	Peoria, IL	10-Feb-1938	Beverly Hills, CA
Wilder, Alec [Alexander LaFayette Chew] (c,a)	16-Feb-1907	Rochester, NY	23-Dec-1980	Gainesville, FL
Wilensky [Vilensky], Moshe (c)	Apr-1910	Warsaw(?), Poland	2-Jan-1997	Tel Aviv, Israel
Williams, Charles (c)	1893	London, England	7-Sep-1978	
Williams, Clarence (c)	6-Oct-1893	Plaquemine, LA	6-Nov-1965	Queens, NY
Williams, Harry (c)	29-Aug-1879	Faribault, MI	15-May-1922	Oakland, CA
Williams, Hugh [Wilhelm Grosz] (c)	11-Aug-1894	Vienna, Austria	10-Dec-1939	NYC
Williams, Spencer (c)	14-Oct-1889	New Orleans, LA	14-Jul-1965	Flushing, NY
Wilson, Jackie (p)	9-Jun-1934	Detroit, MI	19-Jan-1984	Cherry Hill, NJ
Wine-gar, Frank (Fran) (a)	27-Feb-1901	Grand Rapids, MI		
Wise, Fred (c)	27-May-1915	NYC	18-Jan-1966	NYC
Wohl, Herman Zvi (c)	8-Sep-1877	Otynya, Ukraine	1936	NYC?
Wolf, Jack (c)		Paterson, NJ		
Wolfson, Mack (Maxwell A.) (a.k.a. Ronald Marc) (c)	2-Mar-1923			
Wolfstahl, Khona (c)	1851	Myslenice, Galicia	19-Dec-1924	
Wolkoviski, Alex (a.k.a AlexTamir) (c)		Vilna, Lithuania		
Woods, Harry [Harry MacGregor —] (c)	4-Nov-1896	North Chelmsford, MA	13-Jan-1970	Phoenix, AZ
Woods, Leo (c)	2-Sep-1882	San Francisco, CA	2-Aug-1929	NYC
Worth, Bobby (c)	25-Sep-1921	Cleveland, OH		
Wright, Robert (c)	25-Sep-1914	Daytona Beach, FL		
Wrubel, Allie (c)	15-Jan-1905	Middletown, CT	13-Dec-1973	Los Angeles, CA
Yablokoff, Herman [Chaim/Hyman Yablonik] (c,a,p)	1-Aug-1903	Grodno, White Russia	3-Apr-1981	NYC
Yellen, Jack [Jacob Selig Yellen] (a)	6-Jul-1892	Poland	17-Apr-1991	Springville, NY
Youmans, Vincent Millie (c)	27-Sep-1898	NYC	5-Apr-1946	Denver, CO
Young, Joe (Joseph) (c)	4-Jul-1889	NYC	21-Apr-1939	NYC
Young, Victor (c)	8-Aug-1900	Chicago, IL	10-Nov-1956	Palm Springs, CA
Zippel, David (a)	17-May-1954	Easton, PA		

"Yingish" Song Titles—A Selective List

Authors are listed by lyricists (W), then composers (M). Dates given are copyright dates—not necessarily the dates of composition. If no publisher is listed, it is registered at the Library of Congress as unpublished. This supplement does not include well-established songs from Broadway shows.

NINETEENTH CENTURY

Corbin's Idea or No Jews Wanted, a march, (ca.1890s), author unknown, only cover extant; R.A. Sallfield, Pub.

Dot Beautiful Hebrew Gal, 1881, by Henry G. Wheeler (W) & George Schlieffurth (M). Cover spells "kosher" in Hebrew letters; Chicago Music Co. & Wm. A. Pond & Co., N.Y.

Dreyfus, An Innocent Man, ca.1898, by Jere O'Halloran, *Delaney's Song Book,* no. 23, p. 12.

The Dreyfus Court Martial, 1899, by Al Johnson & F.R. Stanley; Al Johnson, Pub.

The Hebrew Fancy Ball, 1892, by Edwin R. Lang, *Delaney's Song Book*, no. 5, p. 14.
Hebrew Maiden, 1869, by Anthony Reiff; Wm. A. Pond & Co., NY.

The Hebrew Mourner, n.d. (ca.1850s), by Rev. J. W. Eastburn (W) & P. K. Moran (M).

The Hebrew Picnic, 1892, by William Jerome. *Delaney's Song Book,* no. 2, p. 26.

The Hebrew Wedding March, 1899, by Max Dreyfus. Instrumental arrangement by the "Dean" of Tin Pan Alley Publishers; T.B. Harms & Co.

Let Us Go to the Sheeny Wedding, 1880s. Cited in Gilbert, *Lost Chords,* p. 181.

Montefiore March, 1885, by Wm. Jonas; J. W. Just & Son, Philadelphia.

Mordecai Lyons, 1882, by Edward Harrigan & David Braham, *Delaney's Song Book,* no. 57, p. 24.

Moses Levi Cohen, 1894, by W. H. Batchelor.

Oh! Such a Business!, 1899, by Arthur Gillespie & Gus Edwards; M. Witmark & Sons.

Paddy Duffy, 1881, by Jerry Cohen (W) & Robert Decker (M). A Jewish-Irish melee; Pauline Lieder, 60 Chatham St., N.Y.

A Rabbi's Daughter, 1899, by Charles K. Harris; Chas. K. Harris Co.

Samuel of Posen, 1880s, by Isaac Schalem & Roger Putnam, cited in Gilbert, p. 179.

Sheenies in the Sand, 1880s, Gilbert, pp. 179-80.

The Sheeny Coon, 1898, by Harry Castling; Francis, Day & Hunter.

Solomon Moses, 1880s, Gilbert, pp. 179-180.

Song of the Hebrew Captive, 1830, by B. Carr, Philadelphia.

The Sorrowing Jew, 1843, Boston.

Wandering Jew Waltz (Bargmüller), 1869, by A. Schwartz, A. E. Blackmer, New Orleans.

TWENTIETH CENTURY

A Bee Gezindt, 1939, by Henry Nemo. Title is corruption of *abi gezint*, Yiddish for "as long as you're healthy"; Melrose Music Corp.

Abie, 1928, by Arthur Arnold.

Abie, 1910, by Rose Berry.

Abie, 1927, by William Russell McDonald.

Abie, Abie You're My Soldier Baby Now, 1941, by Alfred Olenick & David Davis. See "Abie, My Soldier Baby," 1917.

Abie and Me and the Baby, 1915, by Lew Brown & Harry Von Tilzer; Harry Von Tilzer Music Co.

Abie Captured His Wild Irish Rose, 1928, by Edgar Dodson.

Abie Don't Be a Bummer Boy, 1921, by Robert Hyman.

Abie, Dot's Not a Business for You, 1909, by Frank Davis & Jacques Hertzberg; Helf & Hager.

Abie, Maybe, 1924, by Irving Furstenberg.

Abie, My Soldier Baby, 1917, by Alfred Olenick & Leo Bennett, see "Abie, Abie, You're My Soldier Baby Now," 1941; Pub. by authors.

Abie-nu? My Yiddish King, 1931, by Lundi Gilbert; © Samuel Hoffman.

Abie Plays His Scales, n.d., by Agnes Ayars Williams.

Abie Sings an Irish Song, 1913, by Irving Berlin. From show *All Aboard;* Waterson, Berlin & Snyder.

Abie Springer Was a Tenor Singer, ca. 1910, by Jacques Hertzberg, cited in Marks.

Abie Started Running and He Didn't Come Back, 1912, by Pete Hazelwood & George M. Kennedy; Shapiro Music Pub. Co.

Abie, Stop Saying Maybe, 1924, by Jo Swerling, Art Johnson & George Holland; Shapiro, Bernstein & Co.

Abie, Take an Example from Your Fader, 1909, by James Brockman. Also arranged as a barn dance schottische; M. Witmark & Sons.

Abie the Agent, 1931, by Doris Kent; William Morris Agency.

Abie the Agent or Abe Kabbible, 1920, by Harry Hershfield & Eugene Platzman. Six subtitles (e.g. "Abe Kabbible at the Ballgame"), all of it gibberish; Louis Bernstein Pub.

Abie the Sporty Kid, 1909, by Harry W. Fields & Alma L. Russell; Victor Kremer Music Co.

Abie Was a Fighting Guy, 1913, by Joe Helsey. Abie as a boxer, not a soldier.

Abie's Baby, 1926, by John E. Hayes.

Abie's Circus Day, 1926, by W. G. Koepke & M. Arthur Disher; Frank Harding Pub. Co.

Abie's Got a Irish Molly O, 1911, by Raymond Hibbeler & Francis Jean Walz; Southern California Music.

Abie's Irish Nose, 1925, by Gene Austin; Dixon-Lane Music Pub. Co.

Abie's Irish Rose, 1922, by James Howard Flynn & Alfred L. Keefe.

Abie's Irish Rose, 1927, by James R. Hamilton.

Abie's Irish Rose, 1923, by James F. Hanley, from *Fashions of 1924;* Shapiro, Bernstein & Co.

Abie's Irish Rose, 1931, by Emil Lennert.

Abie's Irish Rose, 1928, by Patricia O'Hearn.

Abie's Irish Rose, 1942, by Joe Rines & Rex Irving, arranger. Five piano pieces for radio series; Paull-Pioneer Music Corp.

Abie's Irish Rose, 1927, by Harry Royle & Ervin O. Alley.

Abie's Irish Rose, 1946, by Robert Wells, Mel Tormé, Johnny Burke & Jimmy Van Heusen. From movie of same name.

Abie's Irish Rose O'Day, 1942, by Ted Courtney.

Abie's Lullaby, 1922, by Lee David, Gus Van & Joseph Schenck, arr. by Charles N. Grant; Irving Berlin Pub. Co.

Abie's Wild Irish Rose, 1944, by Edgar Dodson.

Abie's Wild Irish Rose, 1924, by Joseph Mckeon, Ed Moran & Will R. Haskins; Denton & Haskins Music Co.

Abie's Wild Irish Rose, 1922, by Gus Van & Joseph Schenck.

Abraham Riley, 1931, by Michael J. Fitzpatrick; Frank Harding Co.

Abram, Control Yourself, 1916, by Lew Brown & Albert Von Tilzer; Broadway Music Corp.

Abram, I Am Your Wife and Not Your Servant, 1926, by James Kendis. Originally, "Abram, What Do You Want from My Young Jewish Life?"; Kendis Music Pub. Co.

Adam and Eve Had a Wonderful Time, 1913, by Seymour Brown & Albert Gumble; Jerome H. Remick & Co., *Delaney's Song Book,* no. 67, p. 4.

America, 1938, by Alexander Olshanetsky; J. & J. Kammen, Inc.

America, 1924, by Joseph Rosenblatt; Fred Fischer, Inc. Probably the only song printed in English by the celebrated cantor.

And Russia Is Her Name, 1943, by E. Y. Harburg & Jerome Kern. From movie *Song of Russia.* Only known example of Kern's East-European melos; Chappell & Co.

And the Angels Sing, 1939, by Johnny Mercer & Ziggy Elman. Adapted Romanian-Serbian dance. Alternate title: "Freylekh in Swing." For instrumental version, see Kammen Dance Folio I, no.15; Bregman, Vocco & Cohn.

Ask the Stars, 1938, by Alexander Olshanetsky. Not clear if it has Jewish content; Edward B. Marks.

At Abe Kabbible's Kabaret, 1915, by Harry Hershfield & Archie Gottler; Leo Feist Co. Inc.

At That Yiddish Society Ball, 1915, by Sam M. Lewis & Edward Smalle; Broadway Music Corp.

At the Wedding of Sammy and Me, 1917, by Alfred Olenick & Leo Bennett.

At the World's Fair, 1938, by David Meyerowitz, best known as a composer of Yiddish Theater music, was then residing at 2 St. Mark's Place in N.Y.C.

At the Yiddish Cabaret, 1915, by L. Wolfe Gilbert & Lewis F. Muir; F.A. Mills.

At the Yiddish Wedding Jubilee, 1914, by Joe McCarthy, Jack Glogau & Al Piantadosi. *The Soul Kiss.* See "At the Yiddisher Ball"; Leo Feist, Inc.

At the Yiddisha Wedding Dance, 1911, by Arthur Fields & Harry Carroll; Harry Von Tilzer Co.

At the Yiddisher Ball, 1912, by Joe McCarthy & Harry Piani. See "At the Yiddish Wedding Jubilee"; Leo Feist, Inc.

The Ballad of Herman Schlepps, 1954, by Arnold B. Horwitt & Albert Hague. From *Ziegfeld Follies* of 1956.

The Bar Mitzvah Song (A Gift Today), 1962, by Harold Rome. From *I Can Get It for You Wholesale;* Florence Music Co., Inc.

Beckie, Stay in Your Backyard, 1910, by Norman & Young; F. A. Mills.

Becky, 1945, by Gene Dennis.

Becky, 1940, by Jerry Glaser & Elwood Walters.

Becky Do the Bombashay, 1910, by Gus A. Benkhardt & Bobby Heath; Jerome H. Remick & Co.

Becky from Babylon, 1920, by Alex Gerber & Abner Silver. From *The Passing Show of 1921*; M. Witmark & Sons.

Becky Green, the Queen of the Screen, 1920, by Billy Curtis & Harry Von Tilzer; Harry Von Tilzer Music Co.

Becky I Ain't Coming Back No More, 1925, by Harry S. Decker, B. Carlson & Bert H. Carlson, Leo Feist, Inc.

Becky Is Back in the Ballet, 1922, by Blanche Merrill & Leo Robbins, arranged by John Renhauser. From *Ziegfeld Midnight Frolic of 1918*; Shapiro, Bernstein & Co.

Becky Play Your Violin, 1933, by W. Scott & John L. Robinson; John E. Dallas & Sons, London.

Becky Rifkowitz, Tell Me Witz Is Witz, n.d. Listed in Edward Marks, *They All Sang*, p.175, as a number for Belle Baker. See "Sadie Harrovitz, Tell Me Which Is Which."

Becky, Stay in Your Own Backyard, 1910, by Norman Young; F.A. Mills.

Becky Won't You Come Back to Me?, 1921, by Robert Soffer, Canada.

Becky's Got a Job in a Musical Show (or "Becky Joined a Musical Show"), 1912, by Irving Berlin; Waterson, Berlin & Snyder.

Bei Mir Bist Du Schön, 1937, by Sammy Cahn & Saul Chaplin. Adapted 1932 Yiddish song of same title, by Jacob Jacobs & Sholom Secunda; Harms by arrangement with J& J Kammen.

Big Chief Dynamite, 1909, by Jeff T. Branen, Al Piantadosi & Will Rossiter.

Bizzy Izzy, March and Two-Step, 1903, by Charles Kuebler. No words. Cover has sterotypical caricature of the Jew as "shnorrer"; Brehm Bros., Erie, PA.

Blues, 1938, by David Meyerowitz.

Bolshevik, 1926, by Moe Jaffe & Nat Bonx; Shapiro, Bernstein & Co.

Bolsheviki (Jackson), 1928, by George White & Arthur J. Jackson; Jerome H. Remick & Co.

Boombah!, 1958, by Harold Rome. Written for the 10th anniversary of the State of Israel; Chappell & Co., Inc.

Bronx Ballads, n.d., by Harry Hershfield, et al. Titles such as "The Lipschitz Wedding," " Mrs. Shephard Margolies," "Wellington Goldberg," "Big Bouncing Bertha," "Naomi," etc.; 104 pp. with illustrations.

Business Is Business, Rosey Cohen, 1911, by Irving Berlin; Ted Snyder Music Co.

Casey's Wedding Night, 1901, by Vincent A. Bryan & Gus Edwards. Quotes "Khosn kale mazl tov"; Shapiro, Bernstein Co.

Chu Chem, 1966, by Mitch Leigh, Jim Haines & Jack Wohl. Title is a variant of *khokhem*—Yiddish for wise guy. From show of same title.

Chutzpa, 1973, by Leslie Bricusse. From *Feeling No Pain*; Screen Music, Inc.

Cohen and His Friend Meyer, 1920, by Anthony Regina & John Serini.

Cohen and Kelly, 1933, by Thomas Seabury.

The Cohen Family, 1923, by Max Steiner; Sam Fox Pub. Co.

Cohen Has 'Em Going in Hawaii, 1917, by Harry C. Dexter.

Cohen Is Living the Life of O'Reilly, 1927, by Jack Yellen, Lew Pollack, Gus Van & Joseph Schenck; Ager, Yellen & Bornstein.

Cohen Owes Me 97 Dollars, 1915, by Irving Berlin. From *Stop! Look! Listen!* Waterson, Berlin & Snyder.

Cohen the Crooner, 1935, by Ray Sonin & Ronnie Munroe; B. Feldman & Co., London.

Cohen's Nurse, 1919, by Joe Hanobik & E.G. Huntington.

Cohen's the Master, 1936, by Harry Dobkin, Phildalephia; Mills Music.

Cohen's Yiddisha Band, 1912, by Ballard MacDonald & Harry M. Piani. From *Passing Show* of 1912; Joe Morris Music Co.

The Cohens, (ca.1921), Maurice Morris. Words in *Delaney's Song Book,* no. 89.

The Cohens and the Kellys Are Best Friends, 1926, by Aaron Haberman; J & J Kammen Co.

The Cohens and Kellys, They're in Scotland Now, 1929, by Paul Reynolds & Clarence Williams; Clarence Williams Music Co.

Come Back to Aaron, 1911, by Addison Burkhardt & Harry Von Tilzer; Harry Von Tilzer Music Co.

Countess Dubinsky, 1934, Billy Rose, Ballard MacDonald & Joseph Meyer. Fannie Brice song: "Without Her Kolinski, Who's Showing Her Skinski in a Burlesque by Minsky." From *Ziegfeld Follies of 1934*.

Dance, Everyone, Dance!, 1958, by Sid Danoff. Adaptation of "Hava Nagila," Bourne, Inc.

Dance with Me Till I'm Dizzy, Izzy, 1908, by Alfred Bryan & Henriette Bianke-Belcher; Jerome H. Remick & Co.

Dona, Dona, 1940, by Sheldon & Sholom Secunda; Mills Music.

Don't Send Me Back to Petrograd, 1924, by Irving Berlin. Quotes "Der rebe hot geheysen freylekh zayn"; Irving Berlin Music Pub. Co.

Dougherty Is the Name, 1929, by Jack Yellen, Milton Ager, Gus Van & Joseph Schenck; Ager, Yellen & Bornstein.

Ess, Ess Mein Kindt, 1966, by L. Wolfe Gilbert & Josef Myro. Based on book of same title by Harry Golden; Leo Feist, Inc.

Father, Father, 1953, by Edward R. White & Mack Wolfson. Contrafact of "Eli, Eli"; Lear Music, Inc.

Fol De Rol Dol Doi (A Yiddish Serenade), 1912, by Edward Madden & Jean Schwartz; Jerome H. Remick & Co.

The Gazotsky Glide, 1913, by L. B. Goodwin & B.F. Bundy. From the Dartmouth show, *The Golden Isle.*

Get a Girl with Lots of Money, Abie, 1908, by Alfred Bryan, Ben Jansen & George W. Meyer; Harry Cooper Music Pub. Co.

The Ghetto Glide, 1912, by Melville Alexander & Victor Hollis. From *The Charity Girl*; Jos. W. Stern & Co.

Ginzburg's Band, 1924, by James Kendis. Cover: "To the Supreme Comedian of the World, the Honorable Sir Joseph Ginzburg"; Fred Fischer, Inc.

Goldstein, 1928, by Leon De Costa.

Goldstien's [sic] **a Grand Old American Name**, 1927, by Lewis W. Appleton, Philadelphia.

Good-Bye, Beckie Cohn, 1910, by Harry Breen & Fred Fischer. Possibly derived from 1900 song "Good-bye Dolly Gray" by Paul Barnes; Maurice Shapiro.

Gootmon Is a Hootmon Now, 1916, by Sam M. Lewis, Joe Young & Bert Grant; Waterson, Berlin & Snyder.

He Likes Their Jukulele, 1917, by James Kendis. From *The Century Girl*, 1916; Kendis Music Pub. Co.

Hebrew Humorous Melody, 1903, by A. Goldberg, for piano.

The Hebrew Vagabond, 1937, by Cora Marie Loomis & Jacob M. Sokolove, Sedalia, MO.

The Hebrew's Indian Bride, 1916, by Lewis Fuldauer & John Martin; Weber & North Music Pub. Co.

Honey Moneysuckle Baby, 1908, by Alfred Bryan, Addison Burkhardt & Fred Fischer; Fred Fischer Pub. Co.

Honeymoon of Pancho Pincus Rhumba Jake, 1943, by Irving Caesar, from *My Dear Public.*

Hot-House Rose, 1927, by Cole Porter. "Hot-House Rose from God Knows Where," written for Fanny Brice; Harms, Inc.

The House of David Blues, 1923, by Elmer Schoebel, Billy Meyers, Irving Mills; Jack Mills Inc.

How Is Everyt'ing by You, All-Right? By Me It's All-Right Too, 1914, by James Kendis; Maurice Richmond Music Co.

I Ate the Baloney, 1926, by Harry Lee; Edgar Leslie, Inc.

I Can't Believe the Tales of Hoffman, 1927, by Moe Siegel, Jack Meskill, Herman Paley; Edward B. Marks Music Co.

I Knew Him Before He Was Spanish, 1930, by Billy Rose, Ballard MacDonald & Dana Suesse. About Sydney Franklin from Brooklyn who become a popular matador. From *Sweet and Low*, 1930.

I Love to Listen to a Yiddisha Band, 1912, by M. F. Meyers & Lew Evans; M. F. Meyers Music Pub. Co.

I Love You Much Too Much, 1940, by Don Raye, Alex Olshey & C. Towber; Leeds Music Corp.

I Was a Florodora Baby, 1920, by Ballard MacDonald & Harry Carroll. From *Ziegfeld Follies*; Shapiro, Bernstein & Co.

I Wonder What Rebecca Was Doing by the Well, 1936, by Fred Fischer. From a series of tepid Yingish novelties: "Fred Fisher's Funny Folio"; Fred Fischer Inc.

If It Wasn't for the Irish and the Jews, 1912, by William Jerome & Jean Schwartz. From Weber & Fields's *Jubilee*; Jerome & Schwartz Pub. Co.

Ike Don't Make No Strike, ca.1913, by Blanche Merrill & Leo Edwards. Later version published as "Jake! Jake! The Yiddisher Ball-Player" by Blanche Merrill & Irving Berlin.

Ikey, My Baseball Mash, 1907, by Mrs. A. B. McDonald; Madden Music Co.

Ikey Sam, the Paper Rag Man, 1934, by Jimmy Stross, M. Rocke & Joseph E. Zamecnik.

Ikey's Lullaby, 1919, by Wilton Lackaye & Shafter Howard; S. Howard, San Francisco.

Ikey's Wife, 1913, by Harry W. Moorcroft & H. Richard; Harry W. Moorcroft Co.

I'll Open the Door and Close the Door, 1917, by Lew Brown & Maurie Abrams; Kalmar, Puck & Abrahams.

I'll Put the Blame on Mister Rubinstein, 1910, by Eugene Platzmann; Harry Von Tilzer Music Pub. Co.

I'm a Vamp from East Broadway, 1921, by Harry Ruby, Bert Kalmar & Irving Berlin; Waterson, Berlin, Snyder Co.

I'm a Yiddish Cowboy (Tough Guy Levi), 1908, by Edgar Leslie, Al Piantadosi & Halsey K. Mohr; Ted S. Barron Co.

I'm an Indian, 1922, by Blanche Merrill & Leo Edwards. From film *My Man*; Leo Edwards, assigned to Mills Music (1923).

In a Garden of Y'Eden for Two, 1908, by Vincent Bryan & Harry Von Tilzer; Harry Von Tilzer Music Pub. Co.

In My Harem, 1913, by Irving Berlin; Waterson, Berlin & Snyder Co.

Is Izzy Azzy Woz?, 1929, by Irving Caesar, Cliff Friend & George White. From *George White Scandals of 1929*.

Is Izzy Azzy Wozz, 1929, by Arthur Leclerq; Montgomery & Co., London.

Ish-Ga Bibble (I Should Worry), 1913, by Sam M. Lewis & Geo. W. Meyer; Geo. Meyer, Pub.

Isle of Meinisooris, 1943, by Dan Shapiro, Dan Pascal & Phil Charig. Possibly a corruption of Yiddish *tzuris* (trouble).

Israel, 1948, by Al Jolson & Bene Russell. Adaptation of "Khosn kale mazl tov"; ABC Music Co.

Israel, 1948, by Nick Kenny & Joseph M. Rumshinsky. By columnist of the *New York Daily Mirror* and the Yiddish theater composer; Goldmine Music, Inc.

Issy! Issy! Is He Getting Busy?, 1920, by John Neat; Herman Darewski Music Pub. Co., London.

It's Tough When Izzy Rosenstein Loves Genevieve Malone, 1910, by Grace Leboy & Gus Kahn; Will Rossiter, Chicago.

I've Got to See My Partner, 1929, by Jack Yellen, Milton Ager, Gus Van & Joseph Schenck; Ager, Yellen & Bornstein, Inc.

Izzy Get Busy (Write Another Little Ragtime Tune), 1916, by A. Seymour Brown; Jerome H. Remick & Co.

Jake! Jake! The Yiddisher Ball-Player, 1913, by Blanche Merrill (W) & Irving Berlin (M); Waterson, Berlin & Snyder.

Jakey's Vent an' Left Me in the Lurch, 1915, by Dorothy Fyfe.

Jerusalem Rag, 1912, by George Little & Herbert Binner; Betts & Binner Co.

The Jewish Maxixe, 1915, by Cyril Ring. The maxixe was a dance.

The Jewish Wedding Song, 1967, by Sylvia Neufeld. From film *Thoroughly Modern Millie*.

The Jews Have Got Their Irish Up, 1947, by Jack Yellen & Sammy Fain. Published by the authors.

Johnny Mishuga, 1961, by David Rogers & Marc Bucci. From *New Faces of 1962*.

Joseph! Joseph!, 1938, by Sammy Cahn & Saul Chaplin. Adaptation of Samuel Steinberg & Nellie Casman's "Yossel, Yossel," 1923; Harms, Inc.

The Kaddish of My Ancestry (*Der kaddish fun mein shtam*), 1925, by Edward Bennett Marks & Joseph Cherniavsky; Edward B. Marks Co.

Keep Your Rabbits Rabbi, We've Rabbits of Our Own, 1920, by Franklin P. Adams & Jerome D. Kern. Private pub. by T.B. Harms Co.

Kosher Kitty Kelly, 1925, by Leon De Costa; Harms, Inc. From play of the same name. *Queen Kelly*, the unfinished 1928 film by Erich Von Stroheim, starred Gloria Swanson as Kitty Kelly.

Kosher Kleagle, 1926, by J. P. McEvoy & Phil Charig. From *Americana*.

Kosher Politicians, 1937, by Gertrude Marie Haddock Estes, Atlanta.

Kosher Spanish Kid from Madrid, 1929, by Leon De Costa.

Kosher Swing, 1941, by Jimmie Bright.

Leave Abie Alone, 1933, by Joe Pearson; Campbell, Connelly & Co.

Levi Cohen Was a Busy Man, 1914, by A. J. Laugeson. Pub. by the author.

Levine, 1927, by Charlie Tobias & Harry Herschele (pseud. Harry Warren); Shapiro, Bernstein & Co.

Levine! With His Flying Machine, 1927, by Saul Bernie, Joseph Tanzman & Sam Coslow; Spier & Coslow, Inc.

Levinsky's Jubilee, 1921, by William K. Wells, arranged by Louis Katzman; © by Julian Rose.

Levi's Glass Eye Is a Window for His Fox Eye, 1926, by Gus Kirchner.

Little Irish Rose, 1928, by Anne Nichols, J.S. Zamecnik & others. From movie *Abie's Irish Rose*. Nichols is author of the original play; Sam Fox Pub. Co.

Love Me to a Yiddisha Melody, 1911, by Joe Young & Edgar Leslie. Adaptation of "A yor ersht nokh mayn khasene" by Isaac Reingold, in turn adapted from a Hasidic folk song "Der rebe's nigele"; J. Fred Helf Co.

Mahzel (Good Luck), 1928, by James Walsh & Fred Holt; Lawrence Wright Music Co., London.

Mahzel (Means Good Luck), 1947, by Artie Wayne & Jack Beekman; Leo Feist, Inc.

Mahzeltov!, 1967, by Harry James & Rob Turk; Music Makers Pub.

Make Up Your Yiddisher Mind, cited in Edward Marks, *They All Sang*, p.175.

Marry a Yiddisher Boy, 1911, by Seymour Brown & George Botsford; Jerome H. Remick & Co.

Mashuga, 1959, by Eddie White, Mack Wolfson & Sid Danoff; Famous Music Corp.

Matzoh Balls, 1939, by Slim Gaillard & Harry D. Squires; Columbia Music Pub. Co.

Maxie Don't Take a Taxi, 1910, by Sam Lewis & Louis Bennett; Joseph Morris Co.

Maybe You Think I'm Happy, 1911, by L. Wolfe Gilbert & Will Rossiter.

Mazel, 1965, by Luchi DeJesus; Prize Music, Inc.

Mazel Tov, 1964, by Robyn Supraner & Sherman Rothman.

Mazel Tov, 1963, by Charles Gauthier & Sam Everett.

Mazel Tov, 1965, by Dorothy Salus.

Mazeltov, 1979, by Jerry Herman. From *The Grand Tour.*

Mazel Tov Means Good Luck, 1939, by Leo Towers, Ralph Stanley & Spencer Williams; Lion Music Ltd., London.

Mazel Tov Rag, 1964, by Johnny Brandon & Dick Vance; Saturn Music, Inc.

The Mazumah Plant, 1911, by Addison Burkhardt & Melville J. Gideon; Maurice Shapiro Co.

Meyer, 1922, by Willie Raskin & Jack Glogau; Fred Fischer, Inc.

Mighty Like a Rosenbloom, 1920, by Willie Raskin & Fred Fischer; Fred Fischer, Inc.

Minsky, 1937, by Fred Herendeen & Dave Stamper. From *Orchids Preferred.*

Minsky Is Running the Opera Now, 1937, by Henry & Morris Olson, Fargo, ND.

Mischa, Yascha, Sascha, Toscha, 1921, by George & Ira Gershwin; New World Music Corp.

Mister Chamberlain and Mister Levine, 1927, by Harry Pease, Irving Mills & Edward G. Nelson.

Mister (Izzy Always) Bizzy Rosenstein, 1909, by William Jerome & Jean Schwartz. From show *In Hayti.*

Modernistic Moe, 1936, by Ira Gershwin & Vernon Duke. Fanny Brice, "I Give His Highness a Pain Worse Than Sinus," *Ziegfeld Follies of 1936.*

Momele, 1954, by Mitchell Parish, Alex Alstone & Al Goodhart; B. F. Wood Co.

Moses, What's Best for You, Your Mother Knows, 1917, by Felix M. Feist & Joel P. Corin; Leo Feist Co.

Mosha from Nova Scotia, 1915, by L. Wolfe Gilbert & Malvin M. Franklin; Joseph W. Stern & Co.

Moskowitz and Gogeloch and Babblekroit and Svonk, 1927, by Morris Ryskind, Howard Dietz, Henry Souvaine & Jay Gorney; Leo Feist Inc.

Mother's Sabbath Candles, 1950, by Jack Yellen. Pub. by author.

Moysha Machree (They're Proud of Their Irisher, Yiddisher Boy), 1916, by James Kendis; Kendis Music Pub. Co.

My Friends Morris and Max, 1918, by Bert Kalmar, Edgar Leslie & Harry Ruby. Based on characters from plays by Montague Glass, author of the Potash & Perlmutter cycle; Waterson, Berlin & Snyder Co.

My Greene Koseene, 1940, by L. Wolfe Gilbert. Adaptation of "Di grine kuzine" by Prizant & Schwartz. Pub. by the author.

My Kosher Rose, 1926, by A. Leeker & B. Wacht.

My Little Cousin, 1942, by Happy Lewis, Sam Braverman & Cy Coben. Adaptation of "Di grine kuzine" by Schwartz & Prizant; Doraine Music Corp.

My Little Yiddisha Queen, 1909, by Melville J. Gideon & Edgar Selden; Maurice Shapiro Co.

My Little Yiddisher Girl, 1923, by Robert W. McLeod; B. Feldman Co., London.

My Lovin' Yiddisha Queen, 1912, by Ben Rafalo & Homer Denney; Homer Denney.

My Rose of the Ghetto, 1911, by Donaghey, Burkhardt & Ben M. Jerome; Charles K. Harris Co.

My Yankee Yiddisha Boy, 1918, by Florence Phinallo & E.S. Huntington.

My Yiddish Matinee Girl, 1916, by Addison Burkhardt; Shapiro, Bernstein & Co., Inc.

My Yiddisha Butterfly, 1917, by Al Dubin & Joseph A. Burke; M. Witmark & Sons.

My Yiddisha Colleen, 1911, by Edward Madden & Leo Edwards. From *Ziegfeld Follies of 1910*; Gus Edwards Inc.

My Yiddisha Mammy, 1922, by Alex Gerber, Jean Schwartz & Eddie Cantor. From *Make It Snappy*; M. Witmark & Sons.

My Yiddisha Soldier Boy, 1945, by Lani D. Angelo.

My Yiddisha Vampire, 1918, by Hyman Rossman, arr. by Fred J. Fleming.

My Yiddishe Momme (or *A Yiddishe Momme*), 1925, by Jack Yellen & Lew Pollack; DeSylva, Brown & Henderson, Inc.

My Yiddisher Blonde, 1912, by Melville Alexander & Anatol Friedland; Jerome H. Remick & Co.

My Yiddisher Romeo, 1915, by Sam M. Lewis & George W. Meyer; Broadway Music Corp.

Nat'an! Nat'an, Tell for What Are You Waitin', Nat'an?, 1916, by James Kendis; Kendis Music Pub. Co.

Night Shall Be Filled with Music, 1932, by Will Collins, Buddy Fields & Gerald Marks. Verse is adaptation of "Got in zayn mishpet iz gerekht"; Santly-Joy, Inc.

Nize Baby, 1926, by Milt Gross & Benne Russel; Leo Feist, Inc.

Nize Baby (Eet Oop de Oit Mail), 1926, by Jeanette Rosenson.

Nize Baby (MacDonald/Hanley), 1926, by Ballard MacDonald & James Hanley. From *Ziegfeld Revue of 1926*; Shapiro, Bernstein & Co., Inc.

Nize Baby, 1926, by Mac Rutchild & Lenny Whitcup.

Now!, 1963, by Betty Comden, Adolph Green & Jule Styne. A contrafact of "Hava Nagila." Lyrics concern black civil rights; Stratford Music Corp.

Now! Now ! Now!, 1951, by Tom Glazer & Lou Singer. Adaptation of "Hava Nagila." Larry Spier, Inc.

Oh, Mama, I'm So in Love, 1950, by Aaron Schroeder & Abram [sic] Ellstein. Adaptation of "Oy mame bin ikh farlibt" by Abraham Ellstein, J & J Kammen Music Corp.

Oh Yeedle Ay, 1921, by Fred Fischer & Irving Maslof; Fred Fischer, Inc.

Oi Di Quota, 1925, by Leon Kessner & Max L. Schulman.

Oi! Oi! He's Coming Back, 1927, by Larry E. Johnson; T.S. Denison & Co.

Oi, Sadie, 1921, by Perrin W. Jenkins & George Graff, Jr.; World Music Pub. Corp.

Oi, Yoi, To Tell the Tales That Hoffmann Told, 1932, by Gene Edwards; T. S. Edwards & Co.

Oi! Oi! Vat a Lot of Fun!, 1912, by Sidney Davis & T. W. Thurban; Empire Music Pub. Ltd., London.

Oi, Yoi, Yoi, Yoi (A Hebrew Love Song), 1904, by Chris Smith (of Smith & Bowman, a black vaudeville team); Walter Jacobs Co.

Oie Marriage, Yiddish Song, 1920, by William Hood Rhoads.

Oif'n pripetchok [sic], 1920, Yiddish song by Mark Warshawsky, arr. By Max Steiner. Reverted to Southern Music, 1932.

Oy, How I Hate That Fellow Nathan, ca.1920, by Lew Brown & Harry Von Tilzer. Written for Fanny Brice; Broadway Music.

Oy, Yoy Cha-cha, 1936, by H. Nomberg & Samuel Weisser.

Oy Yoy, Mr. Cohen, 1930, by Ralph Stanley & Fred Neville; Music Pub. Ltd., London.

Palesteena, 1920, by Con Conrad & J. Russel Robinson; Shapiro, Bernstein & Co., Inc.

Park Avenue Librettos by Children of the Ghettos, 1932, by Lew Brown. From *Hot-Cha!*—a show "laid in Mexico," with Bert Lahr.

Peace and Love for All (Prayer for Moderns), 1941, by Leo Corday & Leon Carr. Adaptation of "Eli, Eli"; New Era Music Corp.

The Potash and Perlmutter Ball, 1918, by George M. Cohan. From *The Cohan Revue of 1918*.

Potash and Perlmutter Wedding Song, 1914, by Richard Malchien; Jerome H. Remick & Co.

Rachel, 1904, by Collin Davis & Howard Whitney; M. Witmark & Sons.

Rachel Aeroplane's, 1911, by Milton Graber; © David Cohen.

Rachel Lewis, The Sweet Little Jewess, 1911, by Charles Collins & Joe Burley; Francis, Day & Hunter, London.

Rachel O'Toole, 1904, by George De Long & Emile A. Bruguiere. From show *Baroness Fiddlesticks*; M. Witmark & Sons.

Rachel Rubinstein's Rag, 1912, by Sam Lewis & George W. Meyer; Geo. W. Meyer Music Co.

Rebecca, 1908, by Harry Williams & Egbert Van Alstyne. From show *I Was a Hero Too*; Jerome H. Remick Co.

Rebecca Came Back from Mecca, 1921, by Bert Kalmar & Harry Ruby. From show *The Midnight Rounders*; Waterson, Berlin & Snyder Co.

A Refugee's Lullaby, 1947, by Jack Yellen & Sammy Fain.

Rockaway Baby, 1920, by Ballard MacDonald, Harry Piani & Sammy Stept. From *Ziegfeld Midnight Frolic*. Shapiro, Bernstein & Co.

Roll Your Yiddisha Eyes for Me, 1915, by Sam M. Lewis & George W. Meyer; Broadway Music Corp.

Rose of Washington Square, 1920, by Ballard MacDonald & James Hanley. From *Ziegfeld Midnight Frolic*; Shapiro, Bernstein & Co.

Rosenbaum, 1909, by Fred Fischer; Fred Fischer Music Co.

Rosenthal Ain't Rosenthal No More, 1926, by Robert A. Simon.

Rosie Make It Rosy for Me, 1920, by Grant Clarke & J.L. Merkur; Irving Berlin, Inc.

Rosie Rosenblott Don't Make No Theatre with Me, 1915, by Sam M. Lewis & George W. Meyer; Broadway Music Corp.

Rosie Rosinsky, 1904, by William Jerome & Jean Schwartz; Shapiro, Bernstein & Co.

Russian Doll, 1927, by Sonny Miller & Jules K. Stein; Jerome H. Remick & Co.

Russian Lullaby, 1927, by Irving Berlin; Irving Berlin, Inc.

Sadie Harrovitz, Tell Me Which Is Which, 1920, by Alfred Bryan & Harry Tierney; Fred Fischer, Inc.

Sadie Likes It, 1912, by Morris Golden.

Sadie, My Yiddisher Vamp, 1926, by Joe L. Sanders, arr. by Charles Johnson.

Sadie Salome Go Home, 1909, by Edgar Leslie & Irving Berlin; Ted Snyder Co.

Sam, You Made the Pants Too Long, 1940 & 1946, by Fred Whitehouse & Milton Berle. Adapted from "Lawd, You Made the Night Too Long," 1932, by Sam M. Lewis & Victor Young; Shapiro, Bernstein & Co.

Sarah Rosenstein, 1904, by George Whiting & Fred Fischer; Joseph W. Stern & Co.

Sarah the Sunshine Girl, 1934, by Billy Rose, Ballard Macdonald & Joseph Meyer. Fanny Brice as a "noodist," from *Ziegfeld Follies of 1934*.

Sasha, the Passion of the Pasha, 1928, by Jesse Green, Billy Rose & Ballard MacDonald. From the film *Broadway Nights* with Fanny Brice; EMI Robbins, Inc.

Second-Hand Rose, 1921, by Grant Clarke & James F. Hanley. From *Ziegfeld Follies of 1921*; Shapiro, Bernstein & Co.

Serenade Me Sadie, 1912, by Joe Young & Bert Grant; Jerome H. Remick & Co.

Sha-Sha, 1938, by Manny Kurtz & Jimmy Van Heusen. Adaptation of Joseph Moskowitz & Adolph King's *Oi di rebezen,* 1922, changed to "Oi is dus a rebezin" exclusively by Adolph King, 1923; Broadway Music Corp.

The Sheeny and the Lost Shekel, 1921, by J. H. B. Scheuyeaulle & A. Leopold Richard; Letgers Music Co.

The Sheeny's Masquerade, 1919, by Victor K. Nye & Edouard Hesselberg; V. K. Nye.

The Sheik of Avenue B, 1922, by Bert Kalmar, Harry Ruby, Friend & Downing; Parody of "The Sheik of Araby "(1921); Waterson, Berlin & Snyder Co.

Shultzmeier Rag, A Yiddish novelty, 1914, by R. Whitlow. Cover shows wildly gesticulating conductor. Stark Music Co., St. Louis, Mo.

Simon, Healy, and Cohen, 1920, by Henry Creamer & J. Turner Layton; Chas. K. Harris.

Since Henry Ford Apologized to Me, 1927, by Billy Rose, Ballard MacDonald & Dave Stamper; Shapiro, Bernstein & Co.

Since Rosie Joined the Cabaret, 1913, by Ben & Dave Levy & Leo Friedman; Joe Morris Music Co.

Since Sara Saw Theda Bara, 1916, by Alex Gerber & Harry Jentes; Leo Feist, Inc.

Since Yussel Learned to Yodel (He's a Yiddisher Mountaineer), 1935, by James Cavanaugh, Dick Sanford & Sammy Mysels; Rialto Music Pub. Co.

Solomon, 1919, by Alfred Bryan & Jean Schwartz. From *Passing Show of 1919*. Only the music is "Yiddish" inflected; Jerome H. Remick & Co.

Solomon Jock Mackenzie Rubinstein, 1920, by Herbert Rule & Thomas McGhee, Herman Darewski; The Music Pub. Co., London.

Song of the Sewing Machine, 1927, by Billy Rose, Ballard MacDonald & Jesse Greer.

Soul Saving Sadie, 1934, by Billy Rose, Ballard MacDonald & Joseph Meyer. Fanny Brice take-off on Aimee Semple McPherson. From *Ziegfeld Follies of 1934.*

Spanish Jake, 1936, by Irving Caesar, Sammy Lerner & Gerald Marks. From *Transatlantic Rhythm*; Jerome H. Remick & Co.

Stonewall Moskowitz March, 1926, by Irving Caesar, Lorenz Hart & Richard Rodgers. From *Betsy*. Other titles include "The Kitzel Engagement," " Leave It to Levy," " Six Little Kitzels," and the premiere of Irving Berlin's "Blue Skies"; Harms, Inc.

Stop That Bearcat, Sadie, 1912, by Gene Greene; Will Rossiter Co.

Tears of Palestine, 1938, by Richard Sanford, George B. McConnell & Bob Miller.

Telephone Your Rivky, Izzie, 1910, by Addison Burkhardt & Lillian Shaw. From the show *Jumping Jupiter*; Harry Von Tilzer Music Pub. Co.

The Tenement Symphony, 1941, by Sid Kuller, Ray Golden & Hal Borne. From film *The Big Store*; Leo Feist, Inc.

That Eli, Eli Melody, 1920, by Leo Wood & Archie Gottler; Leo Feist, Inc.

That Kazzatsky Dance, 1910, by Irving Berlin; Ted Snyder Co.

That Mittel-Europa European Man, 1943, by Henry Meyers, Edward Elsicu & Jay Gorney. From show *Marching with Johnny*.

That Wonderful Girl of Mine, 1949, by Sammy Gallop. Adaptation of "Mein Shtetele Belz," 1932, by Jacob Jacobs & Alexander Olshanetsky; Supreme Music Corp.

That Yiddish Jazz, 1920, by John Albert; Francis, Day & Hunter, London.

That Yiddisher Tango, 1914, by Robert Watkins & Adolph Deutsch; Denton, Cottler & Daniels Co.

That's Genuine First Class Yiddisha Love, 1910, by Addison Burkhardt & Harry Von Tilzer. From *Ziegfeld Follies of 1910*; Harry Von Tilzer Music Pub. Co.

That's Yiddisha Love, 1910, by James Brockman; M. Witmark & Sons.

There Never Was a White Hope Whose Christian Name Was Cohen, 1912, by Irving Lee & Phil Schwartz. From show *The Charity Girl*; Harold Rossiter Music Co.

There's a Little Bit of Irish in Sadie Cohn, 1916, by Alfred Bryan & Jack Stern; Jerome H. Remick & Co.

They're All Good American Names, 1911, by William Jerome & Jean Schwartz; Jerome H. Remick & Co.

They're Wearing Them Higher in Hawaii, 1916, by Joe Goodwin & Halsey K. Mohr; Shapiro, Bernstein & Co.

To the Steins, 1930, by Walter Doyle; M. Witmark & Sons.

Tzena, Tzena, Tzena, 1950, by Mitchell Parish, Issachar Miron & Julius Grossman. Alternate version with words by Gordon Jenkins claims: "Based on traditional melody"; Mills Music, Inc. (Cromwell Music, Inc.).

Tzotskele, 1958. Recorded by Cab Calloway.

Under the Hebrew Moon, 1909, by Edward Madden & Dorothy Jardon; Maurice Shapiro Co.

Under the Matzos Tree, A Ghetto Love Song, 1917, by Fred Fischer; Fred Fischer, Inc.

Under the Rosenbloom, 1917, by Alfred Bryan & George W. Meyer; Joseph W. Stern & Co.

Utt-Da-Zay, 1939, by Buck Ram & Irving Mills. In 1941, registered as "The Tailor's Song" by Gene Irwin & Manny Young. Adaptation of folk song "Ot azoy"; Mills Music, Inc.

Valeska (My Russian Rose), 1925, by Irving Kahal, Sammy Fain & Irving Mills; Jack Mills, Inc.

What Used to Was, Used to Was, Now It Ain't, 1939, by Sammy Cahn & Saul Chaplin, Adaptation of "Vos iz geven iz geven un nito," by David Meyerowitz; Atlas Music Corp.

When a Kid Who Came from the East Side (Found a Sweet Society Rose), 1926, by Al Dubin & Jimmy McHugh. About the marriage of Irving Berlin to Ellin MacKay; Jack Mills, Inc.

When Gimble Hits the Cymbal, 1932, by Mack Gordon & Harry Revel; Lawrence Music Pub.

When Mose with His Nose Leads the Band, 1906, by Jack Drislane, Bert Fitzgibbon & Theodore Morse; F. B. Haviland Pub. Co.

When Nathan Was Married to Rose of Washington Square, 1923, by Andy Rice & James Kendis; Irving Berlin, Inc.

When Rubinstein and Mendelssohn Played the Wearing of the Green, 1911, by Harry Breen & Jimmy Conlin; Harold Rossiter Music Co.

When They Merge Mazeltoff with the Wearing of the Green, 1930, by Bernie Grossman, Dave Silverstein & Lou Handman; Handman, Kent & Goodman, Inc.

Where Was Moses When the Lights Went Out, 1913, by Joe Goodwin, Edgar Leslie & Al Piantadosi; Leo Feist, Inc.

Who Do You Suppose Went and Married My Sister? Thomâshevsky, 1910, by Nora Bayes & Jack Norworth; Norworth Pub. Co.

Who's Yehoodi?, 1940. Recorded by Cab Calloway.

Whose Izzy Is He Is He Yours or Is He Mine?, 1924, by Lew Brown, Bud Green & Murray Sturm; Shapiro, Bernstein & Co.

Yascha Michaeloffsky's Melody, 1928, by Irving Berlin; Irving Berlin, Inc.

Yenta Power, 1978, by Lee Adams & Charles Strouse. From *A Broadway Honeymoon.*

Yid, 1969, by Stanley A. Robertson.

Yiddische Blues, Yiddische Foxtrot, Yiddische Jazz, Yiddelach Shimmy, 1919, by Joseph Frankel. Unpub. piano pieces.

Yiddische Tate, 1959, by Babe Wallace.

The Yiddish Calypso, 1957, by George W. Painter.

Yiddish Lullabye, 1963, by Roy Reber, George Peace & Whitey Kaufman.

Yiddish Mambo, 1954, by Sanford S. Horowitz.

Yiddish Mambo, 1954, by Max Kalish.

The Yiddish Mambo, 1954, by Ruth Polatschek.

The Yiddish Mambo, 1954, by William H. Walner.

A Yiddish Pot Pie, Or Moses and the Rest of the World, 1908, by George Frank & George E. Castello.

The Yiddish Opera, 1915, by Lew Epstein Richards.

The Yiddish Rag, 1902, by A. Traxler. Piano rag dedicated "To the Hebrews of America." No Jewish content, but cover is caricature of grubby Jewish pawnbroker holding diamonds.

Yiddish Tango Ball, 1914, by Harry H. Hoef; Harry Scharck Music Co., London.

Yiddisha Army Blues, 1928, by Johnny Cooper. Cover shows hooked nose, three pawnshop balls mirrored by three items of men's clothing below; W. A. Quincke & Co.

The Yiddisha Blues, 1929, by Molly Picon & Murray Rumshisky.

Yiddisha Charleston, 1926, by Billy Rose & Fred Fischer; Henry Waterson, Inc.

Yiddisha Eyes, 1910, by Irving Berlin; Ted Snyder Co.

Yiddisha Feet, 1911, by Herman Timberg; Frederick Allen Mills Co.

A Yiddisha Fightin' Man, 1928, by Alfred T. Jacobs, San Fransisco.

The Yiddisha Fruitfly, 1968, by Barry F. Scheifer.

Yiddisha Jazz, 1921, by J. Rose.

Yiddisha Love, 1963, by Lou Grad.

The Yiddisha Lament (Becky From Schenectady), 1926, by Marta Golden Duffy.

Yiddisha Love, 1926, by Louis Chaikin.

Yiddisha Luck and Irisha Love (Kelly and Rosenbaum, That's Mazeltoff), 1911, by Alfred Bryan & Fred Fischer; Maurice Shapiro Co.

Yiddisha Nightingale, 1911, by Irving Berlin; Ted Snyder Co.

The Yiddisha Professor, 1912, by Irving Berlin; Waterson, Berlin & Snyder Co.

The Yiddisha Rag, 1909, by Joseph M. McKeon, Harry M. Piano & W. Raymond Walker; "Respectfully Dedicated to Miss Sophie Tucker"; Harry Von Tilzer Music Pub. Co.

The Yiddisha Rag, for piano, 1910, by Raymond Walker; Harry Von Tilzer Pub. Co.

A Yiddisha Soldier Man, 1918, by Cornelia Fucignas.

The Yiddisha Toreador, 1932, by Mark Beam; Frank Harding Co.

The Yiddisha Turkey Trot, 1912, by Arthur Fields & Harry Carroll; Waterson, Berlin & Snyder Co.

A Yiddisha Wampire, 1918, by Blanche Merrill. From *Ziegfeld 9 O'Clock Frolic.*

Yiddishe Mambo, 1954, by Buddy Feyne & Bill Harrington; Gibralter Music Co.

Yiddisher Aviator Man, 1915, by Alex Gerber & Fred Fischer; Werblow-Fischer Co.

The Yiddisher Baseball Game, 1914, by Aubrey Gittelman & Jay Goldberg.

Yiddisher Bear, 1913, by Charles S. Alberte & Robert D. Cohen.

Yiddisher Blues (Fox Trot), 1921, by Irving Babel.

The Yiddisher Blues, 1931, by Harry Leon & Leo Towbers; Jacques Liber, Ltd., London.

The Yiddisher Foxtrot, 1923, by Joseph Cherniavsky. Piano piece.

Der Yiddisher Fox-Trot, 1929, by Charles Solomon Diamond; Diamond Music Co., London.

Yiddisher Gondolier, 1913, by L. B. Goodwin & B. F. Bundy. From the Dartmouth show *The Golden Isle.*

Yiddisher Irish Baby, 1915, by Morton David, Fred Godfrey & Lawrence Wright; B. Feldman Co., London.

Yiddisher Jazz, 1921, by William K. Wells, ©Julian Rose.

Der Yiddisher Santa Claus (Duet), 1923, by Joseph I. Tanzman, Brooklyn.

The Yiddisher Society Ball, cited in Whitcomb's *After the Ball*, pp. 39, 52.

Yiddisher Tango Ball, 1914, by Harry H. Hoeft; Harry Schorch Co.

Yiddisher Tears, 1954, by Maurice Alfred Cohen [a.k.a. Michael Carr]; Box & Cox Pub. Inc., London.

Yiddle, On Your Fiddle. Play Some Ragtime, 1909, by Irving Berlin; Ted Snyder Co.

Yoi! Yoi! Mister Cohen, 1930, by Ralph Stanley & Fred Neville; The Music Pub. Co. Ltd., London.

Yonkle, the Cowboy Jew, 1917, by Will J. Harris & Harry I. Robinson; Will Rossiter Co.

Musical Example Titles

Abie, Dot's Not a Business for You
Ac-cent-chu-ate the Positive
Addio del passato (Farewell to the Past)
Adio querida (Farewell Beloved)
Adonai malakh (God Is King), scale
    representation
Adonai malakh (Psalm 93)
Adoration Response
The Age of Anxiety Symphony, Epilogue
Ahava raba (With Infinite Love) scale
    representation
Ain't We Got Fun?
Am I Blue?
Amado Mio
American Tune
Among My Souvenirs
Anastasia
Anatevka
And the Angels Sing
Anniversary Waltz
Anstatt-dass (Instead Of)
The Apartment Theme
April Showers
Arbaim shana (Forty Years, Psalm 95)
Arias and Barcarolles
Ashrei yoshvei (Happy Are They)
At Last
At the Yiddish Wedding Jubilee
At the Yiddisher Ball
Avreml der marvikher (Avreml, the
    Pickpocket)
Az der Rebe Elimelekh (When Rabbi
    Elimelekh)
Azoy vi du bist (Just As You Are)

The Ballad of Eldorado
The Ballad of the Social Director
Baltimore Oriole
The Band Played On
The Bar Mitzvah Song
Barbara Song
Bashana haba'a (Next Year)
Basin Street Blues
Bay dem shtetl (In the Small Town)
Bay mir bistu sheyn (To Me You Are Pretty)
Der becher (The Goblet)
Begin the Beguine
Bei Mir Bist Du Schoen [alternate spellings]
Belz [name of a Ukrainian shtetl]
Bernie's Tune
Besamé Mucho

Bess, You Is My Woman Now
The Best Thing for You
Blue Room
Blue Skies
Blues in the Night
The Boulevard of Broken Dreams
A brif tsum liader rebn (A Letter to the
    Liady Rabbi)
Brother, Can You Spare a Dime?

Call to the Torah
Can't Help Lovin' Dat Man
Carioca
A Certain Smile
Chazn oyf shabes (1) (A Cantor on the
    Sabbath)
Chazn oyf shabes (2)
Chichester Psalms, Mvts. I & III
The Coffee in the Army (Campfire song)
Come Rain or Come Shine
Comes Love
El Condor Pasa

Dayeinu (It Is Enough)
Les deux hommes d'armes (Two Soldiers)
Diga-Diga-Doo
Dona, Dona
Don't Send Me Back to Petrograd
Dorogoy dlinoyu (On That Highway)
"Double" Concerto (Concerto for Violin
    and Violoncello with Orchestra, Op.
    102, Brahms)
Dovid un Ester (David and Esther)
Dream Tango
A Dudele (A Thou Song)
Dundai
Dybbuk, Mvts. I & II

Eili, Eili (My God, My God)
Eitz chayim (Tree of Life)
Eitz harimon (Pomegranate Tree)
Embraceable You
The *Exodus* Song

"Fanfares" from *Candide*
Farewell, Amanda
Fascinating Rhythm
Father Abraham
Fiddler on the Roof Theme
For Every Man There's a Woman
Forty-Second Street

The Four Questions
Freylekh [joyful dance]
Freylekh, Romanian-Serbian

Di fir kashes (The Four Questions)
Di gantse velt iz a teater (The Whole World
    Is a Theater)
Gay Caballero
A Gay Ranchero
Get Happy
Geyt a goy in shenkl arayn (A Gentile Goes
    into a Tavern)
A Gift Today (The Bar Mitzvah Song)
The Glory of Love
God Supreme
Golden Earrings
Goldene oyringn (Golden Earrings)
Gone with the Wind Theme
Goodbye, Little Dream, Goodbye
Goodnight Sweetheart
Gootmon Is a Hootmon Now
Got un zayn mishpet (God and His
    Judgment)
The Green Leaves of Summer
Di grine kuzine (The Green Female Cousin)
A Guy Is a Guy

Haftarah (Conclusion)
Hallelujah
Hamavdil (Separation)
Hashiveinu (Cause Us to Lie Down)
Hatikvah (The Hope)
Havu ladonai (Ascribe Unto God, Psalm 29)
Haynt iz Purim (Today Is Purim)
Hello
Hernando's Hideaway
High Noon
Hootchy-Kootchy Dance
How Deep Is the Ocean?

I Feel Like I'm Not Out of Bed Yet
I Hear a Rhapsody
I Met a Girl
If I Were a Rich Man
Ikh hob dikh lib (I'm in Love with You)
Ikh kum yetst fun mayn tsadik (I Just Came
    Back from My Guru)
I'll Be Glad When You're Dead
I'll Build a Stairway to Paradise
I'll Open the Door and Close the Door
I'm a Fool to Want You
In exitu Israel (When Israel Went Out,
    Psalm 114)
Is You Is, or Is You Ain't?
The Isle of Capri
It Ain't Necessarily So
It Only Happens When I Dance with You
It's Fate, Baby

It's Only a Paper Moon

Jake! Jake! The Yiddisher Ball-Player
Jeremiah Symphony, Mvts. I and III
The Jews Have Got Their Irish Up
Joseph, Joseph
Jubilee Games, Mvt. I
Jungle Rose

Kaddish (Sanctification) response
Kaddish Symphony, finale
Kalaniyot (Anemones)
Kazatsky or *Kazatska* [Ukrainian dance]
Kazbeck
Kedusha (Sanctification) Response
A khazn oyf shabes (A Cantor on the
    Sabbath)
Khosn kale mazl tov (Congratulations to the
    Bride and Groom)
Kh'vel shoyn mer nisht ganvenen (I Will No
    Longer Steal)
Kiddush (Sanctification over wine,
    Lewandowski)
Kiddush (Weill)
Kirpitchiki (Little Bricks)
Kol nidrei (All Vows)
Koyft a paper (Buy a Paper)
Kum, Lebke, tantsn (Come, Lebke, Dance)
Kyrie eleison (Lord Have Mercy)

Lawd, You Made the Night Too Long
Lebedik gevandert (Happily I Strolled)
Leonora
Let Me Entertain You
Let Us Adore
Let Yourself Go
Little Egypt Theme
Little Threepenny Music
L'moledet-imah (To the Motherland)
Lonely House
The Look of Love
Love for Sale
Love Is Where You Find It
Love Me to a Yiddisha Melody
Love Thy Neighbor
Luck Be a Lady
Lulu-lulinkee (or *Pipi-pipipee*)

Magnetic Rag
Mah nishtano (Why Is This Different)
Maine Stein Song
Makin' Whoopee
Di mame kokht varenikes (Mama Is Cooking
    Dumplings)
Marche Slav Theme
Maria
Marry a Yiddisher Boy
Mashuga
Mass, Pax: Communion (Bernstein)

Mattathias
Mayko mashmelon (What Is the Meaning)
Mayn Goldele (My Golden One)
Mazl (Luck)
Mein Gmüt (My Courage)
Melinda
Mi chomocho (Who Is Like You)
Mi sheberach (May He Who Blessed)
Mikitka [man's name]
Mikolot mayim rabim (Above the Voices of
     Many Waters, Psalm 93)
Dem milners trern (The Miller's Tears)
Mimkomo (From His Place)
Mischa, Yascha, Sascha, Toscha
Miserlou
Misod chachomim (With Counsel of the
     Wise)
Mit a nodl (With a Needle)
Mixolydian mode
Momele (Little Mother)
Mona Lisa
The Moon Was Yellow
Der morgn shtern (The Morning Star)
Moshe from Nova Scotia
Mrs. Skeffington Theme
My Chrysanthemum Flower
My Favorite Things
My Heart Belongs to Daddy
My Little Yiddisha Queen
My Man's Gone Now
My One and Only
My Yiddisha Mammy

Nat'an! Nat'an!
Nature Boy
Di naye hagode (The New Haggadah)
Der naye sher (The New Sher/Dance; see
     The Wedding Samba)
Near the Woodland a Girl Is Ploughing
Never Said a Mumbalin' Word
The New Suit (a.k.a. Zipper Fly)
New York, New York
Night Shall Be Filled with Music
Nokh a bisl (A Bit More)
Notre Dame Victory March
Numa ferach (Sleep My Flower)

Ochila lael (I Will Hope in God)
The Odd Couple Theme
Oh Lawd, I'm on My Way
Oh, What a Beautiful Mornin'
Oi, nie khody, Hrytsiu (Do Not Go,
     Gregory)
Old King Cole
Omar Rabi Elozor (Rabbi Elazar Said)
Once Too Often
Ot geyt Yankele
Otchi chornyia (Dark Eyes)
Our Director

Out of This World
Over the Rainbow
Overture to Candide
Oy iz dus a meydl (Wow, What a Girl)
Oyfn pripetshik (In the Fireplace)

Padam
Palesteena
Paper Moon
Papirosn (Cigarettes)
The Passion According to St. Matthew,
     Chorale
Piano Concerto in C Minor, K.491
Piano Prelude No. 2 (Gershwin)
The Piccolino
Pipi-pipipee (or *Lulu-lulinkee*)
Poker Chant
Porgy's Theme
Proteger le repos de villes (Protect the Peace
     of the Villages) (See *Les deux hommes
     d'armes*)
Psalms 29, 93, 95, 97, 114
Put the Blame on Mame
Puttin' on the Ritz

Quien será

Rajah Bimmy
Rakhem (Be Merciful)
Reader's *Kaddish*
Der rebe hot geheysn freylekh zayn (The
     Rabbi Has Told Us to Make Merry)
Der rebe iz a baalmelochoh (The Rabbi Is a
     Master of His Craft)
Rebecca
Der rebes nigele (The Rabbi's Little Song)
The Return of the Gay Caballero
Reviewing the Situation
Riff
Roll out the Barrel
Ronde de Florette
A Room without Windows
Roszhinkes mit mandlen (Raisins with
     Almonds)
Russian Doll
Russian Lullaby

The Saga of Jenny
Sam, You Made the Pants Too Long
Sautons valsons (Whirl in Waltzes) (See
     Ronde de Florette)
Send in the Clowns
Shalom chaverim (So Long Friends)
Sham'ah vatismach tziyon (Zion Heard and
     Was Glad, Psalm 97)
Shave and a Haircut
Sheyn vi di l'vone (Beautiful as the Moon)
Shine on Harvest Moon
Shir hashirim (The Song of Songs)

Yidl mitn fidl (Little Jew with a Fiddle)
Yome, Yome [Little Benjamin?]
Yonkle, the Cowboy Jew
A yor ersht nokh mayn khasene (Only One
     Year after My Wedding)
Yossel, Yossel (Joseph, Joseph)
You and the Night and the Music
You Did It!
You'd Be So Nice to Come Home To
Young People's Concert No. 43, "Quiz,
     How Musical Are You?"
You're Breaking My Heart

Zokharti lokh (I Recall You, see *Rakhem)*
Zol zayn (Let It Be)
Der zumer iz gekumen (Summer Is Here)

Acknowledgments

ACCESS TO A WIDE-RANGING, multifaceted set of disciplines was needed to spank this book into existence: knowledge of the Yiddish and Hebrew languages, as well as Russian and other tongues; familiarity with Broadway, Hollywood, and Yiddish theater musical history, along with the pop song literature of Tin Pan Alley; an understanding of Yiddish folk songs, Hazanut, and other areas of synagogue practice; some awareness of jazz, its offshoots and its practitioners; an overview of symphonic and other concert repertoire; at least a passing acquaintance with the sociopolitical history of the Jewish people; and, finally, the ability to have both a compositional and a musicological insight into the structure of music.

Would that I had the polymathic brain to grasp and interpret this vast repository of information. I do not; but I have been fortunate in having friends and colleagues, and in finding strangers via E-mail, snail mail, and by phone, who have been bountiful with their time, energy, and wisdom. My gratitude is extended to them all, as it is to family members: my siblings David and Irene, never "rivals" and always supportive of my musical aspirations; my cousins Sylvia Barchenko Liff and Sonny Warsett (on my father's side) and Sandie Melamed (on my mother's side); and, in particular, my beloved late brother-in-law, Judge Jair S. Kaplan.

The following names, listed alphabetically, are among all the many others without whose "etc." the "etc." would not be "etc." They have contributed to this study in varying ways, large and small. The many citations of "the late," preceding some names, attest to the years devoted to this study. Affiliations given in parentheses were valid at the time of my contact.

Mary Ahern (who hosted a dinner party for me after the lecture I delivered at the Library of Congress), the late Shalom Altman (of Gratz College, where I first saw "Yingish" sheet music), Milton Babbitt (esoteric theorist-composer and enthusiast of popular music).

Ruth and the late Neil Baudhuin (my pals), the late Cantor Ben Zion Belfer and his wife, Florence, Rex Bills (Golden Age Radio), Gerald Bordman (re Jerome Kern), Cantor Richard Botton (coperformer), Joachim Braun (musicologist, Tel Aviv University), Jerome Bunke (Digital Force recordings).

The late Sammy Cahn (the lyricist), Nico Castel (opera singer and Ladino music historian), Schuyler Chapin (Commissioner of Culture, New York City), Ted Chapin (Head of the Rodgers and Hammerstein Organization), Michael Cogswell (Director of the Louis Armstrong Archive, Queens College, New York), Abraham Cohen (Manager of the Israel Philharmonic Orchestra), Robert Cornell (computer programmer), Cantor Don Croll (coperformer), Steven Culbertson (Subito Music Corp.).

Author Christopher Davis (nephew of Marc Blitzstein), Chip Deffaa (pop music author and critic)

Paul Epstein, Esq., Dorothy Etkin (niece of Nellie Casman), the late David Ewen (chronicler of American music).

Frank Fain (Sammy Fain's son), Al Feilich (former BMI vice-president), the late Leonard Feist (National Music Publisher Association), Michael Feinstein (entertainer and Gershwin expert), John Forbes (Boosey & Hawkes, Inc., who rescued me from the recondite intricacies of the ©Score music notation computer system), Betty Fox (daughter of Joseph Rumshinsky), Richard Freed (music critic), Robert and Molly Freedman (Jewish Recorded Music Archive, now housed at the University of Pennsylvania).

Gina Genova (musicologist and indispensable in preparing the manuscript for publication), the late Sylvia Goldstein, Esq. (Boosey & Hawkes, Inc.), Cantor Isaac Goodfriend, Eric Gordon (Marc Blitzstein biographer), Sandra Gorney (concerning her late husband, composer Jay Gorney), Emil Gorovets (Yiddish singer).

Diana Haskell (Newberry Library, Chicago), Jonathan Herzog, Esq. (my lawyer), William Holab (Computer Music Services), Elliot Hurwitt (W. C. Handy scholar).

William Josephson (lawyer and booster), John Joyce (New York Times clipping service), Janet Jurist and Morris Grossman (perceptive readers).

Donald Kahn (Gus's son), Brooks Kerr (stride pianist and jazz expert), Sue Klein (Boosey & Hawkes, Inc. and a fiendish Scrabble player), Barry Kleinbort (composer and music theater history aficionado), Alexander Knapp (Oxford University, Ernest Bloch authority), Mark Korn (MCA-Leeds Music), the Kurt Weill Foundation (with thanks to David Farneth, Kim Kowalke, and David Stein).

The three Robert L's who have been officers of the New York Sheet Music Society (the late Robert Lachman, Robert Lippet, and Robert Lissauer), Michael Leavitt (wise counselor and manager for the lecture-entertainment version of this book).

Robert Mandel (peripatetic university press director), the late Dr. Jacob R. Marcus (American Jewish Archives), the late songwriter Gerald Marks, Pablo Martin (my superb engineer at Digital Force), Dan McCall (sheet music collector), Frankie McCormack (Songwriters Hall of Fame), Paul McKibbins (Director of Publications, Rilting Music, Inc.), the late Stefan Mengelberg, Esq. (conductor, mathematician, and my loyal lawyer), Larry Moore (Theater Books of New York), David Morton (UCLA Library), the late Richard Neumann (Music Director, New York Board of Jewish Education and partisan of my work).

Velvel Pasternak (Tara Publications), the late Molly Picon (inimitable star of the Yiddish stage), Pat Proschina (Balch Institute, Philadelphia).

John and Ruth Rauch (Center for Jewish Culture and Creativity), the late Sylvia Regan (playwright and wife of composer Abraham Ellstein), Fenton Remick (concerning his grandfather, Tin Pan Alley publisher Jerome Remick), Irene Retford (Schauer Music Publishers, for input on European music publishers), Dana Richardson (for translations), the late John W. Ripley of Topeka, Kansas (illustrated song slide collector), Mary Rodgers Guettel (songwriter, Richard Rodgers's daughter), Ned Rorem (prodigious composer and author), Ben Roth (player piano roll collector), Robert Rothstein (Amherst University).

The late Robert Saudek (Chief, Motion Picture, Broadcasting, and Recorded Sound Division, Library of Congress), Edwin Seroussi (Israeli musicologist), the late William Simon (New York Sheet Music Society), Richard Slade and Cynthia Reynolds (for computer expertise), Stephen Sondheim (the one and only), Francis Squibb (Jazz Archive, Tulane University), Steven Sturk (church music scholar).

Michael Tilson Thomas (distinguished conductor and grandson of Boris Thomashevsky), Caldwell Titcomb (musicologist and theater specialist).

The late Eric Werner (preeminent Jewish musicologist), Ruth Wheat (B'nai Brith Lecture Bureau), Anita Willens (daughter of Alexander Olshanetsky), the late Cantor Max Wohlberg (Dean of American cantors, Jewish Theological Seminary), Judd Woldin (composer and pianist), Howard Wolverton ("coon" song collector).

Helen Yablokoff (daughter-in-law of Herman Yablokoff), the late Lucille Yellen (for her husband, composer Jack Yellen), and the late Wolf Younin (Yiddish poet).

In this age of fingertip information on the Internet, old-fashioned libraries have still proven to be equally invaluable. In my case, they include the libraries of Indiana University and of the University of Southern Mississippi, where I was free to roam the stacks; and the full range of the New York Public Library, its local branches, the Performing Arts Division at Lincoln Center, the main branch at 42nd Street, the annex at West 43rd Street, and the uncommon Schomburg Center for Research in Black Culture at 135th Street. For providing me access to rare recordings by African-American performers, I am most grateful to Director Dan Morgenstern and Librarian Vincent Pelote of the exceptional Institute of Jazz Studies at Rutgers University, Newark. Dr. Philip E. Miller, Librarian of Hebrew Union College-Jewish Institute of Religion, was always available to assist me with translations and crucial abstruse data. Other archival resources I have used consisted of reference files at ASCAP (American Society for Composers, Authors, and Publishers, with thanks to Michael Spudic, who cleared a path through the thick jungle of copyright ascriptions), BMI (Broadcast Music, Inc. and its former President, Edward Cramer), and the good people at the New York Philharmonic Archives: Barbara Haws, Richard Wandel, and intern Bernard Behling.

Broadway theater has often been dubbed "The Fabulous Invalid" and like the Yiddish language, it has been perpetually dying. But Yiddish culture will never fade with YIVO, the Institute for Jewish Research, as its advocate. YIVO offered me the riches of its Sound Archive (headed by Lorin Sklamberg) and, most of all, it gave me access to the abundant erudition of musicologist Eleanor (Chana) Mlotek. My deep gratitude goes to her and her conductor-pianist son Zalmen, who keeps Yiddish theater alive. Mlotek means "hammer" in Polish (Macabee in Hebrew). With them I was like the blind man who said: "I see," after he picked up the hammer and saw.

In 1983, Sarah Blacher Cohen, author, playwright, and Professor of English at State University of New York, invited me to do my first lecture on this subject matter for a Modern Language Association of America convention. It was she who cajoled me with persistent advocacy into completing the book. James H. Peltz, Editor-in-Chief of SUNY Press, and has stood by me through thick and thicker. It has been a singular delight to work with him and his enthusiastic staff.

The Library of Congress offer to copublish this book was an unexpected gift of the gods. Working with the team of Iris Bodin Newsom—my indomitable, intrepid, and indefatigable editor—and Jon Newsom, Chief of the Music Division, has truly been a joy. Along with research virtuoso Ruth J. Foss, they have become my boosters and friends. In the early stages of investigation, the Music Division helped me uncover the Jewish ethnic novelty songs that became a basic resource for my work, and I am indebted to Elizabeth Auman, Donor Relations Specialist, James Pruett, former chief, and Raymond White. Samuel Brylawski, head of the Recorded Sound Section, was also most helpful in the early stages of this project. Others at the Library who have given of their time and skills include: Ralph Eubanks, Director of Publishing, Stephen Kraft, designer, who in his eighties has the keenest eye ever, Walter Zvonchenko, research sleuth, and Michael W. Grunberger, Head of the Hebraic Section.

A corner of my heart is occupied by Max Helfman, my first composition teacher. My inner ear still rings with Max's impassioned singing of Moses Milner's classic Yiddish song "In kheder" (In the Classroom), out of which he magically spun the chanting of the Hebrew alphabet into Gershwin's "Summertime." That lesson planted the seeds for this study.

My colleagues, past and present, at the Leonard Bernstein Office, Inc. (formerly the Amberson Group, Inc.), the company that manages Bernstein's multifaceted legacy, could consistently be counted on for their computer talents and for their patience and understanding. They include Maria Bedo, Marie Carter, Rita Davidsen, Charlie Harmon, Harry Kraut, the late Louis Landerson, Esq., Dan Shiffman, Garth Sunderland, Craig Urquhart, and intern Yiyun Wang.

I am forever thankful to Leonard Bernstein—my late daily and dearly lamented teacher, friend, and boss—who not only gave me the leisure to work on this book, but whose teachings have influenced it directly and in not so subtle ways. He read an early draft, and you can be sure his red editorial pencil bled profusely on its pages. In 1969 he made a gift to me of Idelsohn's ten-volume *Treasury of Hebrew-Oriental Melodies* which has proven to be invaluable. His note to me said: "The volumes are my gift to you, with blessings and wishes for you to make great use of them. Amen. L." Thirty-odd years later, I can honestly say: "I have, Maestro, I have."

I am deeply honored that the legacies of three iconic American-Jewish composers helped to fund this publication with generous grants: The Leonard Bernstein Family Foundation, Inc. (Alexander S. Bernstein, President), The Aaron Copland Fund For Music, Inc.(James M. Kendrick, Esq., Secretary), and The Leonore and Ira Gershwin Trust for the Benefit of the Library of Congress. Modesty aside, I believe the immortals would have all been pleased.

Not everyone I approached was happy to cooperate, clearly uncomfortable with my premise that one's Jewishness could have a bearing on creativity. In trying to resolve conflicting evidence about Rudolf Friml's Jewishness, in December 1988 I phoned Robert Wright, of Wright and Forrest fame, who had worked with Friml on the song "Donkey Serenade." His response was: "What has that got to do with music?"[1] The late Irving Caesar was willing to meet with me, but I was told that he was righteously indignant that questions about a songwriter's Jewish background would even be asked.

Mark Twain once said: "All things are mortal but the Jew; all other forces pass, but he remains. What is the secret of his immortality?"[2] Trying to uncover the layers of this secret in terms of music has sometimes led me astray. I would have been left in the dark were it not for the illuminating insights of so many helpful guides. My apologies to anyone whose name I may have inadvertently omitted. All interpretations of received information, errors of judgment, factual mistakes, and the responsibility for gremlins not found in proffreading, are, of course, mine alone.

NOTES

1. Claims that Rudolf Friml was Jewish are found in *The Universal Jewish Encyclopedia*, p. 1059; Saleski, *Famous Musicians of a Wandering Race*, but other sources do not confirm this. Milton Babbitt recalls that when Max Dreyfus was upset with Friml, he disparagingly referred to Friml's Jewish background.

2. Mark Twain, *Harper's Monthly*, September 1899. See *The Complete Essays of Mark Twain*, p. 249.

Bibliography

Autobiographies, Biographies, and Memoirs

Armstrong, Louis, Dan Morgenstern, Introduction. *Satchmo: My Life in New Orleans.* New York: Prentice Hall, 1954.

Bach, Steven. *Dazzler: The Life and Times of Moss Hart.* New York: Alfred A. Knopf, 2001.

Bailey, Pearl. *The Raw Pearl.* New York: Harcourt Brace Jovanovich, 1968.

Barrett, Mary Ellin. *Irving Berlin: A Daughter's Memoir.* New York: Limelight Editions, 1996.

Berg, A. Scott. *Goldwyn: A Biography.* New York: Alfred A. Knopf, Inc., 1989.

Bergreen, Laurence. *As Thousands Cheer: The Life of Irving Berlin.* New York: Viking Penguin, 1990.

————. *Louis Armstrong: An Extravagant Life.* New York: Broadway Books, 1997.

Berle, Milton, with Haskel Frankel. *Milton Berle: An Autobiography.* New York: Delacorte Press, 1974.

Berlin, Edward A. *King of Ragtime: Scott Joplin and His Era.* New York: Oxford University Press, 1994.

Bernardi, Jack. *My Father the Actor.* Foreword by Herschel Bernardi. New York: W.W. Norton, 1971.

Berrett, Joshua, ed. *The Louis Armstrong Companion.* New York: Schirmer Books, 1999.

Biancolli, Amy. *Fritz Kreisler: Love's Sorrow, Love's Joy.* Portland, Oregon: Amadeus Press, 1998.

Bordman, Gerald. *Days to Be Happy, Years to Be Sad: The Life and Music of Vincent Youmanns.* Oxford University Press, 1982.

Burton, Humphrey. *Leonard Bernstein.* New York: Doubleday, 1994.

Cahn, Sammy. *I Should Care.* New York: Arbor House, 1974.

Calloway, Cab, with Bryant Rollins. *Of Minnie the Moocher and Me.* New York: Thomas Y. Crowell Co., 1976.

Cantor, Eddie, as told to David Freedman. *My Life Is in Your Hands.* New York: Harper & Bros., 1928.

Carner, Gary, ed. *The Miles Davis Companion: Four Decades of Commentary.* New York: Schirmer Books, 1996.

Channing, Carol. *Just Lucky I Guess.* New York: Simon & Schuster, 2002.

Chaplin, Saul. *The Golden Age of Movie Musicals and Me.* Norman, Oklahoma: University of Oklahoma Press, 1994.

Colin, Sid. *Ella: The Life and Times of Ella Fitzgerald.* London: Elm Tree Books, 1986.

Comden, Betty. *Off Stage.* New York: Simon & Schuster, 1995.

Coslow, Sam. *Cocktails for Two.* New Rochelle, New York: Arlington House, 1977.

Coward, Noël. *Present Indicative.* Garden City, New York: Doubleday, 1937.

Davis, Jr., Sammy, with Jane and Burt Bryan. *Why Me?: The Sammy Davis, Jr. Story.* New York: Farrar, Strauss and Giroux, 1989.

————. *Yes I Can: The Story of Sammy Davis, Jr.* New York: Farrar, Strauss and Giroux, 1965.

Davis, Tracey, with Dolores A. Barclay. *Sammy Davis, Jr.: My Father.* Los Angeles: Gen. Pub. Group, Inc., 1996.

Douglas, Kirk. *The Ragman's Son.* New York: Pocket Books, 1988.

Drew, David. *The Kurt Weill Handbook.* Berkeley and Los Angeles: University of California Press, 1987.

Eells, George. *Cole Porter: The Life That Late He Led.* New York: G.P. Putnam's Sons, 1967.

Ellington, Edward "Duke" Kennedy. *Music Is My Mistress.* Garden City, New York: Doubleday, 1973; Da Capo, 1985.

Ewen, David. *A Journey to Greatness: The Life and Music of George Gershwin.* New York: Henry Holt & Co., 1956.

Fecher, Charles A., ed. *The Diary of H. L. Mencken.* New York: Alfred A. Knopf, 1989.

Feinstein, Michael. *Nice Work If You Can Get It: My Life in Rhythm and Rhyme.* New York: Hyperion, 1995.

Fisher, Eddie. *My Life, My Loves.* New York: Harper & Row, 1981.

Freedland, Michael. *Al Jolson.* London: Abacus, 1975.

————. *Irving Berlin.* New York: Stein and Day, 1978.

Furia, Philip, with Graham Wood. *Ira Gershwin: The Art of the Lyricist.* New York: Oxford University Press, 1996.

——————. *Irving Berlin: A Life in Song*. New York: Schirmer Books, 1998.

Giddins, Gary. *Bing Crosby: A Pocketful of Dreams—The Early Years, 1903-1904*. New York: Little, Brown, and Company, 2001.

——————. *Satchmo*. New York: Doubleday, 1985.

Goldberg, Isaac. *George Gershwin: A Study in American Music*. New York: Simon and Schuster, 1931; Frederick Ungar Publishing Co., 1958.

Goldman, Albert. *Elvis*. New York: Avon Books, 1981.

Gordon, Eric A. *Mark the Music: The Life and Work of Marc Blitzstein*. New York: St. Martin's Press, 1989.

Gottlieb, Polly Rose. *The Nine Lives of Billy Rose*. New York: Crown Publishers, 1968.

Greenberg, Rodney. *George Gershwin*. London: Twentieth Century Composers Series, Phaidon Press, 1998.

Hamlisch, Marvin, with Gerald Gardiner. *The Way I Was*. New York: Charles Scribner's Sons, 1992.

Haskins, Jim. *The Cotton Club*. New York: Random House, 1977.

Hershfield, Harry. *Laugh Louder, Live Longer*. New York: Gramercy Publishing, 1959.

Holiday, Billie, with William Dufty. *Lady Sings the Blues*. New York: Doubleday & Co., 1956.

Horne, Lena, with Richard Schickel. *Lena*. Garden City, New York: Doubleday & Co., 1965.

Jablonski, Edward. *Alan Jay Lerner*. New York: Henry Holt & Co., 1996.

——————. *Gershwin*. New York: Doubleday, 1987.

——————. *Gershwin Remembered*. Portland, Oregon: Amadeus Press, 1992.

——————. *Harold Arlen: Happy with the Blues*. New York: Doubleday, 1961.

——————. *Irving Berlin, American Troubadour*. Henry Holt & Co., 1999.

Jessel, George, with John Austin. *The World I Lived In*. Chicago: Henry Regnery Co., 1975.

Katkov, Norman. *The Fabulous Fanny: The Story of Fanny Brice*. New York: Alfred A. Knopf, 1952.

Lawrence, Greg. *Dance with Demons: The Life of Jerome Robbins*. New York: Putnam, 2001.

Lawrence, Jerome. *Actor: The Life and Times of Paul Muni*. London: W.H. Allen, 1974.

Lerner, Alan Jay. *The Street Where I Live*. New York: W.W. Norton & Co., 1978.

Levant, Oscar. *The Unimportance of Being Oscar*. New York: G. P. Putnam's Sons, 1968.

Liszt, Franz. *The Gipsy in Music*. Translation by Edwin Evans. London: William Reeves, no date given.

Marx, Groucho. *The Groucho Letters*. New York: Simon & Schuster, 1967.

McBrien, William. *Cole Porter: A Biography*. New York: Alfred A. Knopf, 1998.

McCabe, John. *Cagney*. New York: Alfred A. Knopf, 1997.

——————. *George M. Cohan: The Man Who Owned Broadway*. New York: Da Capo Press, 1973.

McGuire, Patricia Dubin. *Lullaby of Broadway: Life and Times of Al Dubin*. Secaucus: Citadel Press, 1983.

Meeropol, Robert and Michael. *We Are Your Sons: The Legacy of Ethel and Julius Rosenberg*. Boston: Houghton-Mifflin Co., 1975.

Meyerson, Harold and Ernie Harburg. *Who Put the Rainbow in The Wizard of Oz?: Yip Harburg, Lyricist*. Ann Arbor: The University of Michigan Press, 1993.

Milstein, Nathan, with Solmon Volkov. *From Russia to the West: Musical Memoirs and Reminiscences*. New York: Henry Holt & Co., 1990.

Payne, Robert. *Gershwin*. London: Robert Hale, Ltd., 1960.

Picon, Molly, with Jean Grillo. *Molly!* New York: Simon & Schuster, 1980.

Pollack, Howard. *Aaron Copland: The Life and Work of an Uncommon Man*. New York: Henry Holt, 1999.

Pyron, Darden Ashbury. *Liberace, An American Boy*. Chicago: The University of Chicago Press, 2000.

Rodgers, Dorothy. *A Personal Book*. New York: Harper & Row, 1977.

Rodgers, Richard. *Musical Stages*. New York: Random House, 1975.

Rosenberg, Bernard and Ernest Goldstein, eds. *Creators and Disturber:, Reminiscences by Jewish Intellectuals of New York*. New York: Columbia University Press, 1982.

Rosenfeld, Lulla. *Bright Star of Exile: Jacob Adler and the Yiddish Theatre*. New York: Thomas Y. Crowell Co., 1977.

——————, translator and commentator. *Jacob Adler, A Life on the Stage*: *A Memoir*. New York: Alfred A. Knopf, 1999.

Rumshinsky, Joseph. *Klangen fun Mayn Lebn* (Sounds from My Life). New York: Biderman, 1944.

Sanders, Ronald. *The Days Grow Short: The Life and Music of Kurt Weill*. New York: Limelight Editions, 1980.

Schwartz, Charles. *Gershwin, His Life and Music*. Indianapolis: Bobbs-Merrill Co., Inc., 1973.

Secrest, Meryle. *Somewhere for Me: A Biography of Richard Rodgers*. New York: Alfred A. Knopf, 2001.

Secunda, Victoria. *Bei Mir Bist Du Schön: The Life of Sholom Secunda*. New York: Magic Circle Press, 1982.

Smith, Willie "The Lion," with George Hoefer. *Music on My Mind: The Memoirs of an American Pianist*. New York: Da Capo Press, 1975.

Sudhalter, Richard M. *Stardust Melody: The Life and Music of Hoagy Carmichael*. New York: Oxford University Press, 2002.

Suriano, Gregory R., ed., Foreword by Marvin Hamlisch. *Gershwin in His Time: A Biographical Scrapbook, 1919-1937*. New York: Gramercy Books, 1998.

Thomas, Bob. *King Cohn: The Life and Times of Harry Cohn*. New York: G. P. Putnam's Sons, 1967.

Tiomkin, Dimitri, with Prosper Buranelli. *Please Don't Hate Me*. Garden City, New York.: Doubleday & Co., 1959.

Tucker, Sophie, with Dorothy Giles. *Some of These Days*. Garden City, New York: Doubleday, Doran & Co., 1945.

Twain, Mark, "Concerning the Jews," *Harpers Magazine* (September 1899), reprinted in *The Complete Essays of Mark Twain.*, ed. Charles Neider. New York: Doubleday, 1963.

Waters, Ethel, with Charles Samuels. *His Eye Is on the Sparrow*. New York: Da Capo Press, 1951.

Werner, Eric, translated from the German by Dika Newlin. *Mendelssohn: A New Image of the Composer and His Age*. London: Collier-Macmillan, 1963.

Wilson, Mary, with Patricia Romanowski and Ahrgus Juilliard. *Dreamgirl: My Life as a Supreme*. New York: St. Martin's Press, 1986.

Wood, Ean. *The Josephine Baker Story*. London: Sanctuary Publishing, Ltd., 2000.

Yablokoff, Herman. *Arum der Welt Mit Yidish Teater* (Around the World with Yiddish Theater). New York: Workmen's Circle, 1969. Reprinted in English as *Der Payatz* (The Clown), translated by Bella Mysell Yablokoff. Silver Spring, Maryland: Bartleby Press, 1995. Excerpted in Joseph C. Landis, ed., *Memoirs of the Yiddish Stage* (Flushing, New York: Queens College Press, 1984), pp. 156-199.

Ziegfeld, Patricia. *The Ziegfelds' Girl*. Boston: Little, Brown & Co., 1964.

African-American Studies

Allen, Walter L. *Hendersonia: The Music of Fletcher Henderson and His Musicians: A Bio-Discography*. Highland Park: Jazz Monographs no. 4, 1973.

Berman, Paul. *Blacks and Jews: Alliances and Arguments*. New York: Delacorte Press, 1994.

Boyer, Horace Clarence. *How Sweet the Sound: The Golden Age of Gospel*. Washington, D.C.: Elliot & Clark Publishing Co.

Caldwell, Hansonia L. *African American Music: A Chronology 1619-1995*. Los Angeles: Ikoio Communications, Inc., 1996.

Denison, Sam. *Scandalize My Name: Black Imagery in American Popular Music*. New York: Garland Publishing Co., 1982.

Ely, Melvin Patrick. *The Adventures of Amos 'n' Andy*. New York: The Free Press, 1991.

Floyd, Samuel A., Jr., ed. *Black Music and the Harlem Renaissance*. Knoxville: The University of Tennessee Press, 1990.

Giddins, Gary. *Riding on a Blue Note: Jazz and American Pop*. New York: Oxford University Press, 1981.

Haskins, Jim. *The Cotton Club*. New York: Random House, 1977.

Locke, Alain. *The Negro and His Music*. Albany: The Associates in Negro Folk Education, 1936; New York: Arno Press and the *New York Times*, 1969.

————. *The New Negro*. New York: Arno Press and the *New York Times*, 1968.

Lott, Eric. *Love and Theft: Blackface, Minstrelsy, and the American Working Class*. New York: Oxford University Press, 1993.

Machlin, Paul S. *Stride: The Music of Fats Waller*. Boston: Twayne Publishers, 1985.

Melnick, Jeffrey. *Ancestors and Relatives: The Uncanny Relationship of African Americans and Jews*. PhD, Harvard University, 1994.

————. *A Right to Sing the Blues: African Americans, Jews, and American Popular Song*. Cambridge: Harvard University Press, 1999.

Peterson, Bernard L., Jr.. *Early Black American Playwrights and Dramatic Writers: A Biographical Directory and Catalog of Plays, Films, and Broadcasting Scripts*. New York: Greenwood Press, 1990.

Sampson, Henry T. *Blacks in Blackface: A Source Book on Early Black Musical Shows*. Metuchen, New Jersey: The Scarecrow Press, Inc. 1980.

Schiffman, Jack. *Uptown: The Story of Harlem's Apollo Theatre*. New York: Cowles Book Co., 1971.

Williams, Iain Cameron. *Underneath a Harlem Moon: The Harlem to Paris Years of Adelaide Hall*.

London: Continuum, 2002.

Wohl, Allen. *Black Musical Theater: From Coontown to Dreamgirls*. Baton Rouge: Louisiana State University Press, 1989.

Encyclopedias and Other Reference Works

Abravanel, Maurice. "Recollections," *Kurt Weill Newsletter* 5.1, 1987.

The ASCAP Biographical Dictionary, 4th ed. New York: ASCAP, 1980.

Ausubel, Nathan. *The Book of Jewish Knowledge*. New York: Crown Publishers, Inc., 1964.

——. *A Treasury of Jewish Folklore, Stories, Traditions, Legends, Humor, Wisdom, and Folk Songs of the Jewish People*. New York: Crown Publishers, Inc., 1948.

Bartlett, John. *Bartlett's Familiar Quotations*. Boston: Little, Brown & Co., 15th ed.,1980.

Bloom, Eric, ed. *A Dictionary of Music and Musicians*, 5th ed., 9 vols. New York: St. Martins Press, 1954.

Bloom, Ken. *American Song: The Complete Musical Theatre Companion.*, vols. 1 & 2. New York: Facts on File Publications, 1985.

Braun, Joachim. *Jews and Jewish Elements in Soviet Music: A Study of a Socio-National Problem in Music*. Tel Aviv: Israeli Music Publications, Ltd., 1978.

Carlson, Ralph, ed. dir. *American Jewish Desk Reference*. New York: Random House, for the American Jewish Historical Society, 1999.

Downey, James C. and Paul Oliver. "Spiritual," *The New Grove Dictionary of Music and Musicians*, ed. Stanley Sadie, vol.18. London: Macmillan Publishers, Ltd., 1980.

Drew, David. "How Was Weill's Success Achieved?" *Kurt Weill Newsletter* 4.2, 1986.

Eskew, Harry and Paul Oliver. "Gospel Music," *The New Grove Dictionary of Music and Musicians*, ed. Stanley Sadie, vol. 7. London: Macmillan Publishers, Ltd., 1980.

Fuld, James. *The Book of World-Famous Music, Classical, Popular and Folk*. Rev. ed. New York: Crown Publishers, Inc., 1971.

Gammond, Peter. *The Oxford Companion to Popular Music*. London: Oxford University Press, 1991.

Harris, Leon. *Merchant Princes: An Intimate History of Jewish Families Who Built Great Department Stores*. New York: Harper & Row, 1977.

Hummel, David. *The Collector's Guide to the American Musical Theatre*. Metuchen, New Jersey: Scarecrow Press, Inc., 1984.

Jay, Dave. *The Irving Berlin Sonography, 1907-1966*. New Rochelle, New York: Arlington House, 1969.

Lamb, Andrew and Charles Hamm. "Popular Music," *The New Grove Dictionary of Music and Musicians*, ed. Stanley Sadie, vol. 15. London: Macmillan Publishers, Ltd., 1980.

Landau, Ron. *The Book of Jewish Lists*. New York: Stein and Day, 1984.

Larkin, Colin, ed. *The Guinness Encyclopedia of Popular Music*, 6 vols. Middlesex, England: Guinness Publishing, Ltd., 1995.

Levine, Joseph. "Toward Defining the Jewish Prayer Modes: With Particular Emphasis on the *Adonay Malakh* Mode," *Musica Judaica* 3 (1980-1981): 13-32.

Moser, H. J. *Musik Lexicon* [1943]. Reprinted Hamburg: H. Sikorski, 1951.

Nulman, Macy. *Concise Encyclopedia of Jewish Music*. New York: McGraw Hill Book Co., 1975.

Richards, Stanley, ed. *Great Musicals of the American Theatre*, vol. 2. Radnor, Pennsylvania.: Chilton Books Co., 1976.

——. *Ten Great Musicals of the American Theatre*. Radnor, Pennsylvania: Chilton Books Co., 1973.

Roth, Cecil, ed. *Encyclopaedia Judaica*, 18 vols. Jerusalem, New York: Macmillan, 1972-1983, s.v. "Theater," "Music," "Hassidism," "Hazzanim." Reprint edition, New York: Coronet Books, 1994.

Saleski, Gdal. *Famous Musicians of a Wandering Race: Biographical Sketches of Outstanding Figures of Jewish Origin in the Musical World*. New York: Bloch Publishing Co. [1927], 1949.

Sendry, Alfred. *Bibliography of Jewish Music*. New York: Columbia University Press, 1951.

——. *The Universal Jewish Encyclopedia*. [1939-1943], s.v. "Theater," "Music."

Seroussi, Edwin, et al. "Jewish music," *The New Grove Dictionary of Music and Musicians*, 2nd ed. Stanley Sadie, ed, vol. 13. London: Macmillan Publishers, Ltd., 2001.

Shapiro, Nat, ed. *Popular Music: An Annotated Index of American Popular Songs*, 4 vols. [1930-1964]. New York: Adrian Press, 1965.

Singer, Jacob. *The Universal Jewish Encyclopedia* [1939-1943]. s.v. Theater, Music.

Slonimsky, Nicolas, ed. *Baker's Biographical Dictionary of Musicians*, 6th ed. New York: Schirmer Books, 1978.

Stengel, Theophil and Herbert Gerigk, eds. *Lexikon der Juden in der Musik: Mit einem Titelvorzeichnis*

Jüdischer Werke. Berlin: Bernhard Hahnefeld, 1940.

Villiers, Douglas, ed. *Next Year in Jerusalem: Portraits of the Jew in the Twentieth Century.* New York: The Viking Press, 1976.

Werner, Eric. "Jewish Music," *The New Grove Dictionary of Music and Musicians*, ed. Stanley Sadie, vol. 9. London: Macmillan Publishers, Ltd., 1980.

Etymologies

Bratkowsky, Joan G. *Yiddish Linguistics: A Multilingual Bibliography.* New York: Garland Publishing Co., 1988.

Feinsilver, Lillian Mermin. Various articles in *American Speech, The Chicago Jewish Forum, Jewish Heritage,* and *The Jewish Digest.*

Mencken, H. L. *The American Language: An Inquiry Into the Development of English in the United States.* New York: Alfred A. Knopf, 1921 (subsequent editions and supplements 1937-1980).

————. *The Diary of H.L. Mencken.* New York: Alfred A. Knopf, 1989.

Partridge, Eric. *Slang Today and Yesterday.* New York: Macmillan, 1950.

Rosten, Leo. *The Joys of Yiddish.* New York: McGraw-Hill Publishing Co., 1968.

————. *The Joys of Yinglish.* New York: McGraw-Hill Publishing Co., 1989.

Miscellaneous

Adams, Joey, with Henry Tobias. *The Borsht Belt.* New York: Bobbs-Merrill Co., 1966.

Balzell, E. Digby. *The Protestant Establishment Revisited.* New Brunswick, New Jersey: Transaction Publishers, 1991.

Brinkmann, Reinhold and Christoph Wolff, eds. *Driven into Paradise: The Musical Migration from Nazi Germany to the United States.* Berkeley, Los Angeles, and London: University of California Press, 1999.

Epstein, Lawrence J. *That Haunted Smile: The Story of Jewish Comedians in America.* New York: Random House, 2001.

Harmon, Jim. *The Great Radio Comedians.* Garden City, New York: Doubleday & Co., 1970.

Lackman, Ron. *Remember Radio.* New York: G. P. Putnam's Sons, 1970.

Levine, Lawrence. *Highbrow/Lowbrow: The Emergence of Cultural Hierarchy in America.* Cambridge: Harvard University Press, 1988.

Lewis, Thomas P., ed. *An Anthology of Critical Opinion.* White Plains, New York: Pro/Am Music Resources, 1991.

Moore, MacDonald Smith. *Yankee Blues: Musical Culture and American Identity.* Bloomington: Indiana University Press, 1985.

Simon, George T. *The Big Bands.* New York: Macmillan Co., 1967.

Vidal, Gore. *Virgin Islands (Essays 1992-1997).* London: André Deutsch, Ltd., 1997.

Music History, Musicology and Theory

Avenary, Hanoch. "The Concept of Mode in European Synagogue Chant," *Journal of Synagogue Music* 7 (1976): 47-57.

————. *Encounters of East and West in Music.* Tel-Aviv: Tel-Aviv University, 1979.

Beregovski, Moshe. *Old Jewish Folk Music: The Collections and Writings of Moshe Beregovski*, trans. and ed. Mark Slobin. Philadelphia: University of Pennsylvania Press, 1982.

Cohon, Baruch Joseph. "The Structure of the Synagogue Prayer Chant," *Journal of the American Musicological Society* 3 (1950): 17-32.

Forte, Allen. *The American Popular Ballad of the Golden Era, 1924-1950.* Princeton: Princeton University Press, 1995.

————. *Listening to Classic American Popular Songs.* New Haven: Yale University Press, 2001.

Freed, Isadore. *Harmonizing the Jewish Modes.* New York: The Sacred Music Press, 1958.

Gilbert, Steven E. *The Music of Gershwin.* New Haven: Yale University Press, 1995.

Heskes, Irene. *Yiddish American Popular Songs 1895 to 1950: A Catalog Based on the Lawrence Marwick Roster of Copyright Entries.* Washington, D.C.: Library of Congress, 1992.

Holde, Artur. *Jews in Music: From the Age of Enlightenment to the Present.* New York: Philosophical Library, 1959.

Idelsohn, Abraham Zvi. *Jewish Liturgy and Its Development.* New York: Henry Holt & Co., 1932.

————. *Jewish Music in its Historical Development.* New York: Tudor Publishing Co., 1944.

————. "The Kol Nidre Tune," *Journal of Synagogue Music* 3 (1970): 33-49; reprint from Hebrew

Union College Annual, 1931.

Katz, Israel J. "Eric Werner (1901-1988): A Bibliography of His Collected Writings," *Musica Judaica* 10 (1987-1988): 1-36.

Lambert, Constant. *Music Ho!: A Study of Music in Decline*. New York: Scribner, 1934.

Mlotek, Eleanor Gordon. "America in East European Yiddish Folk Song," *Journal of Synagogue Music* 6 (1975): 20-36.

Pasternak, Velvel. *Beyond Hava Nagila: Hasidic Music in 3 Movements*. Owing Mills, Maryland: Tara Publications, 1999.

Rabinovitch, Israel, trans. A. M. Klein. *Of Jewish Music, Ancient and Modern*. Montreal: The Book Center, 1952.

Rubin, Ruth. *Voices of a People: The Story of the Yiddish Folk Song*. New York: Thomas Yoseloff, 1963.

Saminsky, Lazare. *Music of the Ghetto and the Bible*. New York: Bloch Publishing Co., 1934.

Sendry, Alfred. *Music in Ancient Israel*. New York: Philosophical Library, 1969.

————. *The Music of the Jews in the Diaspora (Up to 1800): A Contribution to the Social and Cultural History of the Jews*. New York: Thomas Yoseloff, 1970.

Sendry, Alfred, and Mildred Norton. *David's Harp: The Story of Music in Biblical Times*. New York: New American Library, 1964.

Slobin, Mark. *Chosen Voices: The Story of the American Cantorate*. Urbana: University of Illinois Press, 1989.

————. *Tenement Songs: The Popular Music of the Jewish Immigrants*. Urbana: University of Illinois Press, 1982.

Soltes, Avraham. *Off the Willows: The Rebirth of Modern Jewish Music*. New York: Bloch Publishing Co., 1970.

Somkin, Fred. "Zion's Harp by the East River: Jewish American Popular Songs in Columbus's Golden Land, 1890-1914," *Perspectives in American History*, New Series 2 (1985): 183-220.

Strom, Yale. *The Book of Klezmer: The History, the Music, the Folklore*. Chicago: A Cappella Books, 2002.

Tappert, Wilhelm. *Musikalische Studien*. Berlin: L. Guttentag, 1868.

Weisser, Albert. *The Modern Renaissance of Jewish Music, Events, and Figures: Eastern Europe and America*. New York: Bloch Publishing Co., 1954.

Werner, Eric. "Genealogies of Two Wandering Hebrew Melodies," *Journal of Synagogue Music* 11 (1981): 12-21.

————. *In the Choir Loft*. New York: The Union of American Hebrew Congregations, 1957.

————. *The Sacred Bridge: The Interdependence of Liturgy and Music in Synagogue and Church during the First Millennium*. New York: Columbia University Press, 1960.

————. *The Sacred Bridge: The Interdependence of Liturgy and Music in Synagogue and Church during the First Millennium*, vol. 2. New York: Ktav Publishing House, Inc., 1984.

————. *A Voice Still Heard: The Sacred Songs of the Ashkenazic Jews*. University Park: The Pennsylvania State University Press, 1976.

Wohlberg, Max. "The Hazzanic Recitative," *Musica Judaica* 10 (1987-1988): 40-52.

————. "The History of the Musical Modes of the Ashkenazik Synagogue and Their Usage," [1954] *Journal of Synagogue Music* 4 (1972): 46-61.

————. "The Music of the Synagogue as a Source of the Yiddish Folk Song," *Musica Judaica* 2 (1977-1978): 21-50; reprinted in *MJ* 14 (1999): 33-61.

Prayer Books and Hymnals

Birnbaum, Phillip. *Daily Prayer Book*. New York: Hebrew Publishing Co., 1949.

Campbell-Watson, Frank. *The Catholic Hymnal*. New York: Benziger Editions, 1966.

Central Conference of American Rabbis. *Union Hymnal*. New York, 1932, 1953.

Stern, Chaim, ed. *Gates of Prayer: The New Union Prayerbook*. New York: Central Conference of American Rabbis, 1975.

Song Collections

Algazi, Léon. *Chants Sephardis*. The World Sephardie Foundation, 1958.

Almagor, Gideon, with Moshe Gorali and Moshe Bick. *The Golden Peacock: Yiddish Folk Songs*. Haifa: Haifa Music Museum Library, 1970.

Alter, Israel. *The Sabbath Service*, rev. ed. New York: The Cantors Assembly, 1970.

Baer, Abraham. *Ba-al T'fillah* (Leader in Prayer). Gothenburg, Germany: n.p., 1877;

reprinted in the Out-of-Print Classics Series of Synagogue Music, vol. 1, New York: Sacred Music Press, 1953.

Bart, Jan and William Gunther. *The Yinglish Song Book*. New York: Mills Music, 1964.

Brounoff, Platon. *Yidishe folkslider*. New York, 1911.

Cahan, Yehude Leyb. *Yidishe folkslider mit melodiyes oys dem folksmoyl*, 1912. *Yidishe folkslider: naye zamlungen*, 192719-28. Both collections reprinted in *Yidishe folkslider mit melodiyes*, Max Weinreich, ed. New York: YIVO, 1957.

Camhy, O., ed. *Liturgie Sephardie*. London: Vallentine, Mitchell & Co. for the World Sephardie Foundation, 1959.

Coopersmith, Harry. *Sabbath Service in Song*. New York: Behrman House, Inc., 1955.

—————. *Songs of My People*. Chicago: The Anshe Emet Synagogue, 1937.

—————. *The Songs We Sing*. New York: United Synagogue of America, 1950.

de Butzow, Vladimir. *Nuits Tzigane*. London, New York: Boosey & Hawkes.

Delaney, William W. *Delaney's Song Book* (nos. 1-89), lyrics only. New York: Variety Publication Co., 1892-1922.

Ephros, Gershon. *Cantorial Anthology of Traditional and Modern Synagogue Music*, 6 vols. New York: Bloch Publications, 1941.

—————. *Hassidic Song Festival*. Tel Aviv: Or-Tav, 1970.

Finson, Jon W., ed. *Edward Harrigan and David Braham: Collected Songs I, 1873-1882*. Madison, Wisconsin: A-R Editions, 1997.

Idelsohn, Abraham Zvi. *Hebräisch-Orientalischer Melodienschatz* (*HOM*), 10 vols. Berlin: Benjamin Harz et al., 1914-1932; reprint (10 vols. in 4), New York: Ktav Publishing House, 1973.

—————, A. Irma Cohon, ed. *The Jewish Song Book*. Cincinnati: Publications for Judaism, 1961.

Johnson, J. Rosamond. *American Negro Spirituals*. New York: Viking Press, 1937.

Johnson, James Weldon *The Book of American Negro Spirituals*. 1925; reprint, New York: Viking Press, 1962.

Kammen, Jacob/Jack and Joseph, eds. *International Dance Folios*, nos. 1 and 9. New York: J. & J. Kammen Music Co.[1924], 1937.

—————. *Jewish Theatre Songs*, vols 1 and 2. New York: J. & J. Kammen Music Co., vol. 1, n.d., vol. 2, 1953.

—————. *Most Popular Jewish Songs*. New York: J. & J. Kammen Music Co., 1982.

Katchko, Adolph.. *Services for Sabbath Eve and Morning and Three Festivals*, 3 vols. New York: Sacred Music Press, 1952.

Kimball, Robert and Linda Emmet, eds. *The Complete Lyrics of Irving Berlin*. New York: Alfred A. Knopf, 2001.

Kotylanski, Chaim. *Folks-Gezangen: A Collection of Chassidic Songs and Chants, Yiddish-Ukrainian Folk Songs, and "Shteiger Lieder."* Los Angeles: Chaim Kotylansky Book Committee, with the Alveltlicher Yiddisher Kultur-Farband "YCUF", 1944.

Lefkowitch, Henry. *Jewish Songs, Folk and Modern*. New York: Metro Music Co., 1935.

Levy, Isaac, ed. *Chants Judéo-Espagnole*, 4 vols. Jerusalem: Edition de Pateur, 1973.

—————. *Romanceros Judéo-Espagnole*. Madrid: n.p.,1911; London: World Sephardi Federation, 1959.

Lewandowski, Louis. *Kol Rinnah U't'fillah* (All Songs and Prayers). Reprinted in the Out-of-Print Classics Series of Synagogue Music, vol. 9. New York: Sacred Music Press, 1953.

Lomax, Alan. *American Folk Songs*. Baltimore: Penguin Books, 1964.

Lomax, John and Alan. *American Ballads and Folk Songs*. New York: Macmillan, 1934.

Marek, Peysakh S. and Saul M. Ginzburg. *Evreiskiya narodniya pesni v'Rossii* (Yiddish Folk Songs from Russia). St. Petersburg, Voskhod, Russia, 1901.

Mlotek, Eleanor Gordon. *Mir Trogn a Gezang* (We Carry a Song): *Favorite Songs of Our Generation*. New York: Workmen's Circle Education Department, 1977.

—————. *Songs of Generations: New Pearls of Yiddish Song*. New York: Workmen's Circle Education Department, 1998.

—————. *We Are Here: Songs of the Holocaust*. New York: Workmen's Circle Education Department, 1983.

Mlotek, Eleanor Gordon and Joseph Mlotek. *Pearls of Yiddish Song, Favorite Folk, Art, and Theater Songs*. New York: Workmen's Circle Education Department, 1988.

Mlotek, Eleanor Gordon and Malke Gottlieb. *Twenty-Five Ghetto Songs*. New York: Workmen's Circle Education Department, 1968.

Nathan, Hans, ed. *Israeli Folk Music: Songs of the Early Pioneers*. Foreword and afterword by Philip V. Bohlman. Madison: A-R Editions, 1994.

Nathanson, Moshe. *Manginoth Shireynu*. New York: Hebrew Publishing Co., 1939.

Pasternak, Velvel. *Songs of the Chassidim*. New York: Bloch Publishing Co., 1968.

Putterman, David J., ed. *Synagogue Music by Contemporary Composers: An anthology of 38 Compositions for the Sabbath Eve Service*. New York: G. Schirmer, Inc., 1951.

Roskin, Janot S. *Jüdische Folkslieder*. Berlin-Halensee: Musikverlag fur natzionale Volkskunst, 1917.

Rubin, Ruth, ed. *Jewish Folk Songs*. New York: Oak Publications, 1965.

————. *A Treasury of Jewish Folksong*. New York: Schocken Books, 1950; reprint 1967.

Saminsky, Lazare, transcriber. *Sechs Lieder aus dem Russichen Orient*. Vienna: Universal Edition, 1925-1926.

Schack [Sarah Pitkowsky] and Cohen [Ethel Silberman], eds. *Yiddish Folk Songs*. New York: Bloch Publishing Co., 1927.

Schindler, Eliezer and Joshua Weisser. *Yiddish un Chassidish* (Yiddish and Hassidic). Brooklyn, New York: Schulsinger Bros., 1950.

Siegmeister, Elie, and Olin Downes, eds. *A Treasury of American Song*. New York: Alfred A. Knopf, 1943.

Stone, Gregory. *Gypsy Memories*. New York: Edward B. Marks Corp., 1934.

Warembud, Norman H., ed. *Great Songs of the Yiddish Theatre*. New York: New York Times Book Co., 1975.

Yablokoff, Herman. *Herman Yablokoff Songs*. New York: Joeneil Music Co. (J. & J. Kammen Music Co.), 1962.

Tin Pan Alley, Broadway, and Hollywood

Alpert, Hollis. *The Life and Times of Porgy and Bess: The Story of an American Classic*. New York: Alfred A. Knopf, 1990.

Altman, Richard, with Mervyn Kaufman. *The Making of a Musical: Fiddler on the Roof*. New York: Crown Publishers, 1971.

Burton, Jack. *Blue Book of Broadway Musicals*. Watkins Glen, New York: Century House, 1969.

Cohen, Sarah Blacher, ed. *From Hester Street to Hollywood: The Jewish-American Stage and Screen*. Bloomington: Indiana University Press, 1983.

Corenthal, Michael G. *Cohen on the Telephone: A History of Jewish Recorded Humor and Popular Music, 1892-1942*. Milwaukee: Yesterday's Memories, 1984.

Davis, Sheila. *The Craft of Lyric Writing*. Cincinnati: Writer's Digest Books, 1985.

Engel, Lehman. *The American Musical Theater*. New York: Macmillian, 1967.

Erens, Patricia. *The Jew in American Cinema*. Bloomington: Indiana University Press, 1984.

Evans, Mark. *Soundtrack: The Music of the Movies*. New York: Hopkinson and Blake, 1975.

Ewen, David. *All the Years of American Popular Music*. Englewood, New Jersey: Prentice-Hall, Inc., 1977.

————. *Complete Book of the American Musical Theater*. New York: Henry Holt & Co., 1959.

————. *Great Men of American Popular Song*. Englewood Cliffs, New Jersey: Prentice-Hall, Inc., 1970.

————. *The Life and Death of Tin Pan Alley*. New York: Funk & Wagnalls Co., 1964.

————. *New Complete Book of the American Musical Theater*. New York: Holt, Rinehart & Winston, 1970.

Furia, Phillip. *Ira Gershwin: The Art of the Lyricist*. New York: Oxford University Press, 1996.

Gilbert, Douglas. *Lost Chords: The Diverting Story of American Popular Songs*. Garden City, New York: Doubleday, 1942.

Goldberg, Isaac. *Tin Pan Alley*. New York: John Day Co., 1930.

Gottlieb, Robert and Robert Kimball, eds. *Reading Lyrics*. New York: Pantheon Books, 2000.

Green, Stanley. *Broadway Musicals: Show by Show*. Milwaukee: Hal Leonard Books, 1985.

————. *Ring Bells! Sing Songs!: Broadway Musicals of the 1930s*. New Rochelle, N.Y.: Arlington Books, 1971.

————. *The World of Musical Comedy*, 4th ed. San Diego and New York: A. S. Barnes & Co., 1980.

Guernsey, Jr., Otis, ed. *Broadway Song and Story*. New York; Dodd, Mead & Co., 1985.

Hammerstein, Oscar, ed. *The Jerome Kern Song Book*. New York: Simon & Schuster, Inc., 1955.

Hamm, Charles. *Irving Berlin, Songs from the Melting Pot: The Formative Years 1907-1914*. New York: Oxford University Press, 1997.

————. *Yesterdays: Popular Song in America*. New York: W.W. Norton & Co., 1979.

Hemming, Roy. *The Melody Lingers On: The Great Songwriters and the Movie Musicals*. New York: Newmarket Press, 1986.

Hirschhorn, Clive. *The Hollywood Musical, 1927 to 1981*. New York: Crown Publishing, Inc., 1981.

Hoberman, J. and Jeffrey Shandler. *Entertaining America: Jews, Movies, and* Broadcasting. New York: The Jewish Museum, New York, and Princeton University Press, 2003.

Hyland, William G. *The Song Is Ended*. New York: Oxford University Press, 1995.

Jasen, David A. *Tin Pan Alley: The Composers, the Songs, the Performers, and Their Times, 1886-1956*. New York: Donald L. Fine, Inc., 1988.

Kanter, Kenneth Aaron. *The Jews on Tin Pan Alley: The Jewish Contribution to American Popular Music, 1830-1940*. New York: Ktav Publishing House, 1982.

Kasha, Al and Joel Hirschhorn. *If They Ask You, You Can Write a Song*. New York: Simon & Schuster, Inc., 1979.

————. *Notes on Broadway: Conversations with the Great Songwriters*. Chicago: Contemporary Books, 1985.

Kobal, John. *Gotta Sing, Gotta Dance: A Pictorial History of Film Musicals*. London and New York: Hamlyn Publishing Group, Ltd., 1971.

Marcuse, Maxwe͏ *Tin Pan Alley in Gaslight: A Saga of the Songs that Made the Gray Nineties "Gay."* Watkins Glen, New York: Century House, 1959.

Margolick, David. *Strange Fruit: Billie Holiday, Café Society, and an Early Cry for Civil Rights*. Philadelphia: Running Press, 2000.

Marks, Edward B., as told to Abbott J. Leibling. *They All Sang: From Tony Pastor to Rudy Vallée*. New York: Viking Press, 1935.

Martin, Deac. *Book of Musical Americana*. Englewood Cliffs, New Jersey: Prentice-Hall, 1970.

Mattfield, Julius. *Variety Music Cavalcade, 1620-1961: A Chronology of Vocal and Instrumental Music Popular in the United States*. Englewood Cliffs, New York: Prentice-Hall, 1962.

Meyer, Hazel. *The Gold in Tin Pan Alley*. Philadelphia: J. B. Lippincott, 1958; Westport, Connecticut: Greenwood Press, 1977.

Rose, Al. *Eubie Blake*. New York: Schirmer Books, 1979.

Rosenberg, Deena. *Fascinating Rhythm: The Collaboration of George and Ira Gershwin*. New York: Dutton, 1991.

Schiff, David. *Gershwin: Rhapsody in Blue*. Cambridge: Cambridge University Press, 1997.

Schneider, Wayne. *The Gershwin Style: New Looks at the Music of Gershwin*. New York: Oxford University Press, 1998.

Spaeth, Sigmund, Introduction by Richard Rodgers. *A History of Popular Music in America*. New York: Random House, 1948.

————. *Read 'Em and Weep*. New York: Arco Publishing Co., 1945.

Suskin, Steven. *Show Tunes: 1905-1985*. New York: Dodd, Mead & Co., 1986.

Swain, Joseph P. *The Broadway Musical: A Critical and Musical Survey*. New York: Oxford University Press, 1990.

Thomas, Tony. *Harry Warren and the Hollywood Musical*. Secaucus, New Jersey: Citadel Press, 1975.

Whitcomb, Ian. *After the Ball: Pop Music from Rag to Rock*. New York: Limelight Editions, 1986.

————. *Irving Berlin and Ragtime in America*. New York: Limelight Editions, 1988.

Whitfield, Stephen J. *In Search of American Jewish Culture*. Hanover, New York: University Press of New England (Brandeis University Press), 1999.

Wilk, Max. *They're Playing Our Song*. New York: Atheneum,1973; expanded ed. New York: Zoetrope, 1986.

Witmark, Isidore and Isaac Goldberg. *From Ragtime to Swingtime: The Story of the House of Witmark*. New York: Lee Furman, Inc., 1939.

Zierold, Norman. *The Moguls*. New York: Coward-McCann, 1969.

Yiddish Studies

Dawidowicz, Lucy, ed. *The Golden Tradition: Jewish Life and Thought in Eastern Europe*. Boston: Beacon Press, 1967.

Gold, Michael (b. Irwin Granich). *Jews without Money*. New York: Bard Books, 1958; reissued by Carroll & Graf, 1996; paperback Avon edition, 1965.

Goldsmith, Emanuel S. *Modern Yiddish Culture: The Story of the Yiddish Language Movement*. New York: Shapolsky Publishers and the Workmen's Circle Education Department, 1987.

Hapgood, Hutchins. *The Spirit of the Ghetto: Studies of the Jewish Quarter of New York*. New York: Schocken Books, 1967.

Harshaw, Benjamin. *The Meaning of Yiddish*. Berkeley: University of California Press, 1990.

Hindus, Milton. *The Old East Side: An Anthology*. Philadelphia: Jewish Publication Soc., 1969.

Howe, Irving. *World of Our Fathers: The Journey of the East European Jews to America and the Life They Found and Made*. New York: Schocken Books, 1990.

Landis, Joseph, ed. *The Dybbuk and Other Great Yiddish Plays*. New York: Bantam Books, 1966.

————. *Lexicon fun der Naye Literatur*. New York: Congress for Jewish Culture, 1956.

————. *Memoirs of the Yiddish Stage*. Flushing: Queens College Press, 1984.

Lifson, David S. *The Yiddish Theater in America*. New York: Thomas Yoseloff, 1965.

Lipsky, Louis. *Tales of the Yiddish Rialto*. New York: Thomas Yoscloff, 1962.

Manners, Ande. *Poor Cousins*. New York: Coward, McCann & Geoghegan, Inc., 1972.

Rajzen, Zalmen. *Lexicon fun der Yiddish Literatur, Prese un Filolgia*, 4 vols. Vilna, Lithuania: B. Klatzin, 1926-1929.

Reingold, Isaac, tr. *Tsvey Hundert Lider*. Chicago: *Arbiter Ring Gezungs Fareyn*, 1929.

Rischin, Moses. *The Promised City: New York's Jews, 1870-1914*. Cambridge: Harvard University Press, 1962.

Rumshinsky, Joseph. *Oisgeklibene Shriften: Avrom Goldfaden, di Lieber Plagyator* (Selected Writings: Abraham Goldfaden, the Dear Plagiarist), ed. Shmuel Rozhansky. Buenos Aires, 1963.

Sanders, Ronald. *The Downtown Jews: Portraits of an Immigrant Generation*. New York: Harper & Row, 1969.

Sandrow, Nahma. *Vagabond Stars: A World History of Yiddish Theater*. New York: Harper & Row, 1977.

Sapoznik, Henry. *Klezmer! Jewish Music from Old World to Our World*. New York: Schirmer Books, 1999.

Zylbercweig, Zalmen, ed. *Lexicon of the Yiddish Theater* (in Yiddish), 6 vols. New York: Hebrew Actors Union of America, 1931-1963.

Selected Writings by Jack Gottlieb

"About Leonard Bernstein." Booklet and jacket notes for LP recordings of *The Three Symphonies* and *Chichester Psalms*. Deutsche Grammophon 2709 077.

Blackwell Companion to Jewish Culture. Glenda Abramson, ed., s.v. "Leonard Bernstein," "Popular American-Jewish Music," "Aaron Copland." Oxford: Basil Blackwell Ltd., 1989, 2002.

"Choral Music of Leonard Bernstein: Reflections of Theater and Liturgy," *American Choral Review* (1968):156-177.

"From Shtetl to Stage Door: The Jewish Influence on the American Musical Theater," parts 1 and 2, *Reform Judaism* 1 (1972).

"A Jewish Mass or a Catholic Mitzvah?" *Journal of Synagogue Music* 3 (1971): 3-7.

"A Joyless Noise?" *American Choral Review* 12 (1979): 178-191.

"Leonard Bernstein: *Kaddish* Symphony" (review), *Perspectives of New Music* (1965): 171-175.

Leonard Bernstein: A Complete Catalogue of His Works, ed. Jack Gottlieb. New York: Amberson, Inc., 1998.

Leonard Bernstein: A Jewish Legacy. Liner Notes for CD, co-producer and performer, Naxos label 8.559407, 2003.

"The Music of Leonard Bernstein: A Study of Melodic Manipulations," D.M.A dissertation, University of Illinois, 1964. Available through University Microfilms, Inc. (ProQuest), Ann Arbor, Michigan, Doc. #65-3589.

"Symbols of Faith in the Music of Leonard Bernstein," *Musical Quarterly* 66 (1980): 287-295; updated in *Journal of Synagogue Music* 10 (1980): 45-53.

"Yinglish on Tin Pan Alley," *Jewish Music Notes* (1976).

Lecture-Entertainments by Jack Gottlieb

"From Shtetl to Stage Door." Jack Gottlieb, performer. Indianapolis (Indiana) Museum of Art. 27 November 1972. Later performed with Cantors Don Croll and Richard Botton.

"Funny, It Doesn't Sound Jewish: A Study in American Popular Music." First presented 29 December 1983 for the Modern Language Association convention, Hilton Hotel, New York. First presentation with multimedia: 28 March 1985, Smithsonian Institution, Washington, D.C.

"Sing Along: The Impact of Jewish Life on Tin Pan Alley." Judith Clurman, soprano and Cantor Bruce Ruben, Jack Gottlieb, piano. 13 May 1981, Hebrew Union College-Jewish Institute of Religion, New York.

"The Yiddisha Professor: Early Songs of Irving Berlin." First presented 10 July 2001 for the American Jewish Historical Society at the Center for Jewish History, New York.

Permission Credits for Musical Examples

All copyright notices for song clearances generally include the terms: All Rights Reserved, International Copyright Secured, and Used by permission. Every effort has been made to trace the ownership of all copyrighted material in this book and to obtain permission for its use. Should there be errors or omissions, the author would appreciate notification for inclusion in future editions.

(Listed alphabetically by composer's last name, unless otherwise indicated)

ABRAHAM, MAURICE & LEW BROWN **I'll Open the Door and Close the Door** (1917) Public Domain.

ABREU, ZEQUINHA (M) & ALOYSIO OLIVEIRA (Portuguese words), Ervin Drake (English words) **Tico Tico** (Tico No Fuba) Copyright 1943 by Peer International Corporation. Copyright Renewed.

ACHRON, JOSEPH **God Supreme** (*Union Hymnal*, 3rd ed.) Copyright 1932 by Central Conference of American Rabbis. Copyright Renewed.

ADLER, RICHARD & JERRY ROSS (both W & M) **Hernando's Hideaway** and **There Once Was a Man** (from the stage production *The Pajama Game*) Copyright 1954 Frank Music Corp. Renewed, Assigned to J & J Ross Music Co. and Lakshmi Puja Music Ltd. All rights reserved. Used by permission of Richard Adler and the Estate of Jerry Ross. Warner Bros. Publications U.S. Inc., Miami, FL 33014. **Whatever Lola Wants** (from stage production *Damn Yankees*) Copyright 1955 Frank Music Corp. Renewed, Assigned to J & J Ross Music Co. and Lakshmi Puja Music Ltd. All Rights Reserved. Used by permission of Richard Adler and the Estate of Jerry Ross. Warner Bros. Publications U.S. Inc., Miami, FL 33014.

AHBEZ, EDEN (W & M) **Nature Boy** Copyright 1946 by Golden World Publishing Co. Renewed. All Rights Reserved. Used by permission of David Janowiak.

AHLERT, FRED & EDGAR LESLIE **The Moon Was Yellow** Copyright 1934 (Renewed 1962) by Fred Ahlert Music Corporation and Pencil Mark Music, Inc. Copyright 1934 by Bregman, Vocco and Cohn, Inc. (Renewed 1961 by Edgar Leslie). Edgar Leslie rights administered in the U.S. and Canada by Herald Square Music, Inc. International Copyright Secured. All Rights Reserved.

AKST, HARRY & GRANT CLARKE **Am I Blue?** Copyright 1929 Renewed. Warner Bros. Inc. All Rights Reserved. Used by permission. Warner Bros. Publications U.S. Inc., Miami, FL 33014.

ALTER, ISRAEL **Omar Rabi Elozor** (from *Sabbath Service*) Copyright 1968 by Cantors Assembly. Reprinted by permission.

ARLEN, HAROLD & JOHNNY MERCER **Ac-cent-chu-ate the Positive** (from the film *Here Come the Waves*). Copyright 1944

Renewed. Harwin Music Co. International Copyright Secured. All Rights Reserved. **Blues in the Night**. Copyright 1941, Renewed. Warner Bros. Inc. All Rights Reserved. Used by permission. Warner Bros. Publications U.S. Inc., Miami, FL 33014. **Come Rain or Come Shine** (from the stage production *St. Louis Woman*) Copyright 1946 Renewed. Chappell & Co. All Rights Reserved. Used by permission. Warner Bros. Publications U.S. Inc., Miami, FL 33014. **Out of This World** (from the film *Out of This World*) Copyright 1944 Renewed. Edwin H. Morris & Co., a division of MPL Communications, Inc.

ARLEN, HAROLD & TED KOEHLER **When the Sun Comes Out** Copyright 1941 Renewed 1969. Ted Koehler Music and S. A. Music Co. All rights for Ted Koehler Music administered by Fred Ahlert Music Corporation. International Copyright Secured. All Rights Reserved. **Get Happy** (from the film *Summer Stock*) Copyright 1929 Renewed. Warner Bros. Inc. and S. A. Music Co.

ARLEN, HAROLD & LEO ROBIN **For Every Man There's a Woman** (from the film *Casbah*) Copyright 1948 Renewed. Leo Robin Music Co. & Harwin Music Corp. All rights for Leo Robin Music Co. administered by Music Sales Corp. (ASCAP).

ARLEN, HAROLD & E.Y. HARBURG **Over the Rainbow** (from the film *The Wizard of Oz*) Copyright 1938 Renewed 1966. Metro-Goldwyn-Mayer,Inc. Copyright 1939 Renewed 1967. EMI Feist Catalog, Inc. All Rights Reserved. Used by permission. Warner Bros. Publications U.S. Inc., Miami, FL 33014.

ARLEN, HAROLD/BILLY ROSE & E.Y. HARBURG (W) **It's Only a Paper Moon** (from the film *Paper Moon*) Copyright 1933 Renewed. Warner Bros. Inc. Rights for extended renewal term in the U.S. controlled by Chappell & Co., Glocca Morra Music and S. A. Music Co. All Rights Reserved. Used by permission. Warner Bros. Publications U.S. Inc., Miami, FL 33014.

BACHARACH, BURT & HAL DAVID **The Look of Love** (from the film *Casino Royale*) Copyright 1967 Renewed 1995. Colgems-EMI Music Inc.

BAKER, DAVID & SHELDON HARNICK **A World to Win** (from the stage production *Smiling, the Boy Fell Dead*) Copyright 1961 by Alley Music Corp., Trio Music Co., Carlin America, Inc.

BORNE, HAL/SID KULLER & RAY GOLDEN **The Tenement Symphony** (from the film *The Big Store*) Copyright 1941 EMI-Feist Catalog Inc. All Rights Reserved. Used by Permission Warner Bros. Publications U.S. Inc., Miami, FL 33014.

BOWMAN, EUDAY **12th Street Rag** Public Domain.

BRAND, OSCAR (W & M) **A Guy Is a Guy** TRO—Copyright 1952 Renewed, Ludlow Music, Inc., New York, NY. Used by permission.

BROWN, LEW, WLADIMIR A. TIMM, JAROMIR VEJVODA & VASEK ZEMAN **Beer Barrel Polka (Roll out the Barrel)** based on the European success *Skoda Lasky* Copyright 1934 Renewed. Shapiro, Bernstein & Co., Inc., New York Copyright 1939 Renewed. Shapiro, Bernstein & Co., Inc., New York. International Copyright Secured. All Rights Reserved. Used by permission.

BROWN, NACIO HERB & ARTHUR FREED **Temptation** (from the film *Going Hollywood*) Copyright 1933 Renewed. Metro-Goldwyn-Mayer Inc. All rights controlled by EMI Robbins Catalog Inc. All Rights Reserved. Used by permission. Warner Bros. Publications U.S. Inc., Miami, FL 33014.

BROWN, NACIO HERB & EARL K. BRENT **Love Is Where You Find It** (from the film *The Kissing Bandit*) Copyright 1948 Renewed. EMI-Feist Catalog Inc. All Rights Reserved. Used by permission. Warner Bros. Publications U.S. Inc., Miami, FL 33014.

BROWN, SEYMOUR & GEORGE BOTSFORD **Marry a Yiddisher Boy** (1911) Public Domain.

BRYAN, ALFRED & JACK STERN **There's a Little Bit of Irish in Sadie Cohn** (1916) Public Domain.

CAHN, SAMMY & SAUL CHAPLIN **Bei Mir Bist Du Schon**. See Secunda, Sholom.

CAHN, SAMMY & SAUL CHAPLIN **Joseph, Joseph** (based on "Yossel, Yossel" by Nellie Casman & Samuel Steinberg) Copyright 1938 Renewed. Warner Bros. Inc. All Rights Reserved. Used by permission. Warner Bros. Publications U.S. Inc., Miami, FL 33014.

CAHN, SAMMY & SAUL CHAPLIN **What Used to Was, Used to Was** (based on "Vus iz geven iz geven" by David Meyerowitz) Copyright 1939 Renewed. Warner Bros. Inc. All Rights Reserved. Used by permission. Warner Bros. Publications U.S. Inc., Miami, FL 33014.

CARMICHAEL, HOAGY & PAUL FRANCIS WEBSTER. **Baltimore Oriole**. Copyright 1942, 1944 by Songs of Peer, Ltd. and Warner Bros. Renewed. Warner Bros. Inc. International Copyright Secured. All Rights Reserved. Used by permission. Warner Bros. Publications U.S. Inc., Miami, FL 33014.

CASMAN, NELLIE & SAMUEL STEINBERG (Yiddish version) **Yossel, Yossel** Copyright 1923 Renewed by Music Sales Corp. (ASCAP).

CHAJES, JULIUS. **Let Us Adore** (from *Gates of Song*) Copyright 1987 Transcontinental Music Publications. Used by permission.

COOPERSMITH, HARRY & E. E. LEVINGER **Mattathias** Copyright 1950 United Synagogue of America Copyright assigned to Transcontinental Music Publications. Used by permission.

CRUMIT, FRANK & LOU KLEIN (both W & M) **The Return of the Gay Caballero** Copyright 1929 Renewed 1957 by Jerry Vogel Music Co., Inc.

DABNEY, FORD & JO' TRENT **Jungle Rose** Copyright 1927 Renewed 1955 Leo Feist, Inc. Rights assigned to EMI Catalogue Partnership. All Rights Controlled and Administered by EMI Feist Catalog Inc. All Rights Reserved. International Copyright Secured. Used by Permission. Warner Bros. Publications U.S. Inc., Miami, FL 33014.

DANOFF, SIDNEY/EDWARD WHITE & MAXWELL WOLFSON (all W & M) **Mashuga** Copyright 1959 Renewed 1988 by Famous Music Corp. International Copyright Secured. All Rights Reserved. Used by Permission.

DEUTSCH, EMERY/DICK SMITH, FRANK WINE-GAR & JIMMY ROGERS **When a Gypsy Makes His Violin Cry** Copyright 1935 Renewed. WB Music Corp. All Rights Reserved. Used by permission. Warner Bros. Publications U.S. Inc., Miami, FL 33014. Rights Reserved. Used by permission.

ELLSTEIN, ABRAHAM/JOSEPH LIEBOWITZ & ALAN SMALL **Wedding Samba** (a.k.a. **Wedding Rhumba** and *Der naye sher*) Copyright 1940, 1947. Music Sales Corp. Copyrights Renewed. All rights administered by Universal-Duchess Music Corp.

ELMAN, ZIGGY & JOHNNY MERCER **And the Angels Sing** Copyright 1939 Renewed. WB Music Corp. All Rights Reserved. Used by permission. Warner Bros. Publications U.S. Inc., Miami, FL 33014.

ESPINOSA, JIMENEZ JOAQUIN/FRANCIA LUBAN & ABE TUVIN **A Gay Ranchero** Copyright 1936 by Edward B. Marks Music Company Renewed.

FAIN, SAMMY & PAUL FRANCIS WEBSTER **A Certain Smile** (from the film *A Certain Smile*) Copyright 1958, Renewed Twentieth Century Fox Corp. All rights controlled by EMI Miller Catalog, Inc. All Rights Reserved. Used by permission. Warner Bros. Publications U.S. Inc., Miami, FL 33014.

FAIN, SAMMY & JACK YELLEN **The Jews Have Got Their Irish Up** Copyright 1937 Yellen & Fain. Used by permission of Frank Fain.

FISCHER, FRED & BILLY ROSE (both W & M) **Yiddisher Charleston** Copyright 1926 Henry Waterson. Current copyright holder not found.

FISHER, DORIS & ALLAN ROBERTS **Put the Blame on Mame** and **Amado Mio** (both from the Columbia film *Gilda*) Copyright 1946 Sun Music Co., Inc. Copyright renewed, assigned to Doris Fisher Music Corp. and Allan Roberts Music Co. All rights for Doris Fisher Music Corp. controlled and administered by Universal-MCA Music Publishing, a Division of Universal Studios, Inc. All rights for Allan Roberts administered by Music Sales Corp. (ASCAP). International Copyright Secured. All Rights Reserved. Reprinted by Permission. Warner Bros. Publications U.S. Inc., Miami, FL. 33014.

Copyright 1959 Renewed by Richard Rodgers and Oscar Hammerstein II. Williamson Music is owner of publication and allied rights throughout the world. International Copyright Secured. All Rights Reserved. **Oh, What a Beautiful Mornin'** (from the stage production *Oklahoma!*) Copyright 1943 Renewed by Williamson Music. **Some Enchanted Evening** (from the stage production *South Pacific*) Copyright 1949 Renewed by Richard Rodgers and Oscar Hammerstein II. Williamson Music is owner of publication and allied rights throughout the world. International Copyright Secured. All Rights Reserved.

ROME, HAROLD (W & M) **Ballad of the Social Director** (from the stage production *Wish You Were Here*) Copyright 1952 by Harold Rome Renewed. Assigned to Chappell & Co. All Rights Reserved. Used by permission. Warner Bros. Publications U.S. Inc., Miami, FL 33014. **A Gift Today (The Bar Mitzvah Song)** (from the stage production *I Can Get It For You Wholesale*) Copyright 1962 by Harold Rome Renewed. Publication and allied rights assigned to Chappell & Co. All Rights Reserved. Used by permission. Warner Bros. Publications U.S. Inc., Miami, FL 33014.

ROUBANIS, NICHOLAS, English lyric by S.K. RUSSELL, FRED WISE & MILTON LEEDS **Miserlou** Copyright 1941 Renewed. EMI Grove Park Music Inc. All Rights Reserved. Used by permission. Warner Bros. Publications U.S. Inc., Miami, FL 33014.

RUBINSTEIN, M. J. & CHAIM TOWER **Koyft a Paper** (1934) Copyright holder not found.

RUIZ, PABLO BELTRAN (Spanish words & music) **Quien Será**, NORMAN GIMBEL **Sway** (English words) Copyright 1954 by Peer International Corporation Renewed. International copyright secured. All Rights Reserved.

RUMSHINSKY, JOSEPH & SAM LOWENWORTH **Watch Your Step** (1922) Public Domain.

RUMSHINSKY. JOSEPH & BORIS ROSENTHAL **Yankele** (1924) by permission of Betty Rumshinsky Fox.

RUMSHINSKY, JOSEPH & LOUIS GILROD **Mayn goldele** (1924, 1937) by permission of Betty Rumshinsky Fox.

RUMSHINSKY, JOSEPH & MOLLY PICON **Oy iz dus a meydl** (1927) by permission of Betty Rumshinsky Fox. **Vu iz mayn zivig?** (1925) by permission of Betty Rumshinsky Fox.

RUMSHINSKY, JOSEPH & CHAIM TOWER **Shein vi di l'vone** Copyright 1938 Renewed by Music Sales Corp. (ASCAP). All Rights Reserved. Used by permission.

SANDLER, JACOB KOPPEL **Eili, Eili** (1896) Public Domain.

SCHONBERGER, JOHN & MALVIN SCHONBERGER **Whispering** (1920) Public Domain.

SCHWARTZ, ABE & HYMAN PRIZANT **Di grine kuzine** (1922) Public Domain.

SCHWARTZ, ARTHUR & HOWARD DIETZ **You and the Night and the Music** Copyright 1934 Renewed Warner Bros. Inc. Rights for extended renewal term in U.S. controlled by Warner Bros.

Inc. and Arthur Schwartz Pub. by permission of Paul Schwartz on behalf of Arthur Schwartz Music, Ltd. Canadian rights controlled by Warner Bros. Inc. All Rights Reserved. Used by permission. Warner Bros. Publications U.S. Inc., Miami, FL 33014.

SECUNDA, SHOLOM/SAMMY CAHN & SAUL CHAPLIN (English version based on Sholom Secunda & Jacob Jacobs) **Bei Mir Bist Du Schon** Copyright 1937 Renewed by Warner Bros. Inc. All Rights Reserved. Used by permission. Warner Bros. Publications U.S. Inc., Miami, FL 33014.

SECUNDA, SHOLOM & AARON ZEITLIN (Yiddish version) **Dona, Dona** Copyright 1940, 1956 Renewed. EMI Mills Music Inc. Rights outside U.S. and Canada administered by EMI Mills Music Inc. & Hargail Music Press. All Rights Reserved. Used by permission. Warner Bros. Publications U.S. Inc., Miami, FL 33014.

SILVER, ABNER **Leonora** Copyright 1927 Renewed. Shapiro, Bernstein & Co., New York. International Copyright Secured. All Rights Reserved. Used by permission.

SILVERS, LOUIS & BUDDY DESYLVA **April Showers** (from the stage production *Bombo*, 1921) Public Domain.

SIMON, PAUL (W & M) **American Tune** Copyright 1973 Paul Simon Music, Inc. All Rights Reserved. Used by permission.

SINATRA, FRANK, JACK WOLF & JOEL HERRON (all W & M) **I'm a Fool to Want You** Copyright 1951 Renewed Barton Music Corp. All Rights Reserved. By permission of Joleron Music & Integrity Music Corp. Warner Bros. Publications U.S. Inc., Miami, FL 33014.

SKYLAR, SUNNY & PAT GENARO (both W & M) **You're Breaking My Heart** Copyright 1948 Renewed 1976 by Onyx Music Corp. and Screen Gems-EMI Music, Inc. All rights for Onyx Music Corp. administered by Music Sales Corp (ASCAP). All rights for the world excluding the U.S. controlled and administrated by Screen Gems-EMI Music, Inc. All Rights Reserved. Used by permission.

SONDHEIM, STEPHEN (W & M) **Send in the Clowns** (from the stage production *A Little Night Music*) Copyright 1973 Renewed. Rilting Music, Inc. All rights administered by WB Music Corp. All Rights Reserved. Used by permission. Warner Bros. Publications U.S. Inc., Miami, FL 33014.

STEIN, JULES K. & SONNY MILLER **(My) Russian Doll** Copyright 1927 by Jerome H. Remick & Co. Current copyright holder not found.

STEINER, MAX **Gone with the Wind** (from the film *Gone with the Wind*) Copyright 1940 Renewed Warner Bros. Inc. All Rights Reserved. Used by permission. Warner Bros. Publications U.S. Inc., Miami, FL 33014.

STYNE, JULE/ BETTY COMDEN & ADOLPH GREEN **I Met a Girl** (from the stage production *Bells Are Ringing*) Copyright 1956 Betty Comden, Adolph Green & Jule Styne, Renewed. Publication and allied rights assigned to Stratford Music Corp.

WILLIAMS, HARRY & EGBERT VAN ALSTYNE **Rebecca** (1908) Public Domain.

WILLIAMS, HUGH (pseudonym for WILHELM GROSZ) & JIMMY KENNEDY **The Isle of Capri** Copyright 1934 Renewed Wilhelm Grosz Music Co. and Universal-PolyGram International Publishing, Inc. All Rights Reserved. Used by permission. Warner Bros. Publications U.S. Inc., Miami, FL 33014.

WILLIAMS, SPENCER **Basin Street Blues** Copyright 1928, 1929, 1933 Renewed Edwin H. Morris & Company, a division of MPL Communications, Inc.

WOHL, HERMAN (M) & AARON LEBEDEFF (W) **Slutzk** Copyright 1936 Renewed by Music Sales Corp. International Copyright Secured. All Rights Reserved. Reprinted by permission.

WOODS, HARRY **Side by Side** Copyright 1927 Renewed. Shapiro, Bernstein & Co., Inc., New York.

YABLOKOFF, HERMAN **Papirosn** (Yiddish version) Copyright 1933, 1934 Renewed by Warner Bros. Publications. This edition authorized for sale by Music Sales Corp. (ASCAP) in the U.S. only. **Papirossen (Cigarettes)** Copyright 1933 Renewed WB Music Corp. All Rights Reserved. Used by permission. Warner Bros. Publications U.S. Inc., Miami, FL 33014. **Shvag mayn harts** Copyright 1935 by Herman Yablokoff, assigned to Bergman, Vocco & Cohn, Inc., New York City. Used by permission of Helen Yablokoff.

YOUMANS, VINCENT/CLIFFORD GREY & LEO ROBIN **Hallelujah** (from the film *Hit the Deck*) Copyright 1927 by Warner Bros., Inc., Leo Robin Music Co., Range Road Music & Quartet Music. All rights for Leo Robin Music Co. administered by

Music Sales Corp. (ASCAP) Copyright Renewed. Extended term of copyright deriving from Clifford Grey assigned and effective April 22, 1983, to Range Road Music Inc. & Quartet Music, Inc. All Rights Reserved.

YOUMANS, VINCENT/EDWARD ELISCU & GUS KAHN **The Carioca** Copyright 1933 Renewed T.B. Harms. Rights for extended renewal term in U.S. controlled by WB Music Corp., Gilbert Keyes Music and LSQ Music Co. All Rights Reserved. Used by permission. Warner Bros. Publications U.S. Inc., Miami, FL 33014.

YOUNG, JOE & EDGAR LESLIE **Love Me to a Yiddisha Melody** (1911) Public Domain.

YOUNG, VICTOR/JAY LIVINGSTON & RAY EVANS **Golden Earrings** (from the Paramount Picture *Golden Earrings*) Copyright 1946, 1947 Renewed 1973, 1974 by Paramount Music Corporation. All Rights Reserved. Used by permission.

YOUNG, VICTOR & NED WASHINGTON **Stella by Starlight** (from the Paramount Picture *The Uninvited*) Copyright 1946 Renewed 1973, 1974 by Famous Music Corporation. All Rights Reserved. Used by permission.

YOUNG, VICTOR & SAM LEWIS **Lawd, You Made the Night Too Long** Copyright 1932 Renewed. Shapiro, Bernstein & Co., Inc., New York. International Copyright Secured. All Rights Reserved. Used by permission.

YOUNG, VICTOR/MILTON BERLE & FRED WHITEHOUSE **Sam, You Made the Pants Too Long** (adapted from **Lawd, You Made the Night Too Long** by Victor Young & Sam M. Lewis) Copyright 1932, 1940 and 1966 Renewed Shapiro, Bernstein & Co., Inc., New York. All Rights Reserved. Used by permission.

CD Tracks

Every effort has been made to contact and trace the ownership of all copyrighted recorded material on the CD companion to this book in order to obtain permission for its use. Should there be errors or omissions, the author would appreciate notification for inclusion in future editions. The choice of some tracks was determined strictly by availability. Variants of Yiddish words between printed music examples in book chapters and the texts given below denote the porous nature of folk-songs. Transliteration deviations are explained by a performer's particular dialect.

Chapter 1: Slices of History

1. **A Rabbi's Daughter** (Charles K. Harris)   5:08
   Sarah Sager, soprano, Jack Baras, piano. Hebrew Union College-Jewish Institute of Religion
   (HUC-JIR) Musica Hebraica concert series directed by Jack Gottlieb; NYC, 14 March 1976.

Chapter 2: The Lullaby of Brody

2. **Misha, Yascha, Sascha, Toscha** (George & Ira Gershwin)   3:08
   Paul Whiteman Orchestra: *A Tribute to George Gershwin* Copyright 1938 George and Ira Gershwin,
   CBS Radio and Paul Whiteman. All rights reserved. Used by Permission of the Ira and Leonore
   Gershwin Trusts and Warner/Chappell Music, Inc.

3. **Shlof zhe mayn feygele** (Sleep My Birdie; Abraham Goldfaden) [Ex. 2-3]   1:58
   Belva Spiel, soprano, Suzanne Shulman, flute & Jame Coop, piano (The Pro Arte Trio):
   Folk Songs in Concert Form, arranged by Mieczyslaw Kolinski. Folkways Records SF 31314, provided
   courtesy of Smithsonian Folkways Recordings. © 1979. Used by Permission.

Shlof zhe mayn feygele, makh tsi dayn eygele,	Sleep, my little bird, close your eyes,
Shlof mayn kind, shlof.	Sleep, my child, sleep.
A malakh a giter zol zayn dayn hiter	A good angel will be your guardian
Fun haynt biz morgn fri.	From today until early morning.
Mit zayn fligele iber dayn vigele	With his wings above your cradle
Dekt er shtil dir tsi.	He covers you quietly.
Shlof zhe mayn feygele, makh tsi dayn eygele,	So sleep, my birdie, close your eyes,
Shlof mayn kind, shlof.	Sleep, my child, sleep.
Shlof oys freydn, veys fun keyn leydn,	Sleep in peace, may you never know sorrow,
Shlof mayn tayer kind..	Sleep my dear child.
Makh tsi dayn eygele, mayn tayer feygele,	Close your eyes, my dear little bird,
Shlof zikh oys gezint.	Sleep in good health.

4. **My One and Only** (George & Ira Gershwin) [Ex. 2-4]   1:21
   Ella Fitzgerald, Ellis Larkins, piano: *Ella Sings Gershwin*.
   Originally Decca DL8378, now Universal.

5. **Rozhinkes mit mandlen** (Raisins with Almonds; Abraham Goldfaden) [Ex. 2-8a]   1:08
   Marilyn Michaels: *An Oysher Album*. Michael's Records, MIC 102 LP.

Ay lyu lyu lyu—	Ay, lyu, lyu, lyu—
Unter Yideles vigele	Under Yidele's cradle
Shteyt a shney-vays tsigele.	Stands a snow-white kid.
Dos tsigele iz geforn handlen.	The kid has gone into business.

Dos vet zayn dayn baruf: That will be your calling:
Rozhinkes mit mandlen.   [Trading] in raisins and almonds.
Shlof zhe, Yidele, shlof.   Sleep, Yidele [i.e. the Jewish folk], sleep.

6. **Blue Skies** (Irving Berlin) [Ex. 2-8b]   1:30
     Artie Shaw & His Orchestra. Originally Brunswick 7907 (NYC, 18 May 1937), now Sony.
     Reproduced under license from Sony Music Special Products, a Division of Sony Music Entertainment Inc.

7. **Der rebe hot geheysn freylekh zayn** (The Rebe Has Ordered [Us] to Make Merry; Abraham Goldfaden)
     Yiddisher Orchestra conducted by Abe Schwartz: *Tantz, Tantz Yiddelach.* [Ex. 2-10a]   0:26
     Columbia E3672 mx. 58784-2; NYC, 2 November 1917.
     Reproduced under license from Sony Music Special Products, a Division of Sony Music Entertainment Inc.

8. **Dem milners trern** (The Miller's Tears; Mark Warshawsky) [Ex. 2-15a]   0:39
     Freydele Oysher: *Songs My Brother Moishe Sang.* Tikva Records, T-84 LP.

     Oy, vifl yorn zaynen farforn,   Oh, how many years have flown by,
     Zayt ikh bin milner ot a do?   Since I have been a miller here?
     Di reder dreyen zikh, di yorn geyen zikh   The wheels turn, the years pass,
     Ikh bin shoyn alt un grayz un gro.   I am already old and grizzled and gray.

9. **High Noon** (Dimitri Tiomkin & Ned Washington) [Ex. 2-15b]   1:36
     Frankie Laine. *Greatest Hits.* Original release 1958, Sony 8636. Reproduced under license from Sony
     Music Special Products Division of Sony Music Entertainment, Inc.

Chapter 3: Pathways of Americanization

10. **Vos iz geven iz geven un nito** (What Used To Be, Was, and Is No More; David Meyerowitz)
     Connie Francis: *Connie Francis Sings Jewish Favorites.* MGM 3869, now Universal. [Ex. 3-5a]   1:33

     Vos geven, iz geven un nito.   What was, used to be and is no more.
     Shoyn avek yene yor, yene sho.   Gone are those years, those hours.
     Vi shnel farflit der yunger glik,   How fast has young fortune disappeared,
     Un men ken es nit khapn mer tsurik,   And one cannot retrieve them,
     Vayl vos geven, iz geven un nito.   Since what was, used to be and is no more.

     Di kreftn vern shvakh, di hor vert gro.   The strength diminishes, the hair goes grey.
     Men neyt zikh, men kleyt zikh,   One sews, one dresses up,
     Men mahkt zikh sheyn.   One makes oneself pretty.
     Men nart ober keynem, nor zikh aleyn,   But you don't fool anyone, only yourself,
     Vayl vos geven, iz geven un nito.   Because what was, used to be and is no more.

11. **Oy iz dus a Rebetsn** (Wow, Is This a Rabbi's Wife; Adolf King & Joseph Moskowitz)
     Aaron Lebedeff, Perez Sandler Band. Vocalion 13006 mx. 12553; NYC, December 1923.   0:52

     Sha-sha, es zol zayn shtil, der rebe geyt fin shil.   Shh, be quiet, the Rebe's coming from *shul.*
     Sha-sha, er iz shoyn do, in a guter sho.   Be quiet, he's already here, a time to celebrate.
     Sha-sha, nor, kh'sidim zet, di rebetsn, zi geyt,   Quiet, look Hasidim, the Rebetsn is coming.
     Sha-sha, nor, kukt aykh ayn vi zi shmeykhlt fayn.   Shh, just look at how beautifully she smiles.

     Oy, di rebetsn, oy, iz dus a rebetsn,   Oh, the Rebe's wife, oh, is this a Rebe's wife,
     Vi zi geyt azoy breyt fin der shil aheym.   How she walks so proudly home from *shul.*
     Khasidimlekh, talmidemlekh   Hasidim, talmud-torah students
     Tanstn, zingen kegn ir.   Dance and sing for her.
     Oy, iz dus a rebetsn, aza yor af mir!   Oh, what a Rebetsn, I should be so lucky!
     Fet un kleyn zol zi zen,   Fat and short should see her,
     Vi a Purim-koyletsh sheyn.   As pretty as a Purim-cake.
     Oy, iz dus a rebetsn,   Oh, what a Rabbis' wife,
     Aza yor af mir!   It should only happen to me!

12. **Sha Sha** (Adolph King, Jimmy Van Heusen & Manny Kurtz)   1:48
     The Andrews Sisters, Jimmy Dorsey & His Orchestra. Joker SM3240 33, Milan, Italy, 1972.
     Originally Decca, 1938, now Universal.

13. **Bei Mir Bist Du Schoen** (To Me You're Pretty; Sholom Secunda & Jacob Jacobs/Sammy Cahn & Saul Chaplin).
     Judy Garland. Produced under license from Turner Records 72543. [Ex. 3-4]   2:50

Chapter 4: "Writes" of Passage

14. **Morgn shtern-Di naye zayt** (Morning Star-The New Era, from *Dem rebns nigun*/The Rabbi's Tune)
     Joseph Rumshinsky & Samuel Rosenstein. [Ex. 4-11a]   1:40
     William Schwartz. Columbia E4903 mx 86757-1; NYC, November 1920.
     Reproduced under license from Sony Music Special Products, a Division of Sony Music Entertainment Inc.

Ah–Eyn religyon un eyn natsion,	Ah–One religion and one nation,
Nor libe, libe nor.	Just love, only love.
S'vet zayn glaykh say orem raykh,	It will be the same for poor and rich,
Es kimt, ikh zey es klor.	It is coming, I see it clear.
Kayn grafn, printsn, kayn baronen,	No counts, princes, no barons,
Mentsh, nor mentsh, nit mer.	Just an ordinary man, no more [than that].
Eyns vet hershn, eyns vet hershn,	One will rule, one will rule,
S'is di libe, ikh shver.	It is love, I swear.

15. **The Song Is Ended** (Irving Berlin) [Ex. 4-11b]
     Kiri Te Kanawa: *Kiri Sings Berlin.* Abbey Road Ensemble, Jonathan Tunick, conductor and arranger.
     Angel 72435 50415 2 G.   1:24

Chapter 5: The Wandering Gypsy

16. **Barbara Song** (from *The Threepenny Opera*, Kurt Weill & Bertolt Brecht). [Ex. 5-4a]   0:43
     Lotte Lenya: *Lotte Lenya Sings Berlin Theatre Songs by Kurt Weill.* Columbia KL 5056.
     Reproduced under license from Sony Music Special Products, a Division of Sony Music Entertainment Inc.

Ja, da kann man sich doch nicht nur hinlegen.	Yes, here one cannot just lie down, after all.
Ja, da muss man kalt und herzlos sein.	Yes, here one must be cold and heartless.
Ja, da könnte doch viel geschenhen.	Yes, a lot can happen here.
Ach da gibt's über haupt nur: Nein!	All there is here is 'No!'
Der ershte der kam war ein Mann aus Kent,	The first to come was a man from Kent,
Der war wie ein Mann sein soll.	Who was like a man ought to be.
Der zweite . . .	The second . . .

17. **Azoy vi di bist** (Just As You Are; Alexander Olshanetsky & Jacob Jacobs) [Ex. 5-10a & b]   1:17
     Seymour Rechzteit, Abe Ellstein Orchestra. Columbia 8233-F mx. 34444; NYC, 1940s.
     Reproduced under license from Sony Music Special Products, a Division of Sony Music Entertainment Inc.

Azoy vi di bist, du zolst zikh keyn mol nit baytn.	Just as you are, you must never change.
Azoy vi di bist, nor blayb in mayn gedank.	Just as you are, stay in my memory.
Nor ot azoy iz git far Got in far laytn.	Just like that is good for God and for people.
Farblayb nor hartsik in lib dus gantse lebn lang.	Remain cherished and loving all my life.
Vayl di host mikh batoybt mit dayn shmeykhl,	Because you deafened [blinded] me with your smile,
Vos hot nit kayn glaykn.	Which has no comparison.
Ver hot zikh den gegloybt	Who would have thought
Az ikh zol aza glik gor dergreykhn.	I would have such happiness come to me.
Ikh hob in dir mayn emes glik itst gefinen.	In you I have now found my truest happiness.

| *Gloyb mir, azoy vi di bist,* | Believe me, just as you are, |
| *Bisti mir tayer lib.* | You are dearly loved. |

18. **Besamé Mucho** (Kiss Me Much; Consuelo Velazquez & Sunny Skylar) [Ex. 5-10a & b]   1:27
  Steve Lawrence: *The Best of Steve & Eydie.*
  Curb D2-77316, tracks courtesy of MCA Records, Inc.

19. **Vi iz mayn zivig?** (Where Is My Intended?, from *Der kleynem mazik* (The Little Devil) Joseph Rumshinsky & Isadore Lillian)
  Molly Picon. CO 8121-F mx. W 107097-2; NYC, August 1926. [Ex. 5-11]   0:48
  Reproduced under license from Sony Music Special Products, a Division of Sony Music Entertainment Inc.

Vi iz mayn zivig?, fregt yedes meydele.	Where is my intended?, every young woman asks.
Ver vet mikh rifn zayn ershter leydele?	Who will call me his First Lady?
Vi iz er vus iz mir fin Got bashert?	Where is the one destined for me from God?.
Ikh vil ım zeyn. Tsi hot er mikh di vert?	I must see him. Am I worthy enough for him?
Vi iz mayn zivig?, halt ikh in trakhtn zikh.	Where is my intended? I keep thinking about him.
Er iz der shenster, dus nehmt mir dakhtn zikh.	He is the handsomest, I begin to imagine.
Vi bisti, vi, mayn kavalir?	Where are you, where, my cavalier?
Kim, mayn prints, tsu mir,	Come, my prince, to me,
Dayn printsesn vart af dir.	Your princess awaits you.

Chapter 6: "Yingish Songs"

20. **Yiddle, On Your Fiddle, Play Some Ragtime** (Irving Berlin) [Ex. 6-5 & 8]   1:15
  Albert Whelan, The Australian Entertainer: Music Hall, SHB225H.
  London, January 1912, E. Feldman, Ltd.

21. **My Little Yiddisha Queen** (Melville Gideon & Edgar Selden) [Ex. 6-9]   3:18
  Bruce Benson, baritone, Jack Baras, piano. HUC-JIR Musica Hebraica concert series directed by
  Jack Gottlieb; NYC, 14 March 1976.

Chapter 7: The Mood of Modes

Adonai malakh mode

22. **Khazn oyf shabes** (Cantor On the Sabbath; folksong adapted by Irving Caesar & Robert Katscher)
  Al Jolson: *Memories.* Originally Decca DL90380 LP, now Universal. [Ex. 7-3]   1:30

Si(z) gekimen a khazn in a kleyne shtetele	There came a cantor to a small town
Tsu davenen af shabes, oho.	To chant prayers on the Sabbath, oho.
Hobn gekimen tsu hern	The biggest wheeler-dealers in town,
Di shenste balebatim in shtetl, oho.	Came to hear him, oho.
Eyner, a shnayder, oho,	One of them, a tailor, oho,
Der tsveyter, a shuster, oho,	The second, a shoemaker, oho,
Un der driter, a balagula oho,	And the third, a coachman, oho,
Di shenste balebatim in shtetl.	The biggest wheeler-dealers in town.
Makht der shnayderl: Oho! Ba-ba-ba... ,	The tailor makes [the sound]: Oho! Ba-ba-ba... ,
Hot er gedavnt! Hot er gedavnt!	"How he chanted! How he prayed!
Azoy vi men git mitn nodl a tsi,	As one gives a tug of a needle,
Mit di bigelayzn a for, oho,	With the iron going 'full steam ahead,' oho,
Hot er gedavnt! Oho. Hot er gedavnt!	How he prayed!"

Magein avot mode in films

23. **Skeffington Arrives** (from *Mr. Skeffington,* Franz Waxman) [Ex. 7-18b]   0:49
  Moscow Symphony Orchestra, William T. Stromberg, conductor. Naxos/Marco Polo 8.225037.
  Musical recordings under license from Naxos of America. (P) 2002 HNH International, Ltd. All rights reserved.

24. **Theme of Exodus** (from *Exodus*, Ernest Gold) [Ex. 7-18c]   0:45
    101 Strings Orchestra, Stanley Black, conductor: *The Soul of Israel*.
    Originally Alshire S-5044, now Madacy Records 2856.

25. **For Every Man There's A Woman** (from *Casbah*, Harold Arlen & Leo Robin) [Ex. 7-19a]   1:13
    Peggy Lee & Benny Goodman: *The Complete Recordings, 1941-1947*. Columbia Legacy C2K 6568 6.
    Reproduced under license from Sony Music Special Products, a Division of Sony Music Entertainment Inc.

26. **The Look Of Love** (from *Casino Royale*, Burt Bacharach & Hal David)
    Dusty Springfield. MGM/UA motion picture. [Ex. 7-19b]   1:00
    Courtesy of Metro-Goldwyn-Mayer Music Inc.

Ahava raba mode

27. **Eli, Eli** (Jacob Koppel Sandler) [Ex. 7-7]   2:20
    Belle Baker & Orchestra. Pathé 03655, mx. 68005-3; NYC, November 1919.

Eli, Eli, lomo azavtoni? [repeated]	My God, my God, why hast Thou forsaken me?
In fayer in flam hot men indz gebrent,	In fire and flames they have torched us,
Iberal hot men indz gemakht tsu shand un shpot.	Everywhere they have shamed and mocked us.
Dokh upbtsuvendn hot indz keyner gekent	But no one could turn us away
Fin dir, mayn Got, in fin	From You, my God, nor from
Dayn heyliker toyre, fin dayn gebot.	Your holy Torah, from your commandments.
Hert mayn tfile, hert mayn geveyn	Hear my prayer, hear my cry,
Helfn kensti doch indz aleyn.	You can save us, You alone.
Sh'ma Yisrol, Adoshem elokeynu,	Hear O Israel, the Lord Thy God,
Adoshem echod!	The Lord is one!

28. **That Eli, Eli Melody** (Leo Wood & Archie Gottler) [Ex. 7-37]   2:15
    Elliot Z. Levine, baritone & Jack Gottlieb, piano. Private recording; NYC, 31 May 2002.

Chapter 8: Bits and Pieces

29. **Di grine kuzine** (The Greenhorn Cousin; Hyman Prizant & Abe Schwartz)   0:56
    Abraham Moskowitz, vocalist with Abe Schwartz, violin & Sylvia Schwartz, piano, unknown clarinet.
    Columbia E7553 mx. 88378; NYC, February 1922.
    Reproduced under license from Sony Music Special Products, a Division of Sony Music Entertainment Inc.

Gekimen iz tsi mir a kuzine	My cousin came to me [from the old country,]
Sheyn vi gold iz zi geven, di grine.	Pretty as gold was she, the greenhorn.
Bekelekh vi royte pomerantsn,	Her cheeks were rosy like blood oranges,
Un fiselekh vos betn zikh tsum tantsn. [repeated]	And her feet just begging to dance.

Six verses later:

Yetst, az ikh bagegn mayn kuzine,	Now, when I meet my cousin,
Freg ikh zi: Vos makhsti epes grine?	I ask her: "How are you doing, greenhorn?"
Entfert zi mir mit a troyeriker mine:	She answers me with a sorrowful look:
Az a mazl af Kolombuses medine! [repeated]	"Such luck from Columbus' country!"

30. **My Little Cousin** (Happy Lewis, Sam Braverman & Cy Coben)   0:54
    Peggy Lee & Benny Goodman: *The Complete Recordings, 1941-1947*.
    Columbia Legacy C2K 6568 6; originally on Okeh 6606.
    Reproduced under license from Sony Music Special Products, a Division of Sony Music Entertainment Inc.

Nos. 31 through 34 are arranged as one sequence:

31. **I Met A Girl** (Jule Styne, Betty Comden & Adolph Green) [Ex. 8-7a]   0:23
    Sydney Chaplin: *Bells Are Ringing*. CBS CK 2006.
    Reproduced under license from Sony Music Special Products, a Division of Sony Music Entertainment Inc.

32. **Wedding Samba** (Abraham Ellstein, Joseph Liebowitz & Allan Small) [Ex. 8-7b]　　　　0:31
　　Seymour Rechtzeit, Dave Tarras, Sam Medoff et al. Banner B 580 mx. A-700; NYC, 1940s.

33. **I Feel Like I'm Not Out of Bed Yet** (Leonard Bernstein, Betty Comden & Adolph Green)　　0:32
　　George Gaynes: *On the Town*. CBS CK 2038. [Ex. 8-7c]
　　Reproduced under license from Sony Music Special Products, a Division of Sony Music Entertainment Inc.

34. **If I Were A Rich Man** (Jerry Bock & Sheldon Harnick)　　　　0:32
　　Herschel Bernardi: *Fiddler On the Roof*, Sony Music AZ 5886. [Ex. 8-7d]
　　Reproduced under license from Sony Music Special Products, a Division of Sony Music Entertainment Inc.

35. **Lawd, You Made the Nights Too Long** (Victor Young & Sam M. Lewis)　　　　2:02
　　Louis Armstrong: *Stardust*, Portrait Masters (Sony), RK 44093.
　　Reproduced under license from Sony Music Special Products, a Division of Sony Music Entertainment Inc.

36. **Sam, You Made the Pants Too Long** (Victor Young, Milton Berle & Fred Whitehouse)　　1:12
　　Don Croll, baritone: *Don Alan Croll On Broadway (Addison, Texas)*. Private recording, 2002.

37. **I'm Sam the Man Who Made the Pants Too Long** (Robert Duke Leonard)　　　　1:19
　　Menasha Skulnik with Abe Ellstein's Orchestra, Banner 2022 mx. A-168; NYC, 1940s.
Macaronic text taken from the recording

Let me introduce myself: I was a business man,	The coat, the vest, so finely pressed,
Suits to order, I made them just like a tailor can.	The tall man with the cloak
'Til someone wrote a song on me,	Who chased me 'bout and chewed me out:
And that's the trut'.	"Sam you made the pants too long."
It was my flop, I closed my shop,	
Since then I've been kaput.	My business was spoiled by that song,
	Instead of short, it's better if it's long,
I'm Sam the Man	Were I to make the pants to fit,
That Made the Pants Too Long,	He wouldn't have the song be writ
I'm looking for the guy who made the song.	I'm Sam the Man Who Made the Pants Too Long.

Chapter 9: Sons of Cantors

38. **Haynt iz Purim** (Today Is Purim; Abraham Goldfaden & Mordecai Rivesman) [Ex.9-13a]　　0:44
　　Gladys Gewirtz: *Purim Song Parade*. Menorah Records, Men212 LP.

Haynt iz Purim, brider,	Today is Purim, brothers,
Es iz a yomtev groys.	It is a great holiday.
Lomir zingn lider	Let us sing songs
Un geyn fun hoyz tsu hoyz.	And go from house to house.
Lakh, Mordkhele, lakh, a yomtevl makh.	Laugh, little Mordecai, laugh, make it a festival.
Kinds-kinder gedenken dem nes.	Grandchildren recall the miracle.
Zingt, bridelekh, zingt,	Sing, brothers, sing,
Tantst freylekh un shpringt,	Dance happy and leap,
Dem tayern tog nit farges.	Do not forget the cherished day.

39. **Steppin' Out With My Baby** (Irving Berlin) [Ex. 9-13b]　　　　0:47
　　Fred Astaire: *Easter Parade*. Produced under license from Turner Records R275614.

40. **Shir Hashirim** (Song of Songs; Setting by Lazar Saminsky of a Georgian-Jewish chant)　　2:12
　　Reuven Frankel, baritone & Lazar Weiner, piano: *Out of the Silence, Songs of Russian Jewry*.
　　Famous Records, Fam-1038. [Ex. 9-21a]

Shir hashirim asher lishlomo:	The Song of Songs by Solomon:
Yishakeini min'shikot pihu,	Kiss me with the kisses of your mouth,
Ki tovim dodekha miyayin.	For your love is sweeter than wine.

L'reiakh sh'manekha tovim;	There is a fragrance about you;
Shemen turak shemecha.	The mention of your name brings it to mind.
Al-kein alamot, alamot a-eivukha.	No woman could ever keep from loving you.
Mashkheini akharekha narutza;	Take me with you, and we will run away;
Heviani hamelekh hadarav nagilah.	Be my king and take me to your chambers.
V'nism'kha bakh, natzkirah, dodekha,	We will be happy together,
Meiyayin mesharim aheivukha.	Drink deep and lose ourselves in love.

41. **Come Rain Or Come Shine** (Harold Arlen & Johnny Mercer)
    Lena Horne: *St. Louis Woman.* Angel Broadway ZDM7 64662 2. [Ex. 9-21b]   1:33

Chapter 10: Symbols of Faith in the Music of Leonard Bernstein

<u>Influence of the *Adonai malakh* mode</u>

42. **Ya Got Me** (Leonard Bernstein, Betty Comden & Adolph Green) [Ex. 10-4]   0:54
    Betty Comden & Chris Alexander: *On the Town.* Columbia OL 5540.
    Reproduced under license from Sony Music Special Products, a Division of Sony Music Entertainment Inc.

Chapter 11: Porter's Trunk

43. **Dovid un Ester** (David and Esther; Chaim Towber & Ilia Trilling) [Ex. 11-9a]   1:09
    Rosita Londner & Henry Gerro. Markolit 12036.

Dovid un Ester, vet keyner nit sheydn,	David and Esther, no one shall part them,
Getraye tzvey hertzer in freyd un in noyt.	Two hearts devoted in joy and in poverty.
Dovid un Ester, fun glik a gan eyden,	David and Esther, filled with happiness,
Tsufridn tsu leybn oyf vaser un broyt.	Contented to live on water and bread.
Di emese libe farlangt nisht kayn raykhkayt,	The truest love does not need wealth,
Kayn sheyne palatzn, kayn samet un zayd.	Nor beautiful palaces, nor satin and silk.
Dovid un Ester, zeyer glik hot kayn glaykn,	David and Esther, their joy like no other,
Zeyer libe blaybt heylik oyf eybike tzayt.	Their love is heaven-sent for eternity.

44. **Goodbye, Little Dream, Goodbye** (Cole Porter) [Ex. 11-9b]   1:39
    Jan DeGaetani & Leo Smit, piano: *Classic Cole.* Columbia AL 34533; Columbia Special Products 34533.
    Reproduced under license from Sony Music Special Products, a Division of Sony Music Entertainment Inc.

Chapter 12: Affinities Between Jewish Americans and African Americans

45. **Magnetic Rag** (Scott Joplin) [Ex. 12-1]   0:46
    William Bolcom: *Euphonic Sounds, The Scott Joplin Album.* Omega, OCD 3001.
    Courtesy of the Omega Record Group, Inc.

46. **Avreml der marvikher** (Avreml the Pickpocket; Mordecai Gebirtig) [Ex. 12-2]   0:43
    Ben Bonus with Victor Yampole, piano: *Songs Of Our People.* Tikva T-23 LP, NYC.

Ikh bin Avreml, der feyikster marvikher,	I am Avreml, the finest pickpocket,
A groyser kinstler, kh'arbet laykht un zikher.	A great artist, I work lightly and confidently.
Dos ershte mol, kh'vel es gedenken bizn toyt,	The first time, I'll recall 'til my dying day,
Arayn in tfise far latkhenen a broyt, oy, oy.	I went to jail for stealing a bread, oh, oh.
Kh'for nisht oyf markn vi yene proste yatn,	I don't go to market like other common thieves,
Kh'tsip nor bay karge shmutsike magnatn,	I snatch only from dirty magnates,
Kh'hob lib a mentshen, a voyln a nash-brat,	I love people, a respectable average fellow,
Ikh bin Avreml, gor a voyler yat.	I am Avreml, a really great guy.

47. **Ot azoy neyt a shnayder** (This Is How A Tailor Sews; folk)　　　　　　　　　　　0:27
　　　　Ruth Rubin: *Yiddish Folksongs*, 1968. Private recording.

Ot azoy neyt a shnayder	This is how a tailor sews,
Ot azoy neyt er gut. [repeated]	This is how he sews well.
Er neyt un neyt a gantse vokh,	He sews and sews all week long,
Un fardint a gildn mit a lokh. [repeated]	And he earns a plug nickel.

48. **The Tailor's Song (Utt-da-zay)** (Buck Ram & Irving Mills) [Ex. 12-18]　　　　　1:09
　　　　Cab Calloway. Classics CD595; Vocalion V5062.
　　　　Reproduced under license from Sony Music Special Products, a Division of Sony Music Entertainment Inc.

49. **A [My] Yiddishe Momme** (Jack Yellen & Lew Pollack)　　　　　　　　　　　1:27
　　　　Billie Holiday, Tony Scott, piano; *The Complete Billie Holiday*. Verve (10 CD Box 517 658), Vol. 6.
　　　　Polygram Records, Inc., 1992. Now Universal. Babysitting at William and Marly Duffy's home, NYC, 3 May 1956.
　　　　Note: In this collection, Billy Holiday also recorded "Israel."

50. **The New Suit (Zipper Fly)** (Marc Blitzstein) [Ex. 12-38]　　　　　　　　　4:55
　　　　Leonard Bernstein, singer and pianist.
　　　　Private recording; NYC, ca. 1965.

Total: 73:12 minutes

There are six needle-trades songs in this collection: *Khazn oyf shabes, Sam You Made the Pants Too Long, I Am Sam the Man, Ot azoy, The Tailor's Song* and *The New Suit.* To this could be added *The Song of the Sewing Machine,* performed by Fanny Brice originally on Victor 22169-78rpm, reissued on Vintage Series, RCA-Victor LPV-561.

Index

294